Qualitative Research in Clinical Psychology and Psychotherapy in Latin America

Alemka Tomicic • Javiera Duarte Soto
Editors

Qualitative Research in Clinical Psychology and Psychotherapy in Latin America

Creativity for Studying Complex Objects in Context

Springer

Editors
Alemka Tomicic
Center for Studies in Clinical Psychology and Psychotherapy (CEPPS)
Diego Portales University
Santiago, RM - Santiago, Chile

Javiera Duarte Soto
Center for Studies in Clinical Psychology and Psychotherapy (CEPPS)
Diego Portales University
Santiago, RM - Santiago, Chile

ISBN 978-3-031-90781-4 ISBN 978-3-031-90782-1 (eBook)
https://doi.org/10.1007/978-3-031-90782-1

The original submitted manuscript has been translated into English. The translation was done using artificial intelligence. A subsequent revision was performed by the author(s) to further refine the work and to ensure that the translation is appropriate concerning content and scientific correctness. It may, however, read stylistically different from a conventional translation.

This Springer imprint is published by the registered company Springer Nature Switzerland AG
The registered company address is: Gewerbestrasse 11, 6330 Cham, Switzerland

To Magdalena and Valentina
To Julieta and Amalia

Foreword

There is something sacred about conducting qualitative psychotherapy research. Someone has had an experience that you are interested in understanding, and they are willing to share what it was like for them, what it meant to them, and how they felt during it. This process of exploration can be similar to being a therapist, but I find that clients will sometimes tell researchers things that they might not even share with their therapist. After all, they usually see their therapist every week, but a researcher they may not see again and there can be less to risk.

I think that my favorite part of qualitative research is interviewing a participant and engaging in this deep exploration of an experience together. It can be a moment of profound intimacy. Sometimes I feel that being a qualitative researcher has equipped me with a magic key that allows me to enter into these conversations and examine the vulnerability and complexities that are part of being human. I feel honored and inevitably express sincere curiosity about my participants. I see them as brave people in their willingness to share intimate thoughts, worries, and hopes.

It is always exciting to me to find other researchers who value these same aspects of research and who appreciate these processes. It was wonderful to visit Alemka Tomicic and to meet Javiera Duarte Soto at the University Diego Portales in Santiago, Chile. I was fortunate to hear researcher after researcher present creative ideas for researching a wide range of topics using diverse qualitative methods. I left the meeting feeling excited and invigorated.

Their passion for the work comes through in this volume in a beautiful manner. They are joined in this work by internationally recognized qualitative psychotherapy researchers who are also leaders in this field—producing a book with both great range and depth. I am certain that as you read the studies contained here, you will feel the excitement about qualitative research that I felt on that autumn visit. The studies demonstrate the use of many cutting-edge methodological approaches (including phenomenological, discursive, case study, and biographical methods) and with a range of subject matters related to psychotherapy practice and research. Despite the differences across these chapters, the researchers' valuing of their participants, their respect, and deep understanding of psychotherapy shines through.

Because of this, the book is equally relevant to both researchers and to practitioners wishing to further their conceptualization and psychotherapy interventions.

Qualitative research is a labor of love, but it is not only that. It is also a political act not only because it requires them to educate the field about the necessity and advantage of these methods (Levitt et al., 2024), but also because it is honoring a different way of knowing. Qualitative scientists make a deliberate decision to value the reports of their participants and the close observation of their thoughts and social practices over their own hypotheses. It is a method of learning that is based on humility and dedication to scientific empiricism that can overcome threats to our own assumptions and the limitations of our own lived experiences. Mariane Krause's Chap. 2 speaks beautifully to this attitude. It is a pathway to knowledge that is based on empathy and contextual understanding, as well as on logic (Stige et al., 2024) and leads us to make connections across implicit, contextual, and subconscious experiences.

Because they support research to develop new and unexpected insights, qualitative methods have rapidly grown in their use within qualitative methods across areas in psychology (e.g., Kovács et al., 2019; Sabnis et al., 2023) and within qualitative psychotherapy research (e.g., Levitt et al., 2021). They have led to a new investment in mixed-methods research and the need to consider clients' and therapists' experiences when designing a psychotherapy research study. They raise questions about psychotherapy practices as well as developing outcomes that reflect the experiences of these contributors to psychotherapy (Ladmanová et al., 2024; Levitt et al., 2024). They question fundamental beliefs about psychotherapy and propose new conceptualizations.

This book continues to advance the position and impact of qualitative psychotherapy research in our field and, importantly, in this context as well. It makes clear cultural links and presents demonstrations of how qualitative methods can be of use in a Latin American context. It presents an argument that this way of knowing is not only resonant with Latin American approaches to learning that embrace complexity and local traditions (Altimir, 2025), but also essential in the study of subjectivity and psychotherapy change. This book is positioned to become a cornerstone in its field and to have a lasting impact on psychotherapy science. I hope that you find the sacred and the inspirational in its pages.

Boston, MA, USA
February 19, 2025

Heidi M. Levitt

References

Altimir, C. (2025). Qualitative research on psychotherapeutic change in Latin America: In search of capturing complexity. In A. Tomicic & J. Duarte (Eds.), *Qualitative research in clinical psychology and psychotherapy in Latin America: Creativity for studying complex objects in context*. Springer.

Kovács, A., Kiss, D., Kassai, S., Pados, E., Kaló, Z., & Rácz, J. (2019). Mapping qualitative research in psychology across five Central-Eastern European countries: Contemporary trends:

A paradigm analysis. *Qualitative Research in Psychology, 16*(3), 354–374. https://doi.org/10.1080/14780887.2019.1605271

Krause, M. (2025). Qualitative methods as a road to conceptual innovation. In A. Tomicic & J. Duarte (Eds.), *Qualitative research in clinical psychology and psychotherapy in Latin America: Creativity for studying complex objects in context*. Springer.

Ladmanová, M., Řiháček, T., Timulak, L., Jonášová, K., Kubantová, B., Mikoška, P., Polakovská, L., & Elliott, R. (2024). Client-identified outcomes of individual psychotherapy: a qualitative meta-analysis. *The Lancet Psychiatry*. https://doi.org/10.1016/S2215-0366(24)00356-0

Levitt, H. M., Grabowski, L. M., Minami, T., & Morrill, Z. (2024). An initial validation of the Clients' Experience of Therapy Scale (CETS): Assessing the quality of psychotherapy process and outcome from clients' perspectives. *Counselling Psychology Quarterly, 37*(1) 112–136. https://doi.org/10.1080/09515070.2023.2191171

Levitt, H. M., Hamburger, A., Hill, C. E., McLeod, J., Pascual-Leone, A., Timulak, L., Buchholz, M. B., Frommer, J., Fuertes, J., Iwakabe, S., Martínez, C., Morrill, Z., Knox, S., Langer, P., Muran, J. C., Weie Oddli, H., Řiháček, T., Tomicic, A., & Tuval-Mashiach, R. (2024). Broadening the evidentiary basis for clinical practice guidelines: Recommendations from qualitative psychotherapy researchers. *American Psychologist*. https://doi.org/10.1037/amp0001363

Levitt, H. M., McLeod, J., & Stiles, W. B. (2021). The conceptualization, design, and evaluation of qualitative methods in research on psychotherapy. In M. Barkham, L. Castonguay, & W. Lutz (Eds.), *Bergin and Garfield's handbook of psychotherapy and behavior change* (7th ed., pp. 351–384). Wiley.

Stige, S. H., Oddli, H. W., Hjeltnes, A., Watson, J., & Stige, B. (2024). The researcher as instrument: How our capacity for empathy supports qualitative analysis of transcripts. *Qualitative Research in Psychology*. https://doi.org/10.1080/14780887.2024.2368046

Sabnis, S. V., Newman, D. S., Whitford, D., & Mossing, K. (2023). Publication and characteristics of qualitative research in School Psychology journals between 2006 and 2021. *School Psychology, 38*(5), 330–336. https://doi.org/10.1037/spq0000548

Foreword

The psychotherapist profession is a type of calling for professionals engaged in the practice of psychotherapy. Psychotherapists not only want to help their patients, but they are typically also very passionate about understanding what brings about psychological suffering in their patients and people in general. Psychotherapists also want to understand what processes transform psychological suffering into a more fulfilling life and want to harness these processes in their psychotherapeutic practice. All psychotherapists are thus, in their nature, also researchers. What distinguishes psychotherapy practitioners from formally designated psychotherapy researchers is that psychotherapy researchers go beyond studying, supervision, reflection, and observation in the therapy sessions to design formal methodological (research) procedures that offer an extra perspective on psychological suffering and its transformation, which is not normally available to practitioners-psychotherapists in the sessions they conduct. Psychotherapy researchers apply procedures characterized by rigor in data gathering, observation, and analysis that provide a certain level of confidence that the extra perspective that research may bring can be trusted. In that sense, psychotherapy research can be considered to be a natural extension of the psychotherapists' reflection on their work that utilizes (research) procedures, e.g., interviews with clients about their experience of therapy, that would typically not be available to the therapist.

Psychotherapy research consists of many genres, some of which tend to be referred to by the psychotherapy researchers' community as "qualitative research." Qualitative psychotherapy research (QPR) is popular among many psychotherapy researchers because, in general, psychotherapy researchers are also practicing psychotherapists. The procedures of QPR are typically very similar to the actual practice of psychotherapy, perhaps more so than many of the quantitative procedures. QPR relies on either meticulous observations (e.g., recordings of therapy) or interviews of actors involved in psychotherapy (clients and therapists). The analysis is typically complex, and nuanced, considering context, which are all activities similar to the ones employed by a practicing therapist.

The researchers involved in QPR are typically passionate, driven by their curiosity. They learn about psychotherapy and what works, may work, or may not, in a way that is very similar to how the researcher would practice therapy if they were wearing their clinician's hat. The researchers also want to make sense of what contributes to psychological difficulties and what may be contributing to their alleviation, which is the same thing they are doing as practicing therapists. QPR methodologies, in essence, simply allow the researchers to go about their inquiries, while not losing their practitioner's stance. Thus, QPR allows the researchers to learn about psychotherapy and be better practitioners while engaging in research.

Qualitative research in psychotherapy is a broad umbrella of methodological approaches that examine psychotherapy in a complex, flexible, and open-ended manner (often also a discovery-oriented manner). Over the decades since these types of approaches became clearly recognized in the community of psychotherapy researchers, QPR grew from strength to strength. QPR is currently represented not only by the breadth of approaches but also by the variety of areas of study. QPR has now not only found its way to many scientific outlets, among them also very mainstream journals (e.g., Ladmanová et al., 2024; Levitt et al., 2024), but it has also generated plenty of findings that shape not only the field of psychotherapy research, but also the clinical practice of psychotherapy (McLeod et al., 2021). Indeed, it is an extra benefit if the QPR researchers also know how to share their learnings in a way that the consumers of their research (e.g., students, practicing therapists, other stakeholders) find relevant. Dissemination that stresses immediate relevance is a compelling way of demonstrating the usefulness of psychotherapy research. Examples where this can be seen are represented in some therapeutic approaches such as supportive-expressive psychoanalytic therapy (the research of Lester Luborsky (e.g., Luborsky & Luborsky, 2006) and his colleagues also heavily involved what we would now call qualitative research) or emotion-focused therapy [the task analytic methodological approach that led to the development of this therapy can be considered a mixed-methods approach—Greenberg (2007)].

The edited volume by Alemka Tomicic and Javiera Duarte Soto represents an ensemble of internationally influential psychotherapy researchers (for instance, among the authors we can find several current or past presidents of the international Society for Psychotherapy Research or its Latin American Chapter) who all reside in one of the Latin American countries. The editors succeeded to assemble psychotherapy researchers whose reputation is truly international and reaches well beyond their individual country and Latin America as such. The book thus gives a powerful voice to the community of researchers working in a shared, mutually interactive context. The contribution of this distinct community thus shines strongly and gets its well-deserved recognition and visibility. Indeed, it may not be considered as such within Latin America itself, but looking at the community from a European perspective, it is becoming a stronghold of psychotherapy research (e.g., Gomez-Penedo et al., 2024; Martínez et al., 2023; Paz et al., 2021).

The book presented here is a celebration of qualitative research in Latin American countries. It shows achievements and original contributions. The book divides its chapters into three distinct foci. The first set of chapters focuses on how change comes about in psychotherapy. Methodological considerations as well as examples of exemplary studies are represented here. The chapters show the value of theoretical grounding of some variants of QPR, an area that is sometimes overlooked by the broader psychotherapy researchers' community (Elliott & Timulak, 2021). The second part of the book presents various methodological approaches (e.g., conversation analysis, discourse analysis, systematic observation) to studying diverse phenomena of the psychotherapeutic process. A mixture of self-report, but in particular observer-based approaches (that are often omitted when presenting QPR in other outlets) are presented in this part of the book. The final part of the book looks at methods for studying people's experiences of their inner struggles that can inform psychotherapists in their understanding of what clients may be bringing to psychotherapy. This part of the book also provides a chapter on teaching qualitative methods to an undergraduate audience by psychotherapy researchers and focuses on mixed-methods psychotherapy research, a genre that bridges QPR with a more quantitative paradigm.

This edited book represents a showcase of QPR conducted by psychotherapy researchers residing in Latin American countries. It is a representation of the wealth of knowledge and facts that can serve the whole international community of psychotherapy researchers and psychotherapists. Having it accessible in one volume in an outlet published by a major international publisher makes the book a gift to the international community of psychotherapy researchers and psychotherapists. Congratulations to the editors and to the authors on this significant achievement! I am confident that the book will be a milestone of the further growth of qualitative psychotherapy research in Latin America itself, and across the globe!

Dublin, Ireland
January 3, 2025

Ladislav Timulak

References

Elliott, R., & Timulak, L. (2021). Essentials of descriptive-interpretive qualitative research: A generic approach. *American Psychological Association*. https://doi.org/10.1037/0000224-000

Gómez Penedo, J. M., Errázuriz, P., Coyne, A. E., & Flückiger, C. (2024). Individual risk of not responding to psychotherapy in Latin America: Bringing data-informed precision care to under-resourced clinical settings. *Journal of Consulting and Clinical Psychology, 92*(12), 836–842. https://doi.org/10.1037/ccp0000931

Greenberg, L. S. (2007). A guide to conducting a task analysis of psychotherapeutic change. *Psychotherapy Research, 17*(1), 15–30. https://doi.org/10.1080/10503300600720390

Ladmanová, M., Řiháček, T., Timulak, L., Jonášová, K., Kubantová, B., Mikoška, P., Polakovská, L., & Elliott, R. (2024). Client-identified outcomes of individual psychotherapy: a qualitative meta-analysis. *The Lancet Psychiatry*. https://doi.org/10.1016/S2215-0366(24)00356-0

Levitt, H. M., Grabowski, L. M., Minami, T., & Morrill, Z. (2024). An initial validation of the Clients' Experience of Therapy Scale (CETS): Assessing the quality of psychotherapy process and outcome from clients' perspectives. *Counselling Psychology Quarterly, 37*(1) 112–136. https://doi.org/10.1080/09515070.2023.2191171

Levitt, H. M., Hamburger, A., Hill, C. E., McLeod, J., Pascual-Leone, A., Timulak, L., Buchholz, M. B., Frommer, J., Fuertes, J., Iwakabe, S., Martínez, C., Morrill, Z., Knox, S., Langer, P., Muran, J. C., Weie Oddli, H., Řiháček, T., Tomicic, A., & Tuval-Mashiach, R. (2024).

Broadening the evidentiary basis for clinical practice guidelines: Recommendations from qualitative psychotherapy researchers. *American Psychologist*. https://doi.org/10.1037/amp0001363

Luborsky, L., & Luborsky, E. (2006). *Research and psychotherapy: The vital link*. Jason Aronson.

Martínez, C., Costa, A. B., & Tomicic, A. (2023). Development of a collaborative network: Latin-American network for research in psychotherapy and mental health in sexual and gender diversity. *Trends in psychology, 31*(3), 548–560. https://doi.org/10.1007/s43076-022-00204-4

McLeod, J., Stiles, W. B., & Levitt, H. (2021). Qualitative research: Contributions to psychotherapy practice, theory and policy. In M. Barkham, W. Lutz, & L. Castonguay (Eds.), *Bergin & Garfield's Handbook of psychotherapy and behavior change* (7th ed., pp. 51–86). Wiley.

Paz, C., Mascialino, G., Proaño, K., & Evans, C. (2021). Psychological intervention change measurement in Latin America: Where from? Where to? *Psychotherapy Research, 31*(1), 132–141. https://doi.org/10.1080/10503307.2020.1750728

Preface: Starting with Us

I am a psychologist with a PhD in Psychology, and full professor at Universidad Diego Portales (UDP) in Chile. I have worked at the Center for Studies in Clinical Psychology and Psychotherapy (CEPPS) for over 10 years. I also serve as a principal investigator at the Millennium Institute for Research in Depression and Personality (MIDAP) and have recently taken on the role of co-director. Additionally, I am a regular member of the Society for Psychotherapy Research (SPR) and its Latin American chapter. Currently, I serve as the director of the School of Psychology at UDP's Faculty of Psychology, teaching undergraduate and graduate students how to conduct research using qualitative methods.

As the saying goes, "All roads lead to Rome." This book is my Rome, and although I will not elaborate on what that symbolizes here, I would like to share a brief overview of the academic journey that has brought me to this point, particularly regarding my relationship with qualitative research.

First and foremost, I want to emphasize that learning how to conduct research—especially qualitative research—is deeply rooted in practice, craft, and mentorship. This approach to qualitative research has certainly been my experience. During my undergraduate studies, I met Mariane Krause, a distinguished Chilean researcher, in an elective course within a scientific community that was skeptical about the quality and rigor of findings derived from qualitative research methods. My youthful openness at the time allowed me to set aside such criticisms. Fascinated by the opportunity to understand phenomena through subjective perspectives—both of the participants and my own—I eagerly engaged in constructing inductive understandings and explanatory models by enrolling in the course.

Soon after, I became Mariane's teaching assistant and began conducting research alongside her, as she quickly became my mentor. Since then, I have collaborated with colleagues to transition from applying existing methods to creating new qualitative research methods and techniques. Many of these colleagues, including Claudio Martínez and Javiera Duarte, are featured in this book.

This book does not represent an endpoint, as it may seem; instead, it reflects a journey through "Rome"—or, more accurately, a journey through Santiago, Valparaíso, Buenos Aires, Bariloche, and Lima. It showcases our collective endeavor in researching psychotherapy and clinical psychology using qualitative methods we built together in Latin America.

Alemka Tomicic

My journey is a little different from that of my friend, colleague, and mentor, Alemka. Still, as she says, all roads lead to Rome, well, this path also led me to research and my passion for qualitative research. I have been a clinical psychologist for nearly 20 years and can say that since I began my undergraduate studies in psychology, I knew for sure that being a clinical psychologist and doing psychotherapy was what I wanted to do. What I didn't expect was that shortly after graduating and working for a few years as a clinical psychologist in a public hospital and private practice, I would realize that I needed far more knowledge and evidence to guide my clinical work, much more than what theoretical training or even everyday practice could provide.

Thus, in 2013, I enrolled in the Psychotherapy Doctoral program jointly offered by the University of Chile and the Pontifical Catholic University of Chile to obtain my PhD. There, I discovered a fascinating new world that opened up endless possibilities for me. I quickly understood the importance of answering questions such as why psychotherapy works, what it is that we as clinicians do that makes it effective, and how we can develop psychotherapeutic interventions and psychotherapy processes that, while incorporating the existing body of evidence, also consider the subjective experiences of our patients and are tailored to their needs.

On this journey, I learned from exceptional researchers like Mariane Krause, Juan Pablo Jiménez, Louise Castonguay and my doctoral thesis advisor and now friend, Claudio Martínez. I also became involved with the International Society for Psychotherapy Research (SPR), which allowed me to grow as a researcher and learn from internationally renowned researchers. In this way, I began to forge my path as an independent researcher, well maybe not entirely independent because one of the key things I've learned in this journey is that research is inherently collaborative. Not only is it far too much work to do alone, but it's also more enjoyable when done with others. And I firmly believe that to enjoy what you do genuinely, to be passionate, and be good at it, you have to have fun.

This book is a reflection of that. It has been fun (and challenging), but it has also been collaborative, as each chapter has been written by people we admire, some of whom are even friends. This book shows how we work here in Latin America—with limited resources for research, but with great passion for our work, collaboratively and a strong commitment to advancing clinical psychology and psychotherapy practice.

I hope this book showcases what we do here in Latin America to the rest of the world and serves as a guide for those just beginning their journey in qualitative research in psychotherapy. This book is an opportunity for students and young researchers to envision their paths, challenges, and passions through our work, and a chance for more experienced researchers to get a glimpse of what we've been up to down south. But above all, I just hope you enjoy it.

Javiera Duarte Soto

Santiago, Chile

Alemka Tomicic
Javiera Duarte Soto

Acknowledgments

The idea for this book originated from conversations with members of the Latin-American Chapter of the Society for Psychotherapy Research (SPR) about the contributions of psychotherapy research coming from this region. It was further inspired by Heidi Levitt's visit to Chile at the beginning of the academic semester in 2023, during which her generosity and engaging dialogue motivated us to embark on this endeavor. The project also owes much to the persistent support and encouragement of Claudio Martínez, Director of the Center for Studies on Clinical Psychology and Psychotherapy (CEPPS) at Universidad Diego Portales. We are deeply grateful to him.

We also extend our heartfelt thanks to Bruno Fiuza, Springer's Senior Editor of Behavioral, Health and Social Sciences books for in Latin America, who believed in this project from the very beginning and provided invaluable support. Furthermore, we sincerely thank everyone involved in Springer's production team for their efforts in bringing this book to life.

A significant contribution to the final draft of the manuscript was made by Victoria Díaz, psychologist and assistant at CEPPS. Her meticulous and dedicated work significantly enhanced the quality and organization of the chapters and facilitated communication with the numerous authors involved in this project. Thank you so much, Victoria, for your exceptional commitment and attention to detail!

The Millennium Institute for the Study of Depression and Personality (MIDAP) in Chile has been an essential source of inspiration and support for developing some ideas and research presented in this book. This influence is evident in the contributions of various authors, and we express our gratitude to MIDAP for its ongoing impact on the field.

Furthermore, the authors themselves are the most vital contributors to this book. We are immensely grateful for their willingness to write, commitment to meeting deadlines, and responsiveness during the revision process. Without their dedication, this book would not have been possible, a reason why we honestly appreciate each of their contributions.

We would like to express our heartfelt gratitude to Héctor Fernández-Alvarez, co-author of this volume. His contributions to research and training in psychotherapy have inspired many generations of researchers and therapists in Latin America. Following his heartfelt passing, a significant number of colleagues have shared how deeply he impacted all members of the Society for Psychotherapy Research (SPR). Thus, this book is also a reminder of his legacy.

With gratitude,
Alemka Tomicic and Javiera Duarte, Soto

Contents

Editors and Authors

About the Editors

Alemka Tomicic (Santiago, Chile). She is a psychologist and doctor of psychology at the Catholic University of Chile. She is a Full professor at the University of Diego Portales Faculty of Psychology and Director of the School of Psychology. She is also a researcher at the Center for Studies in Clinical Psychology and Psychotherapy (CEPPS) at the same university. Likewise, she conducts studies on experience in process-outcome research in psychotherapy and the subjective construction of the knowledge of illness and mental health problems. Furthermore, she has participated as a researcher in mental health and culturally competent psychotherapy projects of LGBT+ people, funded by the National Agency of Research and Development (ANID: Agencia Nacional de Investigación y Desarrollo in Spanish). Since 2015, she has been an associate researcher at the Millennium Institute for Research on Depression and Personality (MIDAP) of the Millennium Science Initiative in Chile. Since 2025, she has been co-director of the same institute. alemka.tomicic@mail.udp.cl, https://orcid.org/0000-0003-3272-1198.

Javiera Duarte Soto (Santiago, Chile). She is a psychologist who holds a Master's degree in Adult Clinical Psychology and a Doctorate in Psychotherapy from the University of Chile and Pontificia Universidad Católica de Chile. She has received specialized training in various mentalization-based treatments and is a certified EMDR therapist. With extensive clinical experience, Javiera primarily focuses on mood disorders, anxiety, and personality disorders. Currently, she works as an associate professor and researcher at Diego Portales University and the Center for Studies in Clinical Psychology and Psychotherapy (CEPPS). Additionally, she is a Young Researcher at the Millennium Institute for Research in Depression and Personality. Javiera's research interests center on the subjective experiences of individuals facing mental health challenges and the complex dynamics involved in the psychotherapy process. Through her work, she aims to enhance understanding and treatment approaches in mental health, emphasizing the importance of tailored interventions for various psychological issues. javiera.duarte@mail.udp.cl, https://orcid.org/0000-0002-7569-0048.

About the Authors

Nicolle A. Alamo Anich (Santiago, Chile). She is a psychologist, Postgraduate in Systemic Psychotherapy approach for Children and Adolescents, Master in Clinical Psychology and Doctor of Psychology at Pontificia Universidad Católica de Chile. She is a professor at the School of Social Work at the same university and collaborator professor at the PhD in Psychotherapy program (P. Universidad Católica de Chile-Universidad de Chile). She has conducted studies about change processes in children and their caregivers during psychotherapeutic and clinical-social interventions. She has also participated as a researcher in studies about child abuse, therapeutic relationship, Generic Change Indicators, mental health in first-time and adolescent mothers, and mental health and well-being in migrant and refugee children and mothers. Likewise, she develops research through qualitative methods and integrating different perspectives (children, parents or caregivers, psychotherapists, social workers, and external observers). She is a young researcher at the Millennium Institute for Research on Depression and Personality (MIDAP) of the Millennium Science Initiative in Chile. nalamo@uc.cl, https://orcid.org/0000-0002-3826-1455.

Carolina Altimir (Santiago, Chile). She is professor at the University de Los Andes, and since 2021 Associate Researcher of the Millennium Institute for Research in Depression and Personality (MIDAP). Director of the Latin American Network for Research in Psychotherapy, and member of the Latin American Consortium of Psychotherapy Research. She earned her Ph.D. in Psychotherapy at Pontificia Universidad Católica de Chile. She is a licensed psychologist and psychotherapist in private practice. Dr. Altimir has developed research on the therapeutic relationship, affect regulation within rupture-repair processes, and psychotherapy change process from a microanalytic and events paradigm perspective. She has also developed research on the subjective perspective and lived experience of therapy process and mental health disorders of patients and therapists. Dr. Altimir is currently focusing her research on routine outcome monitoring, based on the paradigm of practice-oriented research, as well as on competence training for clinicians for the treatment of depression in the mental health system. caltimir.colao@gmail.com https://orcid.org/0000-0002-2691-6370.

Doris Argumedo (Lima, Peru). Clinical psychologist and Master in Theoretical Studies in Psychoanalysis from the Pontifical Catholic University of Peru (PUCP). Master in Methodology of Behavioral and Health Sciences from the National University of Distance Education (UNED) and the Complutense University of Madrid (UCM). Associate Professor of the Department of Psychology at PUCP. Coordinator and Researcher of the Research Group in Psychoanalysis at PUCP. Director of the Second Specialty Program in Psychoanalytic Clinic (PUCP) and member of the Advisory Committee of the Master's Degree in Psychoanalytic Clinical Intervention (PUCP). She researches and publishes on topics related to results and processes of change in psychotherapy, gender-based violence and diversity. dargume@pucp.pe, https://orcid.org/0000-0003-4555-2194.

Francisca Avilés (Santiago, Chile). Psychologist from Universidad Diego Portales, with a diploma in Child and Adolescent Psychodiagnostics.For the past 4 years, I have been conducting research on mental health and the well-being of the LGBTQ+ population, focusing on mixed-methods and qualitative studies. My work has explored topics such as the bodily experience of trans individuals, access to mental health services, and the intersection of gender.Currently, I combine my clinical practice with private patients with my work in the legal field, specifically in the area of adolescent criminal responsibility. My approach integrates psychoanalytic and gender perspectives, bridging subjective analysis with the social and legal context. francisca.aviles@mail.udp.cl

Juanpablo Betancourt Canelo (Valparaíso, Chile). He is a psychologist from the University of Valparaíso. He has worked in research focused on observational measures for psychotherapy process research. Currently, he is involved in the Andes project (Assessment of a National DBT Enhanced Skills Training Group), a clinical effectiveness trial of a brief dialectical behavior therapy (DBT) skills training workshop for borderline personality disorder (BPD). juanpablo.bettancourt@alumnos.uv.cl

Claudia Capella (Santiago, Chile). She is a psychologist and a doctor of psychology from the University of Chile. She also holds a Master's in Child and Adolescent Mental Health from King's College London, UK. Furthermore, she is an associate professor at the Department of Psychology of the University of Chile. She has taught child and adolescent clinical psychology and psychotherapy for 15 years. She has led a line of research in healing and psychotherapy from child sexual abuse at the University of Chile. Her clinical, teaching, and research work has been in the area of child and adolescent psychotherapy and sexual abuse, with a special interest in the use of qualitative research methodologies with children and adolescents, that are ethically and developmentally sensitive and include their perspectives. She is part of the nucleus of interdisciplinary studies in childhood at the Faculty of Social Sciences at the University of Chile. She is also a researcher at the Millennium Institute for Research on Depression and Personality (MIDAP). ccapella@u.uchile.cl, https://orcid.org/0000-0002-7252-6605

Mariana Castillo-Hermosilla (Santiago, Chile). She is a psychologist from Diego Portales University (Chile) and a current master's student of Cognitive Science at Osnabrück University (Germany). She is trained as a clinical psychologist at IPRA Chile and has studied philosophy at Diego Portales University. She also did a postgraduate diploma in Psychotherapy Research for Mental Health Professionals at the same university. Likewise, she has participated in qualitative research using art-based methodologies on mental health and gender issues, feminist theories and intersectionality concerning the social and psychological impact of AI, and discrimination interventions. Since 2024 is an Associated Research at the Laboratory of Phenomenology of the Body (LAFEC, Chile). maricastillohermosilla@gmail.com, https://orcid.org/0000-0002-8803-0321

Kene Mike Durand (Lima, Perú). He is a clinical psychologist who holds a Master's in Psychoanalytical Clinical Intervention from the Pontifical Catholic University of Peru (PUCP). He is a psychoanalytic psychotherapist of children, teenagers, and adults in private practice. Furthermore, he is a professor at the Psychology Department of the Peruvian University of Applied Sciences (UPC). Since 2020, he has been a member of a research group formed by Marcos Herrera and his coworkers (A. Ugarte, G. Vásquez-Torres and M. Sánchez), who are graduates and students of the Master's Program in Psychoanalytical Clinical Intervention at the PUCP, to conduct qualitative analysis of psychoanalytic psychotherapy applying Conversation Analysis (CA). Thanks to a grant of the Research Committee of the IPA they have carried out a project to apply CA to study the sequential unfolding of moments of meeting in brief psychoanalytic therapies with female patients victims of domestic violence in Peru. https://orcid.org/0009-0004-7844-4020. mike.durand@pucp.edu.pe

Héctor Fernández-Álvarez (1944–2023) was a Psychologist and Doctor of Psychology. His career spanned five decades. He was an internationally engaged and remarkably accomplished professor, researcher, clinician, supervisor, mentor, and leader who made prolific contributions through his books and articles. In 1977 together with other professionals, he formed the Aiglé foundation, a non-governmental organization in Argentina and thereafter in Guatemala and Spain. Aiglé sought to build bridges through close collaboration with psychologists overseas focused on the professional development of mental health practitioners and the delivery of clinical and community services, both informed by an active research program that evaluated the processes and outcomes of care services and training. He developed a research program on "the personal style of the therapist," which involved international collaborations, and was the coordinator of the working group in Latin America and Spain since 2011. He served as the Honorary President of Aiglé Foundation. Among many of his significant contributions, his integrative model of psychotherapy figured most prominently. Another significant contribution by Dr. Fernández-Álvarez in Aiglé concerned the training of mental health professionals. He developed a research-based, leading-edge graduate psychotherapy training in Latin America and a graduate training program for supervisors. Dr. Fernández-Álvarez's leadership abilities led him to hold significant positions in many scientific and professional organizations. Among others, he was President of the Latin American chapter of the Society for Psychotherapy Research (SPR) (2003–2004). The recognition by his peers made Dr. Fernández-Álvarez the recipient of numerous national and international acknowledgments and awards. https://orcid.org/0000-0002-7781-1165

Martina Fischersworring (Valparaíso, Chile). She is a psychologist at the Ruhr-Universität Bochum, Germany and a doctor of Psychotherapy at the Universities of Chile and the P. Catholic University of Chile. Her doctoral thesis focused on the development of a professional identity of psychotherapists, specifically on the subjective impact of therapeutic success and failure on the therapist's experiences of well-being/discomfort. She is a collaborating researcher at MIDAP Chile (Millennium-Institute for Depression-and-Personality). Trained in conducting and analyzing the Micro-phenomenological Interview (2016). Researcher and postgraduate teacher at different study centers of the Region of Valparaíso. In addition, Martina works as a clinical psychologist and certified EMDR therapist. martinamariafh@yahoo.com

María Isabel Gaete (Valparaíso, Chile). She is a Clinical Psychologist and Doctor in Psychotherapy with a double degree from the University of Chile and the University of Heidelberg, Germany. Young Researcher at the Millennium Institute for the Study of Depression and Personality, MIDAP. Researcher at the Laboratory of Corporal Phenomenology, LAFEC. She has nearly 30 years of clinical experience, in which she has extensively developed Art Therapy to approach psychotherapy with an embodied approach. She has developed and published research in body phenomenology applied to eating disorders and fibromyalgia. Likewise, she has also participated in an international network of researchers to explore the role of language and memory in the study of experience, publishing on micro-phenomenology and qualitative methodologies, and on creative-expressive artistic work as a phenomenological exploration of experience. Currently, she participates as co-investigator, together with the principal investigator Claudio Martínez from the UDP, in the project "El Cuerpo Soñado: Study on the Bodily Experience of Trans* and Gender Non-Conforming People (TGNC)," working and publishing about the Body Map as an art-based methodological tool. isagete@gmail.com, https://orcid.org/0000-0002-7925-872X

Camila Garay Contreras (Valparaíso, Chile). She is a clinical psychologist from the University of Valparaíso, trained in Mentalization-Based Therapy for adolescents by the Anna Freud Centre for Children and Families and in working with individuals diagnosed with Obsessive-Compulsive Disorder by the Latin American Association of Obsessive-Compulsive Disorder (ALTOC). She works as a clinical psychologist addressing patients with depression and participates in research as part of the pilot feasibility study of the MBT-F model for addressing depression in adolescents. ps.camilagaray@gmail.com

Beatriz Gómez (Buenos Aires, Argentina). She is a Clinical Psychology and doctor of psychology. President of Aiglé Foundation in Argentina. Psychotherapist and clinical supervisor. Director and Professor of the Cognitive-Integrative Psychotherapy Graduate Training Program of Aiglé Foundation and the Universidad Nacional de Mar del Plata, Argentina. Member of the Academic Committee and Professor of the Master's Program in Clinical Psychology, with Cognitive-Integrative orientation, Universidad Nacional de San Luis, Argentina. Professor of the Master's Program in Multidisciplinary Interventions for Eating Disorders, Personality Disorders and Emotional Disorders, Universidad de Valencia, Spain. Professor of the Master's degree in Psycho-oncology, Pontificia Universidad Católica de Ecuador. Former Director of the Psychology Degree at Universidad de Belgrano. Co-Coordinator of the Centro de Investigación en Psicoterapia (CIP) in Aiglé. She participates in research programs on treatment outcome monitoring integrating qualitative and quantitative approaches in the context of a Practice Research Network and in a qualitative study on patients' perception of the psychotherapy process at treatment termination. She participated in the research program on the Personal Style of the Therapist of Aiglé. bgomez@aigle.org.ar, https://orcid.org/0000-0002-4908-1169

Marcos Herrera (Lima, Peru). He is a clinical psychologist and doctor of linguistics at the Albert-Ludwigs-University Freiburg, Germany. He is a practicing psychoanalyst, member of the Peruvian Society for Psychoanalysis (affiliated to the International Psychoanalytic Association—IPA). Furthermore, he is an associate professor at the Department of Humanities of the Pontifical Catholic University of Peru (PUCP). He is a member of the Research Group in Psychoanalysis (GIP) of the PUCP. Since 2020 he and his co-workers (A. Ugarte, G. Vásquez-Torres, K. M. Durand and M. Sánchez), who are graduates and students of the Master's Program in Psychoanalytical Clinical Intervention of the PUCP, have formed a research group to conduct qualitative analysis of psychoanalytic psychotherapy applying Conversation Analysis (CA). Thanks to a grant of the Research Committee of the IPA they have carried out a project to apply CA to study the sequential unfolding of moments of meeting in brief psychoanalytic therapies with female patients victims of domestic violence in Peru. mpherrer@pucp.edu.pe, https://orcid.org/0000-0001-6189-3306

Santiago Juan Holds a PhD in Psychology from the University of Buenos Aires (UBA). He is a therapist specializing in psychodynamic psychotherapy, and is a certified trainer in Operationalized Psychodynamic Diagnosis (OPD-2). He is a professor at the School of Psychology at UBA, at the University Institute of Mental Health (IUSAM), and at the Doctorate program in Psychology at the University of Salvador, Buenos Aires.He is senior researcher of the Clinical Psychology Research Team (EIPSI). Also, he is in charge of the Research Department at IUSAM, and is co-director of Arcodinámica, a space dedicated to training and supervision in psychodynamic therapy @drsantiagojuan, @arcodinamica. santiago.juan@iusam.edu.ar, https://orcid.org/0000-0003-1024-1337

Mariane Krause (Santiago, Chile). She is Professor at Pontificia Universidad Católica de Chile's School of Psychology. She obtained her doctoral degree at Freie Universität Berlin (Germany). Her areas of research are change processes in psychotherapy, depression, and the interaction between sociocultural and mental health conditions. She has led several research projects in these areas, with funding from the Chilean Millennium Scientific Initiative (ICM), the Chilean National Committee of Scientific and Technological Research, and the United Nations Development Program, and published around 100 papers in scientific journal, in addition to 3 books and several chapters. Between 2013 and 2016, she was President of the Latin American Chapter of the Society for Psychotherapy Research (SPR). In 2016, she received the National Award of the Chilean Society for Clinical Psychology. Between 2018 and 2019 she was President of SPR. During 2019 she was President of the Chilean Council for Research and Technology. From 2017 to 2019, she was the principal investigator of the Latin American Network in Psychotherapy Process Research. She is involved in international research initiatives in depression and psychotherapeutic change processes and integrates the Council of the Chilean Ministry for Science, Technology, Knowledge, and Innovation. Since 2014, she has been the Principal Investigator of the Millennium Institute for Research in Depression and Personality (MIDAP). Dean of the Faculty of Social Sciences from January 2022 to January 2025, and Provost of the Pontificia Universidad Católica de Chile since April 2025 mkrause@uc.cl, https://orcid.org/0000-0002-1405-8217

Paz Lancho (Lima, Peru). She holds a Master's degree in Psychoanalytic Clinical Intervention and a Bachelor's degree in Clinical Psychology from the Pontifical Catholic University of Peru (PUCP). A psychotherapist with a psychodynamic approach, she works with young people and adults in private practice in Lima. In the academic field, she works at the PUCP as a part-time professor in the Academic Department of Psychology and is a member and researcher in the Psychoanalysis Research Group. paz.lancho@pucp.edu.pe, https://orcid.org/0000-0002-1669-214X

María José León (Santiago, Chile). She is a psychologist with a Master's degree in Clinical Psychology from Adolfo Ibáñez University and a Ph.D. in Psychotherapy from the University of Chile in collaboration with the Pontifical Catholic University of Chile. She is the Co-Founder and Executive Director of Fundación Más Mentes. María José has specialized training in childhood interventions, including Video-feedback Intervention and Mentalization-Based Therapy for Children (MBT-C). She is a researcher at the Millennium Institute for Research on Depression and Personality (MIDAP). She has been the principal investigator of the Fondecyt Postdoctoral Project #3201007 and collaborated as a co-investigator in other projects, including the Priority Research Fund (FIP) of the MIDAP Institute. Her research interests include parenting, co-parenting, early bonds, child socioemotional development, and family interactions. Currently, she teaches and conducts research at the Institute for Socioemotional Wellbeing (IBEM) at Universidad del Desarrollo. mjoseleon@fundacionmasmentes.com

Carla Mantilla (Lima, Peru). Clinical psychologist from the Pontifical Catholic University of Peru (PUCP), member of the Peruvian Society of Psychoanalysis (SPP) and the International Psychoanalytic Association (IPA). She holds a Master's degree in Theoretical Psychoanalytic Studies from University College London (UCL) and a PhD in Philosophy from the PUCP. She is a member of the Psychoanalysis Research Group and the Mind and Language Interdisciplinary Group, both at the PUCP. Furthermore, she is a senior lecturer in the Academic Department of Psychology (PUCP) and director of the Master's Degree in Psychoanalytic Clinical Intervention (PUCP). She is the coordinator for Peru in the Society for Psychotherapy Research Latam and a member of the Research Committee of the IPA. She researches and publishes on topics related to the processes of change in psychotherapy and is co-editor of Cognition and Language: Intersubjectivity in Child Development and the Evolution of the Species (2014, Fondo editorial PUCP). Moreover, she works in private practice with adults. cmantil@pucp.edu.pe, https://orcid.org/0000-0003-1112-479X

Francesco Marinelli (Lima, Peru). Clinical Psychologist with a Master's Degree in Psychoanalytic Clinical Intervention from the Pontifical Catholic University of Peru (PUCP). He is a professor at the Academic Department of Psychology and a researcher at the Psychoanalysis Research Group and at the Research Group on Attachment Relationships and Socioemotional Development at the same university (PUCP). As a professor, he has taught courses on research methodology and thesis seminars at the undergraduate and graduate levels. As a researcher, he is interested in the study of change processes in psychotherapy and also in issues related to the father's involvement in parenting. He works in the clinical field as a therapist for adults and children. fmarinelli@pucp.pe, https://orcid.org/0000-0002-0470-0130

Claudio Martínez, (Santiago, Chile). He is Full Professor of the Faculty of Psychology, Universidad Diego Portales. Doctor in Psychology and a master's in clinical psychology. Director of the Center for Clinical Psychology and Psychotherapy Studies (CEPPS). Director of Project T, a psychological care program for trans* and gender non-conforming people. Clinical psychologist and psychoanalytic psychotherapist.Faculty member and supervisor of the Dynamic Psychotherapy Unit of the Psychiatric Institute "Dr. José Horwitz Barak." Moreover, is a Principal Researcher at the Millennium Institute for Depression and Personality Research (MIDAP). claudio.martinez@mail.udp.cl, https://orcid.org/0000-0001-7866-9124

Augusto Mellado Mora (Santiago, Chile) is a psychologist from Universidad Alberto Hurtado, Master in Clinical Psychology and Doctor in Psychotherapy from the Pontificia Universidad Católica de Chile. Currently, he works as a research professor at the Faculty of Medicine and Health Sciences, in the research group on Mental Health and Wellbeing, Unit for Health Humanization; and Mental Health, Well-being, and Society Research Group of the Institute for Research and Doctoral Studies of the the Universidad Central de Chile. His research primarily focuses on process and outcome variables in psychotherapy, specifically examining processes of subjective transformation from dialogical and systemic perspectives using qualitative and mixed methodologies. He is a collaborating researcher at the Millennium Institute for Research in Depression and Personality (MIDAP) under the Chilean Millennium Science Initiative. augusto.mellado@ucentral.cl, https://orcid.org/0000-0002-2251-4075

Javier Moran-Kneer (Valparaiso, Chile). He is a Clinical Psychologist, holds a Master's degree in Adolescent Psychology, and a Ph.D. in Psychotherapy. Currently, he is a faculty member at the School of Psychology at the University of Valparaíso, where he teaches and conducts research in the clinical psychology department at both undergraduate and postgraduate levels. He also co-directs the Center for Translational Studies in Stress and Mental Health (C-Estres). In addition, he serves as a researcher at the Millennium Institute for the Study of Depression and Personality (MIDAP).As a clinician, he works in psychotherapy with adolescents and families, as well as in the training and supervision of psychologists in the child and adolescent field. He is currently an accredited supervisor by the Anna Freud Centre for Children and Families in the Mentalization-Based Therapy for Families (MBT-F) model.His research trajectory has focused on evaluating the role of mentalization as a process variable in clinical interventions in the child and adolescent field. He is currently conducting a pilot study to evaluate the feasibility of the mentalization-based therapy model for adolescents diagnosed with depression. javier.moran@uv.cl, https://orcid.org/0000-0002-2633-3167

Lucía Núñez (Santiago, Chile). She is a psychologist, Master in Child and Adolescent Clinical Psychology (Universidad de Chile) and PhD in Psychotherapy (P. Universidad Católica de Chile). She is a professor at the School of Psychology at the Pontificia Universidad Católica de Chile. She researches change processes and the therapeutic relationship in child and adolescent psychotherapy, child abuse and neglect, mentalization and clinical and psychosocial interventions in public health. Furthermore, she develops research that promotes children's account of their therapeutic process through qualitative methods, including drawings as an expressive tool that aligns with their development stage. She has also performed longitudinal qualitative research on child psychotherapy and multiple perspective designs, integrating the views of children, parents, and therapists. She is a collaborative researcher at the Millennium Institute for Research on Depression and Personality (MIDAP) of the Millennium Science Initiative in Chile. ltnunez@uc.cl, https://orcid.org/0000-0002-5929-3499

Marcia Olhaberry (Santiago, Chile). PhD in Psychotherapy, Pontificia Universidad Católica de Chile and Heidelberg University, Germany. Psychologist, Bachelor's Degree in Psychology, University of Chile.Associate Professor, School of Psychology, Pontificia Universidad Católica de Chile. Deputy Director and Associate Researcher at the Millennium Institute for Research in Depression and Personality (MIDAP). Director and Supervisor of the Perinatal Mental Health Program, UC Christus Health Network. Academic Director of the Diploma in

Psychopathology of Attachment, PUC. Her main research areas include: Early mental health prevention and intervention, perinatal depression, trauma, attachment and parenting, mentalization, and dyadic and triadic family interactions and bonds. mpolhabe@uc.cl, https://orcid.org/0000-0002-5135-2175

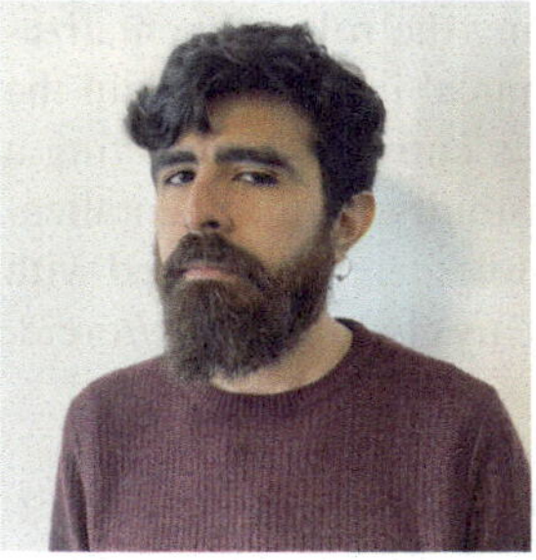

Gian Rasmussen (Lima, Peru). Clinical psychologist and Master in Psychoanalytic Clinical Intervention from the Pontifical Catholic University of Peru (PUCP). Member of the Psychoanalysis Research Group at the same university. In addition to his clinical practice, he works as a professor at the Faculty of Psychology at PUCP. He has taught courses on qualitative research methodology in psychology, psychopathology, and psychoanalysis at the undergraduate and graduate levels. He specializes in studying the influence of sociocultural discourses on subjectivity and the establishment of interpersonal relationships, inside and outside the clinical field, and especially with populations in situations of social vulnerability. gian.rasmussen@pucp.pe, https://orcid.org/0000-0001-7195-5224

Loreto Rodríguez (Santiago, Chile). She is a psychologist from the Universidad de Chile and holds a PhD in Childhood and Youth from the University of Sussex, United Kingdom. She is a professor at the Faculty of Psychology and Humanities at Universidad San Sebastián, Chile. Her work focuses on therapeutic interventions for children who have experienced sexual abuse and on research in this area, employing innovative qualitative methodologies. Loreto's research interests lie in integrating theories from the interdisciplinary field of childhood studies into psychotherapy research with children. She has experience teaching qualitative methods and childhood studies at undergraduate and postgraduate levels, as well as supervising undergraduates in child and adolescent clinical psychology. loreto.rodriguez@uss.cl, https://orcid.org/0000-0002-4988-0147

Andrés Roussos (Bariloche, Argentina). He has a strong background in both research and teaching. He is a Full Professor at the Universidad de Belgrano and chairs the Research Ethics Committee. Dr. Roussos is also a Principal Investigator at CONICET, affiliated explicitly with the Patagonian Institute of Humanities and Social Sciences (IPEHCS-UNCO). Furthermore, he is the Director of the Research Laboratory in Psychology and Information and Communication Technologies (LIPSTIC), an interdisciplinary space investigating the connections between psychology and emerging technologies. On an international level, Dr. Roussos has been President of the Society for Psychotherapy Research (SPR). ajroussos@gmail.com, https://orcid.org/0000-0002-5138-9664

Miguel Sánchez (Lima, Perú). He is a clinical psychologist and student at the Master's Program in Psychoanalytical Clinical Intervention of the Pontifical Catholic University of Peru (PUCP). He is interested in psychoanalytic psychotherapy and experience in working with adult patients with psychosis. Since 2020, he has been a member of a research group formed by Marcos Herrera and his co-workers (A. Ugarte, G. Vásquez-Torres and K. M. Durand), who are graduates and students of the Master's Program in Psychoanalytical Clinical Intervention of the PUCP, to conduct qualitative analysis of psychoanalytic psychotherapy applying Conversation Analysis (CA). Thanks to a grant of the Research Committee of the IPA they have carried out a project to apply CA to study the sequential unfolding of moments of meeting in brief psychoanalytic therapies with female patients victims of domestic violence in Peru. miguel.sancheza@pucp.pe

Catalina Sieverson (Santiago, Chile). She is a psychologist from the Universidad del Desarrollo and Ph.D. from the University of Chile in collaboration with the Pontifical Catholic University of Chile. Catalina works as a perinatal and child and adolescent clinical psychologist. She works as a clinician and professor in the field of perinatal mental health (at the Pontificia Universidad Católica de Chile, UC Christus network, Universidad del Desarrollo and Fundación En Mente), and the use of video-feedback as an intervention strategy in early childhood and mentalization-based interventions (MBT-C) (at the Millennium Institute for Research on Depression and Personality and Fundación En Mente). She researches the same topics of interest. In her postdoctoral research (at PUC and MIDAP) she studied the processes of change in an intervention with video-feedback for mothers with postpartum depressive symptoms and their babies. catasieverson@gmail.com, https://orcid.org/0000-0001-6757-607X

Andrea Ugarte (Lima, Perú). She is a clinical psychologist who holds a Master's in Psychoanalytical Clinical Intervention from the Pontifical Catholic University of Peru (PUCP). She is a psychoanalytic psychotherapist of children, teenagers, and adults in private practice. She is a professor at the Department of Psychology of the PUCP. Likewise, she is a member of the Research Group in Psychoanalysis (GIP) and of the Research Group on Attachment Relationships and Socioemotional Development of the PUCP. Since 2020, she has been a member of a research group formed by Marcos Herrera and his co-workers (G. Vásquez-Torres, K. M. Durand and M. Sánchez), who are graduates and students of the Master's Program in Psychoanalytical Clinical Intervention of the PUCP, to conduct qualitative analysis of psychoanalytic psychotherapy applying Conversation Analysis (CA). Thanks to a grant of the Research Committee of the IPA they have carried out a project to apply CA to study the sequential unfolding of moments of meeting in brief psychoanalytic therapies with female patients victims of domestic violence in Peru. andrea.ugarte@pucp.edu.pe, https://orcid.org/0000-0003-1157-6454

Nelson Valdés Sánchez (Santiago, Chile). He graduated as a Psychologist at the University of Panama (1996). He obtained a master's degree in clinical psychology at the Pontificia Universidad Católica de Chile (2004) and has participated in several government-funded projects since then. Likewise, he obtained the double degree of Doctor of Psychotherapy (2012) awarded by the Pontificia Universidad Católica de Chile and Heidelberg University (Germany) with his doctoral proposal entitled "Patients' Verbal Emotional Expression and their connection with the Psychotherapeutic Change:

A Multi-level analysis of the psychotherapeutic activity." He is currently a Director of the Doctoral Program in Psychological and Social Studies of Well-Being at Universidad Santo Tomás, Santiago, and an Adjunct Researcher at the Millennium Institute for Research in Depression and Personality (MIDAP). He has been dedicated to research in the line of psychotherapeutic processes and outcomes. Moreover, he has used qualitative methodology to analyze relevant segments during the therapeutic conversation and other topics related to mental health. nvaldes.sanchez@gmail.com, https://orcid.org/0000-0001-9583-2667

Gabriela Vásquez-Torres (Lima, Perú). She is a clinical psychologist and psychoanalytic psychotherapist of children, adolescents, and adults. She holds a Master's degree in Psychoanalytic Clinical Intervention from the Pontifical Catholic University of Perú (PUCP). Furthermore, she is a professor at the Department of Psychology of PUCP. She is a member of the Research Group in Psychoanalysis (GIP) at PUCP. Since 2020, she is a member of the Research Group formed by Marcos Herrera and his co-workers (A. Ugarte, K. M. Durand and M. Sánchez) whose aim is to conduct qualitative analysis of psychoanalytic psychotherapy applying Conversation Analysis (CA). Thanks to the IPA Grant, they have developed a project to apply CA to study the sequential unfolding of moments of meeting in brief psychoanalytic therapies with female victims of domestic violence in Perú. gvasquezt@pucp.pe, https://orcid.org/0000-0002-6932-2783

Chapter 1
Introduction: Why Publish This Book?

Alemka Tomicic and Javiera Duarte Soto

Why publish this book? When we decided to embark on this endeavor and invite all the authors who enthusiastically contributed to this volume, we did not think much about it. In the same way, it happens in our daily practice as researchers in psychotherapy. We simply have questions passed down by the tradition in psychotherapy research. We have caught questions that have been transformed and questions that have become personally valuable to us through our experiences as supervisors and teachers, and why not say it, as psychotherapists and patients. Likewise, we are also determined to find the best ways to answer them.

Moreover, we publish these responses when we answer them—always partially, always with new questions. Every time we go down this path and start over, we leave a trace in the methodology section and take away some learnings. When the research is qualitative, methodological development is distributed throughout all the articles, yet in some way, it is nowhere. The above has been concerning us for a while.

In our doctoral studies, a professor used to say: "What is not published does not exist." Furthermore, the word "publish" originates from the Latin "publicus," which means "public" or "of the people." In this etymological meaning, publishing is about making something accessible or known to the public. In this broad sense, publishing involves making information, news, writings, or other content available through various printed or digital media.

In the case of scientific publications, such as the nature of this book, the task is challenging, especially when we gather to write. So, once again, why publish this

A. Tomicic (✉) · J. D. Soto
Faculty of Psychology, Centre for Studies in Clinical Psychology and Psychotherapy (CEPPS), Diego Portales University, Santiago, Chile

Millennium Institute for Research in Depression and Personality (MIDAP), Santiago, Chile
e-mail: alemka.tomicic@mail.udp.cl; javiera.duarte@mail.udp.cl

A. Tomicic, J. D. Soto (eds.), *Qualitative Research in Clinical Psychology and Psychotherapy in Latin America*, https://doi.org/10.1007/978-3-031-90782-1_1

book? Well, it is a rhetorical question. However, we will answer it, nonetheless, and let us show or emphasize how the publication of this book, even if we have yet to fully reflect on it initially, shows a vocation for knowledge construction, disciplinary relevance, and ethical commitment.

Regarding knowledge construction, even though it may be evident when the research findings are made public through a scientific publication, they become available to other researchers in the field and professionals. By critically reading our studies and their results, they can apply and adapt them to evidence-oriented practice. As we mentioned earlier, the knowledge we have produced over the years using qualitative methodology in psychotherapy research is published in this book. This knowledge is made available to the academic community, researchers, professionals, and students, both in Latin America and for those in the global north. They can undoubtedly benefit from our insights.

On the other hand, when thinking about research questions and problems, we take the time to reflect on the relevance of the projects we formulate. You have probably heard that a knowledge gap, a research purpose or question without relevance to others, lacking social and disciplinary significance, is not a research problem (the only problem that makes us happy, by the way). At that moment, we start thinking about ideas such as the knowledge we produce contributing to accumulating knowledge on the subject and deepening our understanding of a less explored topic in a given context, with a particular methodology, or helping to elucidate the replicability of the relationship between certain variables, just to name a few common ideas. However, we less frequently mention the relevance of our progress in developing or refining methodologies in each of our research that make the phenomena we study visible, allowing us to generate evidence. Now, what does this have to do with this publication? It is simple. We have thought that in this book, as in any scientific publication, we can fulfill the "promise" of the methodological relevance of our research that is not always declared. By responding here to this promise or part of it, we make it available to the academic and professional community and, why not, to ourselves.

And what about the ethical aspect? What is it all about? It is about everything, really, and inseparable from the previous points. However, when we think about it from an ethical dimension, one essential aspect of this book is what we could call "transparency."

Transparency is an important topic, particularly in the context of the peer review process, which is an essential aspect of scientific publication. Peer review involves subjecting the manuscript created by the authors to a critical and evaluative analysis. This process aims to enhance the quality of the work and improve the communication of the knowledge generated. On one hand, this scrutiny serves as a quality control measure; on the other hand, it reflects an attitude of humility and openness to feedback, both of which are fundamentally ethical. This is critical because the knowledge produced through research—including the methodologies used—has real effects on how we understand and construct reality. These effects can have both positive and negative consequences.

Then, if it is not published, it does not exist for others, and this existence has, at the very least, a vocation for knowledge construction, disciplinary relevance, and ethical commitment. Why publish this book, then? We believe for these three reasons.

So, let us move forward to two additional questions: What is qualitative research in clinical psychology and psychotherapy? And why qualitative research in clinical psychology and psychotherapy in Latin America?

What is Qualitative Research in Clinical Psychology and Psychotherapy? It Is a Matter of Convenience Between the Method, Theory, and Study Subject

Norman Denzin and Yvonna Lincoln (2005) provided a general and broad definition of qualitative research, indicating that it is a knowledge-producing activity in which the researcher and their positioning in the world are at the center. This implies deploying practices that make the studied phenomena visible, such as interviews, observations, field notes, conversations, photographs, and video recordings. They also pointed out that qualitative research adopt a naturalistic, descriptive, and interpretative approach to these phenomena, studying them in their natural contexts and striving to understand their meaning from the perspective of the individuals who experience them.

This initial approach to a definition of qualitative research also implies a set of beliefs that are not subject to inquiry and that guide the actions of the researchers. These beliefs, which we refer to as research paradigms, involve conceptions about the nature of reality, the relationship of knowledge we establish with it, and confident methodological choices in line with the aforementioned (Guba & Lincoln, 1994). The paradigmatic diversity resulting from these various ontological, epistemological, and methodological conceptions gives rise to different approaches within qualitative research, which are also shaped by disciplinary origins, research purposes, and data collection and analysis procedures. Therefore, to name a few of these paradigmatic and approach variations, we find narrative, phenomenology, ethnography, case study, grounded theory, and discursive analyses (Titscher et al., 2000).

Despite this diversity, as one would expect, qualitative paradigms and approaches share the focus on qualities while simultaneously seeking a comprehensive and holistic understanding of phenomena through detailed description, connecting parts to the whole. The above is achieved primarily through inductive and abductive procedures to build intersubjective meanings and interpretations within the research context (Daher et al., 2017).

Nevertheless, what most characterizes qualitative research is the alignment between method and theory or between method and the subject of study. This alignment gives qualitative research a distinct shape in various disciplinary fields and contexts where its methods are employed. That is why in this book, and others of its kind, we discuss qualitative research in clinical psychology and psychotherapy, not just generic qualitative research. Both the research problems and their areas of study—cognitive, emotional, bodily processes, psychological suffering, adult patients, children and adolescent patients, couples, families, psychosocial interventions, psychotherapy, etc. —demand an application of methodology—the theory of the method—that adapts to the unique nature of the subject.

Regarding those mentioned above, there is a specific consideration for qualitative research in clinical psychology and psychotherapy. According to Stiles (2015), in this context, qualitative research plays a significant role in what he refers to as "Theory Building" and "Enriching Research." The former can be traced back to a long history, notably in the origins recognized today, such as psychoanalysis and the tradition of case studies (McLeod, 2010). This type of research aims to assess, enhance, and expand a specific theory by comparing and reconciling it with observations, striving for a unified and comprehensive explanation within the framework of that theory. Conversely, "enriching research," says Stile (2015), aims to deepen and augment people's understanding or appreciation of a phenomenon by examining it from diverse perspectives and unraveling explicit and implicit meanings. Therefore, although theory building has typically been associated with quantitative and nomothetic methods, while enriching research has leaned toward qualitative and ideographic approaches, at least in psychotherapy research, these prior distinctions are flexible. Thus, Stiles (2015) argued that qualitative and ideographic methods may be especially suitable for theory-building research in psychotherapy; nevertheless, as will be discussed at the end of this book, quantitative data can also be valuable, as evidenced by mixed research designs in clinical psychology and psychotherapy.

Why Qualitative Research in Clinical Psychology and Psychotherapy in Latin America? A Matter of Uniqueness

Qualitative research in psychotherapy has shown significant developments in the context of the Global South. Much of this, in contrast to the strong tradition of Randomized Clinical Trials (RCTs) developed in North America and Europe, is because the origins of psychotherapy research societies in Latin America (e.g., the Society for Psychotherapy Research—SPR) were originally efforts by psychotherapists (Martínez & Tomicic, 2014). This was passed on to many new generations, that is to say, the identity of psychotherapist-researchers (de la Parra, 2013). Furthermore, this dual identity entails the notion that psychotherapy research requires a qualitative dimension, which, among other things, helps bridge the gap between research and the practice of this discipline of psychology (Castonguay & Muran, 2016). The aforementioned is crucial, as discussed at recent annual meetings of the SPR (e.g., Dublin, 2023). The future of psychotherapy demands that research be a part of clinical practice and clinician identity, as well as the training of clinical and scientific therapists, regardless of their theoretical-technical orientations (Lutz, 2023). In this scenario, it can be argued that qualitative research undoubtedly employs scientifically validated methodologies that make it easier to bridge the gap between research and practice in these terms (Levitt et al., 2023).

However, there is another reason to propose qualitative research in clinical practice and psychotherapy as a scientifically valuable and distinctive practice in our continent. As noted by Energici et al. (2025), in Latin America, qualitative research is creative and tends to adhere to principles rather than techniques; the effectiveness of its creative process is about incorporating new approaches rather than maintaining methodological consistency. Additionally, when it comes to studying the complexity of the subject we call psychotherapy (Orlinsky, 2009), as the authors point out, the subject(s) guide the creative endeavor, often in a manner very similar to clinical psychology and a psychotherapeutic process.

This book's edition aims to provide a comprehensive overview, a showcase, and a reference tool for developments in qualitative research for the study of clinical psychology and psychotherapy in Latin America. At the same time, it aims to offer materials to be used in the training of future psychotherapists. It conveys a balance between methodology and creativity that makes it possible, as we said, to bridge the gap between research and practice in clinical psychology and psychotherapy. Following, in part, the traditional division of psychotherapy research, we have organized its chapters into three parts: Change in Psychotherapy, the Psychotherapeutic Process, and Innovative Qualitative Methods for studying complex phenomena in clinical psychology and psychotherapy.

The study of change in psychotherapy, in its origins, was exclusively conducted with qualitative methodologies and serves as a counterpart to outcome studies, predominantly carried out with RCTs and quantitative methods. Chile and other Latin American countries have a long tradition of studying Generic Change Indicators (Krause et al., 2007) and follow-up studies that incorporate the perspectives of both psychotherapists and patients and their families. These research traditions have produced and refined systems of observation and interviews, as well as qualitative analysis, which provide access to various answers—with adults, adolescents, and children—to a fundamental question that is not as obvious as it seems: What changes in psychotherapy?

On the other hand, research on the psychotherapeutic process, rather than asking what changes, questions psychotherapy about how and the way mechanisms of change occur. The tradition of process and process outcome, more recent in the history of psychotherapy research, often combines qualitative and quantitative methods in mixed designs. Regarding qualitative research on psychotherapeutic processes, Latin America stands out in using methods for observing live or recorded therapy sessions. It also distinguishes in using relevant episodes (Duarte et al., 2019) and making visible the micro-processes in the interaction between patient and therapist. According to outcome studies, underlying change mechanisms (e.g., emotional regulation, changes in subjective positions, mentalization, etc.) are also involved.

Finally, the development of innovative qualitative methods for studying complex phenomena in clinical psychology and psychotherapy is distinctive in Latin America. It offers significant opportunities to close the gap between scientific and clinical practice. Due to its contextual nature and the predominance of social determinants, the question, for example, about the subjective experiences of different mental health issues in various population groups is, in its nature, creative and innovative. However, in Latin America, qualitative research designs have been developed—based on what we consider traditional—to incorporate data collection practices and analysis processes that allow for a clinically valuable understanding of these complex experiences.

This Book

In this book, we bring together the work of researchers from Chile, Argentina, and Peru who have generated valuable clinical and disciplinary knowledge using qualitative methodologies. Each chapter includes research lines that illustrate innovative methodological developments that aim to align with their subject of study. Furthermore, throughout its different chapters, it offers a broad perspective of the main traditions of qualitative research in clinical psychology and psychotherapy: change, process, and subjective experience of mental illness and suffering.

In the first part, about research on change in psychotherapy, various approaches have allowed us to elucidate what changes in psychotherapy. Of particular interest is the study of Generic Change Indicators, a method internationally recognized and whose origin comes from Latin America (Chaps. 2 and 3). It has crossed the threshold of studying psychotherapy with adult patients and adapted to the research of the experience of psychotherapeutic change with children and adolescents. In this regard, two chapters of this part present the developments of drawing as a technique for collecting the narratives of children and adolescents and their relationship and tensions with their use as projective techniques in clinical intervention (Chaps. 6 and 7). As a broad framework in which these techniques can be implemented, the developments of researchers from Peru and Argentina with the application of single-case studies for understanding change in highly complex patients are exciting (Chaps. 4 and 5). This qualitative methodology provides generalizations to a phenomenon rather than a population, contributing to the construction of theories.

In the second part, on qualitative research on the psychotherapy process, the most innovative and challenging developments in this landscape are presented to answer how change occurs over time and within sessions—going to the applying of methodologies to making implicit relational change experiences in the psychotherapeutic process explicit to the analysis of conversational interaction and changes in the discursive positioning of the patient and therapist throughout therapy (Chaps. 8, 10, and 12). Therefore, this section presents the developments of Chilean and Peruvian research teams in terms of a robust methodological set of tools (Chaps. 9 and 11). These tools are not only relevant for research but also for clinical practice. Furthermore, one of the chapters in this section incorporates video recording technologies and feedback into both intervention and research, as some authors have called the new materialism in qualitative research (Chap. 13).

The third part, on innovative qualitative methods for studying complex phenomena in clinical psychology and psychotherapy, brings together four works firmly rooted in the most original vocation of qualitative research and its foundation in the social sciences. Therefore, it is unsurprising that one of its chapters references a variation of Grounded Theory (Chap. 14). However, acknowledging the particularity of qualitative research in psychotherapy, the chapter offers an interpretation of this traditional qualitative research method, which allows it to be adapted to the specific requirements of the subject of study. Another chapter in this section presents not only an innovative development but also something original and challenging, focusing on the demands of research in clinical psychology and psychotherapy that have been difficult to grasp: the body (Chap. 15). As its authors suggest, understanding that phenomenology and psychotherapy share an interest in experience, techniques based on art, and phenomenological interviews which can be promising qualitative approaches for psychotherapy and research.

Finally, the last two chapters of this section also have a concluding purpose, since they can be thought of as framing a main narrative or providing the key to interpret the book as a whole (Chaps. 16 and 17). We know this is not a book to read necessarily in a sequential manner; these chapters could be the first or the only reading—just like any of the seventeen chapters that make it up. So why place them here? Well, because these chapters offer a comprehensive, realistic, and critical view of mixed research models on the one hand and the practice of teaching qualitative research on the other. These are essentials for natural development when we are considering what the title of this book promises: Qualitative research in clinical psychology and psychotherapy as a creative study for complex objects in context.

References

Castonguay, L., & Muran, J. C. (Eds.). (2016). *Practice-Oriented Research in Psychotherapy: Building partnerships between clinicians and researchers*. Oxford University Press.

Daher, M., Carré, D., Jaramillo, A., Olivares, H., & Tomicic, A. (2017). Experience and meaning in qualitative research: Conceptual review and a methodological device proposal based on phenomenological-hermeneutic remarks. *Forum: Qualitative Social Research, 18*(3), Art. 9. https://doi.org/10.17169/fqs-18.3.2696

De la Parra, G. (2013). Psychotherapy research in developing countries: The case of Latin America. *Psychotherapy Research*, 609–623. https://doi.org/10.1080/10503307.2013.830794

Denzin, N. K., & Lincoln, Y. S. (Eds.). (2005). *The Sage handbook of qualitative research*. Sage.

Duarte, J., Martínez, C., & Tomicic, A. (2019). Revisión teórica y metodológica de los eventos relevantes en psicoterapia para el estudio del cambio [Theoretical and methodological review of significant events in psychotherapy for the study of change]. *Revista Argentina de Clínica Psicológica, 28*(3), 253–265. https://doi.org/10.24205/03276716.2019.1141

Energici, M., Tomicic, A., & Schöngut-Grollmus, N. (2025). Qualitative research quality in Latin American vulnerable and precarious contexts. In U. Flick (Ed.), *The SAGE handbook of qualitative research design*. Sage Publications. https://doi.org/10.4135/9781529674354

Guba, E. G., & Lincoln, Y. S. (1994). Competing paradigms in qualitative research. In N. K. Denzin & Y. S. Lincoln (Eds.), *Handbook of qualitative research* (pp. 105–117). Sage Publications, Inc.

Krause, M., de la Parra, G., Arístegui, R., Dagnino, P., Tomicic, A., Valdés, N., Echávarri, O., Vilches, O., Ben-Dov, P., Strasser, K., Reyes, L., Altimir, C., & Ramírez, I. (2007). The evolution of therapeutic change studied through generic change indicators. *Psychotherapy Research, 17*(6), 673–689.

Levitt, H. M, Hamburger, A., Hill, C. E., McLeod, J., Pascual-Leone, A., Timulak, L., Buchholz, M., Fuertes, J., Frommer, J., Iwakabe, S., Martinez, C., Morrill, Z., Knox, S., Langer, P., Muran, J. C., Oddli, H., Řiháček, T., Tomicic, A., & Tuval-Mashiach, R. (2023). Broadening the evidentiary basis for clinical guidance: Recommendations from international qualitative psychotherapy researchers. *American Psychologist, under revision.*

Lutz, W. (2023). Presidential address. In *54th International Annual Meeting, Dublin, Ireland*, p. 21 June to 24 June.

Martínez, C., & Tomicic, A. (2014). Mendoza: Un viaje de 20 años (1992–2012) [Mendoza: A 20-Year Journey (1992–2012)]. *Gaceta de Psiquiatría Universitaria, 10*(1), 97–107.

McLeod, J. (2010). *Case study research in counselling and psychotherapy*. Sage.

Orlinsky, D. E. (2009). The "Generic Model of Psychotherapy" after 25 years: Evolution of a research-based metatheory. *Journal of Psychotherapy Integration, 19*(4), 319.

Stiles, W. B. (2015). Theory building, enriching, and fact gathering: Alternative purposes of psychotherapy research. In En O. C. G. Gelo, A. Pritz & B. Rieken (Eds.), *Psychotherapy research: Foundations, process and outcome* (pp. 159–179). Springer. https://doi.org/10.1007/978-3-7091-1382-0_8

Titscher, S., Meyer, M., Wodak, R., & Vetter, E. (2000). *Methods of text and discourse analysis*. Sage.

Part I
Qualitative Research on Psychotherapeutic Change

Chapter 2
Qualitative Methods as a Road to Conceptual Innovation

Mariane Krause

Introduction

Qualitative methodology as a path for the construction of theoretical models dates to the early writings of Glaser and Strauss in the 1960s. However, in clinical psychology, it is possible to trace back to Freud, who indeed, in his studies on hysteria, constructed his impressive theory based on his own systematic observations, although certainly not without criticism (Bogousslavsky & Dieguez, 2014).

Following the logic of Glaser and Strauss (1967), for the evolution of knowledge, there are moments when it is necessary to apply a methodology that promotes discovery, and with it conceptual and theoretical innovation, since, if not done, there is a risk of stagnation in the construction of new knowledge by adhering excessively to the framework of already established theories.

Glaser and Strauss (1967), both sociologists, proposed breaking these barriers to achieve conceptual innovation, which according to their standpoint was inhibited by excessive adherence to the grand sociological theories of the time. For this, they created a methodology that would allow them to generate new concepts and theoretical models from the data through an inductive process that advances from the particular to the more general. These founders of systematic qualitative methodology (Glaser, 1978; Strauss, 1987; Strauss & Corbin, 1991) define it as an inductive method for the development of theoretical models, stating that their procedures were designed to develop a well-integrated set of concepts that provide a detailed and precise theoretical explanation of the social phenomena being studied. They

M. Krause (✉)
Faculty of Psychology, Pontificia Universidad Católica de Chile, Santiago, Chile

Millennium Institute for Research in Depression and Personality (MIDAP), Santiago, Chile
e-mail: mkrause@uc.cl

A. Tomicic, J. D. Soto (eds.), *Qualitative Research in Clinical Psychology and Psychotherapy in Latin America*, https://doi.org/10.1007/978-3-031-90782-1_2

argue that an empirically grounded theory should explain while describing (Corbin & Strauss, 1990).

These authors were successful with their proposal, their most outstanding achievement being precisely the creation of this methodology, which, in line with its mission, they called "Grounded Theory," and which permeated all social sciences, including psychology, particularly clinical psychology and psychotherapy research. Thanks to them, qualitative methodologies began to enjoy increasing acceptance as a legitimate method for accessing knowledge. Hence, their use has proliferated across all continents.

This was the initial impetus for what would later be called "discovery-oriented research" (Mahrer, 1988), instead of "verification-oriented research." As will be seen later in this chapter, these poles, which in the history of qualitative methodology initially represented an irreconcilable epistemological controversy (Guba, 1990), can now be understood as different, both necessary, moments in the process of knowledge generation.

The chapter illustrates—with examples from diverse moments of the construction of the psychotherapeutic change model—the alternation between phases oriented toward discovery, model construction, and stages of validation, showing how in this transition not only qualitative methodology is applied but also quantitative, in a dynamic interplay between both types of methodology.

Qualitative Methods in Clinical Psychology and Psychotherapy Research

In Clinical Psychology, qualitative methods are especially useful for accessing the perspective of people suffering from certain disorders to understand them from their subjectivity. For example, to assess the depressive experience, managing to establish conditions of recovery that from quantitative methods are not entirely accessible (Vásquez et al., 2020), or to investigate little-known topics, such as the psychotherapeutic experience of patients with schizophrenia (Krause et al., 2016). Qualitative follow-up studies post-therapy (Fernández et al., 2020) are also valuable, providing relevant information on the conditions for maintaining psychotherapeutic change over time.

In psychotherapy research, qualitative methods are of great utility to answer basic questions such as: What changes through psychotherapy? And how does the change occur? Thus, they allow us to elucidate phenomena that occur during the therapeutic process and to determine mechanisms of change, such as, for example, the effects of certain therapeutic interventions on the evolution of change (Dagnino et al., 2012).

These two basic questions underlie most studies of the psychotherapeutic process. The first can be addressed with qualitative descriptive analysis; however, the second, more complex, requires relational analyses in which conditions for the occurrence of psychotherapeutic change can be established. For this purpose, it is necessary to work with "emergent designs," where the selection of participants or the sample of therapy segments, data collection, and analysis are not separate but integrated phases. This way, it is possible to work with hypotheses that are successively contrasted to refine the emerging conceptual models.

In operational terms, the primary data of qualitative process research are often observation, interviews, or documents (e.g., therapists' or patients' notes). If the design is "emergent," these data sources will be selected through a "successive strategy," where the analysis of the initial data will generate concepts, conceptual categories, and hypotheses that will be used to create criteria for selecting new data sets that will integrate the sample. This process, in the tradition of Grounded Theory, is called "theoretical sampling," where "theoretical" refers to the theory being constructed. The concepts generated from the initial data are compared with the new evidence and usually corrected until reaching a point called "theoretical saturation," at which new data no longer add additional information. When the goal is the construction of a conceptual model, "theoretical saturation" applies not only to isolated categories but also to the relationships between them (Krause, 1995).

The results of research conducted with this methodology have led to significant advances in the investigation of the psychotherapeutic process, as shown by qualitative meta-analyses (e.g., see Timulák & Lietaer, 2001).

Toward the Psychotherapeutic Change Model

To account for the context of the construction of the psychological change model, a brief historical overview of the different stages of the research program will be exposed.

This research program (www.psicoterapiaycambio.cl) began in the 1990s, starting with the study of change from the perspective of clients with interviews, which allowed the development of a first global model of psychotherapeutic change, followed by the observational study of change (first decade of the 2000s), from which Generic Change Indicators (GCI) were developed. In subsequent years, the study of Change and Stuck Episodes was added, and then the Therapeutic Activity Coding System (TACS) was developed for the microanalysis of therapeutic actions occurring within the episodes. In the next decade, researchers from the Psychotherapy and Change Program developed the study of verbal and non-verbal communication in different episodes (Tomicic et al., 2015; Valdés et al., 2010a); the mutual verbal and non-verbal regulation between patient and therapist (Altimir et al., 2017); the definition and study of mentalization episodes (Morán et al., 2020); and continued with the investigation of therapeutic success and failure (Suárez-Delucchi et al., 2022). Then, greater emphasis was placed again on the subjective experience, in this case of patients with specific disorders, such as depression (Fernández et al., 2022; Vásquez et al., 2020) or schizophrenia (Abarzúa et al., 2016), and distinguishing different age groups (Núñez et al., 2021).

Although the different study topics were developed successively, most of them have been maintained over time, as the team of researchers expanded. This chapter will particularly focus on the development of the change model and the GCI, including the study of episodes, with other topics being addressed in later chapters of this book.

The Initial Model of Psychotherapeutic Change

The construction of the generic psychotherapeutic change model included two qualitative studies. One conducted in Germany, between 1988 and 1991, with participants who were interviewed about their psychotherapeutic experience[1]; another conducted in Chile, between 1993 and 1995[2], also on the psychotherapeutic experience, which was part of a quantitative study on social representations of psychological help in economically disadvantaged sectors. To the data from these two studies, some interviews with Argentine clients facilitated by researchers from that country were added. These initial studies, which laid the groundwork for advancing toward the change model (Krause, 1992a, 1992b, 2005/2011; Krause et al., 1994), focused on reconstructing change from the perspective of the clients, with special emphasis on the development of a conceptual model, based on the methodological proposals of the Grounded Theory (Strauss & Corbin, 1991).

The methodological approach of the study conducted in Germany was narrative and biographical. Life stories of clients were collected with the intention to understand the effects of psychological help in the biographical context of each person and to reconstruct psychotherapeutic changes from their personal subjective experience. In this way, the meanings of personal experience would be in the foreground. This approach is part of a tradition of qualitative research on subjectivity that had its roots in sociology (Denzin, 1989) and was later introduced into psychology (Flick, 1987, 1991). This study included a total of 41 biographical narrative interviews (Schütze, 1983) with 19 clients from diverse socio-economic backgrounds (interviewed two to three times), plus 16 interviews with mental health professionals and 19 detailed descriptions of the interview situations.

The second of these studies included 27 participants from low-income sectors of Santiago, Chile. In both studies, a successive strategy was followed for the selection of participants (Strauss & Corbin, 1991), creating a parallelism between data collection and analysis. The reconstruction of the therapeutic experience of the interviewed individuals, although based on their narratives, included the perspective of their therapists and the researcher herself. The joint analysis of these three

---

[1] Doctoral research by M. Krause funded by the DAAD, with the sponsorship of the Free University of Berlin.

[2] Study funded by the Chilean Science and Technology Fund (FONDECYT, project No. 1930700).

perspectives on the object of study is understood as "triangulation" (Denzin, 1970; Flick, 1990), one of the rigor criteria in qualitative research.

Considerating the aspiration of these studies to generate a transtheoretical model, psychologists and psychiatrists from different therapeutic schools were included, such as Psychoanalysis, Psychodynamic Therapy, Gestalt Therapy, Cognitive Behavioral Therapy, Systemic Therapy, Person-Centered (Rogerian) Therapy, Transactional Analysis, plus some therapists with an eclectic orientation.

In both studies, semi-structured interviews lasting between 60 and 120 minutes were conducted, with an emphasis on "narrative contents" (Schütze, 1983), although the biographical character was deeper in the study conducted in Germany. The interviews were recorded and then transcribed verbatim. Data analysis was conducted according to the procedures of the Grounded Theory (Strauss & Corbin, 1991), considering the stages of "open," "axial," and "selective" coding.

To generate categories for the conceptual model, an alternation between intra-case and inter-case analysis was employed, where each client's experience was analyzed by a team of researchers, considering their life and/or biographical context and generating concepts and categories for labeling the changes and their conditions of occurrence. This "open coding" process is quite similar across qualitative approaches that work with verbal contents.

Then, individual cases were compared with each other to transform specific concepts into more transversal categories. Throughout the analysis, there was an oscillation between particular concepts and more general conceptual categories, that is, between detail and the global perspective. Paraphrasing anthropologist Clifford Geertz (1983), it is permanently jumping from one side to the other, looking at the whole from the perspective of the details, which give it closeness and vitality, and seeing the details from the perspective of the whole, from which they become understandable, which is typical of inductive methods. The categories and questions that arose from the comparative analysis were used for the successive selection of cases and were contrasted in their analyses. With this procedure, a hierarchical system of categories was finally obtained in which all cases were accommodated, and where the same system could be applied to each case to obtain a comprehensive description of their individual change process.

Up to this point, the results were descriptive-interpretative. However, to reach a conceptual model, additional steps of analysis are needed, which involve establishing relationships between the categories extracted from the data. For the establishment of these, the Grounded Theory (Strauss & Corbin, 1991) proposes a "coding paradigm," which contains the following elements: a "phenomenon" (which is the central "object" on which the relational scheme is based), "antecedent conditions" (of the phenomenon), the "context" in which it appears, "intervening conditions" (of the broader context), "action/interaction strategies" that sustain the phenomenon, and "consequences." In practice, depending on the object of study, some of these elements may not appear, but the proposal is to search in the data (or through new data) for empirical elements to establish these conceptual relationships.

In the case of these initial studies of the psychotherapeutic change process, the result was a generic (transtheoretical) model, influenced both by the epistemology of subjectivity and by a contextual understanding of change. The model proposed successive phases in the evolution of psychotherapeutic change and included immediate conditions of the context of appearance, given by the therapeutic structure, but also those of the broader biographical and sociocultural context of the clients. The search for the contents of change was conducted, emphasizing clients' subjectivity beyond their symptoms, which, however, were not excluded. The central conclusion is that generic psychotherapeutic change occurs in the dimension of the representation of reality, very much in line with the assumption that human beings do not behave based on what things "are" but according to their representation of them (Taylor & Bogdan, 1986), representation that includes cognitive, emotional, and evaluative aspects and is implicit in behavior.

In summary, and so was it expressed in the book Psychotherapy and Change, "Generic psychotherapeutic change is primarily related to the subjective perspective of the clients, regarding themselves and their difficulties, their problems, and symptoms, and regarding the relationship of these with the environment in which they occur. This change, which clients express through terms like 'changes in the way of thinking' or 'the way of seeing things,' can be conceptualized as a change in the subjective patterns of interpretation and explanation that lead to the development of new subjective theories" (Krause, 2005, p. 333).

Furthermore, the results of these initial studies also indicate that this change is processual, beginning in the stage before the encounter with professional help, developing throughout the entire helping relationship, and usually continuing to settle afterward. This model of change is one of successive phases, where previous changes constitute the foundation for subsequent ones (Krause, 1992b) (Table 2.1).

According to this model, for the subsequent maintenance of changes, the integration of psychological modes of interpretation (the fact that the clients make them "their own") is crucial, with the consequent development of their autonomy.

This model has demonstrated its conceptual consistency with other models of change progression, emerging from psychotherapy research, such as the Common Therapeutic Components Model applicable to all therapies (Frank, 1971, 1982); the Non-Specific Therapeutic Agents Model by Karasu (1986); the Assimilation of Problematic Experiences Model (APES) (Stiles, 2001); the Transtheoretical Model by Prochaska and Norcross (2002, Prochaska & DiClemente, 1983); or the Two-Stage Semiotic Model (TSSM) by Gennaro et al. (2010).

These models propose that there is a generic psychotherapeutic change, common to different types of therapy, that is progressively constructed and evolves in stages toward transformations of greater complexity and depth.

From the Client's Subjectivity to External Observation

After the first stage of the research program, with qualitative data from retrospective interviews with clients, another stage followed, with a strong emphasis on observation as the primary method of data collection. The mission of this second stage was

Table 2.1 Phases of the change process

Changes before the start of the helping relationship
I. Experience of one's own limits.
II. Acceptance of the need for help.
III. Questioning of personal explanatory models ("unfreezing").
IV. Transformation of the conceptualization of one's own problems and symptoms and the development of goals for therapy.
V. Development of the patient's expectations regarding the role or function of the therapist, regarding their role, and regarding the structure "unfreezing" relationship.
Changes that usually occur during the therapeutic relationship
VI. Acceptance of the (asymmetric) structure of the helping relationship.
VII. First emotional adjustment ("attunement") between the patient and the therapist, which will form the basis for the development of a trusting relationship.
VIII. Acceptance of the therapist's role as "expert."
IX. Visualization of one's own psychological concerns as something "treatable" with defined procedures.
X. Encounter with the therapist's "therapeutic theory" (and first acceptance of it).
XI. Acceptance of a "psychological meaning context" as a framework for working with own concerns and symptoms.
XII. Redefinition and revaluation of own concerns and symptoms.
XIII. Focus on the patient's biography, which will form the basis for a new "self-understanding" and for subsequent therapeutic work.
XIV. Interconnection of problems and symptoms, through which "subjective constructs" about own psychological functioning are formed.
XV. Construction of a subjective theory of a psychological type, grounded in biography, which can be considered the final product of generic therapeutic change.

to operationalize the contents of the change model in the form of observable indicators, which, according to the transtheoretical logic of the model, were called "Generic Change Indicators" (GCI) (Krause et al., 2006, 2007, 2015). In this second stage, three successive studies were conducted between the years 2003 and 2011, funded by Chilean state research funds.[3] The three studies had a longitudinal design for real-time tracking of complete therapeutic processes of around 20 sessions. The therapies were conducted in natural contexts of mental health services in Chile (Krause et al., 2015) and included different theoretical orientations (psychodynamic, systemic, social-constructionist, and cognitive-behavioral) and diverse modalities (individual, couple, family, and group), reaching a total of 39 clients. A

[3] 2003–2005: "Towards an effective practice in psychotherapy: study of relevant episodes of change, in different types of psychotherapy, and their effects on the therapeutic results." Funding: FONDECYT [National Fund for Science and Technology] N° 1030482.

2006–2007: "Facilitating change in psychotherapy: effective and ineffective communicational interactions in different psychotherapeutic modalities" Funding: FONDECYT [National Fund for Science and Technology] N° 1060768.

2008–2011: "Therapeutic interaction, expression of emotions and therapeutic alliance: Study of the essential ingredients of change, in different cultural contexts." Funding: FONDECYT [National Fund for Science and Technology] N° 1080136).

mixed methodology, qualitative and quantitative, was used, oriented toward discovery in the first stage and then mostly toward verification.

Change episodes, moments, and Generic Change Indicators were determined in all therapies (see Fig. 2.1), while simultaneously evaluating psychological well-being and symptomatic evolution through the OQ-45.2 questionnaire, validated for the Chilean population by Von Bergen & de la Parra (2002). This self-report questionnaire, created by Lambert in 1996, evaluates "subjective distress," "interpersonal relationships," and "social role" and is used worldwide.

The first study was mainly focused on the refinement and validation of the Generic Change Indicators that had been developed in the previous stage. The study of Change Episodes was added to the work with the GCI, as it was assumed that the indicators would be housed in these episodes. In the following studies, the validation of the GCI continued, and the study of communication between patients and therapists was added, finally including the therapeutic alliance as well.

All these studies maintained a strong qualitative component in data production, as these were collected through the observation of therapeutic sessions, to which the quantitative evaluation of psychological well-being was added. The analysis of these observational data was initially qualitative and then included quantification to answer some research questions, such as the possible relationship between change in meanings and symptomatic change. Furthermore, the conceptual categories related to therapeutic communication, initially qualitative, were later subjected to quantification to statistically analyze the relationship between therapeutic communication actions and change.

These studies started from the assumption, based on previous literature, that therapeutic change would occur in specific segments of psychotherapy, called "change episodes" (Fiedler & Rogge, 1989). This research tradition gained

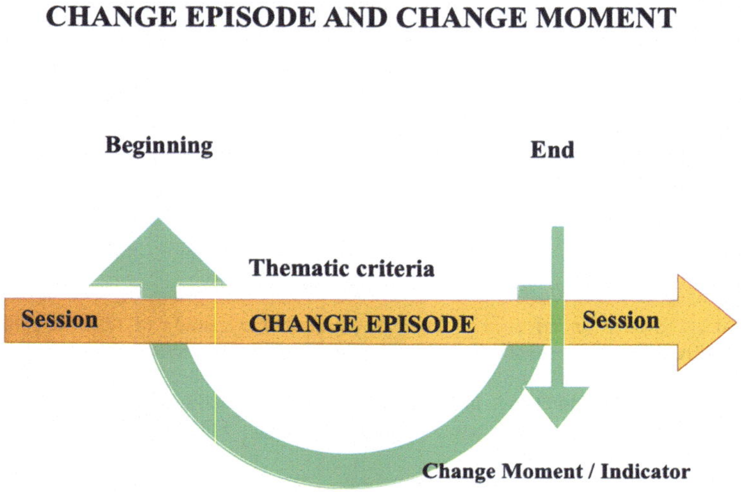

Fig. 2.1 Change episode and change moment

significant momentum in the 1980s, following the studies of Rainer Bastine (1989) in Germany and Robert Elliott (1984) in the USA, and continues to be relevant today, with a certain diversification of types of change episodes (Fitzpatrick & Chamodraka, 2007; Timulák & Lietaer, 2001; Krause, 2023). Currently, these episodes are studied under various names, such as change moments (Gazzolla et al., 2003; Krause et al., 2007), innovative moments (Gonçalves et al., 2009; Matos et al., 2009), moments of connection (McCarthy et al., 2011; Mergenthaler, 2008), events of relational depth (Wiggins et al., 2012), sudden gains (Wucherpfennig et al., 2017), and emotional processing episodes (Watson et al., 2011). Their common characteristic is that they designate segments of positive transformation in the patient's change process. Likewise, there is considerable consensus that the dimension of subjective meanings is crucial in these change segments (Adler et al., 2013).

In the series of three studies, change episodes were first operationally defined, to then relate them the GCI associated with the transformation of meanings that occurred in these episodes. A culminating moment of this transformation was empirically determined, distinguishable by characteristic verbal and non-verbal communication, identified by first-person verbalization, with self-referential content and statements in the present tense (Reyes et al., 2008), and an introspective, quiet non-verbal expression. These change moments, which can last from seconds to a few minutes, were considered as the end of the change episode, assigning them a GCI based on the content of the transformation of meanings. The beginning of the therapeutic work on the content in which the change occurred was traced retrospectively to determine the start of the complete change episode. Figure 2.1 illustrates this procedure:

In the first study of this series, the 19 Generic Change Indicators (GCI) were determined, which were refined and validated in the subsequent studies. For this purpose, the following procedure was carried out: All change episodes of each therapy were selected, with their change moments, to which one of the 19 GCI was assigned. Considering that in the first study (years 2003 to 2005), the GCI and the criteria for the selection of episodes were not yet completely defined, both the final list of GCI and the criteria for the definition and delimitation of change episodes were developed during this stage of the research process.

Crucial for these tasks was the conformation of a team of researchers that had to be heterogeneous in terms of psychotherapeutic schools (psychodynamic, humanistic, cognitive-behavioral, systemic, and social-constructionist) and gender (three men and seven women) and to have training in psychotherapy as well as in qualitative research. This team directly observed (through a one-way mirror or on video) all therapy sessions and conducted the analysis with the videos and session transcripts at their disposal. Change moments were defined via observation, due to their verbal and non-verbal characteristics, while the delimitation of episodes and the final assignment of the GCI were carried out based on the transcripts, as content criteria prevailed for the indicators. The data analysis of this material could be defined as qualitative, intersubjective, and confirmatory (Krause et al., 2006).

The three products of the first study with GCI were: (a) the updated and validated list of GCI with the observation of therapies and intersubjective agreement among researchers; (b) the criteria for the definition and determination of change moments; and (c) a training manual for the determination of episodes, moments, and Change Indicators.

Table 2.2 shows the list of the 19 GCI, published for the first time in 2006 (Krause et al., 2006), indicators that for some subsequent analyses were grouped into three major phases of change (Krause et al., 2015).

This sequence of GCI reflects an "ideal itinerary" of subjective transformation. Subsequent changes implicitly carry the achievement of the previous ones, with the first being considered more basic or superficial in terms of psychic transformation and the later ones more complex and profound (Dagnino et al., 2012).

The criteria for the definition of change moments are presented in Table 2.3.

In summary, the results of the first study in the series with GCI confirmed the possibility of operationalizing the phases of change that had been constructed in the

Table 2.2 List of generic change indicators

I. Initial consolidation of the structure of the therapeutic relationship	1. Acceptance of the existence of a problem 2. Acceptance of his/her limits and of the need for help 3. Acceptance of the therapist as a competent professional 4. Expression of hope 5. Questioning of habitual understanding, behavior, and emotions 6. Expression of the need for change 7. Recognition of his/her own participation in the problems
II. Increase in permeability toward new meanings	8. Discovery of new aspects of self 9. Manifestation of new behavior or emotions 10. Appearance of feelings of competence 11. Establishment of new connections between own aspects (beliefs, behaviors, emotions, etc.); own aspects and the environment (people or events); own aspects and biographical elements 12. Reconceptualization of problems and/or symptoms 13. Transformation of valorization and emotions in relation to self or others
III. Construction and consolidation of a new understanding	14. Creation of subjective constructs of self through the interconnection of personal aspects and aspects of the surroundings, including problems and symptoms 15. Founding of the subjective constructs in own biography 16. Autonomous comprehension and use of the context of psychological meaning 17. Acknowledgment of help received 18. Decreased asymmetry between patient and therapist 19. Construction of a biographically grounded subjective theory of self and of his/her relationship with surroundings (global indicator)

Table 2.3 Criteria for the definition of change moments

Theoretical correspondence	The content of the change must match one of the 19 Generic Change Indicators
Current relevance	The change must be observed within the session (intra-session change) or reported during it when occurring between sessions (extra-session change)
Novelty	It must be the first time this transformation of meanings appears during the psychotherapeutic process
Consistency	There should be no later moments in the session or therapy that contradict the occurrence of this change. The patient's non-verbal behavior should be consistent with the verbal expression

The training manual for the determination of GCI, which was crucial for the following stages of this research program, is accessible at: www.psicoterapiaycambio.cl

nineties based on interviews (Krause, 1992a, 1992b), so that they could be determined by external observers. This study also fulfilled its transtheoretical aspiration by empirically establishing indicators of change common to different schools and therapeutic modalities. However, as the first sample of therapies was small, the question remained open about possible differences in the frequency of the GCI among different psychotherapeutic schools. This question was addressed in a subsequent study where therapies of different theoretical orientations were compared, concluding that there was no significant difference in the occurrence of GCI among them (Echávarri et al., 2009).

It is worth noting that although the three studies in this phase had a "quantitative component," this was initially applied more for the purpose of describing the participants and later gained more prominence with the objective to compare the evolution of subjective change, evaluated through the GCI, with the evolution of psychological well-being, measured through the OQ-45.2. This involved a significant effort to quantify the GCI, which ultimately led to scientifically and clinically relevant conclusions regarding patients' improvement trajectories (Krause et al., 2015). The greater clinical relevance of this result lies in the fact that the evolution of the GCI, at certain stages of therapy, allows predicting both the evolution in subsequent stages and its final outcome (evaluated by the OQ-45.2). Thus, with this tool, therapists could correct the course of their action (e.g., if they were in the eighth session with a patient and had not yet transitioned to mid-stage GCI).

However, this was not the only step from qualitative to quantitative. Once change episodes and change moments were defined (with the help of the GCI), the question about mechanisms of change arose. With the aim of better understanding therapeutic interaction that favors clients' psychological transformation, the focus changed to the investigation of the therapeutic communication associated with change.

Analysis of Therapeutic Communication: The Return to the Qualitative

Intending to elucidate communicational actions—of patient and therapist—associated with change, we started "from scratch," with the transcriptions of therapies and particularly episodes, attempting to categorize from the ground up, with the logic of Grounded Theory (Strauss & Corbin, 1991), what therapists and patients were doing verbally. This was part of the second study in the series (years 2006–2007), conducted in parallel with the study of the GCI, in a research team that had already grown numerically and diversified in terms of areas of interest.

The speech turn was now the unit of analysis, being the verbalizations of patients and therapists labeled in terms of what therapists and patients were doing communicatively, distinguishing whether they were naming something, asking a question, making an interpretation, or expressing an emotion. This led to the development of a complex taxonomy of communicational actions.

In psychotherapy research, there had been previous classification systems for therapeutic verbal communication, some of them published with the concept of "response modes" (Elliott et al., 1987), but most of them focused either only on the verbalizations of therapists or only of patients, or they were associated with a specific disorder, with the exception of the Verbal Response Mode Coding System by Stiles (1992), which seemed fascinating but complex to apply to the training of coders. Based on these precedents, the research team decided to create its own classification system, which soon also demonstrated the inherent complexity of speech and required creating different dimensions to distinguish types of verbalizations.

The Therapeutic Activity Coding System (TACS) is based on a performative notion of language, understood not as a mere reflection of reality, but as constitutive of it, in the sense that "saying something is doing something" (Reyes et al., 2008). Thus, therapeutic conversation configures a new reality, which is part of psychological change (Valdés et al., 2010b). The TACS was developed in two successive phases, one qualitative, in which the coding system was constructed, and one quantitative, aimed at ensuring its reliability. The construction was carried out with episodes of change from five therapies from the same sample of the studies with GCI.

The TACS considers a dimension of speech content, which distinguishes Scope and Reference, and a dimension of action, which includes the categories: Basic Forms, Communicational Intentions, and Techniques. Within each of these five categories, types of communicational actions are distinguished, as shown in Fig. 2.2.

As seen in Fig. 2.2, the content dimension addresses the subject of the verbalization (Reference), that is, whether the protagonist is the patient, the therapist, or another and whether the verbalization refers to actions, ideas, or affects (Domain).

Regarding the types of communicational actions, the TACS distinguishes five Basic Forms (Agreement, Assertion, Denial, Question, and Direction), three Communicational Intentions (Exploring, Attuning, and Resignifying), and 14 Techniques, such as Justification, Reflection, or Interpretation, among others.

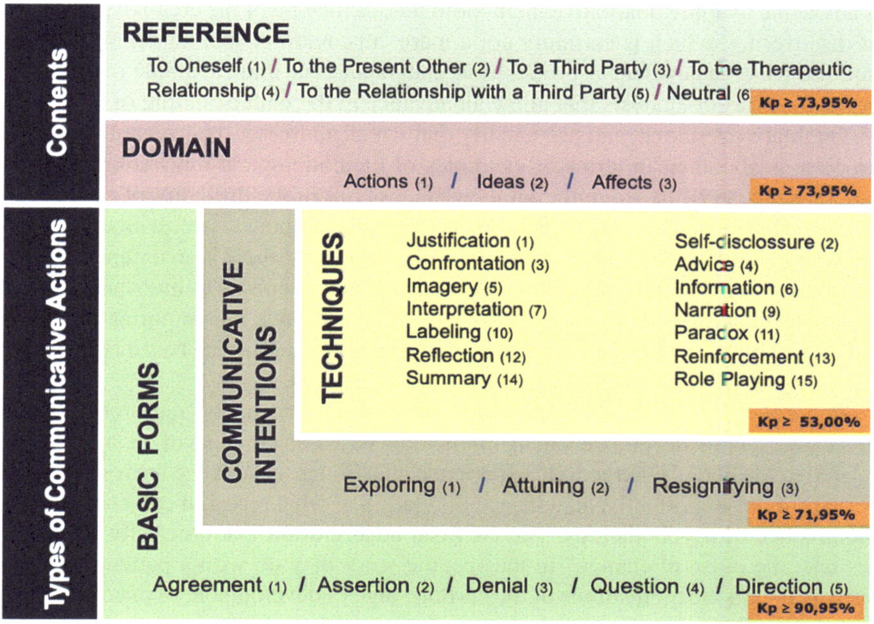

Fig. 2.2 Therapeutic activity coding system

The lessons learned from the TACS are, firstly, the experience of the arduous work to reach a classification system with acceptable levels of reliability among coders (except for the techniques). Secondly, the recognition that the time investment to code small passages of verbal interaction between patient and therapist is high. However, the reward was advancing in the understanding of how therapists' verbalizations transform patients' verbalizations and which verbalizations are more powerful to achieve this effect (Fernández et al., 2012; Valdés et al., 2011). But the application of the TACS also taught that it is not that certain verbalizations are transformative "per se," but rather that this depends on the stage of therapy and the moment of development within the change episode (Dagnino et al., 2012).

Final Reflection

What has been developed in this chapter are the first phases of an ongoing research program, whose most recent developments are reflected in other chapters of this book.

The central message implicit in this narrative is that research is built on a process guided by curiosity and the passion to discover the object of study, in this case, psychotherapeutic change. When the desire to discover prevails over certainties, it is advisable to apply qualitative methodologies, as they favor the creativity of the act of discovering, which is certainly not a mere "uncovering," but an act of creation, through which a new lens is proposed to understand our immeasurable reality, with new categories of analysis that allow an advance in the understanding of it.

Qualitative research, and particularly that which addresses the psychotherapeutic process, is abundant in terms of examples of methodological innovation (Krause, 2023). This can be its strength, but its weakness lies in the difficulty of accumulating knowledge. In the face of this, most recent developments in qualitative meta-analysis (Timulák, 2009) are a promising vein. Evidently, there is an unrenounceable tension between the accumulation of knowledge and openness to innovation, but in this dialectical relationship of the known and the unknown, it is important to keep a balance, which speaks in favor of accumulating more certainties based on research results (even if it is to destroy them with new evidence).

Regarding the specific achievements of the fragment of the research program presented, having developed Change Indicators based on contents of change that are related to the client's therapeutic experience constitutes an advance for research, but perhaps more importantly, an advance in relation to what research can contribute to the practice of psychotherapy. The GCI can be a relevant instrument for therapists to "take the pulse of change" in the specific work they do with a patient. This fits very well with the motivations of the current stage of development of psychotherapy research, where the aim is to strengthen its relationship with practice (Crits-Christoph & Connolly Gibbons, 2021; Espinosa-Duque & Krause, 2020).

On the other hand, having defined and more clearly delineated the Change Episodes could be considered an advance for research, as their previous definitions were ambiguous, but it will only be so to the extent that this definition is disseminated and consensus is reached.

Furthermore, having generated a coding system for therapeutic activity is like recognizing a grain of sand on the vast beach of the ingredients of the psychotherapeutic process. Perhaps the contribution of research with the TACS is having provided evidence of the great complexity involved in this type of research by demonstrating that in psychotherapy it is necessary to make distinctions regarding stages of the process to be able to affirm that something is effective. The same action can promote change at one stage and hinder it at another (Krause, 2023). Thus, the contribution of this phase of our research work has been to remove the veil from our eyes and end the illusion of being able to discover what is effective *per se* in psychotherapy.

A final reflection I would like to share is that, beyond conducting research with scientific rigor and creativity, if we do not manage to share our results with other researchers, to truly accumulate knowledge, and if at the same time we do not channel it so that someone (not necessarily ourselves) transforms it into a useful tool for clinical practice, our endeavor will have been a vain exercise.

References

Abarzúa, M., Silva, M., Navarro, D., & Krause, M. (2016). Psychotherapy from the perspective of Chilean patients with schizophrenia / Psicoterapia desde la perspectiva de pacientes chilenos con esquizofrenia. *Estudios de Psicología, 37(2–3)*, 418–431. https://doi.org/10.1080/02109395.2016.1189204

Adler, J. M., Harmeling, L. H., & Walder-Biesanz, I. (2013). Narrative meaning making is associated with sudden gains in psychotherapy clients' mental health under routine clinical conditions. *Journal of Consulting and Clinical Psychology, 81*(5), 839–845. https://doi.org/10.1037/a0033774

Altimir, C., Capella, C., Núñez, L., Abarzúa, M., & Krause, M. (2017). Meeting in difference: Revisiting the therapeutic relationship based on patients' and therapists' experiences in several clinical contexts. *Journal of Clinical Psychology, 73(11)*, 1510–1522. https://doi.org/10.1002/jclp.22525

Bastine, R., Fiedler, P., & Kommer, D. (1989). Was ist therapeutisch an der Psychotherapie? Versuch einer Bestandsaufnahme und Systematisierung der Psychotherapeutischen Prozeßforschung. [What is therapeutic in psychotherapy? Attempt of stocktaking and codification of the psychotherapeutic process research]. *Zeitschrift für klinische Psychologie, 18*, 3–22.

Bogousslavsky, J., & Dieguez, S. (2014). Sigmund Freud and hysteria: The etiology of psychoanalysis? *Frontiers of Neurology and Neuroscience, 35*, 109–125. https://doi.org/10.1159/000360244

Crits-Christoph, P., & Connolly Gibbons, M. B. (2021). In M. Barkham, W. Lutz, & L. Castonguay (Eds.), *Bergin and Garfield's handbook of psychotherapy and behavior change* (pp. 263–295). Wiley.

Corbin, J., & Strauss, A. L. (1990). Grounded theory research: Procedures, canons, and evaluative criteria. *Qualitative Sociology, 13*(1), 3–21. https://doi.org/10.1007/BF00988593

Dagnino, P., Krause, M., Pérez, J. C., Valdés, N., & Tomicic, A. (2012). The Evolution of communicative intentions during change episodes and throughout the therapeutic Process. *Research in Psychotherapy: Psychopathology, Process and Outcome, 15*, 75–86.

Denzin, N. K. (1970). *The research act*. McGraw Hill.

Denzin, N. K. (1989). *Interpretive interactionism* (Applied social research methods series) (Vol. 16). Sage.

Echávarri, O., González, A., Krause, M., Tomicic, A., Pérez, C., Dagnino, P., de la Parra, G., Valdés, N., Altimir, C., Vilches, O., Strasser, K., Ramírez, I., & Reyes, L. (2009). Cuatro terapias psicodinámicas breves exitosas estudiadas a través de los indicadores genéricos de cambio [Four successful brief psychodynamic therapies studied through the generic change indicators]. *Revista Argentina de Clínica Psicológica, 18(1)*, 5–19.

Elliott, R. (1984). A discovery-oriented approach to significant change events in psychotherapy: Interpersonal process recall and comprehensive process analysis. In L. Rice & L. S. Greenberg (Eds.), *Patterns of change: Intensive analysis of psychotherapy process* (pp. 249–286). Guilford.

Elliott, R., Hill, C. E., Stiles, W. B., Friedlander, M. L., Mahrer, A. R., & Margison, F. R. (1987). Primary response modes: A comparison of six rating systems. *Journal of Consulting and Clinical Psychology, 55*, 218–223.

Espinosa-Duque, D., & Krause, M. (2020). El desafío de integrar teoría, investigación y práctica clínica en psicoterapia. [The challenge of integrating theory, research and clinical practice in psychotherapy.] *Rev. CES Psico, 13*(3), i–ix. https://doi.org/10.21615/%20cesp.13.3.15

Fernández, O., Altimir, C., Reinel, M., Duarte, J., & Krause, M. (2022). "I am strong and I can get on with my life": The subjective experience of recovery of patients treated for depression. *Psychotherapy Research, 33*(5), 625–639. https://doi.org/10.1080/10503307.2022.2147035

Fernández, O., Fernández, S., & Krause, M. (2020). Comprensión del cambio psicoterapéutico en adolescentes: voces de pacientes y terapeutas [Understanding psychotherapeutic change in adolescents: Patient and therapist voices]. *Revista CES Psicología, 13(3)*, 107–123. https://doi.org/10.21615/%20cesp.13.3.7

Fernández, O., Herrera, P., Krause, M., Pérez, J. C., Valdés, N., Vilches, O., & Tomicic, A. (2012). *Episodios de Cambio y Estancamiento en Psicoterapia: Características de la comunicación verbal entre pacientes y terapeutas.* [Change and Stuck Episodes in Psychotherapy. Characterization of the verbal communication between patients and therapists.]. *Terapia Psicológica, 30*(2), 5–22.

Fiedler, P., & Rogge, K. E. (1989). Zur Prozeβuntersuchung psychotherapeutischer Episoden. Ausgewählte Beispiele und Perspektiven [About process research of psychotherapeutic episodes. Selected examples and perspectives]. *Zeitschrift für Klinische Psychologie, 18*, 45–54.

Fitzpatrick, M. R., & Chamodraka, M. (2007). Participants critical events: A method for identifying and isolating significant therapeutic incidents. *Psychotherapy Research, 17*, 622–627.

Flick, U. (1987). Das Subjekt als Theoretiker? Zur Subjektiviät Subjektiver Theorien [The subject as theoretician? On the Subjectivity of Subjective Theories]. In J. Bergold & U. Flick (Eds.), *Ein-Sichten: Zugänge zur Sicht des Subjekts mittels qualitativer Forschung* (pp. 125–134). Forum für Verhaltenstherapie und psychosoziale Praxis, 14.

Flick, U. (1990). Fallanalysen: Geltungsbegründung durch systematische Perspektiven-Triangulation. In G. Jüttemann (Ed.), *Komparative Kasuistik* (pp. 184–203). Asanger.

Flick, U. (1991). *Alltagswissen über Gesundheit und Krankheit: subjektive Theorien und soziale Repräsentationen* [Everyday knowledge about health and disease: Subjective theories and social representations]. Asanger.

Frank, J. D. (1971). Therapeutic factors in psychotherapy. *American Journal of Psychotherapy, 25*, 350–361.

Frank, J. D. (1982). Therapeutic components shared by all psychotherapies. In J. H. Harvey & M. M. Parks (Eds.), *The master lecture series I. Psychotherapy Research and beha-vior change*. APA.

Gazzolla, N., Iwakabe, S., & Stalikas, A. (2003). Counsellor interpretations and the occurrence of in-session client change moments in no-dynamic psychotherapy. *Counselling-Psychology-Quarterly, 16*, 81–94.

Geertz, C. (1983). *Dichte Beschreibung: Beitrag zum Verstehen kultureller Systeme* [Thick description: Contribution to the understanding of cultural systems. Suhrkamp.

Gennaro, A., Al-Radaideh, A., Gelo, O., Manzo, S., Nitti, M., Auletta, A., & Salvatore, S. (2010). Modelling the psychotherapy process as a meaning making dynamics. The Two Stage Semiotic Model (TSSM) and the Discourse Flow Analyzer (DFA). In S. Salvatore, J. Valsiner, J. Travers Simon, & A. Gennaro (Eds.), *Yearbook of idiographic science 2009—Volume 2* (pp. 131–170). Firera Publishing Group.

Glaser, B. G. (1978). *Theoretical sensitivity*. Sociology Press.

Glaser, B. G., & Strauss, A. L. (1967). *The discovery of grounded theory*. Aldine Publishing Company.

Gonçalves, M. M., Matos, M., & Santos, A. (2009). Narrative therapy and the nature of "innovative moments" in the construction of change. *Journal of Constructivist Psychology, 22*, 1–23.

Guba, E. G. (1990). *The paradigm dialog*. Sage.

Karasu, T. B. (1986). The specificity versus nonspecificity dilemma: Toward identifying therapeutic change agents. *American Journal of Psychiatry, 143*, 687–695.

Krause, M. (1992a). *Erfahrungen mit Beratung und Therapie - Veränderungsprozesse aus der Sicht von KlientInnen* [Experiences with Counselling and therapy - change processes from the perspective of clients]. Lambertus.

Krause, M. (1992b). Efectos subjetivos de la ayuda psicológica - Discusión teórica y presentación de un estudio empírico [Subjective effects of psychological help - Theoretical discussion and presentation of an empirical Study]. *Psykhe, 1*, 41–52.

Krause, M. (1995). La investigación cualitativa: Un campo de posibilidades y desafíos [Qualitative research: A field of possibilities and challenges]. *Revista Temas de Educación, 7*, ISSN 0716-7423.

Krause, M. (2005, 2011 - 2nd Ed.). Psicoterapia y Cambio. Una mirada desde la subjetividad. [Psychotherapy and Change. A view from the subjective perspective] Santiago de Chile: Ediciones Universidad Católica (360 pgs.).

Krause, M. (2023). Lessons from ten years of psychotherapy process research. *Psychotherapy Research, 34*(3), 261–275. https://doi.org/10.1080/10503307.2023.220015

Krause, M., De la Parra, G., Arístegui, R., Tomicic, A., Dagnino, P., Echávarri, O., Valdés, N., Vilches, O., Ben-Dov, P., & Altimir, C. (2006). Indicadores de cambio genéricos en la investigación psicoterapéutica. *Revista Latinoamericana de Psicología, 38*(2), 299–325.

Krause, M., Abarzúa, M., Silva, M., Navarro, D., & Altimir, C. (2016). Psychotherapie aus der Sicht von Klienten mit Schizophrenie [Psychotherapy from the perspective of clients with schizophrenia]. *Verhaltenstherapie & Psychosoziale Praxis, 48(1)*, 83–101.

Krause, M., De la Parra, G., Arístegui. R., Dagnino, P., Tomicic, A., Valdés, N., Echávarri, O., Vilches, O., Ben-Dov, P., Strasser, K., Reyes, L., Altimir, C., & Ramírez, I. (2007). The evolution of therapeutic change studied through generic change indicators. *Psychotherapy Research, 17(6)*, 673–689. https://doi.org/10.1080/10503300601158814

Krause, M., Pérez, J. C., Altimir, C., & de la Parra, G. (2015). Generic change indicators in therapeutic processes with different outcomes. *Psychotherapy Research, 25(5)*, 533–545. https://doi.org/10.1080/10503307.2014.935516

Krause, M., Uribe, R., Winkler, M. I., & Avendaño, C. (1994). Caminos en la búsqueda de ayuda psicológica [Paths in the search for psychological help]. *Psykhe, 3*, 211–222.

Lambert, M. J., Hansen, N. B., Umpress, V., Lunnen, K., Okiishi, J., & Burlingame, G. M. (1996). *Administration and scoring manual for the OQ-45.2*. American Professional Credentialing Services.

Mahrer, A. R. (1988). Discovery-oriented psychotherapy research: Rationale, aims, and methods. *American Psychologist, 43*(9), 694–702. https://doi.org/10.1037/0003-066X.43.9.694

Matos, M., Santos, A., Gonçalves, M., & Martins, C. (2009). Innovative moments and change in narrative therapy. *Psychotherapy Research, 19*(1), 68–80. https://doi.org/10.1080/10503300802430657

McCarthy, K. L., Mergenthaler, E., Schneider, S., & Grenyer, B. F. S. (2011). Psychodynamic change in psychotherapy: Cycles of patient–therapist linguistic interactions and interventions. *Psychotherapy Research, 21*(6), 722–731. https://doi.org/10.1080/10503307.2011.615070

Mergenthaler, E. (2008). Resonating minds: A school-independent theoretical conception and its empirical application to psychotherapeutic processes. *Psychotherapy Research, 18*(2), 109–126. https://doi.org/10.1080/10503300701883741

Morán, J., Martínez, C., Díaz, M. F., González, S., Arce, K., & Duarte, J. (2020). Observando la mentalización en psicoterapias con adolescentes: Diseño de un sistema de observación de la interacción terapéutica. [Observing mentalization in psychotherapies with adolescents: Design of an observational system for therapeutic interaction]. *Revista CES Psicología, 13(3)*, 51–75. https://doi.org/10.21615/cesp.13.3.4

Núñez, L., Midgley, N., Capella, C., Alamo, N., Mortimer, R., & Krause, M. (2021). The therapeutic relationship in child psychotherapy: Integrating the perspectives of children, parents and therapists. *Psychotherapy Research, 31(8)*, 988–1000. https://doi.org/10.1080/10503307.2021.1876946

Prochaska, J., & DiClemente, C. (1983). Stages and processes of self-change in smoking: Toward an integrative model of change. *Journal of Consulting and Clinical Psychology, 5*, 390–395.

Prochaska, J. O., & Norcross, J. C. (2002). Stages of change. In J. C. Norcross (Ed.), *Psychotherapy relationships that work: Therapist contributions and responsiveness to patients* (pp. 303–313). Oxford University Press.

Reyes, L., Arístegui, R., Krause, M., Strasser, K., de la Parra, G., Tomicic, A., Dagnino, P., Vilches, O., Valdés, N., Echávarri, O., Altimir, C., Ramírez, I., & Ben-Dov, P. (2008). Language and therapeutic change: A speech acts analysis. *Psychotherapy Research, 18*, 355–362.

Schütze, F. (1983). Biographieforschung und narratives interview [Biography research and narrative interview]. *Neue Praxis, 13*, 283–293.

Stiles, W. B. (1992). *Describing talk: A taxonomy of verbal response modes*. Sage Publications.

Stiles, W. B. (2001). Assimilation of problematic experiences. *Psychotherapy, 38*, 462–465. https://doi.org/10.1037/0033-3204.38.4.462

Strauss, A. L. (1987). *Qualitative analysis for social scientists*. Cambridge University Press.

Strauss, A. L., & Corbin, J. (1991). *Basics of qualitative research*. Sage.

Suárez-Delucchi, N., Keith-Paz, A., Reinel, M., Fernandez, S., & Krause, M. (2022). Failure in psychotherapy: A qualitative comparative study from the perspective of patients diagnosed with depression. *Counselling Psychology Quarterly, 35(4)*, 842–866. https://doi.org/10.1080/09515070.2022.2047614

Taylor, S. J., & Bogdan, R. (1986). *Introducción a los métodos cualitativos de investigación - La búsqueda de significados* [Introduction to qualitative research methods - The search for meanings]. Paidós.

Timulák, L. (2009). Meta-analysis of qualitative studies: A tool for reviewing qualitative research findings in psychotherapy. *Psychotherapy Research, 19*(4–5), 591–600. https://doi.org/10.1080/10503300802477989

Timulák, L., & Lietaer, G. (2001). Moments of empowerment: A qualitative analysis of positively experienced episodes in brief person-centred counselling. *Counselling and Psychotherapy Research: Linking Research with Practice, 1*(1), 62–73. https://doi.org/10.1080/14733140112331385268

Tomicic, A., Martínez, C., Pérez, J. C., Hollenstein, T., Angulo, S., Gerstmann, A., Barroux, I., & Krause, M. (2015). Discourse-voice regulatory strategies in the psychotherapeutic interaction: A state-space dynamics analysis. *Frontiers in Psychology, 6(378)*, 1–17. https://doi.org/10.3389/fpsyg.2015.00378

Valdés, N., Dagnino, P., Krause, M., Pérez, J., Altimir, C., Tomicic, A., Ramírez, I., & de la Parra, G. (2010a). Analysis of verbalized emotions in the psychotherapeutic dialogue during change episodes. *Psychotherapy Research, 20*, 136–150.

Valdés, N., Krause, M., & Alamo, N. (2011). ¿Qué Dicen y Cómo lo Dicen?: Análisis de la comunicación verbal de pacientes y terapeutas en episodios de cambio. [What do they say and how do they say it? Analysis of the verbal communication of patients and therapists in change episodes]. *Revista Argentina de Clínica Psicológica, 20*, 15–28.

Valdés, N., Tomicic, A., Pérez, J. C., & Krause, M. (2010b). Sistema de Codificación de la Actividad Terapéutica (SCAT-1.0): Dimensiones y categorías de las acciones comunicacionales de pacientes y psicoterapeutas. [The Therapeutic Activity Coding System (TACS-1.0): Dimensions and categories of the patients' and therapists' communicational actions]. *Revista Argentina de Clínica Psicológica, 19*, 117–130.

Vásquez, D., Altimir, C. O., Lopera, D. M. R., Pineda, M., Espinosa, H.-D., Mesa, C., Montenegro, C. R., Fernández González, O. M., & Krause, M. (2020). Del malestar a la depresión: dinámicas en la construcción del significado personal de la experiencia de la depresión [From discomfort to depression: Dynamics in the construction of personal meaning from the experience of depression]. *Revista CES Psicología, 13(3)*, 142–161. https://doi.org/10.21615/cesp.13.3.9.

Von Bergen, A., & De la Parra, G. (2002). OQ-45.2, Cuestionario para evaluación de resultados y evolución en psicoterapia: Adaptación, validación e indicaciones para su aplicación e interpretación [OQ-45.2, Questionnaire for the Evaluation of outcomes and evolution in psychotherapy: Adaptation, validation, and indications for application and interpretation]. *Terapia Psicológica, 20*, 161–176.

Watson, J., McMullen, E., Prosser, M., & Bedard, D. (2011). An examination of the relationships among clients' affect regulation, in-session emotional processing, the working alliance, and outcome. *Psychotherapy Research, 21*(1), 86–96. https://doi.org/10.1080/10503307.2010.518637

Wiggins, S., Elliott, R., & Cooper, M. (2012). The prevalence and characteristics of relational depth events in psychotherapy. *Psychotherapy Research, 22*(2), 139–158. https://doi.org/10.1080/10503307.2011.629635

Wucherpfennig, F., Rubel, J. A., Hofmann, S. G., & Lutz, W. (2017). Processes of change after a sudden gain and relation to treatment outcome—Evidence for an upward spiral. *Journal of Consulting and Clinical Psychology, 85*(12), 1199–1210. https://doi.org/10.1037/ccp0000263

Chapter 3
Qualitative Research on Psychotherapeutic Change in Latin America: In Search of Capturing Complexity

Carolina Altimir

Research on psychotherapeutic change is framed in two traditions that relate to each other and constitute different approaches to the phenomenon of change resulting from therapy. One refers to research on therapy outcomes, which seeks to answer the questions: Does psychotherapy have effects? And what are these effects? On the other hand, the process research tradition has posed the question about what changes in psychotherapy, and how does change take place? (Krause & Altimir, 2016).

Psychotherapy outcome research has led to the development of effectiveness and efficacy studies (Krause & Altimir, 2016; Lutz et al., 2021), adopting a quantitative approach. To grant scientific legitimacy to psychological therapies, these studies attempt to establish causal relationships between certain psychological treatments and their effects (Barkham & Mellor-Clark, 2003) through rigorous means of variable control, to achieve high internal validity and attribute the effects on the patient to the specific intervention studied (Altimir et al., 2022). The most used methods are randomized controlled trials (RCTs), quasi-experimental designs, and meta-analyses (Lutz et al., 2021). These methods have received criticism related to the strict inclusion criteria of the participants and the rigorous adherence to treatment protocols, where the independence of other variables is assumed. This results in the findings not being representative of routine clinical practice (Castonguay et al., 2021), limiting the conclusions that can be drawn. Thus, they reduce the ability to account for the complexity of psychotherapy by assuming that the inherent variability of human behavior, which is inevitably present in the way therapists carry out psychotherapy and patients receive it, can be overridden (Barkham et al., 2018).

In response to the limitations of the first studies of effectiveness and efficacy, psychotherapy process research gained relevance during the 1980s, which

C. Altimir (✉)
School of Psychology, University de Los Andes, Santiago, Chile

Millennium Institute for the Study of Depression and Personality (MIDAP), Santiago, Chile

A. Tomicic, J. D. Soto (eds.), *Qualitative Research in Clinical Psychology and Psychotherapy in Latin America*, https://doi.org/10.1007/978-3-031-90782-1_3

prompted the development of the significant therapy events paradigm, suggesting that, instead of trying to demonstrate that one therapy is more effective than another, or to confirm the already proven effectiveness of psychotherapy, the focus should be on examining the change process to be able to arrive at explanations of what really happens in therapy (Greenberg, 1999; Safran, 2003). Since then, there has been a fruitful development of research focused on how psychotherapy works, examining various aspects of therapist's and patient's experiences, actions, and interactions, as well as the mechanisms that are linked to treatment outcomes (Lutz et al., 2021). In turn, process–outcome research seeks to link the events that take place during psychotherapy sessions with the final treatment outcomes (Lutz et al., 2021).

Krause and Altimir (2016) propose a categorization of psychotherapy process research based on the different elements to study: (a) the content of change (what changes); (b) change factors (the individual, contextual, and relational elements through which change is generated and developed); and (c) change mechanisms (the movements that combine and articulate the aforementioned factors for change to occur, as well as their trajectory throughout the process). In turn, they distinguish research according to the unit of analysis they aim to examine. Macro-process research focuses on the complete therapy, where the evolution of change throughout therapy or continuous change, as well as the therapeutic relationship and therapist interventions, becomes relevant. This has allowed the development of various change progression models that include different stages (Krause & Altimir, 2016). On the other hand, micro-process research focuses on specific segments within the sessions, such as change events and their content, difficult events or ruptures, innovative moments, or moments of meeting (Duarte et al., 2019b; Krause, 2023; Krause & Altimir, 2018). In turn, these segments can be analyzed based on the therapeutic communication (verbal and non-verbal) that takes place within them (Krause, 2023; Krause & Altimir, 2018). These events corresponding to the micro-process are related to the macro-process, since they constitute relevant instances and recurrent states that take place in identifiable patterns (Safran, 2003), forming the pieces and gears of the process of continuous change of the macro-process and influencing the final outcome of the therapy (Krause, 2023). Krause (2023) argues that the future development of this field requires models of change of a transtheoretical nature that link the units of the macro-process with those of the micro-process, as well as complex and multi-dimensional designs that consider repeated measures and mixed methods, that connect different characteristics of the phenomenon of change (interpersonal aspects, subjective meaning, verbal and non-verbal communication, and physiological variables), and that incorporate different perspectives (both observational as well as the first- and second-person experience of therapy participants), both during and after the psychotherapy process.

The Value of Qualitative Research for the Study of Psychotherapeutic Change

Both quantitative and qualitative research have addressed the questions posed by studies on psychotherapeutic change. However, in the English-speaking north, there is predominance of quantitative research, which has been influenced by a positivist tradition, as it is considered the way to achieve scientific legitimacy (Lutz et al., 2021), consuming a large proportion of the resources dedicated to psychotherapy research (McLeod et al., 2021).

On the other hand, qualitative research in psychotherapy, although less than quantitative studies, has experienced a progressive growth since the 1980s (Levitt et al., 2024; Lutz et al., 2021). This development has resulted in a significant increase in publications and citations of qualitative studies in mainstream journals in the last 20 years, al beit it continues to represent a smaller percentage compared to quantitative studies (Levitt et al., 2021; Levitt et al., 2024). However, a growing trend and a greater appreciation of the contribution of this type of research to the understanding of psychotherapy (Levitt et al., 2024) is observed.

This greater appreciation of qualitative research is largely due to the postmodern critique of the search for objective knowledge (Rennie et al., 2002). While effectiveness and efficacy studies based on quantitative methods have been key in establishing the benefits and legitimacy of the psychological therapies, qualitative research has argued that such data may be limited in terms of understanding change and what it mean for therapy participants, and therefore to be able to distinguish which changes are clinically significant (Hill et al., 2013).

From this point of view, qualitative psychotherapy research allows access to the complexity of the change process and its different nuances (Elliott et al., 2001) in ways different than quantitative research. As Rennie (2004) points out, since qualitative research is about meaning, which is transmitted and expressed by the language of the participants, it offers deeper insight into subjectivity. This grants qualitative research in psychotherapy an exploratory rahter than confirmatory character, it is more descriptive than explanatory (in terms of causality and prediction), and more interpretive than positivist (Rennie et al., 2002), offering a more differentiated and in-depth understanding of the meaning of therapeutic change from the perspective of patients and therapists. Qualitative research that explores how patients experience psychotherapeutic change and outcome contributes to enriching the understanding not only of the first- and second-hand lived experience of psychotherapy but also of the meaning of change (McLeod et al., 2021), providing a window into the inner experiences of patients and therapists (Levitt et al., 2021). In addition, each actor—researchers, patients, and therapists—can understand change differently, or make different assumptions about what factors and components it involves. At the same time, it provides an account of other aspects related to therapeutic change, such as interaction and intersubjective processes (Altimir et al., 2022), thus constituting an important source of information about the variability associated with the way clinical professionals carry out psychotherapy and how patients receive it.

At the same time, for McLeod et al. (2021), qualitative change research serves as a critical counterweight to the findings and conclusions derived from quantitative methodologies, allowing to refine evaluations on therapeutic outcomes. It allows the development of more differentiated criteria, as well as more valid and reliable evaluation procedures through which treatment protocols can be assessed. Under this logic, Levitt et al. (2024) propose recommendations to expand the evidence base of clinical guidelines that guide practice beyond that stemming from quantitative studies (often based on RCTs), to include the findings of qualitative research. This would enable an expansion of the knowledge and understanding of the processes that are central to psychotherapy, based on results that are not limited to symptomatic improvement and considering the experience of patients and therapists. Thus, this proposal has the value of rescuing experiences, interactions, and processes that quantitative methods based on population averages are unable to account for.

It is also important to point out the value of combining qualitative and quantitative methods in the study of change process in psychotherapy, since the inherent complexity of psychotherapy demands the flexible use of research procedures while allowing the findings of each approach to feed the questions and methods used in the other (Bartholomew & Lockard, 2018). Given that the process of change as an object of study involves variables of diverse nature, it is common to find that a single study can use a combination of different methodologies, applying both qualitative and quantitative devices in the different phases of an investigation (selection of the sample or participants, data collection, and data analysis) (Krause et al., 2018; Lutz et al., 2021; McLeod et al., 2021). Thus, psychotherapeutic change research has been characterized by the use and development of a variety of innovative methods, which seek to capture the contents of change, its mechanisms, and the factors that favor it (Krause & Altimir, 2016). Also, it is common to include the various perspectives involved—those of the patients, the therapists, and the observers of the phenomenon in the study of change (Altimir et al., 2010, 2017; Dos Santos & Dallos, 2012). Another relevant element to consider is that most of the data from change process research is obtained from therapies that take place in natural contexts or from routine practice that takes place in mental health institutions and services. This gives a great external validity to the findings of these studies (Castonguay et al., 2021; Krause et al., 2007, 2018).

The Status of Qualitative Research in Psychotherapy in the Northern Hemisphere

As noted above, qualitative research in psychotherapy has been proportionally less developed than quantitative research at the international level. Although in the countries of the Global North, the former has become increasingly relevant, with more and more studies of this type, it is still less developed than quantitative studies (Krause, 2023; McLeod et al., 2021; Rennie, 2004). To have an overview of how qualitative studies of psychotherapy change have been approached in the Northern Hemisphere, it is convenient to refer to a review conducted by Rennie (2004) on its status in English-speaking northern countries. He distinguishes two groups of methods that have been applied based on this research paradigm in the region. On the one hand, there are methods aimed at analyzing the verbal reports of the experiences of psychotherapy participants. At the time of the review, most adopt a discovery-oriented and open-ended character, until theoretical saturation is achieved. For the data collection procedure, studies conduct semi-structured interviews with the therapy participants, with previously defined questions and favoring the deployment of the interviewee. There are also studies that use unstructured interviews, in which participants address a topic that is presented to them in an open manner. In turn, verbal report studies are distinguished according to whether or not they involve Interpersonal Process Recall (IPR; Elliott, 1986), which can be unstructured or semi-structured. This method consists of recording audio or video therapy sessions or segments of sessions, which are then played back to the therapy participants while the researcher assists the process of eliciting descriptions of experiences, impressions, and fleeting reactions to specific conversational events—which are normally lost when integrating them into episodic memory—as well as the covert processes of the therapist (intentions and decision-making processes) and the patient (intentions and feelings) (Elliott, 1986).

On the other hand, there are methods applied to the analysis of therapy sessions verbatim transcripts. In these, the analysis has often been aimed at the pragmatics of discourse between patient and therapist, through functional analysis applied to the surface of the text and the evaluation of how the responses of the speakers affect each other. Another perspective examines how certain elements of the process that are organized through a particular therapy theory are reflected in the discourse.

With regard to the analytical paradigms commonly employed, Rennie (2004) points out that, in the United Kingdom, largely due to the influence of postmodern thinking, discourse analysis has been relevant for analyzing communication between patient and therapist. This is based on relativist epistemologies, including social constructionism (Gergen, 1996), subject positioning, interpretive repertoires, and ideological dilemmas. It also highlights the use of narrative analysis, based on social constructionism; and the development and flexible application of any method that allows achieving the objectives of the study.

Meanwhile, in the United States and Canada, the focus tends to be on the method, which has been influenced by methodologies close to positivism, although it includes more moderate and critical variants. One of the most commonly used methods is grounded theory (GT) developed by Glaser and Strauss (1967), with various adaptations and emphases given to the different moments and procedures of the research endeavor. A more objectivist version of GT is *Consensual Qualitative Research (CQR)*, systematized by Hill et al. (1997), which emphasizes the categorization of information based on the consensus of the research group.

In relation to the specific study of change process in psychotherapy, and as a consequence of the shift toward this field of study in response to the limitations of effectiveness studies, researchers from the United States have developed various innovative data collection methods (Elliott et al., 2001). Among these is the Change Interview—open-ended interview applied to patients during or at the end of therapy that assesses the changes perceived throughout the course of therapy, their understanding about the origins of these changes, and the facilitating and hindering aspects of the process. Another method is the *Helpful Aspects of Therapy (HAT)* developed by Orlinsky et al. (1994), which consists of a post-session self-report measure and evaluates the immediate effects of the session by asking patients to identify key change events according to their perception. Finally, there are methods of audio- or video-assisted memories (IPR), which produce various formats of information, such as interview transcripts, HAT protocols, and therapy event transcripts.

The data analysis methods that have been applied to the research of change process in psychotherapy have frequently been Grounded Theory (GT), Task Analysis, Discourse Analysis, Conversational Analysis for the transcripts of significant events, and Comprehensive Process Analysis (CPA) of complex event records.

Frommer et al. (2004) conducted a review of qualitative research in psychotherapy in German-speaking countries. In these, the hermeneutic approach has had a significant influence, placing interpretation as a procedure for achieving an understanding of individuals' life expressions. In its application to psychotherapy, research has been characterized by conducting follow-up interviews with therapy participants, with the aim of reconstructing the transformation of psychotherapeutic knowledge in relation to their psychological disorder, their subjective concepts about psychotherapy, and their future orientations. Studies in these countries are characterized by the use of qualitative content analysis, objective hermeneutics, and psychoanalytic understanding, with their usual object of study being hospital psychotherapy and psychosomatic disorders.

Recently, McLeod, Stiles, and Levitt (2021) conducted a review of the main contributions of qualitative research to psychotherapy over the last decade. They point out that different types of qualitative research have generated important knowledge about aspects of how various forms of language use can contribute to the therapeutic process. They highlight that the most applied method for this has been conversational analysis of therapy transcripts. However, other qualitative studies have used thematic analysis or GT to identify patterns of productive language use in therapy associated with change process. They also highlight the contribution of qualitative research on how patients experience therapy outcomes. They thus review the findings of qualitative research aimed at examining the positive outcomes of therapy, negative outcomes, therapy dropout, patient's experience of completing symptom measures, and the implications for the development and verification of overall psychotherapy outcomes.

Qualitative Change Research in Latin America

Latin American countries have not been oblivious to the progressive growth of qualitative research on psychotherapy change process, showing substantive development in the last 20 years. Despite this, Latin American qualitative research remains underrepresented in major publications, such as, for example, the Handbook of Psychotherapy and Behavior Change (60th Ed.), a periodic and reference publication that compiles psychotherapy research carried out in the last ten years (Barkham et al., 2021). In fact, when reviewing the qualitative studies reported in this manual, there is an absence of Latin American authors.

For this reason, to have a more complete perspective of the situation in Latin America, it is important to refer to the reviews carried out by two Latin American and Chilean researchers, both presidents, at different times, of the Society for Psychotherapy Research (SPR). On the one hand, Guillermo de la Parra in 2013 reviews the state of psychotherapy research in Latin America up to that date. Among his results, he points out that the most frequent studies in the region are those focused on process and outcomes (71%), followed by studies on therapists and therapist training (33%), and to a lesser extent outcome studies with control group designs (17%). The majority of the studies are quantitative (59%), followed by a significant proportion of qualitative studies (33%), while mixed methodology represented 8% of the works. In contrast to what was effectively published in the journals reviewed by this study, people in the region with research experience who were surveyed, pointed out as the main study topic therapy process and process/outcome, preferably using qualitative methodology.

On the other hand, Mariane Krause (2023) reviews the state of psychotherapeutic process research in the last ten years worldwide, also accounting for the situation in Latin America. She observes that quantitative methods were not only more frequent for studying psychotherapeutic process, but also placed greater emphasis on macro-process–outcome studies. When analyzing the studies published in Latin American journals, the proportion of studies that include final outcome (linked to the process) is lower. These include more case studies and more qualitative ones. In both reviews, the authors identify contextual barriers-such as economic constraints and the structure of regional health systems-as possible explanations for these trends, which make it more challenging to conduct randomized controlled trials or studies with control groups (de la Parra, 2013; Krause, 2023). At the same time, de la Parra (2013) concludes that his results show the interest of researchers and clinicians in having access to research that is relevant and close to clinical practice, and that is culturally relevant from the point of view of Latin American needs and identity. It is evident through these reviews that in Latin America there is a tendency to carry out more qualitative studies in psychotherapy than in the Northern Hemisphere.

A more detailed look at the qualitative studies on change in psychotherapy in Latin America indicates that they have had considerable development in the past 20 years, particularly in Chile, based on the work of the Chilean Research Group on Psychotherapy and Change led by Mariane Krause (Krause et al., 2006, 2007), which studies change based on Groeben & Scheele's (2000) notion of subjective theories. Subjective theories are understood as a complex set of cognitions or explanatory models about oneself and the world that serve to guide the behavior of individuals and optimize self-assessment. From this conceptualization, psychotherapeutic change is understood as a transformation in the subjective patterns of interpretation and explanation that leads to the development of new subjective theories about oneself and the world, and about the problem that leads to psychotherapy; therefore, it is a model of generic change (Krause et al., 2006). This model has been empirically supported and operationalized through the hierarchy of Generic Change Indicators (GCI) (Krause et al., 2006; Krause et al., 2007) (see Chapter 2 by Krause). Thus, most studies that focus on the micro-process have done so through the study of Generic Change Indicators (GCI) (Krause et al., 2006, 2007). Although the GCI have been used to study the macro-process, a significant portion of the research has approached it from the first- and second-person perspective of patients and therapists, that is, from their subjective experience. These research traditions have produced and refined observation and interview systems, as well as qualitative analysis, sometimes combining them with quantitative methods, which allow access to the question of what changes in psychotherapy?

Most of the research from this group is framed in the paradigm of significant events of therapy and therefore often adopts an observational perspective, that is, therapies are observed, and researchers identify the moments and contents of change—although some include the perspective of the participants to identify moments of change (Altimir et al., 2010). Most of these studies focus on micro-processes, analyzing the content and interactions linked to specific episodes or moments of change. However, some can also be classified as macro-process studies, as the moments of change and the Generic Change Indicator (GCI) reflect ongoing change and its progression throughout the psychotherapeutic process.

Initially, the research carried out by this group sought to apply the GCI to therapy sessions of different orientations, seeking to empirically verify the GCI hierarchy, as well as analyze its generic character (Krause et al., 2006), from a qualitative approach. Later, it combined the observation and analysis of the GCI and moments of change from a qualitative perspective, with quantitative procedures to analyze the frequency of each GCI and account for their evolution throughout the phases of therapy (Krause et al., 2007). Likewise, studies have been developed that seek to identify the components of verbal communication during moments of change (e.g., Valdés et al., 2005). Initially, a qualitative descriptive analysis of the verbal exchange of patient and therapist was carried out. Subsequently, the emotions verbalized by patients and therapists during the psychotherapeutic dialogue within change episodes have been described and compared (e.g., Valdés et al., 2010), using qualitative methodology for the analysis of verbal communication and quantitative methodology for the analysis of its distribution during the psychotherapeutic dialogue. Then, Fernández et al. (2012) analyze therapeutic communication in change episodes and stagnation episodes of 15 therapies, combining qualitative procedures for the identification of episodes and verbal communication, and quantitative for the statistical analysis of different communicational actions according to the type of episode.

Other studies have incorporated the speech acts theory to analyze specific linguistic patterns during moments of change. For example, Reyes et al. (2008) used qualitative procedures for the analysis of patient verbalizations during moments of change, and during random verbalizations. These two groups were then compared by means of quantitative analysis. Later, Arístegui et al. (2009) sought to distinguish recurrent conversational patterns in the verbal exchanges between patient and therapist during change episodes and stuck episodes. In this case, qualitative methodology was used for the identification of the two types of events and for the analysis of the conversation within them. More recently, Gaete et al. (2019) apply an ethnomethodological approach to perform an in-depth discourse analysis, aimed at characterizing micro-conversational practices that contribute to the generation of preferred self-references within change episodes.

Adopting a perspective of discursive positions, Tomicic et al. (2015) describe configurations of recurrent discourse-voice regulation strategies during relevant episodes of therapy. Through qualitative methodology, change and rupture episodes were determined, the discursive positions of the actors of the therapy within these episodes were coded, as well as the patterns of vocal quality. Sophisticated quantitative methods were used to determine the configurations of the patient and therapist's discourse-voice regulatory strategies and their configurations within the episodes. Meanwhile, Mellado et al. (2022) adopt the Model of Analysis of Discursive Positioning in Psychotherapy (MAPP) (Martínez & Tomicic, 2019) to identify the voices and personal positions of patient and therapist in episodes of change.

From practice-oriented research, and combining an observational with a second-person perspective in a qualitative approach, Krause et al. (2018) sought to reconstruct and understand the therapist's subjective experience during change, and stuck episodes, ruptures, and resolutions of the alliance, in a single case of completed psychotherapy. The researchers observed the sessions and identified each type of episode, after which the therapist participated in six sessions of retrospective interview with one of the researchers, where the Interpersonal Process Recall (IPR) was carried out based on a semi-structured interview guide, in order to reconstruct her experience during the session episodes. Finally, the interviews were analyzed using Grounded Theory.

Another relevant development of qualitative research on psychotherapy change in Latin America has focused its interest on the experience and subjective perspective of the participants (patients and therapists). From this point of view, they adopt a first-person and second-person perspective, that is, they examine the perception and narratives elaborated by the same actors of psychotherapy, highlighting the subjectivity of this experience. Since these studies examine the change process based on participants' evaluations—often retrospective—of their experience throughout psychotherapy, their unit of analysis typically focuses on macro-processes. However, some studies also incorporate micro-process analysis (Altimir et al., 2010). In addition, they have focused on the study of specific patient populations.

In Chile, Duarte et al. (2019a) examine the aspects of psychotherapy that contribute to therapeutic change based on the experience of a patient with Borderline Personality Disorder and her therapist, seeking to construct an integrated understanding of the change process. This single case study combined the open coding procedure of Grounded Theory with biographical narration in a discovery-oriented biographical analysis. The study by Besser and Moncada (2013), on the other hand, takes the concept of change from subjective theories to understand the subjective evaluation of therapy and the process of change, as well as the elements that make it possible, from the perspective of female therapists working with female patients with anorexia nervosa. Manríquez-Reyes (2023), in turn, seeks to understand the process of change in psychotherapy with adults who have experienced child sexual abuse, framed in humanistic-existential psychotherapies. Through Grounded Theory analysis, she seeks to understand the processes of change, stagnation, therapeutic alliance, and the effects on patients.

In Peru, Mantilla and Traverso (2021) interviewed 15 people who had completed a psychoanalytic-oriented psychotherapeutic process. The objective was to identify, thematize, and describe the episodes of change, their nature and the relationships between them, based on the patients' retrospective memory. Subsequently, the voices and personal positions of the patient and therapist in these episodes were identified. They used thematic analysis with the aim of assessing whether the users' perspective on the significant moments of the process associated with change contributes to broadening the understanding of the therapeutic action of psychoanalytic psychotherapy. From this point of view, this constitutes a micro-process study, as it seeks to identify specific moments of change in therapy from the patients' perspective, and a macro-process study, as the patients carry out a global evaluation of therapy as a whole.

In Argentina, Olivera et al. (2016) also analyze how people who have completed a psychotherapy process perceive change and how they relate that change to the presenting problem, the therapeutic relationship, and the end of therapy. They used semi-structured qualitative interviews which were then analyzed using the CQR-based approach (Hill et al., 1997).

It is important to note that the studies reviewed in this chapter refer to research conducted with adult participants, so their procedures, as well as their findings, should be considered in relation to that population. More recently, there has been significant development of qualitative research on psychotherapeutic change in therapies aimed at the child and adolescent population, which incorporate their perspectives, as well as that of their caregivers and therapists. In these investigations, innovative devices and procedures have been developed to access the perspective of children, which have been adapted to their evolutionary stages and their natural ways of expression and communication (for more details see Fernández et al., 2015; Núñez et al., 2022).

In summary, the review of qualitative research developed in Latin America shows the development and application of novel and creative approaches to access the complexity of the phenomenon of change in psychotherapy, also considering the particularities and challenges of the context in which it is carried out. All the referred studies have been developed in natural contexts in which routine psychotherapy care is offered, either in university mental health centers, therapist training contexts, or mental health centers that offer psychotherapy services to the general population.

In this sense, they have the richness of capturing the experience, meanings, and characteristics of psychotherapeutic change wherever it takes place, traversed by the sociocultural, institutional, and service delivery contexts that shape the way therapists provide psychotherapy, and patients receive it. Thus, the studies of psychotherapeutic change described capture a local and regional reality, which gives value to this form of research, highlighting its external validity for our Latin American reality.

Change from the Perspectives of Patients, Therapist, and Observers: An Illustrative Case

In order to illustrate in greater detail, the way in which the qualitative study of psychotherapeutic change in Latin America has been approached, and thus exemplify the characteristics and elements of this line of research, a study led by the author of this chapter (Altimir et al., 2010) is described. It applies multi-perspective and multi-dimensional procedures, combining qualitative and quantitative methods, with the aim of accounting for the inherent complexity of the psychotherapeutic change process. The study aimed to deepen the understanding of the degree and type of convergence between patients, therapists, and expert observers in the evaluation of the psychotherapeutic change process. Specifically, this convergence was examined in relation to the amount, temporal location, and content of change, as well as its association with the final therapeutic outcome.

The study sample consisted of nine complete short-term therapies of different modalities and theoretical approaches (three individual psychodynamic, three family social-constructionist, two couples humanistic therapies, and two group therapies for drug abuse). Twenty-seven therapeutic dyads participated, consisting of twenty-seven adult patients and nine therapists with more than ten years of clinical experience. The family, couple, and group therapies carried out by the same therapist or a pair of therapists included more than one patient. These therapies took place in various mental health centers (both university and private) that offer psychotherapy services and ranged between 10 and 23 sessions (average of 18 sessions). All therapies were observed through a one-way mirror and videotaped, to be later transcribed for analysis. The selection of therapies was based on the interest in verifying the generic nature of change, as well as accounting for psychotherapies that take place in natural contexts of routine clinical practice.

The interest in exploring the perspectives of therapy participants and observers is based, first, on the assumption that considering multiple perspectives allows a better understanding of the complex sequences and patterns that constitute and shape the change process (Elliott et al., 2001; Greenberg, 1999). Accessing the experience of patients and therapists about change allows obtaining first-hand information based on the first and second person, about the subjective impact of the process, contributing to determining more precisely which aspects are experienced as useful for the patient's change (Elliott, 1984; Elliott et al., 2001). From the patients' point of view, the memory of significant therapy events accounts for the aspects of it that are mostly remembered and therefore the lasting effect of the first-person psychotherapy experience. From the therapists' point of view, it accounts for their understanding of their patients' experience, contributing to the improvement of therapeutic work (Martin & Stelmaczonek, 1988). Considering the perspective of expert observers constitutes a means of triangulating the information provided by the participants, by allowing a more detailed examination of the elements of the micro-process of change involved in what the participants point out as useful from therapy.

Examining the degree of convergence (or divergence) in the assessment of change made by the different actors is based on the need to deepen previous findings in this line but considering the different dimensions of change (intra-session events, content, and evolution). Previous studies indicate that the agreement between patients and therapists on what is relevant during the therapeutic process is related to therapy outcome, as it accounts for interpersonal attunement and a good working alliance. However, this agreement is greater in terms of the content of change (what changes) than in the identification of significant session events (Cummings et al., 1992; Martin & Stelmaczonek, 1988). That is why the present study seeks to shed more light on these perspectives in relation to the different dimensions of change and their relationship with treatment outcome.

This study also align with the significant therapy events paradigm, as it identifies moments of change as relevant instances within the psychotherapeutic process, which are related to each other, based on their content through the hierarchy of GCI. It also falls within process–outcome research, as it links the elements of the process with treatment outcomes, thus being able to provide relevant knowledge for its application in clinical practice. This study integrates both micro and macro-process analyses of change, since the units of analysis are the moments of change and their content, as well as the entire course of therapy, the progression and evolution of continuous change, and participants' global retrospective evaluation of change.

Qualitative procedures were used to identify and describe moments of change through direct observation of sessions, based on the hierarchy of GCI. This identification was carried out by pairs of researchers, who compared their observations, seeking agreement; otherwise, doubts were reviewed by the research team until an intersubjective agreement was reached (Krause et al., 2007). Subsequently, in-depth retrospective semi-structured interviews were conducted with patients and therapists, which included a series of open-ended questions inviting subjects to talk about their experience: How did you experience the therapy? Did you find it useful in any way? Did you perceive any change throughout the therapy? What changes could you detect throughout the process? They were also asked about specific moments they considered relevant to their change, to account for specific events that participants could retain in their memory. The interviews were conducted between two and three months after the end of treatment, were audio-recorded and transcribed, and subjected to a qualitative content analysis. Each reported change was associated with a single GCI and categorized according to its description as specific moments with a clear temporal location in therapy or as global changes that manifested throughout the ongoing process.

Quantitative methodology was used to analyze the frequency of changes reported by patients, therapists, and observers including their temporal location and content-and its association with treatment outcome. Specific moments as well as global changes reported by therapy participants, and change moments identified by observers were considered for the frequency analysis. For the analysis of the convergence on the content of the identified changes, the degree of representation of each GCI throughout the therapies was considered, regardless of its frequency of appearance, with the aim of accounting for the level of evolution of the reported changes. The frequency of each GCI reported by each perspective was also considered, theoretically grouped based on the phases of evolution and the level of complexity of the indicators: I. Initial consolidation of the structure of the therapeutic relationship, II. Increase in permeability toward new understandings, and III. Construction and consolidation of new understandings (Altimir et al., 2010) (see List of Generic Change Indicators (GCI), Table 1.1 in Chap. 1).

The final therapy outcome was assessed through the Outcome Questionnaire (OQ-45.2) (Lambert et al., 1996), in its adapted and validated version for the Chilean context (von Bergen & de la Parra 2002), which measures patient's change in three areas: (a) subjective distress and symptoms, (b) interpersonal relationships, and (c) social role. The OQ-45.2 was administered to all patients at the beginning and end of therapy. It was considered that patients achieved change when the scores met the criteria of reliable change index or significant improvement. A chi-square quantitative analysis was performed to examine the statistical differences between the quantity, location, and content of the changes identified by each perspective in each therapeutic outcome category (therapy with and without change).

The results of the study indicate that half of the patients (14) achieved clinically significant changes, while the other half (13) showed no changes. The proportion of specific change moments reported by the participants was small compared to the global changes, with no significant differences between them, and without a positive relationship with therapy outcome, so the experience of reconstructing the therapeutic process does not necessarily relate to the level of patient change. Neither did the degree of agreement between patient and therapist in relation to the temporal location of specific moments of change, relate to the therapy outcome.

Upon examining the number of changes reported by the three perspectives, only the patients were able to discriminate between successful and unsuccessful therapies by reporting significantly more changes in the first group. This result makes sense as the changes that occur during therapy take place in the patients, who are the best informants of how this process develops, including those changes that continue consolidating after the end of therapy.

Regarding the content of change, the level of representation of each GCI in the therapeutic processes with and without change was first analyzed, without considering their frequency of appearance; that is, which GCIs appear reported in both outcome groups according to each perspective. For therapies that achieved change, patients, therapists, and observers agree in pointing out the presence of GCI 9

(Manifestation of a new behavior or emotion) as the most represented, followed by the GCI 13 (Transformation of valuations and emotions in relation to oneself and others). For therapies that did not achieve change, the three perspectives agree in pointing out GCI 9 as the most represented. The medium-level indicators (Category II) that account for the "initial cracking" of understanding patterns and increase in permeability toward new understandings could be present in therapies with and without change, as they are not yet consolidated into more robust and complex changes (Category III). In addition, these are changes that can be identified more easily, both from the observational and in the reconstructive process, being more visible or manifest than those that occur in the patient's inner sphere.

The agreement in the frequency of the reported GCI was analyzed, by theoretically grouping these indicators according to the level of evolution of change and according to therapy outcome. Patients and therapists agree on the proportions of each level of GCI present in therapies that achieved change, indicating a greater number of GCI of Category II (medium level), and low frequency of GCI of Category I and III. In the case of therapies without change, therapists report fewer Category III GCI than patients. This suggests that patient–therapist convergence is associated with positive therapeutic outcomes, supporting the assumption of an association between a good therapeutic alliance, agreement on the content of change, and positive therapy outcomes.

In therapies with change, observers identified almost twice the number of Category I changes than patients, however, they agree in reporting more Category II changes, and few Category III changes. In therapies that did not achieve change, there were no statistically significant differences between the proportion of the three categories of GCI reported by patients and observers, showing a general agreement. The evident disagreement in successful therapies is partly explained by the access that observers have from the beginning of the process to the moment-to-moment unfolding of the changes, reporting them in greater quantity as they manifest. These initial changes can be overshadowed, from the perspective of the patients, by the higher-level changes that occur later and that may have more prominence, in addition to the influence of the passage of time on memory.

Finally, therapists and observers agree on the proportions of GCI of each category, regardless of the outcome of the therapies. In both cases, observers reported a significantly higher number of Category I GCI, possibly for the same reasons mentioned above. Thus, the degree of agreement between therapists and observers is not associated to therapeutic change.

Conclusions

The value of the study by Altimir et al. (2010) lies in its multi-dimensional and multi-perspective approach to the study of change events and their evolution in naturalistic contexts with therapies of different modalities and theoretical approaches, using a combination of qualitative and quantitative methods. Few studies to date have addressed change in psychotherapy in this way, so this approach was innovative in terms of its questions and methods. Since different dimensions of change and perspectives were examined, the results can be complex to interpret in a simple and unidimensional way. However, it is possible to suggest that the question about the relationship between agreement on change and therapy outcome is only positively answered when comparing patient and therapist perspectives and when the content dimension of change is considered. This underscores the value of studying the specific content of change moments as a means to better inform clinicians about what may be useful in therapy.

These results support the value of the observational perspective in contributing to the detailed description of the micro-process in psychotherapy and the moment-to-moment unfolding of change, based on what is reported by the participants. The agreement between observational and participant perspectives has limited value, considering the dissimilar access each one has to the unfolding of change. It is very likely that an approach to patient and therapist experience of therapy that captures it at the end of each session could be more easily compared to the observers' perspective. The consideration of the naturalistic contexts in which the therapies were carried out and the ethical sensitivities of therapists and care services limited the possibility of adopting this methodological approach. However, other approaches were chosen, showing flexibility in order to answer the research questions. Finally, the value of the patients' subjective perspective is emphasized to account for change and what is truly useful and beneficial of psychotherapy from their own experience.

This study highlights, even after a decade, that the study of processes and mechanisms of change requires complex and creative designs, in line with the local and contextual reality of therapy delivery, and that they are used with the necessary flexibility to answer and deepen the question about change in psychotherapy.

Considering the review of the status of qualitative research on psychotherapy change, we observe that creativity in the development of methodologies that capture the phenomenon has been present both in the global north and south. At the same time, we observe the influence that the developments of qualitative research on therapeutic process in the north have had on research in Latin America. Nevertheless, we observe how the adoption of these influences has not been alien to an adaptation and transformation of these methods to fit local realities, both from the point of view of the object of study and its actors (patient, therapists, mental health services), as well as of the questions that are asked and the needs that the researchers themselves have. These transformations account for the flexible and creative management that Latin American researchers have made of the investigative tools they have had access to. Likewise, the strong naturalistic base of these studies speaks of the interest and relevance that Latin American researchers have given to clinical practice as it is carried out in the reality of each country. It is possible that this is related, to a large extent, as de la Parra (2013) points out, to the fact that a large part of the researchers in psychotherapy in our region are also psychotherapists, so they are very close and sensitive to the reality in which psychotherapy is provided, and they also ask questions that are relevant for clinicians, and whose answers can contribute significantly to therapeutic practice. Qualitative research on change in psychotherapy has traveled a fruitful path in the last two decades, which has laid the foundations for the formulation of new questions about psychotherapeutic change and its mechanisms. This trajectory evidences a solid development and continuous improvement of methodologies that allow answering these questions, in a situated and contingent way, projecting toward the future with greater developments and contributions to our knowledge about psychotherapy change.

References

Altimir, C., Capella, C., Núñez, L., Abarzúa, M., & Krause, M. (2017). Meeting in difference: Revisiting the therapeutic relationship based on patients' and therapists'' experiences in several clinical contexts. *Journal of Clinical Psychology*, 1–13. https://doi.org/10.1002/jclp.22525

Altimir, C., Krause, M., de la Parra, G., Dagnino, P., Tomicic, A., Valdés, N., Echávarri, O., Vilches, O., Reyes, L., Ramírez, I., & Arístegui, R. (2010). Clients', therapists' and observers' agreement on the amount, temporal location, and content of psychotherapeutic change and its relation to outcome. *Psychotherapy Research, 20*(4), 472–487. https://doi.org/10.1080/10503301003705871

Altimir, C., Mantilla, C., & Serralta, F. (2022). Practice-based evidence: Bridging the gap between research and routine clinical practice in diverse settings (Evidencia basada en la práctica: construyendo puentes entre la investigación y la clínica rutinaria en entornos diversos). *Studies in Psychology*. https://doi.org/10.1080/02109395.2022.2139998

Arístegui, R., Gaete, J., Muñoz, G., Salazar, J. I., Krause, M., Vilche, O., Tomicic, A., & Ramírez, I. (2009). Diálogos y autorreferencia: procesos de cambio en psicoterapia desde la perspectiva de los actos de habla. *Revista Latinoamericana de Psicología, 41*(2), 277–289.

Barkham, M., Delgadillo, J., Firth, N., & Saxon, D. (2018). Practice-based evidence and the law of variability in psychological treatment. *Revista Argentina de Clínica Psicológica, XXVII*(2), 115–135. https://doi.org/10.24205/03276716.2018.1059

Barkham, M., Lutz, W., & Castonguay, L. G. (2021). *Bergin and Garfield's Handbook of psychotherapy and behavior change*. John Wiley & Sons.

Barkham, M., & Mellor-Clark, J. (2003). Bridging evidence-based practice and practice-based evidence: Developing a rigorous and relevant knowledge for the psychological therapies. *Clinical Psychology & Psychotherapy, 10*(6), 319–327. https://doi.org/10.1002/cpp.379

Bartholomew, T. T., & Lockard, A. J. (2018). Mixed methods in psychotherapy research: A review of method (ology) integration in psychotherapy science. *Journal of Clinical Psychology, 74*(10), 1687–1709.

Besser, M. C., & Moncada, L. (2013). Proceso psicoterapéutico desde la perspectiva de terapeutas que tratan trastornos alimentarios: Un estudio cualitativo. *Psykhe, 22*(1), 69–82. https://doi.org/10.7764/psykhe.22.1.633

Castonguay, L. G., Barkham, N., Jeong Youn, S., & Page, A. C. (2021). Practice-based evidence -findings from routine clinical settings. In M. Barkham, W. Lutz, & L. G. Castonguay (Eds.), *Bergin and Garfield's Handbook of psychotherapy and behavior change* (pp. 191–222). John Wiley & Sons.

Cummings, A. L., Martin, J., Hallberg, E., & Slemon, A. (1992). Memory for therapeutic events, session effectiveness and working alliance in short-term counseling. *Journal of Counseling Psychology, 39*(306), 312.

de la Parra, G. (2013). Psychotherapy research in developing countries: The case of Latin America. *Psychotherapy Research, 23*(6), 609–623. https://doi.org/10.1080/10503307.2013.830794

de la Parra, G., von Bergen, A., & del Río, M. (2002). Primeros hallazgos de la aplicacio´n de un instrumento que mide resultados psicoterapéuticos en una muestra de pacientes y de población general. *Revista Chilena de Neuropsiquiatría, 40*, 201–209.

Dos Santos, O., & Dallos, R. (2012). The process of cross-cultural therapy between white therapists and clients of African-Caribbean descent. *Qualitative Research in Psychology, 9*(1), 62–74. https://doi.org/10.1080/14780887.2012.630827

Duarte, J., Fischersworring, M., Martínez, C., & Tomicic. (2019a). "I couldn't change the past; the answer wasn't there": A case study on the subjective construction of psychotherapeutic change of a patient with a Borderline Personality Disorder diagnosis and her therapist. *Psychotherapy Research, 29*(4), 445–462. https://doi.org/10.1080/10503307.2017.1359426

Duarte, S. J., Martínez, G. C., & Tomicic, S. A. (2019b). Revisión teórica y metodológica de los eventos relevantes en psicoterapia para el estudio del cambio [Relevant episodes and events for the study of change in psychotherapy]. *Revista Argentina de Clínica Psicológica, 28*(3), 253–265.

Elliott, R. (1986). Interpersonal Process Recall (IPR) asl psychotherapy process research method. In L. Greenberg & W. Pinsof (Eds.), *The psychotherapeutic process* (pp. 503–527). Guilford.

Elliott, R., Slatick, E., & Urman, M. (2001). Qualitative change process research on psychotherapy. Alternative strategies. In J. Fommer & D. L. Rennie (Eds.), *Qualitative psychotherapy research. Methods and methodology* (pp. 69–111). Pabst Science Publishers.

Fernández, O., Herrera, P., Krause, M., Pérez, J. C., Valdés, N., Vilches, O., & Tomicic, A. (2012). Episodios de cambio y estancamiento en psicoterapia: Características de la comunicación verbal entre pacientes y terapeutas. *Terapia Psicológica, 30*(2), 5–22. https://doi.org/10.4067/S0718-48082012000200001

Fernández, O., Pérez, C., Gloger, S., & Krause, M. (2015). Importancia de los cambios iniciales en la psicoterapia con adolescentes. *Terapia Psicológica, 33*(3). https://doi.org/10.4067/S0718-48082015000300008

Frommer, J., Langenbach, M., & Streeck, U. (2004). Qualitative psychotherapy research in German-speaking countries. *Psychotherapy Research, 14*(1), 57–75.

Gaete, J., Arístegui, R., & Krause, M. (2019). Clarificar para otro: Seis prácticas conversacionales generativas de cambio terapéutico desde la teoría del cambio subjetivo. *Terapia Psicológica, 37*(3), 255–270.

Gergen, K. (1996). *Realidades y relaciones: Aproximaciones a la construcción social*. Paidós.

Glaser, B. G., & Strauss, A. (1967). *The discovery of grounded theory: Strategies for qualitative research*. Aldine.

Greenberg, L. S. (1999). Ideal psychotherapy research: A study of significant change processes. *Journal of Clinical Psychology, 55*, 1467–1480.

Groeben, N., & Scheele, B. (2000). Dialogue-Hermeneutic method and the "Research Program Subjective Theories". *Forum: Qualitative Social Research, 1*(2). https://doi.org/10.17169/fqs-1.2.1079

Hill, C., Chui, H., & Baumann, E. (2013). Revisiting and reenvisioning the outcome problem in psychotherapy: An argument to include individualized and qualitative measurement. *Psychotherapy, 50*, 68–76. https://doi.org/10.1037/a0030571

Hill, C.E., Thompson, B.J., & Williams, E.N. (1997). A guide to conducting consensual qualitative research. *The Counseling Psychologist, 25*(517). https://doi.org/10.1177/011000097254001

Krause, M. (2023). Lessons from ten years of psychotherapy process research. *Psychotherapy Research*. https://doi.org/10.1080/10503307.2023.2200151

Krause, M., de la Parra, G., Arístegui, R., Dagnino, P., Tomicic, A., Valdés, N., Vilches, O., Echávarri, O., Ben-Dov, P., Reyes, L., Altimir, C., & Ramírez, I. (2006). Indicadores genéricos de cambio en el proceso psicoterapéutico. Revista Latinoamericana de Psicología, 38 (2), 299–325.

Krause, M., & Altimir, C. (2016). Introduction: Current developments in psychotherapy process research / Introducción: desarrollos actuales en la investigación del proceso psicoterapéutico. *Estudios de Psicología, 37*(2–3), 201–225. https://doi.org/10.1080/02109395.2016.1227574

Krause, M., & Altimir, C. (2018). El Programa Chileno de Investigación del Cambio en Psicoterapia. *Revista Brasileira de Psicoterapia, 20* (3). https://doi.org/10.5935/2318-0404.2018002

Krause, M., de la Parra, G., Arístegui, R., Dagnino, P., Tomicic, A., Valdés, N., Echávarri, O., Strasser, K., Reyes, L., Altimir, C., Ramírez, I., Vilches, O., & Ben-Dov, P. (2007). The evolution of therapeutic change studied through generic change indicators. *Psychotherapy Research, 17*(6), 673–689. https://doi.org/10.1080/10503300601158814

Krause, M., Venegas, F., Dagnino, P., & Altimir, C. (2018). La experiencia subjetiva del terapeuta durante segmentos significativos en psicoterapia. *Revista Argentina de Clínica Psicológica, 27*(2), 250–273.

Lambert, M. J., Hansen, N. B., Umpress, V., Lunnen, K., Okiishi, J., & Burlingame, G. M. (1996). *Administration and scoring manual for the OQ-45.2*. American Professional Credentialing Services.

Levitt, H. M., Hamburger, A., Hill, C. E., McLeod, J., Pascual-Leone, A., Timulak, L., Buchholz, M. B., Frommer, J., Fuertes, J., Iwakabe, S., Martínez, C., Morrill, Z., Knox, S., Langer, P., Muran, J. C., Weie Oddli, H., Řiháček, T., Tomicic, A., & Tuval-Mashiach, R. (2024). Broadening the evidentiary basis for clinical practice guidelines: Recommendations from qualitative psychotherapy researchers. *American Psychologist, 80*(3), 389–410.

Levitt, H. M., McLeod, J., & Stiles, W. B. (2021). The conceptualization, design, and evaluation of qualitative methods in research on psychotherapy. In M. Barkham, W. Lutz, & L. G. Castonguay (Eds.), *Bergin and Garfield's handbook of psychotherapy and behavior change* (pp. 51–86). John Wiley & Sons.

Lutz, W., Castonguay, L. G., Lambert, M. J., & Barkham, M. (2021). Traditions and new beginnings: Historical and current perspectives on research in psychotherapy and behavior change. In M. Barkham, W. Lutz, & L. G. Castonguay (Eds.), *Bergin and Garfield's Handbook of psychotherapy and behavior change* (pp. 3–18). John Wiley & Sons.

Manríquez-Reyes, K. (2023). Contenidos de cambio y estancamiento en psicoterapias humanistas con adultos que han vivido abuso sexual infantil. *Psicoperspectivas, 22*(3). https://doi.org/10.5027/psicoperpectiva-vol22-issue3-fulltext-2975

Mantilla, C., & Traverso, P. (2021). Momentos significativos asociados al cambio psíquico. *Revista de Psicología, 39*(1). https://doi.org/10.18800/psico.202101.016

Martin, J., & Stelmaczonek, K. (1988). Participant's identification and recall of important events in counseling. *Journal of Counseling Psychology, 35*, 385–390.

Martínez, C., & Tomicic, A. (2019). From dissociation to dialogical reorganization of subjectivity in psychotherapy. In A. Konopka, H. J. Hermans, & M. M. Gonçalves (Eds.), *Handbook of dialogical self theory and psychotherapy: Bridging psychotherapeutic and cultural traditions* (pp. 170–185). Routledge.

McLeod, J., Stiles, W. B., & Levitt, H. M. (2021). Qualitative research: Contributions to psychotherapy practice, theory, and policy. In M. Barkham, W. Lutz, & L.G. Castonguay (Eds.). *Bergin and Garfield's Handbook of psychotherapy and behavior change* (pp. 3–18). John Wiley & Sons (pp. 351–384). John Wiley & Sons.

Mellado, A., Martínez, C., Tomicic, A., & Krause, M. (2022). Identification of dynamic patterns of personal positions in a patient diagnosed with borderline personality disorder and the therapist during change episodes of the psychotherapy. *Frontiers in Psychology, 13*, 716012. https://doi.org/10.3389/fpsyg.2022.716012

Núñez, L., Fernández, S., Alamo, N., Midgley, N., Capella, C., & Krause, M. (2022). The therapeutic relationship and change processes in child psychotherapy: A qualitative, longitudinal study of the views of children, parents and therapists. *Research in Psychotherapy: Psychopathology, Process and Outcome, 25*(1), 103–117.

Olivera, J., Juan, S., & Roussos, A. J. (2016). Las intervenciones terapéuticas desde la perspectiva del paciente: Una aproximación cualitativa. *Anuario de Investigaciones, 23*, 43–51.

Orlinsky, D. E., Grawe, K., & Parks, B. K. (1994). Process and outcome in psychotherapy: Noch einmal. In A. E. Bergin & S. L. Garfield (Eds.), *Handbook of psychotherapy and behavior change* (4th ed., pp. 270–376). John Wiley & Sons.

Rennie, D. L. (2004). Anglo-North American qualitative counseling and psychotherapy research. *Psychotherapy Research, 14*(1), 37–55.

Rennie, D. L., Watson, K. T., & Monteiro, A. (2002). The rise of qualitative research in psychology. *Canadian Psychology, 43*, 179–189.

Reyes, L., Arístegui, R., Krause, M., Strasser, K., Tomicic, A., Valdés, N., Altimir, C., Ramírez, I., de la Parra, G., Dagnino, P., Echávarri, O., Vilches, O., & Ben-Dov, P. (2008). Language and therapeutic change: A speech acts analysis. *Psychotherapy Research, 18*(3), 355–362.

Roussos, A. (2013). Introduction to special section on clients' perspective of change in psychotherapy. *Psychotherapy, 50*(4), 503–504.

Safran, J. D. (2003). The relational turn, the therapeutic alliance, and psychotherapy research: Strange bedfellows or postmodern marriage? *Contemporary Psychoanalysis, 39*, 449–475.

Tomicic, A., Martínez, C., Pérez, J. C., Hollenstein, T., Angulo, S., Gerstmann, A., Barroux, I., & Krause, M. (2015). Discourse-voice regulatory strategies in the psychotherapeutic interaction: A state-space dynamics analysis. *Frontiers Psychology, 6*, 378. https://doi.org/10.3389/fpsyg.2015.00378

Valdés, N., Dagnino, P., Krause, M., Pérez, J. C., Altimir, C., Tomicic, A., & de la Parra, G. (2010). Analysis of verbalized emotions in the psychotherapeutic dialogue during change episodes. *Psychotherapy Research, 20*(2), 136–150. https://doi.org/10.1080/10503300903170921

Valdés, N., Krause, M., Vilches, O., Dagnino, P., Echavarri, O., Ben-Dov, P., Arístegui, R., & de la Parra, G. (2005). Proceso de cambio psicoterapéutico: Análisis de episodios relevantes en una terapia grupal con pacientes adictos. *Psykhe, 14*(2), 3–18.

Chapter 4
The Systematic Case Study in Psychodynamic Focal Psychotherapy with Abused Women: A Context-Sensitive Approach to Understanding Psychological Change

Carla Mantilla, Doris Argumedo, Gian Rasmussen, Francesco Marinelli, and Paz Lancho

The Peruvian social reality is particular and complex. Like in other Latin American countries, factors such as linguistic and ethnic diversity, socioeconomic inequalities, social exclusion, violence based on identity categories, political instability, and the precariousness of mental health services pose significant challenges for researchers. Especially when their task has to do with understanding how to promote positive change in psychotherapy. These challenges unite us and identify us as Latin Americans; in this sense, it is no coincidence that recently, innovative and creative research initiatives for the study of the therapeutic process have emerged in our region, as gathered in this volume.

Researching from our frameworks of reference and with designs adapted to local needs and resources is both relevant and justified on ethical, political, and epistemological levels.

We are not generic subjects; we are shaped by a heterogeneous sociocultural fabric. If we seek to be just in our task of understanding and alleviating the sufferings that inhabit us, it is essential to recognize and consider it to generate evidence that is useful for our reality.

C. Mantilla (✉) · D. Argumedo · G. Rasmussen · F. Marinelli · P. Lancho
Pontifical Catholic University of Peru, Lima, Perú
e-mail: cmantil@pucp.edu.pe; dargume@pucp.pe; gian.rasmussen@pucp.pe; fmarinelli@pucp.pe; paz.lancho@pucp.edu.pe

A. Tomicic, J. D. Soto (eds.), *Qualitative Research in Clinical Psychology and Psychotherapy in Latin America*, https://doi.org/10.1007/978-3-031-90782-1_4

Systematic Single Case and the Research of Dynamic Psychotherapy

For the psychoanalytic approach, the clinical method is considered both a modality of intervention and a resource for researching mental processes; and therefore, it has been the place from which the main theoretical models on the mind and therapeutic action have been constructed (Jiménez, 2007). In this framework, the clinical case is the primary resource for providing evidence to theoretical proposals, as well as a fundamental device for training clinical thinking in training and supervision spaces.

However, the almost exclusive use of narrative reconstructions made by the therapist about the experience of the process, as a platform for evidence and validity, has been the subject of numerous criticisms. These include the presence of confirmation biases, the omission of information, and the exclusivity of one participant's subjective standpoint about what occurred in the therapeutic encounter (Bucci, 2005). In this regard, Kachele et al. (2009) highlight that in the early days of psychoanalysis, case studies showed a high dose of creativity, contribution, detail, and organization. However, over time, a deterioration in their quality became evident due to the absence of rigorous criteria and systematic formats for organizing the reports.

This situation would have contributed to the impoverishment of the device, as instead of being a resource to question, discard, or expand the starting theory, it became an object for its confirmation. Furthermore, the clinical case would have served for the transmission of traditional knowledge within psychoanalytic institutions and as a resource for identity affirmation. In this context, the theory-practice relationship became one where the latter was subjected to the former, thus limiting the possibilities for discovery and questioning (Fonagy, 2003). Therefore, by having the clinical case as the only source of evidence and the absence of a tradition in which rival theories are compared and tested (Fonagy, 2015), a kind of conceptual "babel" (Jiménez, 2005a) was generated due to the multiplicity of explanatory models that often are epistemologically incompatible with each other.

Equally problematic is the fact that the psychoanalytic clinical method, from which the theoretical edifice has been built, was simultaneously the setting for generating and demonstrating hypotheses with universalist pretensions. The absence of other methods to empirically validate the acquired knowledge resulted in an epistemic vicious circle, thus limiting the recognition of psychoanalytic ideas within the scientific world. This situation would have placed psychoanalytic psychotherapy at a disadvantage in accounting for its benefits in a forum broader than its associations, causing a distancing from psychotherapists of other orientations, the academic world, and mental health policies.

The influence of the Evidence-Based Practice (EBP) paradigm and changes in public health systems at the end of the twentieth century aggravated the crisis of the psychodynamic proposal and its permanence in health service systems. In response to this situation, during the 1990s, the International Psychoanalytical Association (IPA) promoted scientific research in psychoanalysis. Among other measures, a research committee, conferences, funds, and training programs were established.

Furthermore, the first edition of the *Open Door Review* (Fonagy et al., 1999) was published, a compendium of the major studies on the effectiveness and efficacy of psychoanalytic psychotherapy across various regions (Leuzingher- Bohleber & Arnold, 2020). Additionally, evidence-based adaptations were made to the brief technique, which is now competitive in public health environments and also amenable to being measured for verifying its effects.

In this context of questioning and change, the clinical case as the sole knowledge-generating device was problematized. Kachele et al. (2009) made a clarifying contribution to this issue by differentiating the reconstructed clinical narrative or clinical case from the systematic or research case. The former involves the reconstruction of the case from the therapist's experience and would mainly serve for formative purposes in supervision and clinical discussion spaces. The latter is based on recording the process in audio or video for research purposes and socialization in scientific spaces. In this sense, the record would be studied from a third-party perspective, using either quantitative or qualitative methods.

According to Leuzingher-Bohleber (2015), the systematic case would be a strategy of extra-clinical research, that is, generated outside the intervention setting. With the case rigorously documented and based on the formulation of questions that go beyond the specific understanding of a particular client, the researched data moves beyond the consulting room to be scientifically studied, undergoing the respective quality controls. Furthermore, within the tradition of qualitative research in psychology and social sciences, the systematic case study holds a paradigmatic importance. It is defined as a methodological strategy aimed at deeply understanding a phenomenon through the generation of detailed, dense, systematic documentation within its natural environment (McLeod, 2010; Stake, 1995).

If we apply this to the field of psychotherapy, the systematic case study allows for the analysis of the therapeutic process's complexity in a contextualized manner, as well as the practical experience in action. This implies a way of constructing knowledge that begins from the practical ground (the therapeutic process as it was conducted) to test explanations that are sensitive to the particularities of the case, thus uncovering what functions optimally to facilitate positive changes. In this way, these studies contribute to generating shared professional and scientific knowledge, allowing both users and clinicians to deepen their understanding of what transpired across different types of therapy and in specific clinical populations. Additionally, they contribute to professional development by providing a source of reflection on practice (McLeod, 2010).

This methodological model aligns with a vision of Practice-Oriented Research (POR) (Castonguay et al., 2013) or Practice-Based Evidence (PBE) (Barkham & Mellor-Clark, 2003). This approach starts from the study of routine processes as a foundation for formulating questions and designing systematic strategies and procedures. The proposed approach contributes to understanding mental health issues in sociocultural realities that are specific and insufficiently represented in the models built in first-world countries, primarily with randomized controlled designs. Thus, to produce useful knowledge that impacts the well-being of clients, the POR approach aims to establish a bridge between research and practice. It aims to capture and represent in a close and creative manner the specific ways in which psychotherapeutic work is carried out (Altimir et al., 2022).

Building on the ideas presented, we could assert, following Altimir and Jiménez (2021), that the use of the systematic case design is an appropriate methodological strategy for the micro-analytic study of complex aspects of therapeutic interaction. Particularly as they unfold during significant events in the dynamic therapy process. Likewise, we consider this device relevant for macro-process studies focused on the evolution of change throughout the therapeutic process (Krause & Altimir, 2016). It is highly sensitive to capturing transformations in clients' psychological functioning, including relational patterns in specific clinical contexts, such as cases of violence against women.

Application of the Systematic Case to the Study of Violence Against Women

One of the main challenges in psychotherapy research within the Latin American context is violence against women. This is a phenomenon that violates the dignity and autonomy of its victims, breaching their human rights and limiting their development and participation in civic life (Grupo de Trabajo de Salud Mental de la Coordinadora Nacional de Derechos Humanos [GTSM-CNDDHH], 2006).

Latin American authors (Berenstein, 2000; Casique & Castro, 2012; Hernández, 2000) argue that acts of violence occur within a relational context influenced by cultural norms shared by human groups. Likewise, various psychodynamic traditions (Layton, 2020a; Safatle et al., 2021) recognize that the social environment plays a fundamental role in the functioning of the individual. In this sense, it is believed that violence against women originates from a social structure characterized by unequal power relationships, where bodies categorized as "masculine" and "feminine" are differently affected.

The Peruvian State has acknowledged that this violence is the result of gender asymmetry, as well as other identity factors, such as skin color and sexual orientation. According to the *Encuesta Demográfica y de Salud Familiar 2022* [*Demographic and Family Health Survey 2022*] (Instituto Nacional de Estadística e Informática [INEI], 2023), nationwide, 56.9% of women aged 15 to 49, who had ever been in relationships with men, have suffered some form of violence (psychological, physical, and/or sexual). To address this issue, the State has implemented various actions through the *Programa Nacional AURORA* [*National Program AURORA*] of the *Ministerio de la Mujer y Poblaciones Vulnerables* [*Ministry of Women and Vulnerable Populations*] (MIMP). Among these, the creation of the *Centro de Emergencia Mujer* [*Women's Emergency Center*] (CEM) stands out, which are specialized services providing psychological, social, and legal assistance to victims, including crisis intervention and psychological support throughout the legal process (MIMP, 2016a, 2016b, 2022). Additionally, the *Ministerio de Salud* [*Ministry of*

Health] (MINSA) has been designated as the entity responsible for providing psychosocial support and counseling for the emotional recovery of victims (MINSA, 2017). These efforts aim to facilitate access to justice and ensure the comprehensive protection of women.

Although the quality of the CEM's model of care for accessing justice is recognized, there is limited evidence regarding the effectiveness of its psychological support. The *Defensoría del Pueblo* [*Ombudsman's Office*] (2018, 2019) noted that many CEMs had only one psychologist, limiting the proper attention to the existing demand. Similarly, concerning the MINSA's health services, it was highlighted that while they facilitated legal processes, they did not address the emotional recovery of the users (Defensoría del Pueblo, 2018, 2019; IWORDS Global, 2020). In general terms, there is a lack of studies on the effectiveness of State-provided psychological support, which tends to focus more on symptom reduction than on the transformation of the relationships that generate violence.

Given this state of affairs, in 2018 the *Programa Nacional Contra la Violencia Familiar y Sexual* [*National Program Against Family and Sexual Violence*] (PNCVFS) of the MIMP expressed interest in establishing an agreement with the master's program in *Intervención Clínica Psicoanalítica* [*Psychoanalytic Clinical Intervention*] of the *Pontificia Universidad Católica del Perú* [*Pontifical Catholic University of Peru*] (PUCP). The goal was to implement psychological support processes for women victims of violence, carried out by psychology graduate students from the master's program, in order to generate changes in their relational dynamics. As a result, psychodynamic interventions based on Interpersonal Dynamic Therapy (DIT; Lemma et al., 2011) were introduced.

The DIT is a focused, individual psychotherapy that centers on conflictual interpersonal patterns (Interpersonal Affective Focus [IPAF]), considered the cause of symptoms. Thus, this therapy has two main objectives: to help the client understand the relationship between their symptoms and their relationships through the analysis of the IPAF and to promote reflective capacity regarding their mental states to improve the management of interpersonal difficulties (Lemma et al., 2011).

The study model presented in this chapter corresponds to a methodological construction effort developed by the *Grupo de Investigación en Psicoanálisis* [*Research Group in Psychoanalysis*] of the PUCP (GIP). This effort was aimed at investigating change in two psychotherapeutic processes with women victims of intimate partner violence in heterosexual relationships, based on the systematic single-case design.

The interventions were conducted by male, cisgender, heterosexual therapists, licensed psychologists, and students in their final year of the aforementioned master's program. The clients (see Table 4.1) were cisgender women who had reported intimate partner violence and were treated at the institutional location of the CEM. They were selected by the institution's psychologists as beneficiaries of psychotherapeutic processes based on the following criteria: (a) being victims of gender-based intimate partner violence; (b) presenting a low or moderate risk of recurrence of violence (i.e., no imminent risk to the integrity of the user); and (c) showing a high level of motivation to work emotionally with them.

Table 4.1 Characteristics of female consultants

	Luz	Muriel
Age	37 years old	35 years old
Place of origin	Northern Highlands of the country	Northern Highlands of the country
Education level	High school completed	High school completed
Number of children	2 (8-year-old daughter and 5-year-old son)	1 (12-year-old daughter)
Marital status	Recently separated (previously cohabited for 8 years)	Married (13 years of marriage)
Economic situation	Economically dependent on ex-partner	Economically dependent on husband
Residence	Living temporarily with her children at a relative's house	Living with partner and daughter
History of domestic violence	Physical violence from her father toward her mother and sisters. Sexual violence by a relative at 8 and 15 years of age	Sexual violence by a relative at age 12
Legal actions	Legal complaint of domestic violence against her ex-partner	Domestic violence complaint against her husband; divorce proceedings initiated
Motives for consultation	Psychological violence by her ex-partner. He insulted her and showed irrational jealousy, accusing her of being unfaithful without foundation	Physical and verbal violence by her husband. He accuses her of infidelity without reason, does not allow her to leave the house, and maintains an extramarital relationship with another woman, with whom she has two children
Interpersonal Affective Focus (IPAF)	She perceives herself as weak, submissive, and dependent, and perceives others as aggressive and unfair. Associated emotions of pain, sadness, and helplessness. Defensively, she assumes a passive and dependent position, hoping that the other will change	She perceives herself as replaceable and dependent. She perceives others as devaluing and inattentive. Associated emotions include rejection, anguish, and sadness, and she fears loneliness and abandonment. Her defense manifests as submissiveness or constant demands

The analyzed material consisted of audio recordings of the sessions and their verbatim transcriptions, donated by both members of the dyad (therapist and client) to the GIP's therapeutic processes archive upon the completion of the intervention. This material was subjected to appropriate ethical protocols for its registration and use in scientific research, publications, and educational activities.

The systematic case studies that informed this chapter (see Table 4.2) were grouped into two lines of research. The first focuses on studying change through the analysis of specific features of the therapeutic interaction and the psychological processes characterizing Episodes of Change (EC), which were identified using the Generic Indicators of Change System (SIG) and capture transformations at a representational level (Krause et al., 2006). The second seeks to identify and characterize clients' relational patterns or configurations to understand their evolution

Table 4.2 Systematic case studies

Line of research	Author	Main subjects	Coding system	Case
Relational patterns, conflict, and structure	Aguirre, M. (2019)	Relational configurations, transgenerational transmission of violence, CCRT-LU-S	Core Conflictual Relationship Theme – Leipzig/Ulm – Spanish version (CCRT-LU-S)	Luz
	Donayre, C. (2019)	Relational configurations, therapeutic change, CCRT-LU-S	CCRT-LU-S	Luz
	Pardo, F. (2019)	Relational configurations, self-other representations, therapeutic change, CCRT-LU-S	CCRT-LU-S Differentiation-Relatedness Scale of Self and Object Representations (D-RS)	Muriel
	Rasmussen, G. (2019)	Relational configurations, class and race power relations, therapeutic relationship, CCRT-LU-S	CCRT-LU-S	Muriel
	Peirano, R. (2021)	Relational configurations, transference, changes in transference, CCRT-LU-S	CCRT-LU-S	Luz
	Topham, S. (2021)	Relational configurations, gender power relations, hegemonic gender discourses, gender narrative change in psychotherapy, CCRT-LU-S	CCRT-LU-S	Muriel
	Alarcón, M. (2022)	Relational configurations, gender power relations, therapeutic relationship, CCRT-LU-S	CCRT-LU-S	Muriel

(continued)

Table 4.2 (continued)

Line of research	Author	Main subjects	Coding system	Case
Study of change through significant moments in the process	Madueño, S. (2019)	Therapist verbal interventions, change episodes	Indicators of generic psychotherapeutic change	Luz
	Marinelli, F. (2019)	Subjective experience of temporality, violence narratives, therapeutic change, agency, affects, change episodes	Indicators of generic psychotherapeutic change	Luz
	Romero, C. (2019)	Affects, therapeutic change, change episodes	Indicators of generic psychotherapeutic change	Luz
	Ugarte, A. (2019)	Co-construction, dialogic interaction between patient and therapist, change episodes, moment of meeting	Indicators of generic psychotherapeutic change	Luz
	Colmenares, M.P. (2021)	Subjective experience, change in interpersonal affective focus, change episodes	Indicators of generic psychotherapeutic change	Muriel
	Luján, J. (2021)	Feminine subjectivity discourse, therapeutic change, agency, change episodes	Indicators of generic psychotherapeutic change	Muriel
	Dam, A. (2021)	Conceptual Metaphor (CM), dialogue analysis, co-construction, therapeutic change	Indicators of generic psychotherapeutic change	Muriel
	Antezana, F. (2022)	Metaphorical conceptualizations, affects, therapeutic change, agency, change episodes	Indicators of generic psychotherapeutic change	Luz
	Gazzo, G. (2022)	Psychotherapy sessions, therapeutic relationship, insights, change episodes	Indicators of generic psychotherapeutic change Psychotherapy Process Q-set (PQS)	Muriel
	González, L. (2022)	Mentalization, patient and therapist interventions, change episodes	Indicators of generic psychotherapeutic change	Luz
	Grández, V. (2022)	Referential activity, therapeutic change, affects, change episodes	Indicators of generic psychotherapeutic change Weighted Referential Activity Dictionary Spanish version (S-WRAD)	Muriel
	Gutiérrez, J. (2022)	Content of communicational actions, therapeutic change, agency, change episodes	Indicators of generic psychotherapeutic change Therapeutic Activity Coding System (SCAT)	Luz
	Lancho, M.P. (2022)	Mentalization, attachment, change episodes	Indicators of generic psychotherapeutic change Patient Attachment Coding System (PACS)	Luz

throughout the intervention process, emphasizing their changes, their relationship with the therapeutic alliance, and cultural context.

The qualitative methodology employed in both research lines ultimately aimed for a deep and contextual understanding of the elements facilitating change. Among the qualitative analysis strategies used were Thematic Analysis, Narrative Analysis, Critical Discourse Analysis, and Conversation Analysis (Pistrang & Barker, 2012). It is worth noting that some studies adopted more inductive categorizations, whereas others relied on various standardized coding systems. These included the System of Coding Therapeutic Activity (SCAT, Krause et al., 2009), the Psychotherapy Process Q-set (PQS, Jones, 1985), the Spanish version of the Core Conflictual Relationship Theme Method (CCRT LU-S, Espinosa & Valdés, 2012), the Patient Attachment Coding System (PACS, Talia & Miller-Bottome, 2014), the Differentiation-Relatedness Scale (D-RS, Diamond et al., 2014), and the Spanish version of the Weighted Referential Activity Dictionary (S-WRAD, Roussos & O'Connell, 2005), among others.

Study of Change Through Significant Moments in the Process

The studies within this line of research, diverse in their questions and qualitative methods, share the commonality of conducting a secondary level of analysis to organize and connect findings related to their constructs of interest with the variable of therapeutic change. These research projects provided valuable insights through the application of Thematic Analysis (TA), which required significant analytical, interpretative, and reflective effort on the part of the researchers (Braun & Clarke, 2006, 2020a, 2020b). In these studies, thematic development was conducted afterward and used to construct emerging patterns of meaning around various organizing concepts.

Moreover, the methodological characteristics of TA (Braun & Clarke, 2006, 2012, 2020a, 2020b) are closely aligned with the Practice-Oriented Research (POR) approach, as well as with the systematic case study design. There is a privileged intersection between (a) the design's provision of rich and rigorously documented data and (b) the interpretative procedures of inductive analysis techniques (such as TA), which offer systematic yet flexible and reflective approaches for a deep and contextualized understanding of the data.

To organize the results of this first line of investigation and transfer them into contributions to clinical practice, the studies can be grouped according to their focus of interest: (a) interactional processes within the therapeutic dyad; (b) the development of complexity in the client's mental functions; and (c) dialogical elements[1].

The first grouping stems from the principle that therapeutic interaction is a central aspect for understanding significant moments in the process. These studies

[1] The research employing conversation analysis approach used by this line is discussed in Chap. 7.

focused on interactional processes, adopting the perspective of two-person psychology (Aron, 1990; Kirman, 1998), and sought to explore the association between various types of exchanges (e.g., verbal, mentalizing, and affective) and significant therapeutic events, mainly Episodes of Change (EC).

Madueño (2019), who focused on therapeutic interventions, suggests that alternating between questioning and recognizing the client's perspective, as well as formulating proposals in a non-conclusive manner and using metaphors, contributed to representational change. These findings align with those of Gazzo (2022), who observed that the client's insights emerged from therapeutic interventions involving relational acts (Mitchell, 1993). These acts aimed to convey to the client that they were being heard, thought about, and understood within a safe framework (Seligman, 2000). The client's responses to such interventions—whether accepting, rejecting, elaborating, or reformulating them—also contributed to insight and change. Notably, Ugarte's (2019) findings emphasized the client's active position, revealing that moments of change were not the product of unilateral action by the psychotherapist. Instead, both the client and therapist actively contributed to constructing meanings associated with representational change.

Grández (2022) studied the Referential Activity, a psycholinguistic tool that evaluates the affective charge in the communication between client and therapist, and the possibility of evoking a corresponding experience in the interlocutor (Maskit et al., 2015). She emphasized that the client's dialogue on painful or conflictive topics is more supported in moments where the subjectivity of the therapist is evident, which challenges the ideal of psychotherapy based on neutrality.

Regarding the concept of mentalization, the following studies focused on the relational and fluctuating nature of this construct: a vehicle in the interaction that allows for relational engagement between one's own mental states and those of an interlocutor (Bromberg, 2008) and the interpretation of one's own and others' behavior in a coherent experience (Bateman & Fonagy, 2012). This ability changes according to the demands and complexity of the meeting between minds (De la Cerda et al., 2019).

Lancho (2022), who conducted an analysis of two sessions (from the initial and the final phase), found that resistance to mentalization was associated with therapeutic interventions formulated in the present tense and directed at having the client clarify or explain their point directly, creating a sense of false attunement. In contrast, interventions formulated in the past tense and inviting the client to imagine or open new content were associated with positive responses in terms of mentalization. In the work with victims of violence and apparently complex trauma, the first type of intervention would be counterproductive in the early stages of the process.

Finally, González (2022) selected episodes of mentalization from the final phase of two therapeutic processes for analysis and found that these tended to coincide with EC, showing a higher level of complexity toward the end of the process. In particular, associations between affect and behavior allowed for approaching active mentalization processes. It was also found that in higher-level mentalization episodes, early experiences of violence were mentioned, and these verbalizations allowed for the observation of the client's thought processes in action.

The second grouping consists of research that sought to understand the psychological processes that add complexity to the mental functioning of clients and contribute to or are linked to subjective representational change. The results of these investigations highlight that the transformations in the affective experience, as well as the construction of a sense of agency, are central aspects that helped to understand the clients' change processes.

Regarding the complexity of the affective experience, the studies employed various methodological approaches to select and systematize the data related to affect. Some studies used EC as the initial unit of analysis to delve into aspects of the affective experience (Colmenares, 2021; Gutiérrez, 2022; Romero, 2019), while others focused on different significant segments of the process, such as narratives about situations of violence (Marinelli, 2019) or metaphors (Antezana, 2022; Dam, 2021) that were later linked to the EC.

The results highlighted that the clients expanded their subjective understanding of their affective states, showing greater self-reflection and finding communication through affect a valuable meeting point to connect with their own thoughts and actions. In this line, Colmenares (2021) noticed that the client began incorporating the possibility of questioning and challenging her own affective states, which would have allowed her to broaden her perspective on what she feels and value previously obscured aspects of the same experience. Similarly, in Romero's (2019) research, it was emphasized that the client began linking her affective states with internal aspects, rather than only external ones. For example, fear was no longer seen solely as related to external violence but also linked to her own fragility and impulsive, reactive aspects. Additionally, Marinelli (2019) stressed that change occurred as the client found opportunities to incorporate her affective experience into her narratives about violence. In this way, having gained greater understanding about what happened and her own actions, the client would have built new perspectives and understandings about herself, which were recorded as moments of change.

Other studies highlighted the use of metaphors as a tool to connect affect with symbolic processes, contributing to the expansion of affective understanding. In this line, Antezana (2022) emphasized that metaphors were an important means for the client to express the nuances of her affective experience, thus providing an intermediate space for representation and expression. Moreover, Gutiérrez (2022) observed that metaphorical resources became a new way of communicating from the affective domain as the therapeutic process progressed. Specifically, Dam (2021) conducted a study on metaphorical conceptualizations in the final session of the therapeutic process, highlighting that these facilitated the construction of new understandings and meanings about the client's experiences, affections, and the therapeutic experience. Her analysis also highlighted that these metaphorical conceptualizations were co-constructed in an active and cooperative dialogue between therapist and client.

In summary, the various results from this second group of studies emphasized that, in the therapeutic process of these clients, the expression, recognition, and articulation of affect, initially confused, inhibited, or unrecognized, were a central element in the construction of new understandings about themselves and their issues. Specifically, the important role that metaphors played in this process of affective complexity was highlighted. Thus, metaphors turned out to be a significant way to communicate the affective states of one's own experience, and at the same time, the very construction of certain metaphors formed part of the change process deployed by the clients.

Regarding the construction of a greater sense of agency, the studies pointed out its importance in the change process. It was defined both as the ability to feel as the author of one's own mental states (Fonagy et al., 2002), as well as the development of a sense of strength, the adoption of a more active position regarding one's own change process, and the taking of actions concerning one's own issues and life situation.

In Luján's (2021) study on the discourse of feminine subjectivity in the EC at the start and end of the therapeutic process, it was identified initially that the client, when referring to herself, used discourse marked by devaluation and difficulty with agency. In response, the change process was accompanied by the client's appropriation of the meaning-making process, as well as a transformation in her sense of agency, reaching a point where she described herself as responsible for her actions and decisions and was able to positively value her decision to report the violence of her partner. In the same line, the studies of Colmenares (2021) and Romero (2019) suggested that the recognition of one's own strength and autonomy, as well as the construction of new meanings related to these, were some of the axes around which the change was articulated. Specifically, Colmenares (2021) observed that, as the client linked her actions to her mental states or affective needs, she was able to adopt a different perspective in dealing with her issue and feel competent to take care of herself.

Finally, regarding the development of a more active position in one's own change process, Gutiérrez (2022) highlighted that from the middle phase of the process, episodes were identified where change was constructed as the client integrated her experience from different domains (cognitive, affective, and behavioral) in a more active and autonomous manner. Similarly, Marinelli (2019) pointed out that the process of articulating affect, thought, and actions, as well as greater flexibility in self-evaluations, allowed the client to take a more active position in the construction of her experience and the meanings associated with herself and her issues.

Relational Configurations: Change and Content

Relational patterns or configurations are schemas that help the subject interpret their attachment experiences, thereby constructing their internal and motivational world in relation to others (Ávila, 2013; Bedoya, 2012; Liberman, 2013; Mitchell, 1993, 2000; Rodríguez, 2014a). Adopting Mitchell's (1993) perspective, we assume that the human psyche is consolidated based on a relational matrix, and in this process, it becomes relational; therefore, all psychic phenomena and human behaviors can be understood as interactive experiences in which others occupy an essential and constitutive role. Understanding violence as a relational phenomenon, we consider that the construct of relational configurations is particularly relevant for capturing the specific relational dynamics with significant others of women subjected to violence within the context of a psychodynamic intervention focused on relational aspects.

Under this framework, and with the aim of investigating the possibilities for change in the relational patterns of these women, seven studies were conducted, which can be grouped into two areas according to their focus of interest: (a) characterization of relational configurations throughout the therapeutic process, and (b) power relations in culture and their role in therapeutic interventions with women who have experienced violence.

A characteristic of the relational configurations is that they express attachment patterns originating in the past that seek to be repeated in current relationships. In this regard, Aguirre (2019), in her research on transgenerational elements in relational patterns, highlighted that the violent narratives from the past occupied an important space in the client's mind. Moreover, these narratives seemed to be split, as her relationships—both past and present—were experienced with others who were either violent or offered support.

As mentioned earlier, the intervention received by the clients followed the guidelines proposed by DIT (Lemma et al., 2011), a therapy that focuses on the elaboration of the IPAF, which can also be understood as a prevalent and pathological relational configuration in the client's experience. With this in mind, three of our studies explored changes in these configurations by comparing them at the start and end of treatment.

The studies by Donayre (2019) and Pardo (2019) identified that, at the start of the process, clients tended to seek recognition and validation from their violent partners, who subjected them to domination dynamics. Additionally, there was a significant difficulty in expressing their own desires. In contrast, by the end of the process, a greater ability to express their desires was observed, along with a reduction in the need for external recognition, giving way to a new one: self-determination. In this sense, both studies emphasized that the changes in the clients involved a break from previous dynamics of subordination and a reclamation of their sense of agency.

Pardo (2019) also investigated changes in the qualities of the representations of the self and the other. Initially, the client had a static and degrading view of herself, along with an ambivalent and poorly integrated image of her partner. By the end of treatment, there was a perception of the self that incorporated elements of strength and enjoyment, though still weakly integrated. The representation of the other, on the other hand, was organized according to their differentiated roles: as a partner and as a father. Thus, the author highlighted the importance of studying changes in relational patterns alongside the process of reorganizing the representations of the self and the other.

When considering the transformation of relational patterns as an indicator of change, the therapeutic relationship becomes relevant as it is understood as an agent of transformation in psychotherapeutic processes. With this in mind, Peirano's (2021) study aimed to characterize the qualities of the relational pattern with the therapist and how it transformed throughout the process. The author identified the need for recognition as the matrix from which three relational patterns initially unfolded.

At the beginning, the client showed a desire to be close to her therapist, seeking elements of identification with him. Later, a second pattern emerged in which the client wanted the therapist to tell her what to do, putting him in a dilemma of either positioning himself as the subject of knowledge or redirecting the focus of the work so she could think through her own experience. Finally, indicating the progressive recognition of her own power and autonomy within an asymmetrical relationship, the client's desire to take action in response to her situation emerged. However, this time without self-judgment, without feeling powerless or overburdened, and with a greater willingness to receive whatever the therapist could offer to her (Peirano, 2021).

On the other hand, when considering the process of formation (and transformation) of relational configurations, contemporary psychodynamic literature highlights not only the importance of early experiences but also the cultural and contextual signifiers that color the significant relational experiences that give rise to these patterns (Layton, 2020a; Mitchell, 1993, 2000; Roseneil & Ketokivi, 2016; Segal, 2013; Watchel, 2014).

Taking this into account, two of our studies aimed to understand the presence of cultural signifiers related to gender, class, and race in the relational configurations of these women. To do so, qualitative analysis strategies were designed to explore sociocultural elements in relational patterns, based on the conceptualization of relational configurations (Mitchell, 1993), the operationalization of relational patterns from the CCRT-LU-S method (Espinosa & Valdés, 2012), and the guidelines of AT (Braun & Clarke, 2012).

In Alarcón's (2022) research on gender in relational configurations, it was pointed out that in the self-representations of the client, there were narratives alluding to her woman's condition as a "victim" of violence and "in need of others." It was also indicated that her previous history of sexual violence placed her in a position of feeling like a woman who was "already used." In contrast, the other was perceived as someone powerful due to his strength, sense of agency, and ability to provide for the family nucleus and herself, characteristics primarily associated with masculine figures. This representation made of the object someone from whom recognition, closeness, and containment were desired; however, given her previous experiences of violence with other men, he was also felt to be potentially dangerous.

Regarding class relations in these configurations, Rasmussen's (2019) study identified that narratives about material resource possession were central to differentiating the self from the other. Her own lack of economic and social resources was translated into a sense of incapacity, turning the other into someone powerful, from whom she was dependent, a situation that legitimized the abuse. Furthermore, with respect to race-related discourses, it was highlighted that the client devalued characteristics of herself related to being a migrant woman with Andean accent and non-white physical traits. The other, being perceived as someone from the capital with a phenotype closer to the idea of "whiteness" (e.g., skin color, English fluency), was idealized. This gave rise to a relational dynamic where the self (she) sought to "improve" by identifying with the idealized aspects of the other.

Since relational patterns tend to seek continuity in the social world, various authors emphasize that they also manifest in the therapeutic relationship (Ávila, 2013; Mitchell, 1993; Rodríguez, 2014b; Segal, 2013). Additionally, considering that the therapeutic encounter occurs within a specific social context, cultural signifiers would emerge in the interaction between client and therapist (Aggarwal, 2011; Altman, 2010; Aron, 1999; Ávila, 2013; Bonovitz, 2005; Hadley, 2008; Layton, 2020a; Leary, 2002; Rodríguez, 2014a; Zeddies, 2000).

Thus, Alarcón (2022) and Rasmussen (2019), in their studies, presented the relational configurations of the client with the therapist and how their understanding can become more complex if cultural narratives are considered. Initially, the therapist figure was idealized by the client as a man with traditional masculine characteristics and both material resources (e.g., class markers) and immaterial resources (e.g., professional knowledge). In contrast, the client saw herself as lacking and dependent, without the internal resources to address her own distress, which led to a passive and demanding stance toward the therapist. This dependency made her strictly adhere to the framework, as she feared rejection and reinforced her negative self-perception.

Rather than responding to this dependency, the therapist promoted the possibility for the client to think through her own distress. With this openness from the therapist to listen without imposing, the client began to see him as a "good" masculine figure who could offer support without expectations of submission. This would have facilitated the development of the client's desire to become a strong woman capable of managing her own problems, thus fostering a process of autonomy and personal empowerment (Alarcón, 2022; Rasmussen, 2019).

After reviewing these studies, we observe that in the psychotherapeutic process, the client-therapist relationship was permeated by a broader social context (Altman, 2010). However, rather than being a relationship that repeated pathological cultural patterns, in the investigated case, we observed the construction of new, healthier relational experiences within the therapy. In this regard, we align with authors like Aguiar (1996), Benjamin (2013), and Harris (2008), who argue that cultural relational patterns can be addressed and worked through in the therapeutic process.

From this perspective, Topham (2021) conducted research with the same case as the two previous studies, with the aim of understanding the discourses of masculinity and femininity in the relational patterns. She also explored the changes in these discourses throughout the therapeutic process. The author emphasized the presence of hegemonic and non-hegemonic gender narratives throughout all the sessions of the process. However, a change was identified in the proportions of appearance of these discourses. At the beginning of the treatment, there was a higher proportion of hegemonic narratives. However, from the sixth session onward until the end, these narratives began to decrease, while non-hegemonic narratives emerged, maintaining an equitable proportion between these two discourses. In this regard, it is assumed that, throughout the therapy, the client seems to have been weaving less rigid relational narratives, with desires that also broke with the hegemonic gender norms.

Discussion

In this chapter, we aimed to review the relevance of the systematic single-case design to establish a dialogue between research and clinical practice with the goal of contributing to the implementation of intervention frameworks and clinical competencies that are pertinent and sensitive to the needs of this vulnerable population. We will begin by highlighting the main contributions of psychodynamic work with this population and then assess the potential of the single-case design as a vehicle for constructing knowledge of change processes in women who have experienced intimate partner violence.

The results of the studies presented have allowed us to identify the marks of violence in the participants at the intra-subjective, intersubjective, and trans-subjective levels (Berenstein, 2000). Violence occurs in the qualities of various psychological aspects (e.g., weak sense of agency, intense emotional activation, difficulty in capturing mental states), as well as in relational patterns that seem to repeat forms of bonding marked by violence and social exclusion.

The first point to highlight is the relevance of the relational approach in addressing the most urgent needs of this specific population. The cases reviewed in this chapter encompass different traumatic events stemming from human relationships and a continuous delegitimization of the participants' subjective experiences. Thus, issues related to the bonds are extensive and must be the core of therapeutic work (Bromberg, 2008).

Regarding change, the findings suggest that interventions that alternate between questioning and recognizing the client's perspective, the formulation of inconclusive proposals inviting the imagination or the opening of new content, and the use of metaphors are effective in enhancing various processes linked to representational change (mentalization, emotional experience complexity, and the sense of agency).

With this in mind, we emphasize two aspects of the therapeutic approach that facilitate change in these women's processes. First, the therapeutic attitude is characterized by openness and flexibility in making continuous adjustments, prioritizing the creation of a unique rhythm within the dyad. In this way, the therapists' stance is emphasized, maintaining a progressive and proactive approach, rather than a prescriptive one, in the possibility of addressing their issues from a psychological and relational model. In this sense, we engage with Jiménez's (2005b) proposal regarding a technique tailored to the client's needs, as well as the premises on the therapist's capacity to function within a zone of proximal development (Leiman & Stiles, 2001).

Second, and in line with the previous point, we can suggest that the therapeutic process constituted an experience of recognition and validation for the clients. This is particularly relevant as they were women in situations of violence, seeking help for issues related to a relational pattern characterized by dynamics of devaluation, dependence, and submission, with a desire for recognition. The research findings align in proposing that the therapeutic processes themselves were, in fact, an emotionally corrective experience (Mitchell, 1997) for these women, in addition to the transformations achieved at the representational level. In this sense, promoting listening and recognizing the clients' perspective, attuning to their affective experience, and not engaging with the initially presented relational offer likely contributed to the clients positioning themselves in a more active role.

The discussed studies have also allowed us to observe that violence does originate in the social world and perpetuates normative unconscious processes (Layton, 2020a) that are lived by our dyads at various levels. The problematic aspects that were found seem to sustain an ideologically abusive system, historically inherited, and tainted with sexism, racism, and classism. This calls on us, as psychotherapists, to incorporate a culturally sensitive perspective (Tummala-Narra, 2018) and to commit to clinical practices that break the ideological split between the subject and their context (Layton, 2006/2020b). It is not just about seeing that a person is within a social context, but that this person lives the social environment in their psychic reality (Frosh & Baraitser, 2008).

After presenting the systematization of our research experience in psychotherapy, we want to highlight the relevance and usefulness of the systematic single-case design, approached qualitatively and within the POR framework. In line with Altimir et al. (2022), we believe that this platform offers a sensitive framework to deeply understand the particularities of therapeutic work and change processes in specific populations, such as women victims of violence, within an inter-institutional agreement involving the university and the State. This context required adaptations to the brief technique used (DIT) in terms of (a) duration (12 sessions instead of 16) and (b) training of therapists in dealing with gender-based violence cases, since the DIT was originally designed for depression and anxiety cases. Additionally, the naturalistic intervention context, upon which the presented results were based, focused on dyads composed of male therapists and female clients. This particular angle of inquiry had the potential to creatively contribute to the understanding of change processes in diverse and unequal realities such as ours, emphasizing the importance of considering variables such as gender, race, and class, which urgently need to be addressed and included.

Regarding the scope and limitations of the main systems used (CCRT LU-S and Generic Indicators of Change System [SIG]), we must note that their use involved adaptations and adjustments within the context of the systematic case design and the qualitative approach to knowledge production. In this sense, the SIG (Krause et al., 2006) was not used to describe the pattern of representational change of the clients, but rather to identify useful units of analysis for understanding aspects of therapeutic interaction and the clients' mental functioning. That is, to "question" these in relation to the actions of other variables (e.g., mentalization, referential activity, therapeutic activity, among others) is important for understanding change. Therefore, rather than describing the phenomenon of representational change, our interest was in analyzing and understanding what happens in the therapeutic exchange in these fragments, in terms of the processes and mechanisms that facilitate it. The result of this approach was the creation of a methodological working model, which, with the limitations of any attempt to combine resources and time within the university context, allowed us to return useful reflections and tools to clinical practice (Altimir et al., 2022; Barkham & Mellor-Clark, 2003).

On the other hand, we consider that the CCRT-LU-S method (Espinosa & Valdés, 2012) was a system that allowed us to approach the study of relational experience in a deep and thorough manner. In line with a theoretical position that acknowledges the inherently relational nature of human experience (Mitchell, 1993), this coding method enabled us to operationalize a variable that is difficult to "capture" in systematic research. Moreover, as a method that is based on interactional narratives (Relational Episodes) as the unit of analysis, it also allowed us to ask questions about the qualities that permeate this relational experience, which fall outside the method strictly speaking. In this way, by adopting a qualitative methodology, we made creative use of it to open ourselves to exploring what emerges from the interactional experience. The CCRT-LU-S served as a method that allowed us to organize the data, yet did not limit us in questioning the discourses and narratives that colored the content of these Relational Episodes.

The experience outlined in this chapter allows us to point out that the effort to bring together clinical work and research in our contexts requires not only creativity, flexibility, and ingenuity. It also requires an ethical and political commitment to guarantee the construction and sustainability of a common ground of interests, with the ultimate goal being the psychological well-being of the clients. In this endeavor, the university plays a fundamental role, both as a guarantor of its quality and fertility and as a translator in communication with the State for the implementation of public mental health policies.

References

Aggarwal, N. (2011). Intersubjectivity, transference and the cultural third. *Contemporary psychoanalysis, 47*(2), 204–223.

Aguiar, E. (1996). Violencia y pareja [Violence and couple]. In I. Izaguirre (Comp.), *Violencia social y derechos humanos* [Social violence and human rights] (pp. 15–37). Eudeba.

Aguirre, M. (2019). *El lugar de lo transgeneracional en las configuraciones relacionales de una mujer violentada por su pareja* [The place of the transgenerational in the relational configurations of a woman abused by her partner]. [Master's thesis, Pontificia Universidad Católica del Perú]. Repositorio de Tesis PUCP.

Alarcón, M. (2022). *Relaciones de poder basadas en género en las configuraciones relacionales de una mujer violentada, en el contexto de un proceso de psicoterapia breve de orientación psicoanalítica* [Gender-based power relations in the relational configurations of an abused woman, in the context of a brief psychoanalytic-oriented psychotherapy process]. [Master's thesis, Pontificia Universidad Católica del Perú]. Repositorio de Tesis PUCP.

Altimir, C., & Jiménez, J. P. (2021). The clinical relevance of interdisciplinary research on affect regulation in the analytic relationship. *Frontiers in Psychology, 12*, 1–16. https://doi.org/10.3389/fpsyg.2021.718490

Altimir, C., Mantilla, C., & Serralta, F. (2022). Practice-based evidence: Bridging the gap between research and routine clinical practice in diverse settings (Evidencia basada en la práctica: construyendo puentes entre la investigación y la clínica rutinaria en entornos diversos). *Studies in Psychology, 43*(3), 415–454. https://doi.org/10.1080/02109395.2022.2139998

Altman, N. (2010). *The analyst in the inner city*. Routledge.
Antezana, F. (2022). *"Siempre he tratado de disfrazar mi tristeza con otra cara". La transformación de las expresiones metafóricas sobre afectos como parte del cambio subjetivo en un proceso focal* ["I have always tried to disguise my sadness with another face.' The transformation of metaphorical expressions about affects as part of subjective change in a focal process]. [Master's thesis, Pontificia Universidad Católica del Perú]. Repositorio de Tesis PUCP.
Aron, L. (1990). One person and two person psychologies and the method of psychoanalysis. *Psychoanalytic Psychology, 7*(4), 475–485. https://doi.org/10.1037/0736-9735.7.4.475
Aron, L. (1999). Clinical choices and the relational matrix. *Psychoanalytic Dialogues, 9*(1), 1–29.
Ávila, A. (2013). *La tradición interpersonal. Perspectiva social y cultural en psicoanálisis* [The interpersonal tradition. Social and cultural perspective in psychoanalysis]. Ágora Relacional.
Barkham, M., & Mellor-Clark, J. (2003). Bridging evidence-based practice and practice-based evidence: Developing a rigorous and relevant knowledge for the psychological therapies. *Clinical Psychology & Psychotherapy, 10*(6), 319–327. https://doi.org/10.1002/cpp.379
Bateman, A., & Fonagy, P. (2012). *Handbook of mentalizing in mental health practice*. American Psychiatric Publishing.
Bedoya, M. (2012). *La noción de matriz relacional y sus implicaciones para el ejercicio clínico de la psicología dinámica* [The notion of relational matrix and its implications for the clinical practice of dynamic psychology]. *Psicología desde el Caribe, 29*(3), 1–9.
Benjamin, J. (2013). *Shadow of the other: Intersubjectivity and gender in psychoanalysis*. Routledge.
Berenstein, I. (2000). *Notas sobre la violencia* [Notes on violence]. *Psicoanálisis, 22*(2), 257–271.
Bonovitz, C. (2005). Locating culture in the psychic field. *Contemporary Psychoanalysis, 41*(1), 55–75.
Braun, V., & Clarke, V. (2006). Using thematic analysis in psychology. *Qualitative Research in Psychology, 3*(2), 77–101. https://doi.org/10.1191/1478088706qp063oa
Braun, V., & Clarke, V. (2012). Thematic analysis. In H. Cooper, P. M. Camic, D. L. Long, A. T. Panter, D. Rindskopf, & K. J. Sher (Eds.), *APA handbook of research methods in psychology, Vol. 2. Research designs: Quantitative, qualitative, neuropsychological and biological* (pp. 57–71). American Psychological Association. https://doi.org/10.1037/13620-004
Braun, V., & Clarke, V. (2020a). Can I use TA? Should I use TA? Should I not use TA? Comparing reflexive thematic analysis and other pattern-based qualitative analytic approaches. *Counseling and Psychotherapy Research, 21*(1), 37–47. https://doi.org/10.1002/capr.12360
Braun, V., & Clarke, V. (2020b). One size fits all? What counts as quality practice in (reflexive) thematic analysis? *Qualitative Research in Psychology, 18*(3), 328–352. https://doi.org/10.1080/14780887.2020.1769238
Bromberg, P. M. (2008). Mentalize THIS!: Dissociation, enactment, and clinical process. In E. Jurist, A. Slade, & S. Bergner (Eds.), *Mind to mind: Infant research, neuroscience, and psychoanalysis* (pp. 414–434). Other Press.
Bucci, W. (2005). Process research. In E. Person, A. Cooper, & G. Gabbard (Eds.), *The American psychiatric publishing textbook of psychoanalysis* (pp. 317–333). American Psychiatric Publishing Inc.
Casique, I., & Castro, R. (2012). *Claroscuros en el conocimiento sobre la violencia contra las mujeres* [Shadows and lights in the knowledge about violence against women]. In I. Casique & R. Castro (Eds.), *Retratos de la violencia contra las mujeres en México. Análisis de los resultados de la Encuesta Nacional sobre la Dinámica de las Relaciones en los Hogares, 2011* [Portraits of violence against women in Mexico. Analysis of the results of the national survey on the dynamics of relationships in the households, 2011] (pp. 9–39). Instituto Nacional de las Mujeres.
Castonguay, L. G., Barkham, M., Lutz, W., & McAleavy, A. (2013). Practice oriented research: Approaches and applications. In M. J. Lambert (Ed.), *Bergin & Garfield's handbook of psychotherapy and behavior change* (6th ed., pp. 85–133). Wiley.

Colmenares, M. (2021). *Análisis de las variaciones en el patrón afectivo interpersonal del foco terapéutico a partir de los episodios de cambio en un proceso de psicoterapia psicoanalítica breve* [Analysis of variations in the interpersonal affective pattern of the therapeutic focus based on change episodes in a brief psychoanalytic psychotherapy process]. [Master's thesis, Pontificia Universidad Católica del Perú]. Repositorio de Tesis PUCP.

Dam, A. (2021). *"Voy a hacer como si tú fueras ese foquito": Conceptualizaciones metafóricas, momentos de cambio e interacción dialógica en la sesión final de un proceso psicoterapéutico psicoanalítico focal* ["I will act as if you were that little light": Metaphorical conceptualizations, moments of change, and dialogical interaction in the final session of a brief psychoanalytic psychotherapy process]. [Master's thesis, Pontificia Universidad Católica del Perú]. Repositorio de Tesis PUCP.

De la Cerda, C., Martinez, C., & Tomicic, A. (2019). *La función reflexiva como aprendizaje procedural en la interacción terapéutica: el funcionamiento reflexivo-relacional* [The reflective function as procedural learning in therapeutic interaction: Reflective-relational functioning]. *Revista Argentina de Clínica Psicológica, 28*(3), 285–294.

Defensoría del Pueblo. (2018). *Vigésimo segundo informe anual* [Twenty-second annual report].

Defensoría del Pueblo. (2019). *Centros Emergencia Mujer. Segunda supervisión a nivel nacional 2018* [Women's Emergency Centers. Second national supervision 2018].

Diamond, D., Blatt, S. J., Stayner, D. A., Kaslow, N. J., Auerbach, J. S., Luyten, P., & Lowyck, B. (2014). *Manual for the Differentiation-Relatedness Scale*. Yale University.

Donayre, C. (2019). *Una mirada a los cambios en las configuraciones relacionales de una mujer violentada participante de un proceso psicoanalítico breve* [A look at the changes in the relational configurations of an abused woman participating in a brief psychoanalytic process]. [Master's thesis, Pontificia Universidad Católica del Perú]. Repositorio de Tesis PUCP.

Espinosa, D., & Valdés, N. (2012). *Codificación de Episodios Relacionales a partir de la versión en castellano del Método del Tema Central de Conflicto Relacional CCRT- LU-S: Manual de Procedimiento* [Coding of relational episodes based on the Spanish version of the central conflict relational theme method CCRT- LU-S: Procedural Manual]. [Unpublished manuscript]. Proyecto Fondecyt N°3130367. Comisión Nacional de Investigación Científica y Tecnológica, Santiago de Chile.

Fonagy, P. (2003). Some complexities in the relationship of psychoanalytic theory to technique. *The Psychoanalytic Quarterly, 72*(1), 13–47. https://doi.org/10.1002/j.2167-4086.2003.tb00121.x

Fonagy, P. (2015). Research Issues in Psychoanalysis. In M. Leuzinger Bohleber & H. Kachele (Eds.), *An open door review of outcome and process studies in psychoanalysis* (3rd ed., pp. 42–60). International Psychoanalytic Association.

Fonagy, P., Gergely, G., Jurist, E. L., & Target, M. (2002). *Affect regulation, mentalization and the development of the self.* Routledge.

Fonagy, P., Kachele, H., Krause, R., Jones, E., Perron, R., & Lopez, L. (1999). *An open door review of outcome studies in psychoanalysis*. International Psychoanalytical Association.

Frosh, S., & Baraitser, L. (2008). Psychoanalysis and psychosocial studies. *Psychoanalysis, Culture & Society, 13*, 346–365. https://doi.org/10.1057/pcs.2008.8

Gazzo, G. (2022). *Caracterización de dos sesiones de un proceso de psicoterapia psicoanalítica focal en una mujer víctima de violencia y su relación con los Episodios de Cambio* [Characterization of two sessions of a focal psychoanalytic psychotherapy process in a woman victim of violence and its relation to Change Episodes]. [Master's thesis, Pontificia Universidad Católica del Perú]. Repositorio de Tesis PUCP.

González, L. (2022). *Un análisis de las intervenciones de paciente y terapeuta en los episodios de mentalización y su contribución a la complejización de la teoría subjetiva de dos mujeres en situación de violencia en el curso de una psicoterapia psicoanalítica focal* [An analysis of patient and therapist interventions in mentalization episodes and their contribution to the complexification of the subjective theory of two women in a situation of violence during a focal psychoanalytic psychotherapy]. [Master's thesis, Pontificia Universidad Católica del Perú]. Repositorio de Tesis PUCP.

Grández, V. (2022). *Actividad referencial en el intercambio verbal terapéutico durante los episodios de cambio de un proceso psicoterapéutico psicoanalítico breve* [Referential activity in therapeutic verbal exchange during change episodes of a brief psychoanalytic psychotherapy process]. [Master's thesis, Pontificia Universidad Católica del Perú]. Repositorio de Tesis PUCP.

Grupo de Trabajo de Salud Mental de la Coordinadora Nacional de Derechos Humanos. (2006). *Salud mental comunitaria en el Perú. Aportes temáticos para el trabajo con poblaciones* [Community mental health in Peru. Thematic contributions for working with populations]. Ministerio de Salud; Proyecto AMARES.

Gutiérrez, J. (2022). *Un análisis del ámbito y la referencia a partir de las funciones de las verbalizaciones en los Episodios de cambio de un proceso de psicoterapia psicoanalítica focal en una mujer víctima de violencia* [An analysis of scope and reference based on the functions of verbalizations in Change Episodes of a focal psychoanalytic psychotherapy process in a woman victim of violence]. [Master's thesis, Pontificia Universidad Católica del Perú]. Repositorio de Tesis PUCP.

Hadley, M. (2008). Relational theory: Inside out, outside in, in-between and all around. In J. Berzoff, L. Flanagan, & P. Hertz (Eds.), *Inside out and Outside in* (pp. 205–228). Jason Aronson.

Harris, A. (2008). *Gender as soft assembly*. Routledge.

Hernández, M. (2000). *¿Es otro el rostro del Perú? Identidad, diversidad y cambio* [Is another face of Peru? Identity, diversity, and change]. Agenda.

Instituto Nacional de Estadística e Informática. (2023). *Encuesta Demográfica y de Salud Familiar 2022* [Demographic and family health survey 2022].

IWORDS Global. (2020). *Evaluación de los Centros de Emergencia Mujer (CEM)* [Evaluation of the Women's Emergency Centers (CEM)].

Jiménez, J. P. (2005a). *Después del pluralismo: hacia un nuevo paradigma psicoanalítico integrado* [After pluralism: Towards a new integrated psychoanalytic paradigm]. *Revista de Psicoanálisis, 4*, 67–90.

Jiménez, J. P. (2005b). *La investigación empírica apoya una técnica psicoanalítica relacional y flexible* [Empirical research supports a relational and flexible psychoanalytic technique]. *Aperturas Psicoanalíticas, 21* https://aperturas.org/articulo.php?articulo=0000349&a=La-investigacion-empirica-apoya-una-tecnica-psicoanaliticarelacional-y-flexible.

Jiménez, J. P. (2007). Can research influence clinical practice? *The International Journal of Psychoanalysis, 88*(3), 661–679.

Jones, E. (1985). *Manual for the psychotherapy process Q-sort* [Unpublished manuscript]. University of California, Berkeley

Kachele, H., Schachter, J., & Thoma, H. (2009). *From psychoanalytic narrative to empirical single case research*. Routledge.

Kirman, J. H. (1998). One-person or two-person psychology? *Modern Psychoanalysis, 23*(1), 3–22.

Krause, M., & Altimir, C. (2016). Introduction: Current developments in psychotherapy process research. *Estudios de Psicología, 37*(2–3), 201–225. https://doi.org/10.1080/02109395.2016.1227574

Krause, M., de la Parra, G., Arístegui, R., Dagnino, P., Tomicic, A., Valdés, N., Vilches, O., Echávarri, O., Ben-Dov, P., Reyes, L., Altimir, C., & Ramírez, I. (2006). Indicadores genéricos de cambio en el proceso psicoterapéutico [Generic indicators of change in the psychotherapeutic process]. *Revista Latinoamericana de Psicología, 38*(2), 299–325.

Krause, M., Valdés, N., & Tomicic, A. (2009). *Sistema de Codificación de la Actividad Terapéutica (SCAT): Manual de Procedimiento* [Therapeutic Activity Coding System (SCAT): Procedure Manual] [Unpublished manuscript]. Proyecto Fondecyt N°1080136. Psychotherapy and Change Chilean Research Program.

Lancho, M. P. (2022). *El lugar de la mentalización en la interacción terapéutica y su relación con el cambio psíquico en un proceso de psicoterapia psicoanalítica breve* [The place of mentalization in the therapeutic interaction and its relationship with psychic change in a brief psycho-

analytic psychotherapy process] [Master's thesis, Pontificia Universidad Católica del Perú]. Repositorio de Tesis PUCP.
Layton, L. (2020a). *Toward a social psychoanalysis: Culture, character, and normative unconscious processes* (M. Leavy-Sperounis, Ed.). Routledge/Taylor & Francis Group. https://doi.org/10.4324/9781003023098
Layton, L. (2020b). Attacks on linking: The unconscious pull to dissociate individuals from their social context. In L. Layton, *Towards a social psychoanalysis. Culture, character and normative unconscious processes* (M. Leavy-Sperounis, Ed., pp. 34–44). Routledge/Taylor & Francis Group. (Reprinted from *Psychoanalysis, class and politics: Encounters in the clinical setting*, pp. 107–117, by L. Layton, N. C. Hollander & S. Gutwill, Eds., 2006, Routledge)
Leary, K. (2002). Response to Layton. In S. Fairfield, L. Layton, & C. Stack (Eds.), *Bringing the plague. Toward a postmodern psychoanalysis* (pp. 225–232). Other Press.
Leiman, M., & Stiles, W. B. (2001). Dialogical sequence analysis and the zone of proximal development as conceptual enhancements to the assimilation model: The case of Jan revisited. *Psychotherapy Research, 11*(3), 311–330.
Lemma, A., Target, M., & Fonagy, P. (2011). *Brief dynamic interpersonal therapy: A clinician's guide*. OUP Oxford.
Leuzingher- Bohleber, M. (2015). Development of a plurality during the one hundred year old history of research of psychoanalysis. In M. Leuzinger Bohleber & H. Kachele (Eds.), *An open door review of outcome and process studies in psychoanalysis* (3rd ed., pp. 18–36). International Psychoanalytic Association.
Leuzingher- Bohleber, M., & Arnold, S. (2020). Introduction. Outcome research and the future of psychoanalysis. In M. Leuzinger-Bohleber, M. Solms, & S. Arnold (Eds.), *Outcome research and the future of psychoanalysis. Clinicians and researchers in dialogue* (pp. 1–25). Routledge.
Liberman, A. (2013). Stephen A. Mitchell. Del psicoanálisis interpersonal al psicoanálisis relacional: de idas y vueltas [Stephen A. Mitchell. From interpersonal psychoanalysis to relational psychoanalysis: Of comings and goings]. In A. Ávila (Ed.), *La tradición interpersonal. Perspectiva social y cultural en psicoanálisis* [The interpersonal tradition: Social and cultural perspectives in psychoanalysis] (pp. 367–421). Ágora Relacional.
Luján, J. (2021). *El discurso sobre la subjetividad femenina en los episodios de cambio de un proceso de psicoterapia psicoanalítica focal con una mujer en situación de violencia de pareja* [The discourse on female subjectivity in the change episodes of a brief psychoanalytic psychotherapy process with a woman in an intimate partner violence situation] [Master's thesis, Pontificia Universidad Católica del Perú]. Repositorio de Tesis PUCP.
Madueño, S. (2019). *La trayectoria de las intervenciones verbales de un terapeuta y su contribución al cambio psíquico en un proceso de psicoterapia psicoanalítica focal* [The trajectory of a therapist's verbal interventions and their contribution to psychic change in a brief psychoanalytic psychotherapy process] [Master's thesis, Pontificia Universidad Católica del Perú]. Repositorio de Tesis PUCP.
Marinelli, F. (2019). *Cambios en la experiencia subjetiva de la temporalidad a partir de las variaciones en la narrativa de un evento de violencia: Un análisis desde los relatos de una paciente en el contexto de una psicoterapia psicoanalítica focal* [Changes in the subjective experience of temporality based on variations in the narrative of a violence event: An analysis from the accounts of a patient in the context of a brief psychoanalytic psychotherapy] [Master's thesis, Pontificia Universidad Católica del Perú]. Repositorio de Tesis PUCP.
Maskit, B., Bucci, W., & Murphy, S. (2015, June 5). A computer program for tracking the evolution of a psychotherapy treatment. In M. Mitchell, G. Coppersmith, & K. Hollingshead (Chairs), *From linguistic signal to clinical reality. Proceedings of the Second Workshop* [Symposium]. Computational Linguistics and Clinical Psychology, Denver, CO, United States. https://doi.org/10.3115/v1/w15-1216
McLeod, J. (2010). *Case study research in counselling and psychotherapy*. Sage Publications.

Ministerio de la Mujer y Poblaciones Vulnerables. (2016a). *Lineamientos para el desarrollo de acciones preventivo-promocionales en los Centros Emergencia Mujer* [Guidelines for the development of preventive-promotional actions in the Women's Emergency Centers].
Ministerio de la Mujer y Poblaciones Vulnerables. (2016b). *Guía de atención integral de los Centros Emergencia Mujer*[Comprehensive care guide of the Women's Emergency Centers].
Ministerio de la Mujer y Poblaciones Vulnerables. (2022). *Guía de atención del Centro Emergencia Mujer en estado de emergencia* [Care guide for the Women's Emergency Center in a state of emergency].
Ministerio de Salud. (2017). *Guía técnica para la atención de salud mental a mujeres en situación de violencia ocasionada por la pareja o expareja* [Technical guide for mental health care for women in situations of violence caused by a partner or ex-partner].
Mitchell, S. A. (1993). *Conceptos relacionales en psicoanálisis. Una integración* [Relational concepts in psychoanalysis. An integration]. Siglo XXI.
Mitchell, S. A. (1997). *Influence and autonomy in psychoanalysis*. The Analytic Press.
Mitchell, S. A. (2000). *Relationality. From attachment to intersubjectivity*. The Analytic Press.
Pardo, F. (2019). *Cambio en las configuraciones relacionales en un proceso de psicoterapia psicoanalítica breve de una mujer violentada en el contexto de pareja: Una integración entre los patrones relacionales y las representaciones Self/Otro* [Change in relational configurations in a brief psychoanalytic psychotherapy process of a woman subjected to partner violence: An integration between relational patterns and Self/Other representations] [Master's thesis, Pontificia Universidad Católica del Perú]. Repositorio de Tesis PUCP.
Peirano, R. (2021). *Cambio en la transferencia en un proceso de psicoterapia psicoanalítica breve con una mujer violentada: Un abordaje desde las configuraciones relacionales y la mirada del terapeuta* [Change in transference in a brief psychoanalytic psychotherapy process with a woman subjected to violence: An approach from relational configurations and the therapist's perspective] [Master's thesis, Pontificia Universidad Católica del Perú]. Repositorio de Tesis PUCP.
Pistrang, N., & Barker, C. (2012). Varieties of qualitative research: A pragmatic approach to selecting methods. In H. Cooper, P. M. Camic, D. L. Long, A. T. Panter, D. Rindskopf, & K. J. Sher (Eds.), *APA handbook of research methods in psychology, Vol. 2. Research designs: Quantitative, qualitative, neuropsychological, and biological* (pp. 5–18). American Psychological Association. https://doi.org/10.1037/13620-001
Rasmussen, G. (2019). *Relaciones de poder de clase y raza en la relación terapéutica en un caso de psicoterapia psicoanalítica breve con una mujer violentada* [Class and race power relations in the therapeutic relationship in a brief psychoanalytic psychotherapy case with a woman subjected to violence] [Master's thesis, Pontificia Universidad Católica del Perú]. Repositorio de Tesis PUCP.
Rodríguez, C. (2014a). *Psicopatología psicoanalítica relacional. La persona en relación y sus problemas* [Relational psychoanalytic psychopathology. The person in relationship and their problems]. Ágora Relacional.
Rodríguez, C. (2014b). ¿Cuál es la técnica en psicoanálisis relacional? [What is the technique in relational psychoanalysis?] In J. Coderch (Ed.), *Avances en psicoanálisis relacional* [Advances in relational psychoanalysis] (pp. 287–318). Ágora Relacional.
Romero, C. (2019). *Contenidos afectivos en los Episodios de Cambio a lo largo de un proceso psicoterapéutico psicoanalítico de corte focal* [Affective contents in the Episodes of Change throughout a brief psychoanalytic psychotherapy process] [Master's thesis, Pontificia Universidad Católica del Perú]. Repositorio de Tesis PUCP.
Roseneil, S., & Ketokivi, K. (2016). Relational persons and relational processes: Developing the notion of relationality for the sociology of personal life. *Sociology, 50*(1), 143–159.
Roussos, A., & O'Connell, M. (2005). *Construcción de un diccionario ponderado en español para medir la actividad referencial* [Construction of a weighted dictionary in Spanish to measure referential activity]. *Revista del Instituto de Investigaciones de la Facultad de Psicología / uBa, 10*(2), 99–119.

Safatle, V., da Silva Junior, N., & Dunker, C. (2021). *Patologias do social. Arqueologias do sofrimento psíquico* [Pathologies of the social. Archaeologies of psychic suffering]. Autêntica.

Segal, E. (2013). Beyond the pale of psychoanalysis: Relational theory and generalist social work practice. *Clinical Social Work Journal, 41*, 376–386.

Seligman, S. (2000). Clinical implications of current attachment theory. *Journal of the American Psychoanalytic Association*, 48 (4), 1189–1194.

Stake, R. (1995). *The art of study case research.* Sage Publications.

Talia, A., & Miller-Bottome, M. (2014). *Patient attachment coding system 2.0. Coding manual* [Unpublished manuscript]. Department of Psychology, University of Copenhagen.

Topham, S. (2021). *Feminidad y masculinidad hegemónica en las configuraciones relacionales de una consultante víctima de violencia de pareja en el curso de un proceso terapéutico* [Hegemonic femininity and masculinity in the relational configurations of a client victim of partner violence during a therapeutic process] [Master's thesis, Pontificia Universidad Católica del Perú]. Repositorio de Tesis PUCP.

Tummala-Narra, P. (2018). Considering culture from a psychoanalytic perspective. In R. E. Barsness (Ed.), *Core competencies of relational psychoanalysis. A guide to practice, study and research* (pp. 283–301). Routledge.

Ugarte, A. (2019). *La co-construcción de los momentos de cambio: Una aplicación del análisis del diálogo a la sesión final de un proceso de psicoterapia psicoanalítica focal* [The co-construction of moments of change: An application of dialogue analysis to the final session of a brief psychoanalytic psychotherapy process] [Master's thesis, Pontificia Universidad Católica del Perú]. Repositorio de Tesis PUCP.

Watchel, R. (2014). *Cyclical psychodynamics and the contextual self.* Routledge.

Zeddies, T. (2000). Within, outside, and in between. *The relational unconscious. Psychoanalytic psychology, 17*(3), 467–487.

Chapter 5
Depression and Personality Dysfunctions Treated with Cognitive-Integrative Psychotherapy: Researching Change Throughout Qualitative Case Study Method

Beatriz Gómez, Santiago Juan, and Héctor Fernández-Álvarez

Case, Context and Method

The present case study examines the treatment of "Leonor," a 59-year-old patient diagnosed with depression and personality disorder. The study took place at the Aiglé Foundation,[1] a naturalistic context where research is conducted within the framework of Practice-Oriented Research (POR) (Castonguay & Muran, 2017; Fernández-Álvarez et al., 2015). Leonor received psychotherapeutic treatment based on the Cognitive-Integrative model of the Aiglé Foundation (Fernández-Álvarez et al., 2008; Fernández-Álvarez & Fernández-Álvarez, 2017), and it was carried out by Héctor Fernández-Álvarez, with an intermediate duration. In this context, Leonor signed a consent to allow the recording of her treatment material and make it available for educational and research purposes. It was explained to her

The Aiglé Foundation is a Non-Governmental Organization, founded in 1977 in Argentina, with branches in Spain and Guatemala. It is dedicated to promoting actions in the field of health and education to improve people's quality of life. Its programs are aimed at the development of resources through: education and training, research, community outreach plans, support for care programs, and publications.

B. Gómez (✉) · H. Fernández-Álvarez
Aiglé Foundation, Buenos Aires, Argentina
e-mail: bgomez@aigle.org.ar

S. Juan
Research Department, University Institute of Mental Health (IUSAM), Buenos Aires, Argentina
e-mail: santiago.juan@iusam.edu.ar

A. Tomicic, J. D. Soto (eds.), *Qualitative Research in Clinical Psychology and Psychotherapy in Latin America*, https://doi.org/10.1007/978-3-031-90782-1_5

that the confidentiality of sensitive data would be safeguarded and that all circulating material would be masked. She was also informed that she was free to interrupt the recording of the material at any time, without this affecting the continuity of her treatment in any way. Finally, the recording of the sessions was contextualized as part of the usual functioning of the Aiglé Foundation.

The case illustrates the work, in the psychotherapeutic approach, of articulating dysfunctions at the symptomatic level and the level of basic patterns of personal identity. Its selection sought to be representative of the described diagnosis, and the case was evaluated as successful in meeting the objectives.

Cognitive-Integrative Model

The fundamental purpose of the Cognitive-Integrative Model of psychotherapy is to articulate the different levels of biopsychosocial organization, with the dysfunctional dimensions and the appropriate therapeutic interventions that promote change. The model converges and synthesizes the conceptual contributions of the four traditional approaches: psychodynamic, cognitive-behavioral, humanistic-existential, and systemic, integrating the distinctive strengths of each into a broader approach (Fernández-Álvarez & Fernández-Álvarez, 2017). The model articulates the different approaches in a common axis, based on the cognitive-behavioral approach where the different mental operations can be integrated into a hierarchical scheme that accounts for the multiple levels of organization that characterize the architecture of psychological phenomena (Fernández-Álvarez et al., 2016). It is a comprehensive model that considers the individual, the context, and the levels of personal organization, from the most peripheral aspects to the deepest patterns of personality. Clinical judgment, in relation to the psychopathological condition, includes both the affected behaviors and the evolutionary moment and vital circumstances, as well as the contextual variables that sustain dysfunctionality and the cultural characteristics that frame patients´ expectations. The aim is to provide treatment adjusted to the needs and characteristics of each patient (Fernández-Álvarez, et al., 2020).

Intake Process

The intake process consisted of a first interview to explore the relevance of the consultation for psychotherapy by studying the content of the demand. The Admission Form developed at Aiglé was completed, a registration system to collect relevant data, including (a) the characteristics of the problem, (b) the evolution of the request for by care, (c) the patient's attributional hypothesis about the problem, and (d) expectations regarding psychotherapy. It also contains information related to other significant variables such as clinical evolution, life and family history, and treatments previously carried out. As a result of the corresponding exploration, presumptive diagnosis, therapeutic indication, and prognosis are formulated.

In the case of Leonor, as psychotherapy was evaluated as the most appropriate indication, the routinary assessment with psychological tests was carried out, which includes questionnaires to assess symptomatology of emotional disorders, a dimensional assessment of personality pathology, difficulties in emotional regulation, interpersonal problems, and general clinical distress, to arrive at a diagnosis and design a treatment plan (Fernández-Álvarez, 2018a; Fernández-Álvarez et al., 2008). In a second interview, the results of the tests were shared, and the treatment objectives were agreed upon: to improve mood, regulate emotions, and make certain personality patterns more flexible that were linked to the relational modality causing her suffering.

Summary of the First Interview

Leonor has been married for 36 years and has three children aged 30, 28, and 22; the two eldest are sons, and the youngest is a daughter and lives with her and her husband. She works with her husband, who is 12 years older, in a cheese factory that he owned when she met him. She presents herself at the meeting well-groomed but with signs of depression. Her expression is sad, and she states that she feels tired, "down." She says she looks in the mirror and sees herself overwhelmed. She cries during the interview. From the beginning, she focuses her discomfort on her relationship with her husband. She feels very dissatisfied, although her husband does not express discomfort, as he does not express what he thinks or feels. This is precisely what makes Leonor suffer, as she is very communicative and lively: "Could it be that I want something I can't expect from him?"

Her husband Tomás has become increasingly isolated, and although she is willing to accompany him in his activities, both professionally and socially, her husband openly refuses to do the same with her. Her husband's routine is to work and stay at home; he does not participate in family gatherings, including birthdays, and according to Leonor, he never responds to her requests or complaints. He remains silent in the face of any expression of displeasure from her. The patient says this makes her furious, and she does not speak to him. Tomás continues to address her as if there were no disagreements and never asks how she is or revisits the topic of discussion. He only waits for her anger to dissipate. She says, "At times, I get anxious and cry every day… I cry in the street, on the bus, wherever I am, when I'm working." Her own children suggest that she separate, but Leonor says she feels guilty about doing so and "breaking the family," even though she does not even want to resume her sexual life with him. In fact, she often responds poorly when he approaches. Even so, she cannot face a possible separation from her husband. She states that this difficulty is what led her to seek consultation.

Her family of origin lived in the countryside in a province of Argentina, far from urban areas. Her parents worked in the fields and had serious economic difficulties in supporting their nine children. Furthermore, her father was an alcoholic and violent man, and her mother was very submissive and dependent. When Leonor was 11 years old, during her mother's sixth pregnancy, she was sent to a town to work as a live-in domestic employee for an elderly woman, in exchange for food and schooling. From that moment, she seldom saw her family again. Nostalgia and pain accompanied her intensely during the first years. After the elderly woman passed away, she worked in other houses, and in the last one, at 16, she met the man who became her husband, as he supplied the household with cheeses from his production. At 17, she went to live with him, escaping a life of limitations and lack of freedom, and married at 23. Currently, she has little relationship with her siblings, several of whom were also raised outside the home. Regarding her current family, she highlights the good relationship with her three children, saying they have a great time together and have very fluid communication. She also has good friends. Working with her husband is unsatisfactory for her, as he makes all the decisions. Economically, she depends on him for any expenses.

Second Interview: Feedback

Feedback is provided with the objectives of establishing the therapeutic alliance, checking the stage of change (Prochaska et al., 2013), preparing the patient to face difficulties, identifying her resources, reinforcing strengths, and proposing a treatment plan. The feedback includes (a) the diagnostic summary, (b) clinical criteria, and (c) the prognosis. In this sense, through clinical evaluation and the results of the administered instruments, signs of depression and emotional dysregulation are detected in Leonor, which are linked to basic dysfunctional personality patterns. Furthermore, a moderate degree of severity is considered, with intermediate complexity, as there are vital areas with a good level of functioning in the patient. At the same time, the level of chronicity is high, and significant effects on daily life are observed, given the high level of emotional discomfort. Finally, the prognosis includes a positive expectation of improvement and recovery.

Case Formulation

Leonor's disorder is rooted in vulnerability factors linked to an upbringing marked by emotional detachment, devaluation, and economic hardships. These elements led the patient to establish a marital relationship that ensured emotional support and security, at the expense of emotional and economic dependence that condemned her to a chronic feeling of helplessness and self-devaluation. For many years, while raising her children and under the protection of a sense of security for her family's development, Leonor endured this form of relationship without questioning it. The trigger for the disturbance is situated at the moment she completes her secondary school studies and, for the first time, believes in her worth. From that moment, she begins to suffer from submission, generating feelings of anger and frustration. The critical cycle gives rise to a chronic disorder because maintenance factors of dysfunction were established: Leonor keeps her discomfort to herself, discussing it with her children more than with her husband, ruminates about past and current situations, and cries alone, thus promoting a feeling of helplessness and anger that floods her daily life. These ideas contribute to establishing a depressive disorder that in turn reinforces the basic cores of lack of recognition and personal autonomy.

Treatment Plan

The work model indicates that it is advisable to first aim to reduce symptomatic manifestations to immediately improve the patient's clinical condition. It promotes an increase in adherence to a treatment aimed at addressing work on the deeper levels of experience. The therapeutic process is designed in consecutive phases that are articulated to help the patient establish a connection between the presenting complaint, her behaviors and emotions, and a way of being that has dysfunctional effects. Achieving the link with basic patterns of the organization of her experience, which are usually far from her consciousness, is one of the key points of the treatment program (Fernández-Álvarez, 2010).

The indication for this case was individual psychotherapy with a weekly frequency with two main objectives: symptomatic relief and changes in the organization of experience, with an open intervention program, in accordance with the process' progress. The duration was set as intermediate, of a year and a half.

Intervention Program

The integrative therapeutic approach establishes the need to install a sufficiently structured framework, which implies a clear therapeutic contract (setting well-defined objectives and tasks) and building a strong therapeutic alliance.

The intervention design is adjusted to two fundamental principles: the gradualness of changes and the application of a phased design. The interventions are deployed in three progressive levels based on the depth of the changes pursued (Fernández-Álvarez, 2010, 2018b). The first level refers to *peripheral interventions*, which promote changes at the symptomatic level. In this case, fundamentally the reactions of distress and anger. A second level lies in *regulation interventions*, which enhance the regulation of emotions by increasing awareness of the emotional experience and teaching skills to promote more functional regulation strategies in the cognitive, emotional, and behavioral areas. The third level involves *core interventions* aimed at making the basic dysfunctional personality patterns more flexible. In this case, a high level of negative effectivity, particularly in the facet of

Table 5.1 Progressive levels of intervention applied to the case of Leonor as part of the cognitive-integrative model (Fernández-Álvarez, 2010)

Levels of intervention	Application to the case
(1) Peripheral: promote symptomatic changes	Reactions of distress and anger
(2) Regulation: increase awareness of emotions and teach skills for their regulation	Cognitive, emotional, and behavioral regulation focused on the couple's relationship
(3) Core: flexibilize basic dysfunctional patterns of personality	Negative affectivity and dependence, based on low self-esteem and attachment problems

vulnerability, and a high degree of conformity and dependence based on low self-esteem and basic attachment problems.

These three levels are deployed gradually and overlap during the process. Thus, as emotional distress is reduced, it is possible to advance in the levels of depth of the core meanings of the identity that sustain them. Table 5.1 offers a synthesis of the levels of intervention applied to the case of Leonor.

Treatment Phases

The treatment had two phases. First, the aim was to reduce emotional symptoms to strengthen the patient and develop strategies to promote better regulation and modulation of emotions in the different areas of mental functioning. Additionally, during the first phase, work began to help the patient understand the presence of personality dysfunction, urging her to recognize the signs of these dysfunctional aspects. This was implemented by appealing to records that allowed Leonor to verify the persistence of facets of traits such as submission and the way they are expressed through a multiplicity of behaviors. These behaviors were distributed over time and extended in the different areas of her personal functioning (Belloch Fuster et al., 2019).

In the second phase, the work of flexibilizing core dysfunctional personality patterns was deepened.

First Phase

Sessions 1 and 2: Clarification and Awareness of the Scope of the Problem, Addressing Symptoms and Maintenance Agents, and Generating Positive Expectations Regarding the Treatment

In the first session, the patient elaborates on the reasons for her difficulties in making decisions and how these might relate to her feelings of guilt for *"undoing the family."* The therapist encourages Leonor to reflect on these aspects to gain a more in-depth understanding of her situation and to prepare for future sessions. This approach aims to build her capacity gradually to address the issues she faces, fostering a sense of empowerment and autonomy in her decision-making process. She closes the first meeting with an empathetic farewell. The cordial treatment fosters a climate of trust in a person who has just shown pain for the way she feels treated by close people.

Leonor begins her second session by saying that she feels she cannot separate, and this causes her distress; she is sure that her husband knows it. She describes it as if she were trapped in a situation without escape, feels that something is preventing her, becomes anxious, and cries. She says: *"I feel like I'm useless... that I can't do it alone, that I can't solve things on my own... it's like a dependency."*

In response to the assignment of an intersession task, she reports in the second session that she thought of eight reasons why she believes she could not separate. She reported that (1) it would destroy the family she built with much effort and of which she feels proud, (2) fear of the consequences on her economic situation, as she does not know how to handle economic matters, (3) fear of living alone, and (4) fear that her children will feel they have to take care of her because she is left alone. The patient becomes anxious and cries while sharing her thoughts. The therapist reinforces the good work she did and at the same time supports her and invites her to move forward slowly. He tries an intervention to help her mitigate the anxiety:

> *One very important thing you can already incorporate is that when you feel that anxiety is taking over, don't try to keep moving forward, relax, you can think that anxiety is not something negative, but something you need to feel at this moment, you feel it, and it passes, you feel it, and it passes.*

Following this intervention, the patient continues listing the reasons: (5) fear of criticism from the extended family, (6) feeling disloyal because together with her husband they made the factory grow with much effort and started their life together from a situation of much emotional and material lack, (7) fear that he will feel abandoned in the last stage of life, (8) feeling panic about everything. The therapist's feedback aims to deepen the understanding of the problem:

Therapist (T): *There are several things I want to comment on. Firstly, I think the work you did is excellent, it is very useful and positive for us. There are some reasons associated. For example, the one where the children might think you are selfish or that other family members might criticize you. Those two somehow have points in common. Secondly, some situations are very linked to each other, one is these reactions of anxiety you have or the fear, that physical sensation of restlessness, that is, there are a series of distressing sensations that affect you day by day. The second is this feeling that the life you are living is not the life you want to live, that you would like to live another life, but you don't know how, it's as if you have the feeling that you are trapped, imprisoned in something you would like to get out of, isn't it? And I say that anxiety is related to this because this feeling of being trapped generates anxiety* (links the symptom with dysfunction in the experience).

P: *Yes*

T: *That is, having a little anxiety is a normal thing, that is, anxiety is not necessarily a disease, it all depends on how much anxiety we have. The way you tell me, that you are at the dentist or walking down the street, and you start crying, already indicates that there is something to improve. So one of the first things we are going to do is help you better regulate the anxiety, and one of the first things that is important for you to incorporate is that when you feel that this feeling is starting to arise, try to relax, to feel it, to loosen up, to contact yourself. Because the first thing one tends to do is escape from that feeling."*

At the end of the session, the therapist says:

T: *Well, from now until we see each other again, I propose you remember what we are talking about. I am simply interested in you recording it and seeing how you experience it, that you write down what you remember we talked about, do I make myself clear?*
P: *Yes, yes.*
T: *Perfect, perfect. We will also work on the issue of being able to live another life, it is probably the most significant thing because when I asked you why you came, the first thing you told me was that.*
P: *Yes*
T: *So we will also achieve that, and for your peace of mind, although of course, we have to see it in practice, I believe that you will achieve a lot in this direction, that you will achieve a turn in your life. If you were to ask me if what I mean is that you are going to separate from your husband, I, as a therapist, have to honestly tell you that I don't know. Maybe you can lead a better life in another way, or perhaps you will separate. What I do know is that the eight reasons you thought of are all associated, all linked to each other. They all contain feelings of impotence, of incapacity, that is what we can modify, the way you see yourself in your relationship with others. I want to convey from my experience that you have many possibilities to achieve it.*
P: *That's great.*
T: *Because things are as one sees them ultimately, that's why it is said that things are the color of the glass through which one looks at them, so let's try to start putting on different lenses to see things differently… this work is a bit slower. I want you to be less distressed on the one hand, to have more control over yourself, and the explanations for why things happen to you will probably also emerge.*

Session 4: The Work Focuses on the Level of Emotional Regulation

Leonor elaborates on the anger she feels daily and does not communicate. She feels overwhelmed, cries for hours at night, and is overcome by despair. The therapist begins by validating her sharing these feelings. Then, he formulates an intervention to help her face it differently:

"Leonor, first, when all this makes you angry daily, you have to try to reduce it, dilute it because anger unbalances you. That is, when you feel you are starting to get angry, you have to work on yourself to lower that anger. As if you were sweating it out. Let it leave your body. Because when you get angry, you have two problems: what makes you angry, plus the anger. Therefore, everything is more complicated. When you feel you're going to get angry, connect with that and try to tell yourself: no, Leonor, this doesn't serve you. Because your goal is to get out of where you are, to get out of this situation where you feel you've wanted to say something for a long time and can't say it. You wish to have a different relationship, living with him or not, but what you want is to change your way of life. But if you're angry, you can never start because anger makes you escalate to a tense situation. Then you have to come down from that, and all that makes you waste time. That can become a habit, and one finally ends up in an endless cycle. If you remove the anger, what you'll be left with, as you're telling me now, is the pain. Anger is to cover the pain. Many things have happened in your life that you were able to overcome, so not being able to now doesn't mean you'll never be able to. You can't today, do not worry about speaking up today, don't demand or force yourself, try to connect with what I'm telling you, try to keep in mind what we talked about, and think that you'll achieve it. Just as you achieved other things in your life, and just as you were able to finish high school or go to the gym to improve your body, being able to convey to him the things that distress you will take you several days, weeks, and months of treadmill and weights, but you will achieve it. Don't demand yourself to do it today or tomorrow. Because if you demand yourself to do it today or tomorrow, you'll feel like you failed. Don't expose yourself to the feeling of failure. Because there are many things, we're referring to how you see yourself, that are obstacles for you to be able to communicate exactly what distresses you. It's like seeing a plant on the surface, which has enormous roots below. Moreover, those roots are things from different sources, in which you have the feeling that you are unable, you're incapable... All that set of situations in which you see yourself insufficiently valued is what makes it that when you decide to tell him, you can't."

The patient's response indicates progress in processing the problem. The attribution becomes more internal, shifting from placing it on her husband to her own inaction. *She then says: "I never used to have these breakdowns of... I used to get angry and whatever... it would pass, and I would move on. Now, maybe it's me who gets upset about something, and he doesn't even notice, he sleeps peacefully. How is he going to know I'm upset if I don't show it?"*

Second Phase: Flexibility of Dysfunctional Core Personality Patterns

Session 10

The work in this session illuminates the problem from a new perspective. Leonor says that Tomás was interested in her, but he lost his interest, and this is what makes her suffer the most. As she grew in autonomy and personal grooming, she felt Tomás distanced himself from her. She says: *"It went beyond the body. It was a change of image, of attitude, of wanting to be differently, of showing myself differently, of presenting a different image to Tomás and others."*

However, this change caused Tomás, who had known her when she had no autonomy and had "rescued" her by providing emotional and financial support, not to like this new, more self-sufficient image. The conflict that sustains the problems and is expressed in symptoms of depression is clarified: being a dependent woman and once again having Tomás's sexual-affective closeness, or being more independent and tolerating his lack of interest and possible separation. In another fragment, the therapist illuminates the conflict between becoming the submissive person she assumes Tomás expects to get closer again or being an independent woman and tolerating a possible separation:

T Do you remember you had told me several reasons why you didn't separate? You had listed eight reasons why you didn't, and maybe you're finding a ninth reason that is the most important of all, much more important to you than being able to separate, feel like a woman, and start all over, is the desire for Tomás to become interested in you again.
P Yes, perhaps. I'm always waiting.
T That's the conflict to solve here. This is very interesting, Leonor. We're making a critical discovery. But you have to… to take care a lot, not to rush because we have to go step by step.
P: *Right, that is what he said. He once told me that if, maybe, I were the same, he wouldn't distance himself from me…*

Session 18

Leonor reports that she is taking an English course, and when she makes a mistake, she gets furious with herself. Her daughter reproaches her for being self-critical. Similarly, she criticizes herself when she looks in the mirror despite others telling her she is pretty. The therapist summarizes what was worked on in the session:

T Thinking about everything we are talking about, I believe we have a critical task. Clearly, you have an image of yourself that is more negative than the one others have. Evidently, since other people have a better image than you do, your image can only come from somewhere else. Because people do nothing but tell you that you are nice, that you are capable, that you are pretty, that you are good, in general, people esteem you, value you, and say good things to you. Not only your children but also your surroundings. So if all that you hear all the time doesn't weigh as much as what you think of yourself, it means it comes from previous times, and you haven't managed to change it. It's like going to a place with a certain idea of how that place will be, and no matter how different it is, you still have the previous idea. Maybe this idea you have is, to some extent, because you have a temperament that leads you to see yourself that way, it may also be that things have happened throughout your life that reinforced that. What is certain is that to some extent, this discrepancy between how you see yourself and how others see you is a source of distress. With our work, we are managing to keep the distress at bay. We are handling it better so it does not affect you. Nevertheless, this is always there, latent, so we have to try to align your perception of yourself with the perception of others. We have to give more impor-

tance to what others think because, ultimately, by criticizing yourself you put yourself more in the center of the scene; do you understand what I mean?
P Yes, now that you put it that way, yes. Of course, give importance to what others say.

Session 26

At this point in the treatment, Leonor expresses her progress:

T: *How have you been this week?*
P: *Really well, honestly, I feel like… it's like I don't recognize myself.*
T: *I told you on the first day you would have another life.*
P: *I'm doing really well, if I get angry, I say it's not worth it, it lasts two seconds and I'm fine again, I try not to let it impact me, I don't let myself get carried away.*

At a later moment, Leonor continues to express her progress:

P: *Yes, now at least I've started to talk about it and I want him to leave the house, I didn't dare to say that before, but now I do, I tell the children that I think he shouldn't be where I am.*
T: *On one hand, you would like him to see you as a woman and show some desire for you, and on the other hand, you want him to leave, those two things collide with one another, don't they?*
P: *Yes, and I think the one that will win is the one that leaves.*
T: *Well, that is already…*
P: *Also for my pride and my dignity, I think.*

In the following section, Leonor describes certain behaviors of Tomás that she relates to those of her father:

P: *When my family to visit, he would even decide the topics that could be talked about. Then he would go to sleep. He wasn't violent, but what he said was law: at 9 you have to go to sleep, and that was it: at 9 you have to go to sleep, maybe it has to do with my dad, I was always afraid of my dad. I always wanted to be good, do everything my dad wanted, to be the good daughter, and might be that's why I wanted to be like that with him, I accepted everything from him.*
T: *How was the relationship you established with your dad?*
P: *Terrible to the point that I never confronted him with anything, I was terrified of him.*
T: *And you say that when you met Tomás, it seemed to you that with him…*
P: *Yes, I think I idolized Tomás. It was the first time I felt I had someone who loved me, my father didn't love me, and my dad told me I was useless and stupid, never a word of encouragement, so I felt that Tomás gave me love, that he cared for me, that he accepted me as I was.*

T: *He valued you... I understand, it seems to me that this must explain largely why there were situations at different times when you got angry because when you have things inside that fight against each other that generates tension. What will make your life better is to solve this tension, and to be able to see with which of these two things you stay, or how you live with those two things well, without it distressing you.*
P: *Now it doesn't happen to me, it's been 5 weeks: Any little thing from him would generate tension in my stomach, now it doesn't, presently when I get angry about something that irritates me, I think, this is the way it is... it won't change. I am now accepting that it won't change because he is not interested in changing anything, or because maybe it shouldn't change because I shouldn't change for him either. I wouldn't want to change things about myself because I have already suffered a lot, I gave in a lot, and now I want to do what I want, what makes me feel good.*

Discussion

Based on the case report format, the present discussion: (a) offers a qualitative characterization of a clinical situation focusing on the approach to depressive symptoms and their interaction with personality variables, and (b) analyzes the evolution of the case considering the perspective of the patient, the therapist, and external evaluators. In this last section dedicated to the discussion, all the clinical information developed throughout the chapter is integrated qualitatively, showing convergences and divergences between the different perspectives (patient, therapist, follow-up evaluator). The chapter concludes by analyzing a possible construction of the success factors of the treatment.

The Leonor Case and Her Process of Change from Different Perspectives

What Led Leonor to Treatment?

According to the patient, she approached therapy because *"I was in a relationship...since I was 16 years old I was with him...we dated for 7 years, and then we were married for 36 years... I was tired of the relationship, of things I had been enduring, accommodating myself... I couldn't separate... I wasn't doing well, and I was already in a lamentable state...I cried every day... I was very distressed... I had chest pain, back pain, a lot of physical pain, a lot of migraine... I cried...."*

The treating therapist considered Leonor's initial situation as that of a woman "trapped in frustration." In his report, the clinician added: *"Leonor expressed that she had been entangled for a long time in a conflict regarding the will to separate from her husband and the impossibility of doing so, and this generated a state of enormous tensions, which were accompanied by very acute emotional symptoms, particularly depressive ones."* In his case, formulation, the clinician considered that the patient's situation reflected a fairly high level of dysfunction, with evident alterations in the daily functioning of both elements that configure personality functioning: the Self and interpersonal relationships.

Beyond the obvious differences in the organization of the data between the patient and therapist, it is worth highlighting the high convergence in the interpretation of the patient's initial situation. We believe that this alignment has been one of the axes that marked the success of the process throughout the entire treatment.

What Did the Treatment Consist Of?

According to the therapist, Leonor's situation was highly representative, as it had a sufficiently significant degree of dysfunctionality to suffer a lot in day-to-day life and have her quality of life very affected, sometimes even approaching risky situations, but which did not require the implementation of safety strategies. The intervention program advanced over the three dysfunctional domains of personality that are hierarchically structured. This led to a therapeutic journey from the symptoms, the problems with regulation and modulation of behavior and experience, to the exploration and flexibilization of interpersonal pathology underlying the symptoms and the problems that hinder adjustment. The most relevant constellation worked on with Leonor was the emotional dependency expressed in insecure attachment, submission, and fear in interpersonal matters.

Once again, here, it is important how the views of the patient and therapist coincided on the central aspects to work on. Thus, from the patient's perspective:

> *I felt like the doctor provided me an orientation... I felt that in each session I would take away something. And it was incredible. I would say to myself: how could it be that I alone couldn't realize things? Like for example, I always thought I was useless because I was always in the shadow of my husband, and then I started to see the doctor, telling him my life, listening to my life, the story of my life through the sessions... I realized that I had always been strong... I learned to see that my three children are excellent and that I could raise them. I always did it alone, besides working, because I am strong not only physically also I have something in my head... and then I started to get rid of that idea that I was dumb... I spoke with the doctor about all those things, and then they stayed in my head, it was like being a spectator of those things I said about myself: Yes, I am a nice person, I don't have to feel less, nor bad, nor sad, and it was unbelievable how I was strengthening myself.*

Beyond these areas of convergence, we also consider it indispensable to highlight how, for the patient, the therapist played a guiding role, an aspect that was not explicitly declared in those terms by the clinician in charge of the case.

What Changed in Leonor as a Result of the Psychotherapy?

As part of the treatment design, at the beginning and end of the process, Leonor completed a series of scales that evaluate symptomatology, personality variables, interpersonal problems, and general clinical distress.

As expected, at the beginning of her psychotherapy, Leonor exhibited a combination of anxiety and depressive symptoms, with a clear predominance of the latter. Additionally, the initial assessment revealed the presence of some dysfunctional personality traits, which made the patient feel vulnerable, insecure, and fearful. On an interpersonal level, it was noted that Leonor felt insecure and vulnerable, especially if the other person had a more assertive position than she did. In contrast to this initial information, upon being re-evaluated during the follow-up of the treatment, it was concluded that the patient did not present any significant subjective distress. All the results in the symptomatology tests showed extremely low scores. No significant difficulties were observed in her daily functioning either. Regarding her personality profile, a way of being has been observed that had more functional resources to adapt to her environment. Toward the end of the process, her self-concept appeared strengthened, indicating that Leonor had been able to soften traits that were more rigid before starting the treatment. She now felt more self-assured, with more confidence in her abilities and decisions and with fewer fears, worries, and feelings of guilt. On an interpersonal level, she could now set clearer boundaries with others and express what she thought and felt more assertively. This more quantitative information was entirely consistent with what was qualitatively investigated in the follow-up interview of the process. Thus, taking the perspective of the patient and the interviewer from the evaluation session, both agreed that the treatment helped Leonor to "learn to see and accept herself." Thus, the patient was able to recap at the end of the treatment:

> *Being able to confront my husband and talk about it, even though the separation couldn't happen, I was capable of talking to him, be honest, and let him know how bad I felt and that it wasn't worth continuing the relationship... I have been able to face all those situations, and that's where I noticed that I already felt good, that I felt strong already... although that still costs me... Furthermore, feeling good about my body. The worst thing for me was my face, I couldn't look at myself. I saw myself as ugly, and the more I looked in the mirror, the uglier I saw myself, and now this doesn't happen. Now I accept myself, I like myself, I see myself, and occasionally, I even see myself as pretty and say you are 60 years old, and you are doing very well.*

In that sense, the evaluation made by the therapist included a summary of the case's evolution involving: the symptomatic relief achieved, the expansion in the ability to develop better ways of organizing daily life, and the improvement in social skills in general. In the clinician's words, these aspects were "*very important in terms of her quality of life and promoted the motivation to move towards a deeper change*." Thus, according to the therapist, the therapeutic plan advanced in the last phase toward more core areas of the personality system that sustain the dysfunctional organization of experience.

Regarding the flexibility of pathological traits, there were two significant achievements: the significant reduction in trait anxiety levels and especially insecure attachment. In this regard, the therapist's report included: "*We aimed for the patient to achieve a transformation that would allow her to soften the rigid patterns that persistently projected into her existence. We addressed the generation of changes, always ensuring they did not alter the backbone of the personal style that sustained the patient's identity. The intervention program was guided by the premise of helping Leonor find alternatives to operate within the framework of her idiosyncratic way of being. This involved a change in the way she saw herself, composed the landscape of her environment, and the chance of thinking about future scenarios as a space that made personal and social fulfillment possible.*"

Again, here, it is very important to highlight an area of agreement between what the patient and therapist believe has been achieved with the process. Of course, each part of the dyad uses its narrative, but the axis of the changes achieved is similar.

How was the process evaluated once completed? A month after her therapeutic process ended, an interview was held with Leonor in which a professional from the institution reviewed the reasons that had led her to seek consultation and her reconstruction of the treatment. In the words of this clinician: "*I met a jovial 60-year-old woman, very well-disposed for the meeting and with a high appreciation of the process she underwent. The signs of emotional distress she reported that initially led her to the consultation were not observed during the follow-up interview. She presents as a cheerful and relaxed person. An improvement in her general well-being is inferred. She has an excellent record of the therapy and describes with satisfaction and humility the achievements reached during the process. It is observed that she has integrated the strategies and tools learned in therapy into her daily life. She has discovered new aspects of herself and significantly increased her sense of competence; a significant decrease in self-criticism and devaluation can also be observed, showing a positive and constructive view of herself. It is inferred that during the process, a strong therapeutic alliance was established that allowed her to challenge new alternatives. It can be inferred that the patient exceeded the objectives she had set at the beginning of the therapy.*"

In summary, from the follow-up interview, an improvement in her emotional well-being could be concluded. Moreover, throughout the process the proposed therapeutic goals have been met, both through symptomatic improvement and by increasing flexibility in personality patterns. Finally, for the professional who conducted the evaluation interview, Leonor struck her as "*deeply grateful for the therapeutic process and her therapist, who by her description... seems to have been responsive and respectful of her own timing and availability for change.*"

As a Final Reflection: A Possible Construction on the Success Factors of the Treatment

The Importance of a Good Therapeutic Alliance

After having analyzed the different elements of the case, we can conclude that the construction and development of a good therapeutic alliance was fundamental for achieving Leonor's objectives.

On one hand, this alliance was built in the relational aspect, as it was an empathetic and responsive relationship with repeated manifestations of validation of the experience. Likewise, there was an effort by the therapist to generate a corrective emotional experience by helping the patient face extremely painful emotional situations from the past and reverse the adverse influences in her primary relationships through a very understanding attitude with affectionate displays.

On the other hand, we also speak of a good alliance concerning the agreement of goals, working in psychoeducation to keep the patient clearly informed of the treatment steps and their foundations to achieve the goals, as well as a work rhythm in tune with the predisposition to change and the resistance aspects.

Concerning the means, there seems to have been an adjustment of the intervention forms to the patient's preferences and those that supported her self-esteem, promoting an active attitude, for example, through between-session activities.

The Role of a Structured, Hierarchical, and Flexible Care Setting

Another key element for success in Leonor, we believe, lies in a staged and flexible treatment plan, according to the vicissitudes of the patient's life. Thus, early interventions could be implemented to alleviate symptoms, basically the signs of depression and the vicious circle of irritability and increased discomfort from not being able to regulate her anger. These interventions aimed at behavioral changes that could have effects as quickly as possible and beneficially impact the social environment to reinforce them.

Then, interventions that aimed at a deeper level could be applied, promoting self-observation gradually. This process seems to have been achieved by reiterating the interventions in different ways and with between-session activities, adjusting very patiently to the patient's availability for change, and protecting the basic cores of her identity.

A Continuous Evaluation Setting to Enhance Results

Finally, the role of continuous evaluation that took place throughout Leonor's treatment is not minor. Evaluation that involved, as already analyzed, various perspectives (patient, therapist, evaluator). Originally, the evaluation was both clinical and with instruments. Throughout the process, the state of the therapeutic alliance was also monitored, checking the availability for change, the degree of understanding of the interventions, the pace of change processes, and the adjustment of interventions. At the end of the treatment, a clinical and instrument assessment was again implemented, to which a follow-up interview conducted by a therapist who had not been responsible for the patient could also be added. In this sense, it is worth noting that this case report is inserted in current trends in psychotherapy research, which aim to systematically and repeatedly analyze the mechanisms of change within clinical cases to identify what types of treatments best benefit what kind of patients (Juan et al., 2023; Montesano & Scherb, 2023).

To close, we would like to reproduce a fragment of the report made by Leonor's therapist, Héctor Fernández-Álvarez: "*Accompanying Leonor on the path to improvement was a stimulating challenge to the extent that her willingness to seek a better life and her personal qualities, such as resilience, persistence in the effort, and the ability to develop a trusting therapeutic relationship, constituted a solid foundation for sustaining the changes.*" Ultimately, a joint work in which the patient was the architect of her achievements.

References

Belloch Fuster, A., Fernández-Álvarez, H., & Pascual-Vera, B. (2019). Guía de intervención en trastornos de la personalidad. Síntesis.

Castonguay, L., & Muran, J. C. (2017). *Practice-oriented research in psychotherapy: Building partnerships between clinicians and researchers*. Routledge.

Fernández-Álvarez, H. (2010). Modelo integrativo de psicoterapia para los trastornos de la personalidad. En: A. Belloch & H. Fernández-Álvarez (Comps.). *Tratado de Trastornos de Personalidad* (pp. 337–354). Madrid: Síntesis.

Fernández-Álvarez, H. (2018a). La organización de Aiglé y la investigación orientada por la práctica- POR. *Revista Brasileira de Psicoterapia, 20*(3), 215–228.

Fernández-Álvarez, H. (2018b). Todo o nada. Las disfunciones de la personalidad a la luz de un caso clínico. En: T. Zohn Muldoon, E.N. Gómez Gómez, & R. Enríquez Rosas (Eds.). *Los estudios de caso en psicoterapia. Desafíos y posibilidades* (pp.129–165) Universidad Jesuita de Guadalajara (ITESO).

Fernández-Álvarez, H., Consoli, A., & Gómez, B. (2016). Integration in psychotherapy: Reasons and challenges. *American Psychologist, 71*, 820–830.

Fernández-Álvarez, H., & Fernández-Álvarez, J. (2017). Terapia cognitivo conductual integrativa. *Revista de Psicopatología y Psicología Clínica, 22*(2), 157–169.

Fernández-Álvarez, H., Gómez, B., & García, F. (2015). Bridging the gap between research and practice in a clinical and training network: Aigle's Program. *Psychotherapy Research, 25*(1), 84–94.

Fernández-Álvarez, H., Pérez, A. y Fraga Míguez, M. (2008). Modelo de abordaje y diseño de tratamientos. En H. Fernández-Álvarez (comp.) *Integración y Salud Mental. El proyecto Aigle 1977–2008*, 423–452. : Desclée de Brouwer.

Fernández-Álvarez, J., Prado-Abril, J., Sánchez-Reales, S., Molinari, G., Martín Gómez Penedo, J., & Jeong Youn, S. (2020). La brecha entre la investigación y la práctica clínica: hacia la integración de la psicoterapia. *Papeles del psicólogo, 41*(2), 81–90.

Juan, S., Manubens, R., Muiños, R., Babl, A., & Penedo, J. M. G. (2023). Mechanisms of change in focused psychodynamic therapy: A systematized single-case time-series analysis. *Cogent Mental Health, 2*(1). https://doi.org/10.1080/28324765.2023.2266229

Montesano, A., & Scherb, E. (2023). Teamwork for complex clinical situations in psychotherapy: Introduction to the issue. *Journal of Clinical Psychology, 79*(6), 1515–1520. https://doi.org/10.1002/jclp.23518

Prochaska, J. O., Norcross, J. C., & DiClemente, C. C. (2013). Applying the stages of change. *Psychotherapy in Australia, 19*(2), 10–15.

Chapter 6
Approaching Child and Adolescent's Perspectives of the Psychotherapeutic Change Process Following Sexual Abuse Through Drawings

Claudia Capella and Loreto Rodríguez

Introduction

In recent years, the progress of research in child and adolescent psychotherapy has been highlighted (Midgley et al., 2018; Salcuni et al., 2015). However, there is still a recognized need for more research with this population, which is necessary due to the high prevalence of child and adolescent mental health problems (Midgley et al., 2018) and the fact that research with this population remains less than that with adults, despite their differences and specificities (Salcuni et al., 2015).

Specifically, qualitative research in psychotherapy with children and adolescents has traditionally included the use of verbal methods, such as interviews, which has led to the consideration of the perspective of adults (caregivers or therapists), young people, or children with greater verbal abilities (Midgley, 2004). Thus, the perspective of children in psychotherapy research is still scarce, requiring their inclusion (Capella et al., 2015; Carlberg et al., 2009). The best informants regarding children's experiences are the children themselves (Groundwater-Smith et al., 2015).

It has been suggested that methodological innovations, such as the use of drawings and other non-verbal methods, allow access to the meaning children and adolescents provide to the psychotherapeutic process (Capella et al., 2015; Carlberg et al., 2009). However, these innovations bring with them ethical and methodological challenges that will be addressed in this chapter, especially when children and adolescents who have experienced traumatic experiences, such as child sexual abuse (CSA), are involved.

C. Capella (✉)
Department of Psychology, Universidad de Chile, Santiago, Chile
e-mail: ccapella@u.chile.cl

L. Rodríguez
Faculty of Psychology and Humanities, Universidad San Sebastián, Santiago, Chile
e-mail: loreto.rodriguez@uss.cl

A. Tomicic, J. D. Soto (eds.), *Qualitative Research in Clinical Psychology and Psychotherapy in Latin America*, https://doi.org/10.1007/978-3-031-90782-1_6

Thus, in this chapter, the research work carried out will be addressed, which includes drawings made by children and adolescents who have been victims of sexual abuse to access their view on psychotherapeutic change, analyzed from a narrative framework. In previous studies by the research team, we have used this technique (Capella et al., 2015, 2018). However, one of the pending challenges that we will address in this chapter is how to access their views of different moments of the psychotherapeutic process through drawing (Capella et al., 2015), understanding that narratives, and therefore narratives about psychotherapy, evolve and change (Capella & Boddy, 2021).

The first section of the chapter briefly shows the findings of research on psychotherapeutic change in sexual abuse in children and adolescents. Subsequently, the use of drawing is supported by research in childhood studies and ethical and methodological discussions as a valuable way to explore the perspectives of children and adolescents, especially on sensitive topics and in contexts of vulnerability. Then, the drawing technique that has been used in cases of children who have been victims of sexual abuse—the "before and after" drawing—will be briefly presented as a methodology to explore children's views on psychotherapeutic change. Later, the process and evolution of psychotherapeutic change in a sample of children and adolescents who have been victims of sexual abuse will be studied, analyzing drawings made by them at different moments of their therapies as part of a longitudinal research to finally bring some final reflections regarding the use of this methodology.

Change in Psychotherapy for Child Sexual Abuse

The field of research in psychotherapy with children who have been victims of sexual abuse at an international level has assessed change mainly in the symptomatological sphere, with meta-analyses in this area showing the effectiveness of psychotherapeutic interventions in overcoming the symptomatic consequences of these experiences (Sánchez et al., 2011; Tichelaar et al., 2020). Most of the research included in these meta-analyses has been conducted in Western Anglo-Saxon countries, where the extent of sexual abuse and their treatment may differ from countries in other regions (Tichelaar et al., 2020). On the other hand, reports of changes are often from the perspectives of the adult caregivers of the children and adolescents and not directly from the latter (Tichelaar et al., 2020). International studies on psychotherapy in sexual abuse that include the perspectives of children and adolescents are scarce, with some exceptions (Farr et al., 2021; Foster & Hagedorn, 2014; Jessiman et al., 2017; Nelson-Gardell, 2001).

The inclusion of the perspectives of children and adolescents could be relevant to address aspects that are still pending in research, such as the components of interventions linked to therapeutic change (Tichelaar et al., 2020). For example, in these international studies in Anglo-Saxon countries, children and adolescents express the importance of achieving a therapeutic relationship of trust, the relevance of addressing the experience of sexual assault during psychotherapy despite it being difficult and painful, and the use of various playful and creative techniques preferred by children and adolescents (Farr et al., 2021; Foster & Hagedorn, 2014; Jessiman et al., 2017; Nelson-Gardell, 2001).

In Latin American countries, such as Chile, a high prevalence of sexual assaults against children and adolescents has been evidenced, being reported by 26% of adolescents surveyed in a recent large study (Pinto-Cortés & Guerra, 2019). However, more research is still needed to inform intervention guidelines with this population (Gabriel-Vacher & Capella, 2024; Guerra & Arredondo, 2017).

In recent years in Chile, there has been significant development by the research team in which the authors of this chapter participate, regarding the process of psychotherapy, healing, and change in children and adolescents who have been victims of sexual abuse, including the perspectives of psychotherapists, caregivers, and the children and adolescents themselves (Capella et al., 2016, 2022; Dussert et al., 2017; Águila et al., 2016). In those studies that focus on the perspectives of children and adolescents, the findings show a positive view of participation in psychotherapeutic processes, visualizing psychotherapy as a space of help that favors the development of changes in different spheres, including the re-signification and overcoming of sexual abuse. The factors that children and adolescents most highlight as favoring change include the support of others, especially family, friends, and caregivers, the relevance of the therapeutic bond developed with their psychologists, as well as the use of various techniques in psychotherapy, such as play and drawing, in addition to being able to address the experience of sexual assault at a time when the bond of trust is established, which favors a respectful and gradual approach to the topic (Capella et al., 2016, 2018; Gómez et al., 2021; Madrid et al., 2022).

Along with this, the results of these studies with different participants, such as children and adolescents, caregivers, and therapists, describe change as a gradual process (Capella et al., 2018), identifying various phases of psychotherapy, with the initial phase being a complex phase in which children and their caregivers present fears and resistances. However, as the intervention process progresses and a therapeutic relationship based on trust is achieved, these fears decrease, favoring motivation toward the intervention process. Then, a second phase in which the experience of abuse is addressed, both verbally and non-verbally, contributes to the process of re-signifying that experience. However, this is a phase in which setbacks are often observed. Finally, in the last stage of the intervention, children and their families experience a sense of accomplishment and empowerment for the changes achieved (Águila et al., 2016; Capella et al., 2022).

Children and their caregivers identify the achievement of different changes during psychotherapy, which are maintained once it is completed, such as emotional changes, in interpersonal relationships, behavioral and identity-related changes, changes in their relationship with caregivers, and changes linked to the abusive experience (Capella et al., 2018, 2021). Concerning the abusive experience, with the support of psychotherapy, it is possible to overcome the experience, which implies a greater sense of well-being, an integration of it into one's own life, being able to resume life's challenges, and achieving growth and empowerment to cope with future challenges (Capella et al., 2016). Distinct changes are observed in different cases, which are associated with the psychosocial characteristics of these and the psychotherapeutic process (Capella et al., 2022), being necessary for the overcoming of the abusive experience of some factors such as the stability of the therapy and the therapist and longer therapies (18 months or more), in which the experience of abuse is addressed in depth in a context of familial support from caregivers (Capella et al., 2022).

The Study of the Perspectives of Children and Adolescents Through Their Drawings

In the field of childhood studies in social sciences, the relevance of the participation of children and young people in different areas, including research, is highlighted. This is even established in the Convention on the Rights of the Child, to the extent that it is recognized as a right for children to be heard in matters that affect them (Groundwater-Smith et al., 2015). This implies a recognition of the voice of children as valid and different from that of adults and, in turn, considers children as effective communicators and as agents of their lives in the sociocultural network (Clark, 2017; Fuentes-Peláez et al., 2023; Groundwater-Smith et al., 2015).

It is recognized as a challenge for researchers to support children in communicating their perspectives, especially for those for whom verbal communication is more challenging, providing contexts and resources to do so (Clark, 2017), and adapting research methodologies to favor their participation (Fuentes-Peláez et al., 2023). In this way, non-verbal techniques have been used in childhood studies in the social sciences as a way to facilitate the construction of meanings by children by aligning with their usual communicative resources. Thus, non-verbal techniques can help approach children's perspectives, considering that verbal expression often proves to be a challenge, especially for younger children (Capella et al., 2015).

Among the benefits of using non-verbal techniques, such as visual ones, is that participants can create images of their experiences (Clark, 2017), being able to elicit tacit aspects, symbols, and other forms of meaning through them (Bell, 2013; Capella et al., 2015). Specifically, in children, its potential has been considered because it can help ideas that are not clearly articulated or easily articulate to be made explicit, helping those who create them to construct their meanings (Bell, 2013). In this line, a child-centered methodology has been considered (Capella & Boddy, 2021; Fuentes-Peláez et al., 2023), which implies that the researcher provides the participant with the necessary tools to assist them in their efforts to narrate (Hydén, 2013). Different art techniques have been used with children and young people, including drawing as a way for them to express their emotions and communicate their perspectives and personal experiences, which might have been difficult to do purely verbally (Fuentes-Peláez et al., 2023). In this way, the use of visual narratives allows us to approach their "voices" (Luttrell, 2010).

However, one element that has been highlighted is the relevance of the interaction between verbal and non-verbal aspects in the production of narratives (Bell, 2013). Thus, when working with images created by the participants themselves, one of the aspects to safeguard is the interpretation made by the adult researcher and that the meanings may emerge from the children themselves. In this way, different researchers (Bell, 2013; Capella et al., 2015; Fuentes-Peláez et al., 2023) mention, as a fundamental methodological aspect, the dialogue with the child regarding the drawing produced so that they can comment on what has been produced and clarify its meaning. In this way, verbal and visual aspects are complemented in understanding the child's vision, which is essential to understanding what the child wants to express.

Another benefit of using non-verbal techniques is linked to ethical aspects. Within narrative research, the approach to sensitive topics, such as sexual abuse, has been discussed. Topics are considered sensitive when addressing them can be threatening for those involved in the narration—in a specific relational and cultural context—in the sense that they are topics that can leave them vulnerable (Hydén, 2013). This is especially true when, as adults and researchers, we find ourselves in a position of power over the participants (Capella & Boddy, 2021). For this, the importance of various ethical safeguards has been highlighted, within which it is essential to give participants control both in the decision-making of their participation (in addition to that of their caregivers) and also regarding the topics to be addressed and the way of addressing them, where the construction of an adequate relational context (Hydén, 2013) and a sensitive interaction that minimizes the risks of emotional distress is crucial (Groundwater-Smith et al., 2015). In that sense, the construction of narratives occurs in a particular relational context, being essential not only to the methodology used but also to the characteristics of the interaction and its context (Capella & Boddy, 2021); it is necessary to construct clear protocols to minimize emotional destabilization, as well as to act in response to it. Along with this, researchers have highlighted that one of the essential ethical aspects, especially when working with sensitive topics, is to generate beneficial participation, and for this, it is not only necessary to talk about complex aspects but also about the possibilities of resistance or recovery processes (Groundwater-Smith et al., 2015; Hydén, 2013).

Specifically, when working with children living in conditions or contexts of special vulnerability, a discussion has arisen regarding the difficulty of creating a balance that safeguards their protection and well-being while simultaneously ensuring their participation (Fuentes-Pelaéz et al., 2023; García-Quiroga & Salvo, 2020; Groundwater-Smith et al., 2015). This has often led to not including them in research processes. However, in this discussion, it has been argued that protection and participation are not opposites, as one of the benefits of children's participation is being heard, which will be relevant for their protection, in the sense of reinforcing their agency and understanding their perspectives. Furthermore, the ethical safeguards taken by research teams will protect the safety and privacy of their participation, without limiting or excluding them (Fuentes-Pelaéz et al., 2023; García-Quiroga & Salvo, 2020; Groundwater-Smith et al., 2015). In this way, the participation of children in vulnerable contexts is possible and desirable (García-Quiroga & Salvo, 2020).

Taking all these elements into account, it is considered that including children as participants, especially in vulnerable contexts or when addressing sensitive topics, is challenging for researchers, which can be remedied by developing appropriate research techniques for them (García-Quiroga & Salvo, 2020). In this context, it is emphasized that the role of researchers is to adjust to participants' needs and resources and that a non-intrusive technique for working on sensitive topics that may be difficult to discuss is non-verbal methods, giving control to the children and providing a way of expression appropriate to their developmental resources.

The "Before and After" Drawing as a Research Methodology to Explore Psychotherapeutic Change in Children and Adolescents Who Have Experienced Sexual Abuse

In this section, we will present the "before and after therapy" drawing technique—and its adaptation "how were you at the beginning of therapy and how are you now?"—which has been previously used in qualitative studies of the current line of research with the aim of exploring the views of children and adolescents regarding the process of healing from sexual abuse and psychotherapeutic change after these experiences (Capella et al., 2015, 2016, 2018).

The technique consists of dividing a blank sheet into two sections, where the left side section indicates "before therapy" or "how were you at the beginning of therapy?," while the right side indicates "after therapy" or "how are you now?" (see Fig. 6.1). The child or adolescent is invited to draw themselves on each of the two sides of the drawing. Colored pencils and other art materials are provided to promote creativity and expression. This drawing technique has been used in Chile in the context of psychotherapy with children and adolescents who have been victims of CSA (Capella et al., 2014). In the context of clinical practice, it has been described as a technique that favors the integration of the therapy process as a period of recovery and personal strengthening, thus promoting the recognition of achievements and resources developed during psychotherapy, as well as the assimilation of the process of overcoming the abusive experience into the self-view (Capella et al., 2015). The adaptation of this drawing for research purposes is recent and represents a methodological contribution to the field of child psychotherapy and CSA research.

In research, this technique seeks to explore the notion of psychotherapeutic change in children and adolescents, as they are invited to draw themselves in relation to how they perceived themselves before or at the beginning of therapy and how they consider themselves during the process or at the end of it. In this way, it is a technique that, through its prompt, proposes the creation of a visual narrative of change (Capella et al., 2015). Additionally, this drawing methodology presents the possibility of being adapted depending on the research design. In previous studies

Fig. 6.1 Example of "before and after therapy" drawing and its adaptation "How were you at the beginning of therapy? (¿Cómo estabas al principio de la terapia?) and How are you now?" (¿Cómo estás ahora?)

of the research line (Capella et al., 2015, 2016, 2022), the prompt for applying this technique has been adapted depending on the study's objectives and whether it sought to explore the views of children and adolescents regarding psychotherapeutic change at a single moment in therapy (at the end, for example) or to examine this notion longitudinally through different moments of psychotherapy (for example, at the beginning, during, and at the end of the process).

In previous studies of this line of research, semi-structured qualitative interviews were conducted with each of the participating children and adolescents, using an interview script focused on exploring how they evaluated the therapy process and psychotherapeutic change after experiences of CSA. At the beginning of the interview, the child or adolescent was invited to perform the "before and after therapy" drawing technique (or its variation) as a way to facilitate the construction of their verbal narrative during the interview (depending on the case, the drawing could also be done in the middle or at the end of the interview). After the child completed the drawing, open-ended questions about their visual creation were asked, allowing the participant to develop a free narrative about the elements of the illustration, which was followed by more focused questions about the general composition of the drawing and contextual aspects. Additionally, based on what the participant indicated about the drawing, the interviewer also integrated into the conversation questions related to the topics of the interview script.

Narrative analysis is a method that has been used to study the emerging data from the interviews and drawings. According to Bruner (2004), individuals narratively organize reality through the telling of their experiences. A narrative is central to the process of making sense of life experiences and stories (Bruner, 2004; Squire et al., 2014). Engel (2005) points out that the stories children tell about their daily lives and significant experiences reveal how they organize and make sense of their worlds. Consequently, narrative analysis is the systematic study of narrative data, and it is interested in exploring how an individual organizes events using verbal or non-verbal language to communicate meanings (Riessman, 2008). McLeod (2001) highlights the usefulness of this approach for studying narratives developed in the context of psychotherapy.

Esin and Squire (2013) adopt a broad definition of narrative, noting that narratives involve a meaningful succession of signs and symbols that can be verbal, visual, and enacted through activities and actions. In the case of children, narrative construction can be better understood as multiple forms of embodied expression through action (play), images (drawing), sounds, expressions, and body movements, rather than solely the use of words (Engel, 2005). Under this consideration, narrative data can come from various sources, whether interviews, drawings, or play, among others (Capella et al., 2016; Crossley, 2007), and can also be non-verbal. This is a notion of narrative that goes beyond the traditional view that primarily associates it with the verbal world. Thus, in recent years, the development of narrative analysis focused on the study of visual material such as photographs and drawings has emerged (Capella et al., 2015; Luttrell, 2010, 2020; Riessman, 2008). Like verbal narratives, visual narratives are means of narrative construction, as they contain theories based on the understanding that their creators possess (Luttrell, 2010, 2020; Riessman, 2008), being a way to symbolize and make visible aspects of the self in social environments and circumstances (Harrison, 2002).

Visual narrative analysis is understood as the interpretation of the image itself, the context in which it is produced, and the context in which this narrative is "read" or viewed (Bell, 2013; Riessman, 2008). Regarding the context in which the image is produced and in which it is read, it is necessary to ask about how and when the image was made, the social identity of the creator, the initial responses of the observers about the visual creation, and the stories they create regarding the image, as well as other aspects of the visual creation and perception process (Riessman, 2008). Regarding the analysis of the image itself, it inquiries the story that the image suggests, which includes how the elements of the image are organized, the use of color, and other relevant aspects depending on the type of visual creation (drawing, photography, filming) (Riessman, 2008). The analysis methodology used in our studies is positioned within this latter approach, as it pays particular attention to how graphic components are organized and related, as well as what the drawing suggests about the therapeutic change process. A visual narrative analysis procedure has been developed by the research team to study the "before and after therapy" drawing and its variation "How were you at the beginning of therapy and how are you now?" (Capella et al., 2015, 2022). This analysis proposal consists of a process that can be carried out in two stages:

In the first stage of analysis, an intra-case study is conducted, in which each drawing made by a participant case at a specific moment of therapy is analyzed, integrating the analysis of both sides of the visual creation (the "before" or "how were you at the beginning of therapy" and the "after" or "how are you now?"). In this stage, the analysis of each drawing is conducted around the following four axes of analysis: (1) Elements of the self; (2) Contextual elements; (3) Formal characteristics of the drawing; and (4) Connections between the visual narrative and the verbal narrative of the drawing. The focus is primarily on the study of the graphic and elements of the self, as it would be the central focus of the illustration on each side of the drawing. Consequently, axis 1 analyzes how the child draws themselves on each side of the drawing. Axis 2 focuses on the contextual elements that accompany the central illustration on each side of the drawing, what role they play in the configuration of the complete visual narrative, and what these elements might mean in that context. The third axis integrates the observation of the formal elements of the drawing on each side, which includes aspects such as the use of color, size, details, and position of the drawing, among others. Then, differences, similarities, and changes between the drawings on each side are analyzed, contrasting the central element (drawing of the self) and the contextual aspects between both sides of the drawing.

From a narrative constructivist framework, we understand that the meaning of a drawing does not lie solely in the image itself, but rather in how the individual perceives and talks about it (Luttrell, 2010, 2020; Squire et al., 2014). Several authors point out the existence of a blurry line between verbal and visual narrative, which is why they use both together (Bell, 2013; Radley et al., 2005; Squire et al., 2014). For example, Radley et al. (2005) explain that while some images can be understood independently, others can be better analyzed in relation to what the individual narrates about them. Thus, in the search to construct a more complete and integrated narrative for each case, the verbal narrative that the child provides about their drawing is integrated at different moments of analysis of their drawing. Thus, axis 4 of the intra-case analysis stage also considered more specifically the complementary study of the visual narrative of the drawing and the emerging verbal narrative regarding the drawing during the interview as a way to contrast similarities and differences between both means of narration (Luttrell 2010, 2020).

Centrally, this first stage of intra-case analysis includes consideration for the variations, similarities, and changes in visual narrative over time for a case. Thus, after analyzing the drawing from a specific moment in psychotherapy, the drawings made by a case at different moments of therapy (for example, at the beginning, middle, and end of therapy) are jointly analyzed. This allows exploring the narratives of change in a case not only at a specific moment in therapy but also studying how change evolves at different moments of the psychotherapeutic process for a case. This analysis of the evolution or progression of change among the different drawings of a case at various moments of therapy is also conducted based on the 4 axes mentioned earlier.

Finally, in search of providing a more complete context to the analysis conducted, the analysis also integrates variables associated with the singularity of each

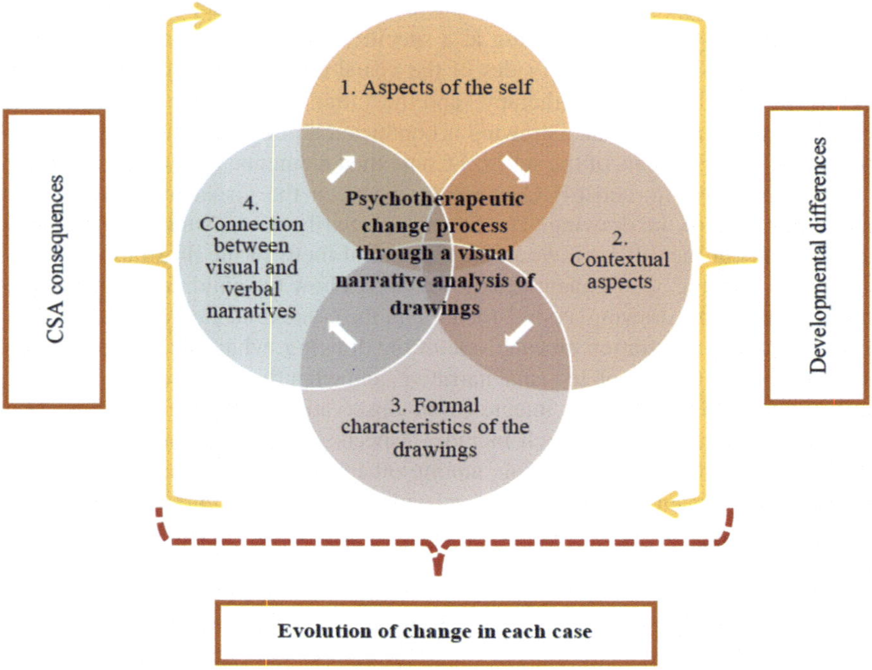

Fig. 6.2 Proposed procedure for visual narrative analysis to study psychotherapeutic change through the analysis of drawings in a case

case, including aspects such as the characteristics of the abusive experience lived by the participants (type of abuse, relationship with the offender, frequency, among others), and developmental variables associated with the life stage of the child or adolescent. Figure 6.2 illustrates the proposed methodology for visual narrative analysis to study psychotherapeutic change through the study of drawings in a case.

A second stage of analysis is possible when the study consists of different participating cases. Thus, an inter-case analysis procedure is conducted by analyzing the drawings of all participating cases, considering all the different moments of psychotherapy in which they were interviewed. This stage seeks to explore possible connections and divergences among the participants' drawings concerning each of the four axes and the moments of psychotherapy.

A joint analysis work by different members of the research team was carried out, which is recommended as a way to provide different perspectives that favor the criteria of rigor and validity regarding the visual analysis conducted and to broaden its complexity.

The Process of Psychotherapeutic Change of a Group of Children and Adolescents Who Were Victims of Sexual Abuse Through the Analysis of Their "Before and After" Drawings

In this section, we will present an example of an analysis in which the drawing technique and the methodological proposal already described have been used. This example derives from a larger qualitative and longitudinal research study (Fondecyt 11140049), in which children and adolescent victims of CSA who were undergoing psychotherapy in public centers specialized in treating CSA and maltreatment in Chile participated, as well as their parents/caregivers and their psychotherapists (Capella et al., 2022). It should be noted that the project had the approval of the ethics committee of research in Social Sciences of the University of Chile (Code 003_07/2014).

As the objective of this chapter is to show the use of drawing to understand the experiences of children and adolescents in relation to therapy and psychotherapeutic change, we will present the analysis of the drawings of a sub-sample from the bigger project of 10 participating children and adolescents.

The participants were between 6 and 14 years old when they started their therapies, eight were female, and two were male. Regarding the psychotherapy process, six participants had therapeutic processes that extended between 6 and 12 months, and for four participants, the therapy extended 18 months or more. The research methods with the ten children and adolescents—semi-structured qualitative interview and the drawing "How were you at the beginning of therapy and how are you now?"—were applied at different moments of psychotherapy to each participant, that is, at approximately 6 months after starting therapy, then at approximately 12 months, and at a final third moment when the child was discharged from therapy if it extended for more than 12 months. All participants and their caregivers initially provided their informed assent and consent to participate in the research, as well as a special assent and consent authorizing the use of the drawings by the research team for analysis and to be shown in publications and presentations of research findings. Special considerations regarding the use of visual material were included to protect the confidentiality and anonymity of the participants, as well as ethical safeguards to protect the emotional stability of the children and adolescents during their participation.

The analysis of the drawings was conducted according to the described proposal: (1) in the first intra-case stage, the drawings from different moments of therapy of each participant were analyzed; (2) in the second inter-case stage, the drawings from different moments of therapy of the ten children and adolescents were jointly analyzed. The results presented here are the outcome of the inter-case analysis and are organized according to the four axes of analysis. It is possible to mention that the visual narratives of the participating children clearly express their vision of change in relation to the experience of sexual assault.

1. **Elements of the Self**

Regarding the first axis, it is possible to identify four predominant visual narratives in the participants' drawings: (a) affective changes and mood improvement; (b) changes in attitude toward therapy; (c) changes associated with growth; (d) permanence of aspects of the self-representation despite experiencing changes.

(a) **Affective changes:** The visual narratives of the participants predominantly reflect the presence of changes and improvements in mood during the therapeutic process, observed in the three stages. By comparing both sides of the drawing, it is possible to see that in the drawings of "How were you before therapy?", children and adolescents visually describe the existence of feelings of sadness and discomfort, which can be identified through facial expressions (see Fig. 6.3). In the drawings of "How are you now?" or during therapy, feelings of sadness seem to evolve, making way for mood improvements observed in facial expressions of happiness and calm, which could indicate a general sense of well-being. Both child and adolescent participants use facial expressions as a resource to account for these affective changes at different moments of therapy.

Fig. 6.3 Detail of the drawing of two participants that accounts for affective changes through their visual narratives

(b) **Changes in attitude toward therapy:** Another predominant narrative is linked to changes in participants' orientation, availability, and feelings toward the therapy space from the beginning of the process to the current moment. On the side of the beginning of therapy, several participants express feelings of nervousness, distrust, and shyness. These feelings are present at different moments of therapy. However, on the side of the current moment of therapy, it is possible to observe an increased interest in the therapy process and feelings of motivation to attend the space.

Figure 6.4 presents the drawings of two 10-year-old girls, one at 6 months of therapy and the other at the time of discharge, respectively. In their drawings on the left side, it is possible to read "how nervous!" and "nervous," while in the drawings of the current moment of therapy, they indicate "how good I feel when I go to the psychologist" and "I am happy." Thus, some participants report feeling happier and better when attending therapy, which is visualized in the facial expressions and verbal narratives of the drawing.

Fig. 6.4 Changes in attitude toward therapy

(c) **Changes associated with growth:** Changes associated with growth are also observed in relation to how participants draw themselves, showing how human figures at the initial moment of therapy tend to increase in size at the current moment through the different moments of psychotherapy. Additionally, participants possibly experienced changes associated with aging, as some who started therapy as children transformed into pre-adolescents or adolescents during the therapy and research process. In their drawings, physical changes are observed that make them look different (see Fig. 6.5). This increase in size and growth could be linked to a sense of greater empowerment and autonomy.

(d) **Permanence of aspects of self-representation despite experiencing changes:** According to Draucker et al. (2009), the recovery process of those who have experienced CSA would not harm their identities but rather strengthen them. The visual narratives of the participants show that, despite glimpsing changes regarding their self-view, overcoming some of the negative effects of CSA (such as a sad mood), and undergoing a therapy process, there is a perception of continuity of the self, as there are aspects that do not change through the different moments of therapy (see Fig. 6.5). This would not imply returning to who they were before, but rather they would be visualized with more resources and strengthened.

Fig. 6.5 Drawings at three different moments of therapy—6 months, 12 months, and end of therapy—of an 11-year-old girl. The six-month drawing is included in the article by Capella et al. (2018, p. 31)

Figure 6.5 shows the drawings of the three different interview moments of a girl who was 11 years old at the start of therapy and successfully discharged from the process at 14 years old. Through her drawings, we can observe changes in the different sizes of the drawings (from smaller to larger), different use of color as therapy progresses, and changes in clothing style and some physical characteristics. Changes in attitude toward therapy are also observed, indicating in the first drawing "what a drag to go" on the left side and "it's finally Wednesday" (the day she went to therapy) on the right side; in the drawing at the second interview, "what a bore to go" and "where do I find more time to go" and, in the last drawing on the left side, she wrote "why do I have to go?" (Capella et al., 2018). However, we can also see that some characteristics remain similar through the different moments, indicating that, although she is or has changed, she also remains the same.

2. **Contextual Elements**

In the second axis of contextual elements, it is possible to identify two main characteristics in the visual narratives of the participants. On one hand, the presence of other people in the drawings—different from the child or adolescent—tells a perception of changes at the family level, feeling socially more supported by others, and the notion of greater openness to relate and connect with others. Additionally, some of the contextual elements seem to empathize with the emotional tone of the central drawing of the self (facial expressions, sun, clouds). The second characteristic in the visual narratives of the participants shows how, from the initial moment of therapy to its final stage, the contextual elements (such as people and pets) decrease in presence as the process progresses, which would indicate feelings of autonomy, independence, and less need for social support. Figure 6.6 shows the drawings of a teenage girl and a teenage boy, both aged 14 years old. Both drawings were made at the final stage of therapy, where it is possible to observe, for example, a greater openness to connecting with others and significant changes in the emotional state. For instance, the teenage boy explains regarding his drawing (the second one), "Before when I came, I felt closed off in front of people (...) and then when I started coming around six, seven months, I began to socialize with people, to talk to them, and that's when I started making more friends." His visual narrative reveals his perception of feeling distant from connecting with others on the left side of the drawing. In contrast, a greater openness to connection with others is evident on the right side of the drawing, represented by hand contact between two characters.

3. **Formal Aspects of the Drawing**

It is possible to visualize changes in relation to the formal quality of the drawings, as the visual narratives associated with the drawing of oneself and contextual elements become enriched as therapy progresses, with further graphic details in the drawings—such as, for example, increased use of color—which is especially significant in the final stages of therapy (see Fig. 6.5). In addition, some graphic changes could possibly be associated with the passage of time and, therefore, developmental and age changes. These can also be linked to feelings of greater well-being in the participants.

Fig. 6.6 Changes associated with contextual elements

4. **Connections Between the Visual and the Verbal Narrative of the Drawing**

In most participant cases, it was possible to identify connections between the verbal and visual narratives associated with the drawing. Similarities were observed between what the participants verbally explained about the drawing and the story that the image itself conveyed. Figure 6.7 displays the drawing and verbal narrative of a 9-year-old girl at the end of therapy, showing the similarities between the visual and verbal.

Interviewer: 'How were you before therapy?'
Girl: 'At the beginning of therapy, I was sad, uh, nervous (...), that's why the girl in the drawing is showing you her nervous face.'
Interviewer: 'And how do you feel now?'
Girl: 'I feel good (...) I feel better now.

It was possible to observe changes in all the visual narratives of the participants, although associated with different aspects. This would be influenced by factors such as the developmental characteristics and age of the participants, the impact of CSA, and the subjective experience of each child, as well as the characteristics of the

Fig. 6.7 Example of connection between verbal and visual narratives of the drawing

therapy process. Developmental differences in the visual narratives of the participants were mainly observed in that children tended to use a simpler formal structure at the graphic level than adolescents, although they used various colors in their drawings compared to older participants, who generally used one or two tones. In terms of the content, adolescent participants tended to include contextual aspects associated with the presence of other people (and pets), while child participants included details such as the sun, clouds, and flowers. Additionally, the change in visual narratives is also linked to the subjective experience associated with the consequences of CSA, with specific changes visualized for each case regarding dynamics of traumatic sexualization, betrayal, stigmatization, and helplessness.

Final Thoughts

In this chapter, we have described and analyzed the use of drawing in psychotherapy research with children and adolescents who have been victims of sexual abuse, showing how drawing, as a non-verbal, non-intrusive technique, is close to the usual forms of communication of children and allows exploring narratives of change and evolution of change.

In this way, the possibility of "listening" to the perspectives of children and adolescents through drawings is highlighted as a sensitive technique in ethical, methodological, and developmental terms, especially for those who have experienced traumatic experiences such as sexual abuse.

Furthermore, the relevance of integrating the verbal and visual narratives of the participants is emphasized as a methodological resource, as this allows a more comprehensive approach to their perspectives, enabling children and adolescents to express their meanings in other ways, producing a more complete visual-verbal narrative of their psychotherapeutic change process. This intends to prevent the sometimes biased interpretation of their graphic productions by adult researchers.

Another central element described is how change and its evolution, observed through drawings, account for a change process that is particular to each case. Not all participants change in the same way and at the same pace (Capella et al., 2022), as the psychotherapeutic change process is progressive but not linear (Krause, 2011) and can take different directions. There are different characteristics of the child, their particular context, and the psychotherapeutic process itself that could influence the change in each case (Capella et al., 2022), which should be considered in the analysis.

The use of the drawing described in this chapter contributes as a research methodology of interest for researching the experiences of children and adolescents, as an easy-to-use and accessible technique. This is of particular relevance in research contexts in psychotherapy in Latin America, where there are often scarce resources for research, requiring the search for accessible and creative methods. Moreover, the potential and richness described in the analysis of this technique also allow for projecting its use in other contexts, contributing from Latin America with creative methodologies for the field of child and adolescent psychotherapy research.

While this chapter describes a proposal for the use of drawing and visual narrative analysis, it can continue to be adapted considering the particular characteristics of each research, allowing researchers flexibility in its applications. Along with this, we can also observe the contributions of the technique of using drawings, and specifically the "before-after" drawing and its variations, not only in research but also in its therapy use, aiming to approach the experiences of children and adolescents. In this sense, using this technique in clinical practice can help to observe during therapy the view that the child has of their change and the progress of the therapeutic process and for the child to visualize their own changes. Furthermore, just as in this case we explain its use with sensitive topics, such as sexual abuse, it could also be applicable in working with other populations with experiences of vulnerability, such as, for example, children who have lived through other traumatic experiences.

At the same time, future challenges remain, such as developing different methodologies for research in child psychotherapy, which are also sensitive and allow for the expression of children, even the youngest ones, such as, for example, play. This is especially relevant in research with children who have been victims of sexual abuse, as other studies in the field have particularly noted the difficulty of accessing the perspectives of the youngest children (Capella et al., 2022).

References

Águila, D., Lama, X., Capella, C., Rodríguez, L., Dussert, D., Gutiérrez, C., & Beiza, G. (2016). Narratives from therapists regarding the process of psychotherapeutic change in children and adolescents who have been victims of sexual abuse / Narrativas de terapeutas sobre el proceso de cambio psicoterapéutico en niños, niñas y adolescentes que han sido víctimas de agresiones sexuales. *Estudios de Psicología, 37*(2–3), 344–364. https://doi.org/10.1080/02109395.2016.1204780

Bell, S. (2013). Seeing narratives. In M. In Andrews, C. Squire, & M. Tamboukou (Eds.), *Doing narrative research* (pp. 142–158). Sage.

Bruner, J. (2004). Life as narrative. *Social Research, 71*(3), 691–710. https://doi.org/10.1353/sor.2004.0045

Capella, C., Azócar, E., Gómez, C., Albornoz, S., Pitron, D., Pizarro, R., Vega, M., & Rodríguez, L. (2021). *Cambio Psicoterapéutico en niños, niñas y adolescentes que han sido víctimas de agresiones sexuales: Evaluación de la continuidad y caracterización del cambio posterior a la psicoterapia* [Psychotherapeutic change in children and adolescents who have been victims of sexual assault: Evaluation of the continuity and characterization of change after psychotherapy]. *Terapia Psicológica, 39*(3), 329–352. https://doi.org/10.4067/S0718-48082021000300329

Capella, C., & Boddy, J. (2021). Listening to the opinista? Relational understandings of voice and silence in a multiperspective narrative study of child psychotherapy. *Children & Society, 35*, 835–849. https://doi.org/10.1111/chso.12458

Capella, C., Escala, C. L., & Núñez, L. (2014). *Intervención psicoterapéutica con niños y niñas que han sido víctimas de agresiones sexuales: Profundización en el uso de técnicas* [Psychotherapeutic intervention with boys and girls who have been victims of sexual assault: Deepening the use of techniques]. Postgraduate refresher course, University of Chile.

Capella, C., Gutiérrez, C., Rodríguez, L., & Gómez, C. (2018). Change during psychotherapy: The perspective of children and adolescents who have been sexually abused. *Research in Psychotherapy: Psychopathology, Process and Outcome, 21*(1), 24–39. https://doi.org/10.4081/ripppo.2018.288

Capella, C., Lama, X., Rodriguez, L., Aguila, D., Beiza, G., Dussert, D., & Gutierrez, C. (2016). Winning a race: Narratives of healing and Psychotherapy in children and adolescents who have been sexually abused. *Journal of Child Sexual Abuse, 25*(1), 73–92. https://doi.org/10.1080/10538712.2015.1088915

Capella, C., Rodriguez, L., Aguila, D., Dussert, D., Lama, X., Gutierrez, C., & Beiza, G. (2015). Storied images of psychotherapeutic change: Approaching children´s voices through drawings. *Research in Psychotherapy: Psychopathology, Process and Outcome, 18*(2). https://doi.org/10.7411/RP.2015.109

Capella, C., Rodríguez, L., Azócar, E., Lama, X., Núñez, L., Águila, D., Gómez, C., Espeleta, M., & Vásquez, V. (2022). Psychotherapeutic change in children and adolescents who have been sexually abused: A model from participants' perspectives. *Research in Psychotherapy: Psychopathology, Process and Outcome, 25*(1), 95–107. https://doi.org/10.4081/ripppo.2022.583

Carlberg, G., Thoren, A., Billstrom, S., & Odhammar, F. (2009). Children's expectation and experiences of psychodynamic child psychotherapy. *Journal of Child Psychotherapy, 35*(2), 175–193.

Clark, A. (2017). *Listening to young children: A guide to understanding and using the mosaic approach*. Jessica Kingsley Publishers.

Crossley, M. (2007). Narrative analysis. In E. Lyons & A. Coyle (Eds.), *Analysing qualitative data in psychology*. Sage Publications.

Draucker, C. B., Martsolf, D., Ross, R., Cook, C. B., Stidham, A., & Mweemba, P. (2009). The essence of healing from sexual violence: A qualitative metasynthesis. *Research in Nursing and Mental Health, 32*, 366–378.

Dussert, D., Capella, C., Lama, X., Gutiérrez, C., Águila, D., Rodríguez, L., & Beiza, G. (2017). *Narrativas de Padres de Niños, Niñas y Adolescentes que Han Finalizado Psicoterapia por Agresiones Sexuales: Un Proceso de Superación Conjunta* [Narratives of parents of boys, girls and adolescents who have completed psychotherapy for sexual assaults: A joint overcoming process]. *Psykhe, 26*(1), 1–14. https://doi.org/10.7764/psykhe.26.1.916

Engel, S. (2005). Narrative analysis of children's experiences. In S. Green & D. Hogan (Eds.), *Researching children's experiences: Methods and approaches* (pp. 199–216). SAGE Publications.

Esin, C., & Squire, C. (2013). Visual autobiographies in East London: Narratives of still images, interpersonal exchanges, and intrapersonal dialogues. *Forum Qualitative Sozi-alforschung / Forum: Qualitative Social Research, 14*(2), Art.1.

Farr, J., Edbrooke-Childs, J., Town, R., Pietkiewicz, D., Young, I., & Stapley, E. (2021). Counseling for young people and families affected by child sexual exploitation and abuse: A qualitative investigation of the perspective of young people, parents, and professionals. *Journal of Child Sexual Abuse, 30*(1), 102–123. https://doi.org/10.1080/10538712.2020.1848959

Foster, J., & Hagedorn, B. (2014). Through the eyes of the wounded: A narrative analysis of children's sexual abuse experiences and recovery process. *Journal of Child Sexual Abuse, 23*, 538–557. https://doi.org/10.1080/10538712.2014.918072

Fuentes-Peláez, N., Mateos, A., Balsells, M. A., & Rodrigo, M. J. (2023). Arts based research with children in program evaluation in Spain. In K. Kriz & M. Petersen (Eds.), *Children and young people´s participation in child protection* (pp. 182–200). Oxford University Press.

Gabriel-Vacher, N., & Capella, C. (2024). Neglected caregivers: Analysis of the technical guidelines of child maltreatment and child sexual abuse programs (Cuidadores descuidados: Análisis de las orientaciones técnicas de programas de maltrato y abuso sexual infantil). *Ibero-American Journal of Psychology and Public Policy, 1*(1), 9–32. https://doi.org/10.56754/2810-6598.2024.0005

Garcia-Quiroga, M., & Salvo, I. (2020). Too vulnerable to participate? challenges for meaningful participation in research with children in alternative care and adoption. *International Journal of Qualitative Methods, 19*, 1–11. https://doi.org/10.1177/1609406920958965

Gómez, C., Lama, X., & Capella, C. (2021). *Psicoterapia y Superación de Agresiones Sexuales: Mensajes de Niños/as y Adolescentes a Pares y Psicoterapeutas* [Psychotherapy and overcoming sexual assaults: Messages from children and adolescents to peers and psychotherapists]. *Psykhe, 30*(2), 1–15. https://doi.org/10.7764/psykhe.2019.22385

Groundwater-Smith, S., Dockett, S., & Bottrell, D. (2015). *Participatory research with children and young people*. Sage.

Guerra, C., & Arredondo, V. (2017). *Investigación sobre psicoterapia en abuso sexual infantil: ¿una tarea pendiente en Chile?* [Research on psychotherapy in child sexual abuse: A pending task in Chile?]. *Summa Psicológica UST, 14*(1), 1–11. https://doi.org/10.18774/summa-vol14.num1-227

Harrison, B. (2002). Photographic visions and narrative inquiry. *Narrative Inquiry, 12*(1), 87–111.

Hydén, M. (2013). Narrating sensitive topics. In M. Andrews, C. Squire, & M. Tamboukou (Eds.), *Doing Narrative research* (pp. 223–239). Sage.

Jessiman, P., Hackett, S., & Carpenter, J. (2017). Children's and carers' perspectives of a therapeutic intervention for children affected by sexual abuse. *Child & Family Social Work, 22*(2), 1024–1033. https://doi.org/10.1111/cfs.12322

Krause, M. (2011). *Psicoterapia y cambio. Una mirada desde la subjetividad* [Psychotherapy and change. A view from subjectivity](2nd ed). Universidad Católica Editions.

Luttrell, W. (2010). "A camera is a big responsibility": A lens for analyzing children´s visual voices. *Visual studies, 25*(3), 224–237.

Luttrell, W. (2020). *Children framing childhoods: Working-class kids' visions of care*. Policy Press.

Madrid, M., Rodríguez, L., & Capella, C. (2022). *Relación terapéutica, juego y abordaje de la experiencia de agresiones sexuales en psicoterapia: la perspectiva de niños/as y adolescentes* [Therapeutic relationship, play and addressing the experience of sexual assault in psychotherapy: The perspective of children and adolescents]. *Revista de Psicología, 31*(1), 1–14. https://doi.org/10.5354/0719-0581.2022.64715

McLeod, J. (2001). *Qualitative Research in Counseling and Psychotherapy*. London: Sage.

Midgley, N. (2004). Sailing between Scylla and Charybdis: Incorporating qualitative approaches into child psychotherapy research. *Journal of Child Psychotherapy, 30*(1), 89–111.

Midgley, N., Capella, C., Goodman, G., Lis, A., Noom, M., Tishby, O., & Weitkamp, K. (2018). Introduction to the special section on child and adolescent psychotherapy research. *Psychotherapy Research, 28*(1), 1–2. https://doi.org/10.1080/10503307.2017.1380864

Nelson-Gardell, D. (2001). The voices of victims: Surviving child sexual abuse. *Child and Adolescent Social Work Journal, 18*(6), 401–416. https://doi.org/10.1023/A:1012936031764

Pinto-Cortez, C., & Guerra, C. (2019). *Victimización sexual de niños, niñas y adolescentes chilenos: prevalencia y características asociadas* [Sexual victimization of Chilean children and adolescents: Prevalence and associated characteristics]. *Revista de Psicología, 28*(2), 1–12. https://doi.org/10.5354/0719-0581.2019.55658

Radley, A., Hodgetts, D., & Cullen, A. (2005). Visualizing homeless: A study in photography and estrangement. *Journal of Community & Applied Social Psychology, 15*, 273–295.

Riessman, C. K. (2008). *Narrative methods for the human sciences*. Sage Publications.

Salcuni, S., Capella, C., & Lis, A. (2015). Introduction to the special issue on qualitative and quantitative research in child and adolescent psychotherapy. *Research in Psychotherapy: Psychopathology, Process and Outcome, 18*(2), VIII–XI.

Sánchez-Meca, J., Rosa-Alcázar, A., & López-Soler, C. (2011). The psychological treatment of sexual abuse in children and adolescents: A meta-analysis. *International Journal of Clinical and Health Psychology, 11*(1), 67–93. Recuperado de https://bit.ly/3BghDF3

Squire, C., Andrews, M., Davis, M., Esin, C., Harrison, B., Hyden, L., & Hydem, M. (2014). *What is narrative research?* Bloomsbury.

Tichelaar, H., Deković, M., & Endendijk, J. (2020). Exploring effectiveness of psychotherapy options for sexually abused children and adolescents: A systematic review of randomized controlled trials. *Children and Youth Services Review, 119, 105519*. https://doi.org/10.1016/j.childyouth.2020.105519

Chapter 7
Qualitative Analysis of Drawings of the Process of Psychotherapeutic Change: Proposal to Promote the Participation of Children in the Research Context

Nicolle Alamo and Lucía Núñez

Introduction

Incorporating the perspective of children in child psychotherapy research is not always easy and requires methodologies that favor their expression and access to other forms of analysis and conceptualization by the researcher (Carlberg et al., 2009; Carroll, 2002). In this context, children's drawings are a possible tool, as drawing is a natural, non-threatening activity for children and is very useful when language development has not yet surpassed graphic expression or when there are aspects that the child cannot (or does not want to) express in words (García-Arzeno, 2007; Koppitz, 1995; Widlöcher, 1988).

Drawing as a means of evaluation in the field of clinical psychology has followed a long tradition of projective interpretation, which seeks to understand psychological functioning and areas of conflict or psychopathology through the exploration of aspects of unconscious life projected in the drawings (de Santiago et al., 1999).

Within the tradition of projective interpretation, authors like Hammer (1969/2016) and Machover (1974) propose four levels of analysis: (a) Gestalt, which corresponds to a general or global impression of the drawing (style, degree of organization, and sensations it generates); (b) Graphic, in which the lines and strokes are analyzed; (c) Formal structures, in which size, placement, sequence, among other elements, are considered; and (d) Content, which corresponds to the main theme

N. Alamo (✉)
School of Social Work, Pontifical Catholic University of Chile, Santiago, Chile
e-mail: nalamo@uc.cl

L. Núñez
School of Psychology, Pontifical Catholic University of Chile, Santiago, Chile
e-mail: ltnunez@uc.cl

A. Tomicic, J. D. Soto (eds.), *Qualitative Research in Clinical Psychology and Psychotherapy in Latin America*, https://doi.org/10.1007/978-3-031-90782-1_7

and accounts for the narrative value of the drawing. The posture and/or action of the figures, facial expression when it is an animated being, and the importance given to different details of the drawing are also included. In addition to these elements, authors like Celener (2003) pay special attention to spontaneous verbalization during the activity, the attitude, and the content of the verbalized narrative.

Thus, drawings are generally used as part of a psychodiagnostic battery, which implies the use of various techniques (graphic, thematic, and play) along with the clinical interview with the child and their caregivers. The interpretation and conclusions derived from the projective analysis of the drawings and other tests are framed in this global process and do not constitute conclusive diagnostic sources by themselves (Febbraio, 2007; García Arzeno, 2007).

In the context of research, the objective of using drawings is different from that of a psychodiagnostic, as it seeks to provide the child with an expressive medium complementary to the purely verbal narration of their experience. Following this aim, in such a context, a psychodiagnostic battery is not applied, which is necessary for a correct projective interpretation (García-Arzeno, 2007). In this line, Driessnack (2005) highlights the tension of conducting a projective analysis of the drawing in the research context, as the goal is not to diagnose but to approach the child's subjective experience regarding a topic or experience and remain as close as possible to their narrative intention.

In the field of research, it is emphasized that the analysis of drawings should be conducted with the children's verbalization of them (Driessnack, 2005; Esin & Squire, 2013). Furthermore, the thematic and visual narrative analysis proposed by Reissman (2008) stands out, focusing on the content and significance of the drawing, considering: (a) the history of the graphic production: context, instruction, and question it responds to; (b) the production itself: characteristics of the central figure and the environment, components, and use of color; and (c) the dialogue constructed from the visual production. These guidelines represent a significant contribution to graphic analysis but do not present a detailed guide of the specific elements of the drawing that can be analyzed, that is, the components of the graphic production itself. This could lead to an interpretation that strays from the child's narrative intention.

In the field of research in child clinical psychology, it is possible to identify the development of some strategies and analysis scales, highlighting, for example, the study of attachment patterns in children based on the Family Drawing, which has supported an important research tradition in this area (Fury et al., 1997; Jin et al., 2018; Madigan et al., 2003; Procaccia et al., 2014). Analysis guidelines have also been used to study children's drawings about specific events, such as research on the COVID-19 pandemic and mitigation measures (Bray et al., 2021). However, in the field of child psychotherapy, the development of studies that have used children's drawings to access their subjective experience in psychotherapy is rather incipient (e.g., Alamo et al., 2022; Capella et al., 2015, 2022; Núñez et al., 2021, 2022). These studies have been developed in Chile, and some of them have been accompanied by the generation of a qualitative analysis guideline for drawings of change in psychotherapy and therapeutic relationships (Alamo, 2019; Núñez, 2021), which is further developed and applied in a revised version in the present chapter.

The research by Capella et al. (2015, 2022) and was developed in psychotherapy with children who have been victims of sexual assault to understand their perspective regarding therapeutic change processes. To this end, they incorporated the drawing called "Before/After therapy" in the context of a semi-structured interview. In subsequent studies, its use was expanded in processes with different consultation reasons (e.g., Alamo et al., 2022; Núñez et al., 2022). The analysis was based on Reissman's (2008) verbal and visual thematic narrative technique. Capella et al. (2015) were pioneers in the national context in incorporating children's drawings as a data collection technique for psychotherapy research; however, in their results, they do not fully detail some criteria used for certain interpretations.

In the research by Alamo (2019), Alamo et al. (2022), Núñez et al. (2021), and Núñez et al. (2022), a qualitative analysis guideline for drawings of change and therapeutic relationship was developed and implemented, using some central elements of classic graphic and thematic narrative analysis, but subordinated to the visual and verbal narrative intention of the children in their drawings (Driessnack, 2005). In these studies, the drawings were used in the context of a semi-structured interview, following the model of Capella et al. (2015). From the results, it was concluded that the drawings significantly enriched the child's overall narrative regarding their subjective experience in psychotherapy, specifically in relation to the content of change and characteristics of the therapeutic relationship. However, in all these investigations, the central unit of analysis was the semi-structured interview, with the drawing being a complementary element. Additionally, the analyses of the interviews with the drawings of the group of participants were conducted jointly, so the results account for findings in an integrated manner.

The purpose of the present chapter is to delve into the use of the Qualitative Analysis Guideline for Drawings of the Therapeutic Change Process developed by the authors in a revised version. The guideline is presented, and its use is exemplified through the analysis of a case to facilitate its dissemination in the scientific community.

Qualitative Analysis Guideline for Drawings of Therapeutic Change Process

The Qualitative Analysis Guideline for Drawings of Therapeutic Change Process, developed by Alamo (2019) and Núñez (2021), in a revised version (see Table 7.1) is presented below. This version seeks to improve its use and replicability. The detailed construction process of this Guideline, in its original version, and its first applications were reported in Alamo (2019), Alamo et al. (2022), Núñez et al. (2021), and Núñez et al. (2022).

Table 7.1 Qualitative analysis guideline for drawings of therapeutic change process

Category	Subcategories
1. Context of graphic production: it is the general frame of reference from which the drawing is analyzed	1.1 Age and sex/gender of the child 1.2 Consulting reason 1.3 Moment in the therapeutic process 1.4 Instruction given 1.5 Place and circumstances in which the drawing is made 1.6 Child's receptivity to the instruction
2. Content of the drawing and its narration: what is represented in general terms and the particular elements that compose the visual and verbal production associated. Includes the child's spontaneous narrative about their drawing and the dialogue with the researcher during and after its creation	2.1 Central theme and gestalt of the drawing: central theme and the general impression conveyed by the drawing. The research team can give each drawing a title, which allows for synthesizing the central theme 2.2 Characteristics of central figures: the perception or representation of the child and others in the context of the graphic production. Includes the posture of the figures, their attitude, facial expression, and the action they might be performing 2.3 Characteristics of the environment: the representation of the environment or context in the graphic production. It accounts for how much detail is given to the environment in the drawing 2.4 Characteristics of the interaction and relationship between graphic elements: the interactions and relationships of the figures with each other and with the environment 2.5 The use of color as a tool of graphic expression: the use or non-use of color to represent what is experienced or perceived is analyzed from the child's narrative intentionality. In general, this analysis is integrated into the dimensions of the central theme, figures, and environment
3. Contributions of the drawing beyond the verbal narrative: if the drawing expands or adds content of the change or process experienced by the child, beyond what is expressed verbally, is considered	No subcategories

In this revised version, some subcategories were added in the Context of graphic production category (age and sex/gender of the child, moment in the therapeutic process in which it is applied, and child's receptivity to the instruction) and the Elaboration of the narrative or visual representation associated with the drawing was removed as a separate category, since, in light of previous applications of the Guideline in its original version (Alamo et al., 2022; Núñez et al., 2021, 2022), it was observed that this category already appeared in the Content of the drawing and its narration, so it was included there.

For the creation of the drawing regarding the therapeutic change process, the child is given a letter-sized white sheet, a graphite pencil, colored pencils, an eraser, and a sharpener. The instruction is: "*I would like to ask you to make a drawing called "Before/After," which has to do with how you were and felt before therapy, and after, when it ended. First, we are going to make a line here in the middle* [the sheet is placed horizontally, and a dividing line is drawn in the middle]; *then here, on the left side, we will put "Before coming to the psychologist" and on the right side we will put "After coming to the psychologist." The drawing I am going to ask you to make then has two parts, one where you can draw how you were and how you felt before starting to come to the psychologist, and how you feel after having come, that is, now.*" If the child has not verbalized or generated a spontaneous narrative in relation to the drawing while making it, at the end they are asked to talk about it: *What can you tell me about this drawing?* Subsequently, other types of open questions are asked to delve into the narrative and specific elements of the drawing (e.g., *Tell me, what did you draw here? How did you feel at this moment? What did you draw in this other part? How did you feel at this other moment? Do you feel that something changed, What do you feel changed?*).

The drawing, with the application of the Guideline, is analyzed together with the narrative, following the arguments presented by authors such as Driessnack (2005) and Esin and Squire (2013).

To ensure the quality of the results and inter-rater reliability of the analyses, a researcher triangulation strategy is employed, which involves two or more trained researchers analyzing the data. This strategy allows for minimizing potential biases derived from a sole researcher's perspective, increasing the reliability of the analyses (Denzin, 2009). In the investigations conducted so far, the participation of a pair of researchers has been considered, who analyze the drawings based on the Guidelines separately and then meet to triangulate their analyses. In this way, the final analyses in relation to the drawings are established through intersubjective agreement (Flick, 2007).

Use of the Guideline: Example of Analysis in a Retrospective Application

The detailed use of the Qualitative Analysis Guideline for Drawings of the Therapeutic Change Process is presented based on the analysis of a case in which the study was conducted in a cross-sectional and retrospective manner; that is, at a single moment, once the psychotherapy was completed.

Context of the Graphic Production

The analyzed case corresponds to a 6-year-8-month-old girl whose parents consulted due to low frustration tolerance. The therapist's main diagnosis was not harmonic development, also adding emotional dependence on parental figures and difficulties in establishing interpersonal relationships with peers. The therapist was 26 years old, had one year of clinical experience, and followed a constructivist-developmental theoretical approach. The therapy was conducted at a university psychological care center, with an extension of one year, with generally weekly sessions (38 sessions), and the condition for termination was the completion of treatment goals.

It should be noted that this case participated in a larger research project that had the approval of an Accredited University Scientific Research Ethics Committee. Among the ethical safeguards, ensuring the delivery of information and full understanding regarding participation in the study, voluntariness, anonymity, and the adequacy of language and instruments to the developmental stage of the participants were considered, all of which were noted in the respective informed consents and assents.

The drawing was made in the context of a semi-structured qualitative interview (Taylor & Bodgan, 1987; Flick, 2007), which was conducted two weeks after the therapy ended. The interview mainly explores the girl's experience in relation to psychotherapy, delving into her subjective experience of her change process, mainly in its content (what changes during psychotherapy). In this context, the drawing was used to deepen the narrative regarding the changes perceived and/or experienced in herself due to psychotherapy.

The interview with the application of the drawing was conducted by a psychologist researcher specialized in child and adolescent psychotherapy and with previous research experience at the same psychological care center where the girl attended.

The girl was very receptive to the proposed activity. She was cooperative, motivated, and talkative, made the drawing with much pleasure, made spontaneous verbalizations about it, and also answered all the questions.

Content of the Drawing and Its Narration

The drawing made by the girl is presented in Fig. 7.1.

Table 7.2 summarizes the differences in the content of the drawing observed between the before and the after-therapy moment, according to the subcategories of the analysis guideline.

Regarding the *central theme and gestalt of the drawing*, when integrating and comparing the two depicted moments, the affective change and the improvement in the girl's mood stand out the most as the content of the perceived change. Regarding the drawing, the girl says:

Fig. 7.1 Drawing "How I was before/How I am after therapy" (Alamo et al., 2022)

> That (after) is paradise, and these (before) are the ruins (…) The paradise is very beautiful (…) (The before) is a very sad, very ugly place, and this (the after) very beautiful place. This is called 'ruins', and that would be 'paradise'.

Integrating the girl's metaphorical narrative about the depicted change, the research team titled her drawing "From the ruins to the emotional paradise."

The affective and mood changes are also observed in the characteristics of the central figure, changing her face and clothing from "sad" to "happy." The aspects of the drawing related to the face and clothing also appear in the girl's verbal narrative:

> (This is) a broken heart, which seems like sad. I will draw it on the shirt, so you will know how I feel (…). A broken heart (…) is not pretty at all (…). This is in 'before', sad (…), sad face, crying (…), the face looks sad-like (…) (E: And what difference is there between these two girls?) This one is happier, this one is sadder.

In addition to the affective changes, it is possible to visualize identity changes in the central figure, represented through differences in physical appearance, going from one that we could call more "unkempt" to another that for the girl is more "pretty" and "cared for." Regarding this change, the girl says:

> Before I had another look (…) bangs like normal (…) Mmm, nothing pretty about that look… (…) it is not pretty at all (…). And I will make a different look (…) mmm, here eyelashes are missing (…) (E: You were telling me you had made a different look) yes, this is the different look (E: what is different?) in this (pointing to the hair of the central figure) to this. (E: Okay, the hair) yes, I mean the bangs. (E: And what else is different between

Table 7.2 Description of the content of the drawing and its narration before and after therapy

Subcategory	Before therapy	After therapy
2.1. Central theme and gestalt of the drawing	"The ruins." Personal experience of emotional distress and sadness	"The paradise." Personal experience of emotional well-being and happiness
2.2 Characteristics of the central figures	The girl draws herself alone, with a sad face, represented by tears in her eyes and a concave mouth (downward). Her hair is messy. On her shirt, there is a broken heart as a symbol of sadness. The figure (skin) is colored, but not her clothing. The narrative accompanying the drawing describes feelings in the same direction	The girl draws herself alone with a happy face, a smiling mouth painted red, combed hair, and highlighted eyelashes. Her clothing, including shoes, has varied and striking colors. The narrative accompanying the drawing describes feelings in the same direction
2.3 Characteristics of the Environment	Darkened clouds, rain, thunder. A bat flying and a broken heart next to the girl. A withered flower on the ground. Absence of color. The story accompanying the drawing describes feelings in the same direction	A big sun and a white cloud. A butterfly flying and a heart with many hearts inside next to the girl. A living flower on the ground. Absence of color. The story accompanying the drawing describes feelings in the same direction
2.4 Characteristics of the interaction and/or relationship between the graphic elements	There is no major interaction between the figures and the environment or any story about it. However, there is coherence among the elements as they all represent dysphoric affects and emotional distress	There is no major interaction between the figures and the environment or any story about it. However, there is coherence among the elements as they all represent affects linked to happiness and emotional well-being
2.5 The use of color as a tool for graphic expression	Only the skin of the central figure is colored, not her clothing or the environment. There is no verbalization of the color	The skin of the central figure is not colored, but her clothing and mouth are colorful. She verbalizes that she will color the mouth

> those two girls?) mmm… wait, something is missing (…) draw her skirt (…). I will put on like lipstick (…) I must paint the mouth red (…) and I will paint this dress (…).

The differences between the central figures of both moments, in terms of the details and varied colors used in the "after," would indicate an improvement in self-concept, although more from the metaphor and visual representation than from a self-perception explicitly stated in the narrative.

Like the central figures, the characteristics of the environment also reflect the previously mentioned affective changes, moving from an "ugly," sad, threatening, and devitalized environment to a more "beautiful," happy, and vital one. This is symbolized in the narrative and through various elements of the drawing, as the girl describes below:

> (In the before) The clouds (...) a bat... it is not beautiful at all. Crushed flower... Here you see nothing pretty (...). Another lightning (...) rain, thunder. This is in 'before'. Sad. (In the after) A sun! Very cheerful (...) Now the flower (...) this one is happier and this one (before) is sadder (...). Look, in this there are clouds and in this (after) sun (...). Here there is something different flying. Look, difference between bat and this butterfly (...). This is... an evil place. And this is a good place. Something else is missing (...) A little cloud. But it is very different from the other, look (E: What difference do those two clouds have?) that one is prettier, and that one is more horrible (...). I missed something. A broken heart, which seems sad. So, you will know how I feel (...) I will make it bigger (...) it is not pretty at all. Look, there is something different about that broken heart from this heart (after) (E: And how is that other heart?) happy, and is not broken, it's united (...) with much love (...). Here there are many hearts.

Although an interaction between the graphic elements is not explicitly appreciated, the coherence of the affective tone between the central figures and the environment of each represented moment stands out.

Regarding the use of color as a tool of graphic expression, as already mentioned, the girl uses it only in the central figure to represent her experience of affective and some identity changes.

Contributions of the Drawing: Beyond the Verbal Narrative

Although most elements of the drawing are complemented by a verbalization, the graphic production allows, on one hand, to highlight what is most important for the girl regarding her experience of change, which fundamentally had to do with feeling better, happier, and more joyful after therapy. On the other hand, the drawing adds, beyond the associated narrative, details of the central figures that enable us to visualize identity changes. Likewise, the use of color was employed by the girl to represent or symbolically portray affective and self-concept changes.

Other Uses of the Qualitative Analysis Guideline for Drawings

The Qualitative Analysis Guideline for Drawings of the Therapeutic Change Process can also be used for drawings of other moments of the psychotherapeutic process and in longitudinal studies of change. Núñez et al. (2022) used the guidelines for drawings that explored therapeutic change expectations in children through the instruction: "How I am before/how do I want to be at the end of therapy," a variation of the drawing "How I was before/how I am after therapy" (Capella et al., 2015). They also used the guideline for a longitudinal study, comparing the drawings of children in two moments, the first was "How I am before therapy," made at the beginning of the process, and the second was the drawing "How I am after therapy," created once the therapy concluded. This allowed analyzing the therapeutic change process from a longitudinal perspective and not only retrospectively, comparing the child's self-perception when starting therapy with their self-perception at the end of the process based on the Guideline.

Another use given to the Guideline is to analyze drawings of the therapeutic relationship, following the instruction "My psychologist/and me" (Núñez et al., 2021, 2022). In these drawings, the guideline has proven very useful for exploring aspects of the relationship between child and therapist, observing elements of the relational dynamic that were not verbalized by the children, for example, the emphasis on material elements of the therapy room at the start of therapy beyond the figures of the child and therapist, and the relational symmetry when playing in advanced stages of the psychotherapy process.

Additionally, the Guideline was used in a study aimed at analyzing the subjective experience of children from migrant families regarding their psychological and emotional well-being during the health crisis caused by COVID-19 (Alamo et al., 2023). Semi-structured interviews were conducted, including the Before/After Drawing, with a prompt adapted to the research objective: *"How you were and how you felt before the pandemic/How you are and how you feel now, during the pandemic."* In the drawings, the guideline helped to evidence the extensive presence of emotional distress in the children, accounting for feelings and emotions such as fear, sorrow, sadness, boredom, and a sense of confinement, among others, all related to the pandemic and confinement measures. These feelings and emotions were mainly represented through changes in faces (mouth, eyes, tears) and the action and body posture of the central figures (figures in action and movement versus static figures), as well as changes in the environments (open spaces, outdoors, with vegetation and other elements, versus closed spaces, like rooms, without much detail or ornamentation).

Discussion

Drawings prove to be a rich and developmentally sensitive tool for approaching the subjective experience of children in child psychotherapy research, as they open a door to their inner world and provide greater metaphorical richness to their verbal narrative, as evidenced in the analyzed case, where the drawing facilitates the reflection and expression of the girl about her own psychotherapeutic change process.

Regarding the use of the Guideline, it allows integration of both visual and verbal elements, enabling both dimensions to complement. It also allows deepening, organizing, highlighting, and synthesizing the main findings related to the researched topic.

The Guideline was constructed to systematize and unify criteria for the application and analysis of drawings in the research context to favor its replicability and use by other researchers. Therefore, it is meant to be used in the research field and is not intended for a clinical or psychodiagnostic analysis. For this reason, levels of analysis that involve a projective interpretation were set aside, and the Guideline proposes the analysis of drawings together with the child's narrative, as suggested by other authors (Driessnack, 2005; Esin & Squire, 2013).

This does not disregard other systematizations or positions concerning the analysis of drawings in research contexts, but it is considered that the greater the degree of projective interpretation, the greater the risk of straying from the child's narrative intention, and the more difficult it would be to disseminate the use of the Guideline for purely investigative purposes. In this sense, by not intending to perform a clinical or projective analysis, the application of the Guideline does not require knowing more details of the case than those specified in it, such as the reason for consultation or aspects of the therapeutic process. It can be used to study the processes of change in psychotherapies of different theoretical approaches and does not require training in projective test interpretation, which allows it to diversify its use and ease training costs.

So far, the "Before/After" drawing has been used within the framework of semi-structured interviews (e.g., Alamo et al., 2022, 2023; Capella et al., 2015; Núñez et al., 2022). However, the proposed Guideline could also be used without a full interview but with a brief inquiry that includes the questions presented in the instruction and aims to obtain a verbal narrative as detailed as possible of what was drawn. This would favor a more extensive use, enabling studies with a larger number of participants and also making comparisons between cases, using, for example, comparative tables.

In addition, as future uses of the Guideline, longitudinal studies could be increased, where the process of change is studied at different moments of psychotherapy and not just at the end. The analysis Guideline would facilitate conducting intra-case comparative studies, analyzing changes in the drawings and in the elements that the Guideline explores at different moments of its application.

It would also be interesting to test the applicability of the Guideline in drawings that inquire about other processes of change in children, not only psychotherapeutic, in various contexts or concerning other situations, events, or experiences, as done by Alamo et al. (2023) regarding COVID-19. Studies, for example, about how children experience migratory experiences, natural disasters, catastrophes, significant losses, and changes in family configuration, in the school context, among others.

It is worth remembering that this is a very incipient area of development, so the objective of this chapter is to propose an analysis Guideline and exemplify its use in detail so that it can be replicated and thus provide greater support to this type of analysis.

Although the Guideline is qualitative in nature, quantitative studies could also be conducted; for example, regarding the different categories and subcategories contemplated in it and how these are presented in different populations and age groups, among others, moving toward mixed analyses that contribute to encompassing the complexity of research in socio-emotional health and psychotherapy with children.

Acknowledgments This research has been conducted within the project CONICYT-PCHA/National Doctorate/2013-21130261 funded by CONICYT [National Commission for Scientific and Technological Research of Chile], and the project IS130005 funded by the Innovation for Competitiveness Fund (FIC) of the Ministry of Economy, Development and Tourism, through the Millennium Scientific Initiative.

References

Alamo, N. (2019). *Contenidos y evolución del cambio en la psicoterapia con niños y niñas: propuesta de un modelo genérico y de proceso* [Contents and evolution of change in psychotherapy with boys and girls: Proposal of a generic and process model]. (Thesis to qualify for the academic degree of Doctor in Psychology). (Pontificia Universidad Católica de Chile. Escuela de Psicología. Santiago. https://repositorio.uc.cl/handle/11534/22501

Alamo, N., Grau-Rengifo, O., Fernández, S., & Veas, A. (21–24 de junio de 2023). Mental health, pandemic, and migration: Rescuing the voice and subjectivity of children. En N. Alamo (coordinator), *Mental health and psychosocial well-being in immigrants and refugees: Experiences and challenges for intervention.* 54th International Annual Meeting of the Society for Psychotherapy Research (SPR), Dublin, Ireland.

Alamo, N., Núñez, L., Bräutigam, B., & Krause, M. (2022). *Der Einsatz von Kinderzeichnungen zur Analyse von Veränderungsprozessen in der Kinderpsychotherapie: empirische Beispiele* [The use of children's drawings to analyze change processes in child psychotherapy: Empirical examples]. In M. Kekeritz, & M. Kubandt (eds.), *Kinderzeichnungen in der qualitativen Forschung* [Children's drawings in qualitative research] (pp.355–375). Springer VS, Wiesbaden. https://doi.org/10.1007/978-3-658-34885-4_14

Bray, L., Blake, L., Protheroe, J., Nafria, B., Garcia de Avila, M., Ångström-Brännström, C., Forsner, M., Campbell, S., Ford, K., Rullander, A., Robichaud, F., Nolbris, J., Saron, H., Kirton, J., & Carter, B. (2021). Children's pictures of COVID-19 and measures to mitigate its spread: An international qualitative study Children's pictures of COVID-19 and measures to mitigate its spread: An international qualitative study. *Health Education Journal, 1–22.* https://doi.org/10.1177/00178969211019459

Capella, C., Rodríguez, L., Águila, D., Dussert, D., Lama, X., Gutiérrez, C., & Beiza, G. (2015). Storied images of psychotherapeutic change: Approaching children's voices through drawings. *Research in Psychotherapy: Psychopathology, Process and Outcome, 18*(2), 141–151. https://doi.org/10.7411/RP.2015.109

Capella, C., Rodríguez, L., Azócar, E., Lama, X., Núñez, L., Águila, D., Gómez, C., Espeleta, M., & Vásquez, V. (2022). Psychotherapeutic change in children and adolescents who have been sexually abused: A model from participants' perspectives. *Research in Psychotherapy: Psychopathology, Process and Outcome, 25*(1), 95–107. https://doi.org/10.4081/ripppo.2022.583

Carlberg, G., Thoren, A., Billstrom, S., & Odhammar, F. (2009). Children´s expectations and experiences of psychodynamic child psychotherapy. *Journal of Child Psychotherapy, 35*(2), 175–193. https://doi.org/10.1080/00754170902996130

Carroll, J. (2002). Play therapy: The children's view. *Child and Family Social Work, 7*(3), 177–187. https://doi.org/10.1046/j.1365-2206.2002.00234.x

Celener, G. (2003). *Técnicas Proyectivas: Actualización e interpretación en los ámbitos Clínico, Laboral y Forense* [Projective techniques: Update and interpretation in the Clinical, Labor and Forensic areas]. Lugar Editorial.

de Santiago, F., Fernández, M., & Guerra, L. (1999). *Psicodiagnóstico dinámico a través de las técnicas proyectivas.* [Dynamic psychodiagnosis through projective techniques.] Amarú Editions.

Denzin, N. K. (2009). *The research act. A theoretical introduction to sociological methods.* Routledge.

Driessnack, M. (2005). Children's drawings as facilitators of communication: A meta-analysis. *J. of Pediatric Nursing, 20*(6), 415–423. https://doi.org/10.1016/j.pedn.2005.03.011

Esin, C., & Squire, C. (2013). Visual autobiographies in east London: Narratives of still images, interpersonal exchanges, and intrapersonal dialogues. *Forum: Qualitative Social Research, 14*(2) https://doi.org/10.17169/fqs-14.2.1971

Febbraio, A. (2007). *Desarrollo y actualización de la evolutiva gráfica* [Development and updating of the evolutionary graphic]. In G. Celener (Ed.), *Projective techniques. Update in interpretation in the clinical, labor and forensic fields.* Lugar Editorial.

Flick, U. (2007). *Introducción a la investigación cualitativa* [Introduction to qualitative research]. Morata.
Fury, G., Carlson, E., & Sroufe, L. (1997). Children's representations of attachment relationships in family drawings. *Child Development, 68*(6), 1154–1164. https://doi.org/10.1111/j.1467-8624.1997.tb01991.x
García Arzeno, M. (2007). *Nuevas aportaciones al psicodiagnóstico clínico* [New contributions to clinical psychodiagnosis]. Nueva Visión.
Hammer, E. F. (1969/2016). *Aspectos expresivos de los dibujos proyectivos* [Expressive aspects of projective drawings]. En E. F. Hammer (ed.), Test *proyectivos gráficos* [*Graphic projective tests*] (2nd ed., pp. 61–74). Paidós.
Jin, M., Chung, U., & Hazen, N. (2018). Attachment representations of school-aged Korean children: Comparing family drawing and narrative assessments in a clinical and a community sample. *Attachment & Human Development, 20*(1), 43–61. https://doi.org/10.1080/14616734.2017.1371781
Koppitz, E. M. (1995). *El dibujo de la figura humana en los niños* [*Drawing the human figure in children*]. Guadalupe.
Machover, K. (1974). *Proyección de la personalidad en el dibujo de la figura humana* [*Projection of personality in the drawing of the human figure*]. Cultura.
Madigan, S., Ladd, M., & Goldberg, S. (2003). A picture is worth a thousand words: Children's representations of family as indicators of early attachment. *Attachment & Human Development, 1*, 19–37.
Núñez, L. (2021). *The therapeutic relationship as a change facilitator in child psychotherapy: A multiple perspective study of children, parents, and therapists* (Tesis para optar al grado académico de Doctora en Psicoterapia). Pontificia Universidad Católica de Chile. Escuela de Psicología. Santiago. https://repositorio.uc.cl/handle/11534/63072
Núñez, L., Fernández, S., Alamo, N., Midgley, N., Capella, C., & Krause, M. (2022). The therapeutic relationship and change processes in child psychotherapy: A qualitative, longitudinal study of the views of children, parents and therapists. *Research in Psychotherapy: Psychopathology, Process and Outcome, 25*(1), 67–81. https://doi.org/10.4081/ripppo.2022.556
Núñez, L., Midgley, N., Capella, C., Alamo, N., Mortimer, R., & Krause, M. (2021). The therapeutic relationship in child psychotherapy: Integrating the perspectives of children, parents, and therapists. *Psychotherapy Research, 28*, 1–13. https://doi.org/10.1080/10503307.2021.1876946
Procaccia, R., Veronese, G., & Castiglioni, M. (2014). The impact of attachment style on the family drawings of school-aged children. *The Open Psychology Journal, 7*, 9–17.
Reissman, C. (2008). *Narrative methods for the human sciences*. SAGE.
Taylor, S. J., & Bodgan, R. (1987). *Introducción a los métodos cualitativos de investigación: la búsqueda de significados* [*Introduction to qualitative research methods: The search for meanings*]. Paidós.
Widlöcher, D. (1988). *Los dibujos de los niños. Bases para una interpretación psicológica* [*Children's drawings. Basis for a psychological interpretation*]. Herder.

Part II
Qualitative Research on Psychotherapy Process

Chapter 8
The Sequential Emergence of New Forms of Relatedness in Moments of Meeting: Applying Conversation Analysis to Psychoanalytic Therapy Sessions

Marcos Herrera, Miguel Sánchez, Andrea Ugarte, Gabriela Vásquez-Torres, and Kene M. Durand

Conversation Analysis and its Application to Psychotherapy Research: An Overview

The term "Conversation Analysis" (CA) refers to the tradition initiated in sociology in the 1960s by the pioneering work of Harvey Sacks and his collaborators Gail Jefferson and Emanuel Schegloff, which then extended its influence in linguistics and psychology. It can be defined as the study of *talk-in-interaction* (Schegloff, 2007), or more precisely, as the discipline and method for studying talk and other behaviors in interaction and of how participants in that interaction manage the formation and attribution of social actions (Raymond & Olguín, 2022). Through the analysis of recorded and transcribed naturally occurring conversations, CA discovered that there is order in talk-in-interaction, underpinned by a multiplicity of organizations (Ten Have, 2007), such as the organization for turn-taking, the construction of sequences, the design of individual turns, repairs, and the global management of conversation. CA is grounded in a detailed analysis of particular instances rather than its categorization or codification, considering subtle details that could get lost in other investigative practices.

CA does not focus on isolated words or utterances but on sequences of linguistic utterances produced by different participants and the sequences of social actions brought about by such linguistic utterances. In so doing, CA follows the principle that every linguistic utterance and the action it brings about has a reflexive relation with the one that precedes it and with the one that follows it (Deppermann, 1999),

M. Herrera (✉) · M. Sánchez · A. Ugarte · G. Vásquez-Torres · K. M. Durand
Pontifical Catholic University of Peru, Lima, Peru
e-mail: mpherrer@pucp.edu.pe; miguel.sancheza@pucp.pe; andrea.ugarte@pucp.edu.pe; gvasquezt@pucp.pe; mike.durand@pucp.edu.pe

A. Tomicic, J. D. Soto (eds.), *Qualitative Research in Clinical Psychology and Psychotherapy in Latin America*, https://doi.org/10.1007/978-3-031-90782-1_8

or principle of *nextness*: "Next turns are understood by co-participants to display their speaker's understanding of the just-prior turn and to embody an action responsive to the just-prior turn so understood" (Schegloff, 2007, p.15). This focus on sequential organization distinguishes CA from other investigative approaches centered on isolated individual linguistic utterances or expressions. When a CA researcher analyzes a transcript, his/her sight does not stay fixed on the isolated contribution of one participant: it always goes back and forth, looking at how it relates to the contribution of the former participant and how it relates to the next one.

A basic assumption of CA (Willig & Stainton-Rogers, 2008), integrating a fundamental contribution of Speech Acts Theory (Austin, 1962), is that we can do things with words: speaking is acting. Every time a speaker says something, they bring about a (social) action with their utterance, like *requesting*, *greeting*, *complaining*, *offering*, *promising*, *thanking*, etc. (Hindelang, 1994). Thus, by producing the linguistic utterance *"Hello!"* a speaker can bring about the action of *greeting*, or by producing the linguistic utterance *"Do you want more coffee?"* a speaker can bring about the action of *offering* (Fig. 8.1).

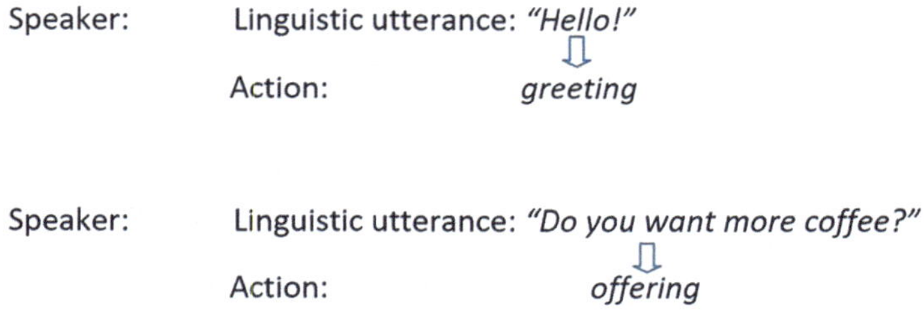

Fig. 8.1 Speech acts

CA elaborates on this basic assumption: the things we can do with words, we do them *together with others* through action sequences brought about by the exchange of linguistic utterances in talk-in-interaction. Thus, after in turn (01) participant P1 produces the linguistic utterance *"Hello!"*, thereby bringing about the action of *greeting*, in turn (02) participant P2 produces the linguistic utterance *"Hi!"*, thereby bringing about the corresponding next action, which in this case is also *greeting*, and by which a sequence [*greeting-greeting*] is completed (Fig. 8.2).

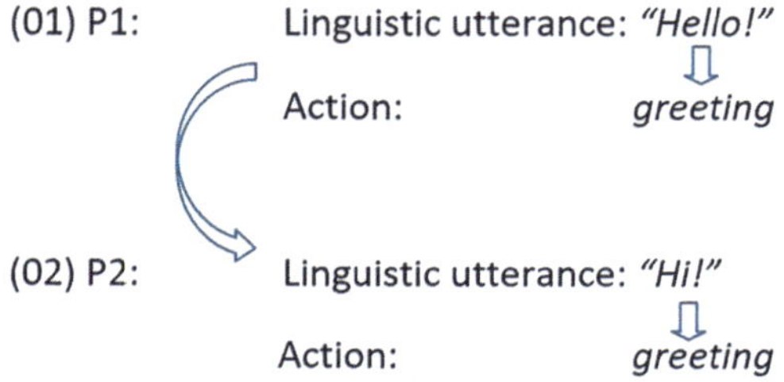

Fig. 8.2 Sequences (i): [greeting-greeting]

Likewise, after in turn (01) participant P1 produces the linguistic utterance *"Do you want more coffee?"* thereby bringing about the action of *offering*, in turn (02) participant P2 produces the linguistic utterance *"Okay!"*, thereby bringing about the corresponding next action, which in this case is *accepting*, and by which a sequence [*offering-acceptance*] is completed (Fig. 8.3).

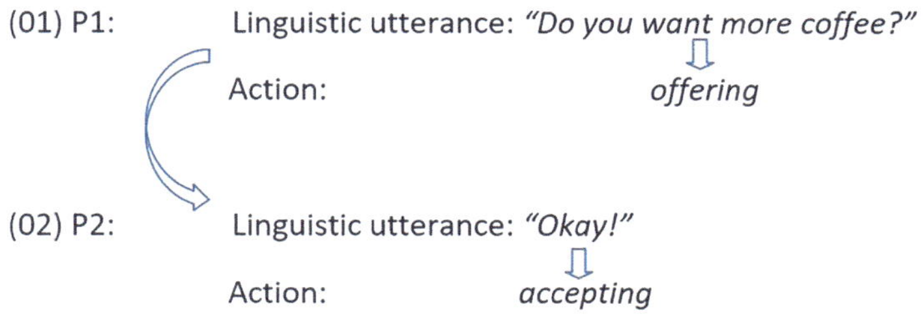

Fig. 8.3 Sequences (ii): [offering-acceptance]

Thus, the central tenet of CA is that talk-in-interaction is organized sequentially (Stivers, 2013). The basic unit of sequential organization is the so-called *adjacency pair*, a sequence like the ones we have just examined, where the first action is the First Pair Part (FPP) and the second action is the Second Pair Part (SPP). The FPP makes relevant the SPP. Therefore, when a participant produces an FPP of an adjacency pair, the next participant is normatively expected to produce the second one (Schegloff, 2007; Ten Have, 2007). In most adjacency pairs, like [*offerance-acceptance*], FPP and SPP are different, and there are usually two options for the SPP, one of which is the *preferred* one (which completes the sequence) and the other, the *dispreferred* one (Fig. 8.4).

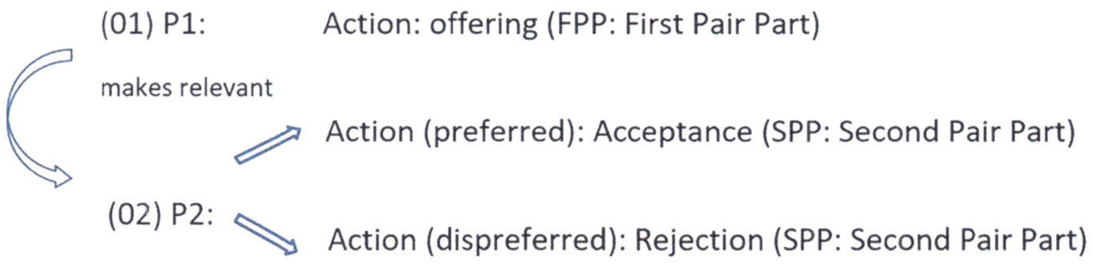

Fig. 8.4 Sequences (iii): Adjacency Pairs

During the last decades, CA has extensively studied *talk-in-interaction*, both informal, non-structured, and symmetrical verbal interactions (what we typically call "conversations") and verbal interactions in institutional settings, which involve institutional goals, themes, roles, and interactional patterns, such as a medical consultation or a job interview. A particular kind of institutional interaction that has attracted the attention of CA is *psychotherapy*. The application of CA to psychotherapy research is a field that has witnessed significant development lately, with a growing number of publications (Peräkylä, 2008, 2013; Buchholz & Kächele, 2013; Muntigl, 2020; Scarvaglieri, 2020; Guxholli et al., 2021; Peräkylä & Buchholz,

2021). The *International Conference on Conversation Analysis and Psychotherapy*, held every two years, gathers researchers in the field to share their data and investigations.

CA has identified two important sequences in psychotherapy interaction, triggered by two kinds of action that psychotherapists bring about: *formulations* and *interpretations* (Antaki, 2008). The goal of *formulations* is to express, usually in other words, contents from the patient's mental life that are already known to them. In the design of their turns, therapists display that the content is presented *from the patient's perspective*, through expressions like *"Maybe what you feel is..."* Sequentially, formulations by the therapist make it relevant for patients to produce a ratification or a denial (Antaki, 2008). The goal of *interpretations* is to put into words contents from the patient's mental life that are unknown to them. In the design of their turns, therapists display that the content is new and presented *from the therapist's perspective* through expressions like *"I think that..."* or *"I believe that...."* Sequentially, interpretations by the therapist make it relevant for patients to produce an agreement or acceptance and then a further elaboration, or a rejection (Bercelli et al., 2008; Peräkylä & Antaki, 2008; Peräkylä, 2013).

A central goal of CA in its application to psychotherapy research is to investigate how therapeutically relevant change takes place in and through action sequences (Peräkylä, 2019), which can be analyzed by applying a sequential model of psychotherapy interaction, consisting of a *Prior Action* (PA), an initiating *Target Action* (TA) (the focus of the analysis), a responding action or *Response* (RE), and a *Third Position Action* (TP), which closes the exchange (Peräkylä, 2019). Using this model, the CA researcher can take an interpretation of the therapist as a Target Action. Accordingly, the previous contribution of the patient would be the Prior Action, about which the interpretation has been offered by the therapist. The patient's reaction to it would be the Response. The sequence is closed by a Third Position Action by the therapist. For instance, if the Response of the patient has been an agreement with the interpretation and further elaboration of it, then in the Third Position the therapist can intersubjectively ratify their reciprocal agreement.

Finally, two important themes in CA psychotherapy research are *affiliation* and *alignment*. Affiliation refers to the display by the recipient that they support the affective stance of the speaker (Lindström & Sorjonen, 2013). Alignment is a feature of an interaction in which participants go along reciprocally with the direction that the other is proposing (Voutilainen et al., 2011). In psychotherapy interaction, it means the collaboration of participants to maintain actions and activities in therapy (Peräkylä & Buchholz, 2021).

Applying CA to Psychotherapy Process Research: The Sequential Unfolding of Two Moments of Meeting in Psychoanalytic Therapy Sessions

Next, we will present two examples of our research to illustrate how CA can be applied to examine in detail the interactional unfolding of two *moments of meeting* (Stern et al., 1998; Stern, 2004) in psychoanalytic therapy sessions.

Traditionally, changes in psychoanalytic therapy have been attributed to the self-knowledge (insight) in the patient, which is provided by the therapist's interpretations. However, there has been a growing realization in recent decades that changes can also result from developing new forms of relatedness (Mitchell, 1997) or ways of being with the other (Stern et al., 1998) through patient-therapist interaction. Those changes occur particularly in and through special intersubjective moments, in which mutuality is achieved through practices of "doing we" (Buchholz, 2022). Standing among such intersubjective moments are so-called *moments of meeting* (Stern, 2004), which resolve a challenge to the intersubjective relationship posed by so-called *now moments*. In our research, we use CA to examine how therapists can promote changes in their patients not primarily through the content of their interpretations but rather through interactional moves in significant intersubjective episodes like moments of meeting, which foster temporary but significant changes in the interactional pattern of the patient in the here-and-now of the session. We have applied Peräkylä's (2019) sequential model to analyze the interactional unfolding of two moments of meeting and the sequential transformations of the here-and-now relationship between patient and therapist that takes place in such moments, as manifested in changes in their interactional pattern. The data belong to three brief psychoanalytic therapies with female patients who were victims of domestic violence in Peru (in Spanish). The three psychotherapies were conducted by male therapists with training in psychoanalytic therapy, ages around 30–35. The psychotherapies comprised 12 sessions of Brief Dynamic Interpersonal Therapy (DIT). Only audio recording of the sessions was feasible[1].

Example 1: Luz—"ya pues hijita" [Come on, girl]

The patient, "Luz," is a 37-year-old migrant woman who lives in Lima in an economically precarious situation and who has been a victim of domestic violence. The episode belongs to the last session of the therapy and has been extensively analyzed in Herrera et al. (2023). Next, we will analyze two segments of this episode.

[1] This data has been taken from our research project Dialogic Moments of Meeting. An Application of Conversation Analysis to Sessions of Brief Psychoanalytic Psychotherapy, supported by a Grant of the Research Committee of the International Psychoanalytic Association in cooperation with the Pontifical Catholic University of Peru.

At the beginning of the episode, the therapist addresses the difficult issue of the imminent separation, pointing to the agency and autonomy of the patient as resources that should allow her to continue the work they have been doing together. Their interaction already is typical from most of the session up to this point: the therapist, who has the turn most of the time, talks to the patient in a rather didactic style and just gives weak signals of acknowledgment. Here, we recognize an implicit relational pattern, where the therapist has an active role while the patient remains passive, which is at odds with his explicit goal during the treatment, which is to foster the patient's agency and to change her passive attitude toward others. The relational pattern that the therapist is trying to change shapes their relationship in the here-and-now of the session, which is manifested in their interaction. Then comes the following segment (the lines belong to the whole extract of the episode) (Table 8.1):

Table 8.1 Segment 1 (Luz)

12		(7.4)
13	P:	ay .hh **ay [sighs]**
14		(5.2)
15		lo único que le pido a dios es quem (2.0) que me dé fuer£za **the only thing I ask god is that (2.0) that he gives me £strength**
16		.hh£ (2.2) °que no me suelte° **.hh£ (2.2) °that he doesn't let me go°**
17		(5.8)

Instead of affiliating with the stance of the therapist in his previous turn, after an expression of pain, the patient invokes in this segment the help of God as an external force, presenting herself in an extremely vulnerable position, which is at odds with the agency that he credits her with. This can be considered as a now moment, which represents a challenge to the intersubjective relationship (Stern, 2004). After this segment, to cope with this now moment, the therapist proposes an interpretation to the patient, telling her that despite her feelings of helplessness, she possesses strength. However, she is not aware of it. If the patient affiliates herself with this therapist's stance, we should have a moment of meeting to resolve the crisis created by the now moment. However, her answer is ambiguous, and the moment of meeting is not accomplished sequentially. Next comes the following segment (Table 8.2):

Here we have a second attempt by the therapist to achieve a moment of meeting, which this time is successful. We apply Peräkylä's (2019) sequential model to analyze its interactional unfolding. In our analysis, we identify two overlapping sequences that share the patient's turn (28) (Herrera et al., 2023). We lean on CA's proposal that every contribution in a conversation has both a reactive and an initiating aspect (Deppermann, 1999). Turn (28) is the Response RE in the first sequence in its reactive aspect and the Target Action (TA) in the second sequence in its initiating aspect.

Table 8.2 Segment 2 (Luz)

24	T:	a lo mejor Dios lo que tiene que decirle es (.) a↑cuérdate **may be God what he should tell you is (.) re↑member**
25		Luz que=ya=las tienes(.) yo no tengo [que] **Luz that=you=already got it (.) I don't have [to]**
26	P:	[°haha°]
27	T:	dártelas, **give it to you,**
28	P:	he o (.) £ya pues hijita,£= **or (.) £c'mon girl,£=**
29	T:	ya pues hij[ita] **c'mon [girl]**
30	P:	[hahaha ha:]

Sequential Analysis of the Moment of Meeting in Segment 2: First Sequence

The first sequence is triggered by the therapist's initiating Target Action TA in turn (24, 25, 27). The now moment in Segment 1 is the Previous Action PA for this sequence. Here, the therapist departs from the interaction style he has displayed so far in the session, playfully resorting to the figure of God, which was introduced by the patient in the now moment, and makes him convey to her the content of his previous interpretation. In so doing, the therapist is employing the practice of animation (Cantarutti, 2022), which introduces a moment of intense emotion, affiliation, and intimacy. The patient responds to this move with a laugh in (26), an expression of this different *way of being with her* by the therapist (Vásquez-Torres, 2021). Her Response RE in (28) is highly affiliative, but she does not limit herself to expressing her agreement with the stance of the therapist: she also animates God herself. Thereby, she turns the practice of animation of the therapist into a shared practice of co-animation (Cantarutti, 2022). Furthermore, in her co-animation she does not just repeat the words of the therapist but formulates it with other, more familiar words, conveying to herself a powerful message of encouragement: "¡Ya pues hijita!" ("c'mon, girl!"). In this way, she affiliates with the stance expressed by the therapist's interpretation.

In our opinion, the alignment between the complementary practices of animation by the therapist and co-animation by the patient leads to a moment of meeting. In the Third Position Action TP (29), the therapist repeats the patient's words "Ya pues hijita" ("c'mon, girl"). This practice of repetition reinforces the affiliation prompted by the therapist's animation in his initiating Target Action TA and the patient's co-animation in her Response RE. By echoing the patient's co-animation the therapist intersubjectively ratifies the moment of meeting in the Third Position TP, closing this first sequence (Herrera et al., 2023) (Table 8.3).

Table 8.3 Sequential Analysis of Segment 2 (Luz)– First Sequence

24TA	T:	a lo mejor Dios lo que tiene que decirle es (.) a↑cuérdate **may be God what he should tell you is (.) re↑member**
25		Luz que=ya=las tienes(.) yo no tengo [que] **Luz that=you=already got it (.) I don't have [to]**
26	P:	[°haha°]
27	T:	dártelas, **give it to you,**
28RE	P:	he o (.) £ya pues hijita,£= **or (.) £c'mon girl,£=**
29TP	T:	ya pues hij[ita] **c'mon [girl]**
30	P:	[hahaha ha:]

Sequential Analysis of the Moment of Meeting in Segment 2: Second Sequence

The second sequence is triggered by the initiating aspect of the patient's co-animation in (28), the Target Action TA. The Previous Action PA is the therapist's animation in (24,25,27), and the therapist's repetition of the patient's co-animation in (29) is the Response RE, which "meets" the initiating Target Action TA of the patient. This meeting of actions also leads to a moment of meeting. With her gleeful laugh in (30), the patient intersubjectively ratifies the moment of meeting in the Third Position, closing this second sequence (Herrera et al., 2023).

We conclude that in and through these two overlapping sequences, a moment of meeting emerges between therapist and patient. It is a moment characterized by "intersubjective fittedness" (Stern, 2004), where a significant connection takes place (Duarte et al., 2020) and "something fits," allowing a special understanding and complicity between them (Duarte et al., 2021). In this moment of meeting, therapist and patient successfully solve the challenge posed to the intersubjective relationship by the now moment.

Moreover, through the shared practice of co-animation, sequentially accomplished, a momentary yet significant change takes place in the relationship between patient and therapist in the here-and-now of the session: the patient moves away from her previously passive role and actively engages in the interaction, a shift that is acknowledged and affirmed by the therapist. The patient exercises her agency in interacting with the therapist in this sequence, embodying the essence of the therapist's interpretation that she possesses agency and strength in the here-and-now interaction between them. We are witness to a momentary change in the patient's way-of-being-with-another, or a transformation of relation, emerging in this sequence (Herrera et al., 2023). It has been pointed out that moments of meeting can potentially change the relationship between patient and therapist, enabling the transformation of the ways patients typically relate with others, providing changes in their implicit relational knowledge (Duarte et al., 2021). We claim that our analysis applying CA shows empirically how such a transformation can take place sequentially through the verbal interaction between patient and therapist (Table 8.4).

Table 8.4 Sequential analysis of segment 2 (Luz) - Second Sequence

24PA	T:	a lo mejor Dios lo que tiene que decirle es (.) a↑cuérdate **may be God what he should tell you is (.) re↑member**
25		Luz que=ya=las tienes(.) yo no tengo [que] **Luz that=you=already got it (.) I don't have [to]**
26	P:	[°haha°]
27	T:	dártelas, **give it to you,**
28TA	P:	he o (.) £ya pues hijita,£= **or (.) £c'mon girl,£=**
29RE	T:	ya pues hij[ita] **c'mon [girl]**
30TP	P:	[hahaha ha:]

Example 2: Muriel—"What does stability mean?"

The patient, "Muriel," is also a 35-year-old migrant woman who also lives in Lima in an economically precarious situation and who has a history of domestic and sexual violence. The episode belongs to the last part of the first session of the therapy. For our analysis, we have divided the transcript of this episode in seven segments (Table 8.5).

Table 8.5 Segment 1 (Muriel)

08	T:	[y me cuentas] que AHORA (.) también estás buscando **and you tell me that now you are also looking for**
09		algo para ti. **something for you**
10	P:	mhm,
11	T:	no? e:, (.) algo que tal vez sientes que puedes haber cómo: (.) e, **right? something that you perhaps feel that you**
12		no PODIDO (.) tener o::, o SER, digamos, °no?=° **could not have had or have been so to speak**

In this first segment at the beginning of this episode, the therapist points to the session's closing and that they will see each other again next week. Then, he poses a crucial question to the patient regarding what she seeks in therapy (8–12). This is a First Pair Part (FPP). Next comes a very significant segment (Table 8.6):

Table 8.6 Segment 2 (Muriel)

13_{PA}	P:	=no sé si estará correcta, la palabra lo que digo? o, a ver corríjame **I don't know if it is right, the word what I am saying? or you correct me**
14		usted?
15_{TA}	T:	>no, no,< dilo, **no no say it**
16_{RE}	P:	e:, Estabilida'. **stability**
17_{TP}	T:	estabilidad. **stability**

An important intersubjective moment occurs in this segment because the patient does not produce the corresponding Second Pair Part (SPP) immediately. Instead, she initiates in (13–14) what CA calls an "insert expansion," which explores a condition to bring forth the SPP (Schegloff, 2007; Stivers, 2013). In the FPP of this insert expansion, she asks the therapist emphatically to tell her if the word she will use is right (that word should describe what she is looking for herself). From an interactional viewpoint, with this move, the patient puts the therapist in a position of authority regarding the language she is going to use to speak about her mental state. Applying Peräkylä's sequential model, this turn of the patient is the Previous Action PA. From Stern's (2004) perspective, this Prior Action PA corresponds to a now moment because it contains a relational challenge for the therapist. In that regard, the next turn of the therapist in (15) is critical. He refuses to assume such a role in the SPP of the insert expansion. Instead, he returns to her the authority over the words she will use to refer to her mental states. This turn is the Target Action TA.

After this insert expansion is completed, the patient produces in (16) the SPP of the sequence initiated by the previous question of the therapist (the FPP). This turn comprises a single lexical unity, the word "estabilidad" (stability). This turn is the Response RE of the patient to the Target Action TA of the therapist: I accept and assume my authority over the words I use to speak about my mental state. In his next turn in (17), which is the Third Position TP of this sequence, the therapist repeats the word "estabilidad" (stability), ratifying the role of the patient. Despite the difference in the pronunciation, which is due to sociolinguistic factors, both "meet" in the use of that word. Through the repetition of the word, the therapist displays that this linguistic sign also belongs to his vocabulary, that both belong to the same linguistic community, that the way she uses that word follows the conventions of that community, and that she does not need his correction. We may say that through this repetition in (16–17), a moment of meeting takes place, which resolves the tension introduced by the now moment. By not assuming a role of authority regarding the language the patient is using to refer to her mental states and giving her that authority back, the therapist fosters a new form of relatedness, of being with the other, in which she passes from a position of dependence to a position of autonomy.

However, this transitory moment of meeting does not resolve definitively the now moment introduced by the patient in (13–14), which keeps on returning, as we will see in the next segments (Table 8.7).

Table 8.7 Segment 3 (Muriel)

18_{PA}	P:	está bien lo que digo? (.) que busco eso? **is it right what I am saying (.) that I am looking for that?**
19_{TA}	T:	si es lo que buscas, es lo que- cómo lo sientes, no? **if that is what you are looking for, it is what- how you feel it, right?**
20	P:	sí.= **yes**
21	T:	=iremos descubriendo: qué significa esa es[tabilidad para ti] **we are going to discover what that stability means for you**
22_{RE}	P:	[di ( ) de qué es] QUÉ **say (of what it is) what**
23		significa. [↑eso] es lo que justamente también QUISIERA QUE ME HAGAN **it means that is precisely what I want someone to do to me**
24_{TP}	T:	[aja,]

In (18) the patient asks again the therapist to ratify if what she has said is right, forcing him once more, and now with more intensity, to assume the role of authority he had refused to take in the previous sequence. It is a kind of "return" of the now moment, which reveals how difficult it is to change relational patterns. Applying the sequential model, this new patient turn corresponds to the Prior Action PA. In his next turn in (19), which is the Target Action TA, the therapist tries to cope with this return of the now moment. However, the design of his turn shows that he hesitates and changes his plan. The result is somehow incoherent. But he recovers, and in (21) he can convey the message that it is not his role to teach her the "correct" meaning of the term "stability," but that as a result of their cooperative work, they are going to find out together what that word means for her. In her next turn (22–23), the Response RE, the patient repeats the expression of the therapist, apparently ratifying his stance, and in (24), the therapist produces a feedback signal of agreement "ahá," the Third Position TP, which ratify their presumed intersubjective agreement, thereby closing this sequence (Table 8.8).

Table 8.8 Segment 4 (Muriel)

23_{PA}		significa. [↑eso] es lo que justamente también QUISIERA QUE ME HAGAN **it means that is precisely what I want someone to do to me**
24	T:	[aja,]
25	P:	entender- **understand**
26_{TA}	T:	mhm,
27	P:	qué es- qué es la estabilidad. **what is- what is stability**
28	T:	mhm,

The moment of meeting that would resolve the challenge of the now moment does not occur, because in (23–27) the patient repeats her request to the therapist that he should assume the position of authority and help her to understand the meaning of the word. This is a second coming-of-the-now moment and, from a sequential standpoint, a new Prior Action PA. But the therapist responds now using a different strategy. Instead of taking the turn, he stays in the position of hearer, producing a continuator in (26), which is the TA of a new sequence, and displaying thereby again to the patient that he is not willing to assume that role. The RE of the patient in turn (29–31) is noteworthy because she suddenly begins to describe what she wants, using the word "stability" in a competent way (Table 8.9):

Table 8.9 Segment 5 (Muriel)

29_{RE}	P:	o sea, quiero (.) una estabilidad (.) emocional, **I mean, I want an emotional stability**
30_{TP}	T:	mhm,
31	P:	y quiero una estabilidad económica que no tenga que: (.) depender **and I want a financial stability that I must not (.) depend**
32		de alguien más. **on someone else**
33	T:	mm,

If we consider Wittgenstein's proposal that the meaning of a word is its use, then the patient clearly displays in this turn that she "knows" the meaning of the word "stability." Through his continuators in (30 and 33) the therapist ratifies in the Third Position TP the authority of the patient to use that word to refer to her mental states, promoting a new way of relating with the other from a position of autonomy and agency. This can be considered a new moment of meeting that resolves the challenge of the second coming of the now moment.

Nevertheless, after having assumed temporarily that position of autonomy and agency, in her next turns, so to speak, a new "regression" to the former position of dependency takes place (Table 8.10).

Table 8.10 Segment 6 (Muriel)

34	P:	me entiende? **you understand me?**
35	T:	mhm,
36_{PA}	P:	£no sé, si estaré bien lo que estoy£ (.) lo que estoy diciendo? (.) **I don't know, if I am right what I am (.) what I am saying?**
37		po' eso le pido que me corrijas si es:- si es correcto o no. **that is why I ask you to correct me if it is- it is right or not**
38_{TA}	T:	está bien lo que estás diciendo si es lo que sientes, **what you are saying is right if that is what you are feeling,**
39	P:	sí, eso es lo que quiero. **yes, that is what I want.**
40	T:	[digamos aquí un] **let's say here a**
41_{RE}	P:	[O SEA NO QUIERO] SENTIRME (0.3) si el piso está acá, **I mean I don't want to feel (0.3) if the floor is here,**

The patient first (34) asks the therapist if he understands her, and then (36–37) she requests him again emphatically to take the role of authority and to confirm if she is correctly using that word. This turn, the Prior Action PA, represents a third return of the now moment. The next turn of the therapist in (38) is very significant in this sequential context. In a noteworthy move, the therapist finally accepts the role of authority. However, he uses this role to give back to the patient her authority regarding the language she uses to refer to her mental state. With a calm and confident voice, he tells her: "está bien lo que estás diciendo si es lo que sientes" (what you are saying is right if that is what you are feeling). The impact of this action on the therapist and the patient is significant. In her Response RE in (39), she ratifies emphatically and in a highly affiliative way that she agrees with the previous turn of the therapist: "sí, eso es lo que quiero" (yes, that is what I want). Moreover, from that moment on, she assumes an active role in the interaction, initiating a long turn, which begins in (41), where overlapping with the turn of the therapist in (40) occurs, interrupting him, and which goes until the end of the extract (Table 8.11):

Table 8.11 Segment 7 (Muriel)

42	T:	mhm,
43	P:	no quiero sentirme acá. **I don't want to feel myself here**
44	T:	ya, **yes**
45	P:	me entiende? quiero sentirme, en el piso. **you understand me? I want to feel, on the floor**
46	T:	mhm,
47	P:	bien parada. **standing right**
48	T:	mhm,
49	P:	y yo ahorita me siento como si estuviera este (.) caminando sobre **and I now feel as if I was walking upon**
50		huecos. **holes (on the ground)**
51	T:	ya. **yes**
(lines 52-56 omitted)		
57	P:	en cambio quisiera ser así, COMO UNA PARED, NO? QUE NO SE MUEVE. **instead of that I wish to be like a wall, yes? which doesn't move.**
58		FUERTE, **strong**
59	T:	mhm,
60$_{TA}$	P:	que está ahí: b↑ien este:, cómo se llama:? este:, es↑table, no? **which is there very how is the word stable yes?**
61$_{RE}$	T:	mhm,
62$_{TP}$	P:	eso es lo que quiero. más (.) °por mi hija°. **that is what I want specially because of my daughter**
63	T:	mm,
64	P:	o sea no me quiero derrumbar. (.) y trato de: (.) de: s- de salir, **I mean I don't want to crumble and I try to go out**

In this complex turn, the patient displays with confidence her authority over the words she uses to refer to her mental states and she even develops a very elaborate conceptual metaphor (Lakoff & Johnson, 1980, 1999): I feel like I were walking upon holes, but I want to feel that I am like a strong wall that does not crumble. During this long turn of the patient, the therapist only produces continuators, by which he ratifies in Third Position the authority of the patient over the words she uses to refer to her mental states, and, in this way, her autonomy and agency. Then in (60) she looks for a word to designate the mental state she has just described with the metaphor and picks precisely "stability," this time as an adjective ("stable"), adding a tag for ratification: "yes?". If we take the whole turn (60) as the Target Action TA of a new sequence, this time by the patient, then in his next turn (61), the Response RE, the therapist ratifies. This has a noteworthy consequence because in her next turn (62), the patient permits herself in the Third Position TP to finally answer, clearly and emphatically, the question posed by the therapist at the beginning of this episode: "That is what I want." This represents a significant step in the direction of self-affirmation and agency, an important goal of the therapy. Additionally, this complete segment can be considered as a new moment of meeting, which finally resolves the now moment.

The Contribution of CA to Qualitative Research of Psychotherapy Process

In the second part of this chapter, we have employed a sequential model (Peräkylä, 2019) to examine in detail the interactional unfolding of two moments of meeting to illustrate the application of CA as a qualitative method in psychotherapy research. We have shown how new forms of relatedness emerge sequentially in and through the interaction between patients and therapists in these moments of meeting. Such new ways of being with the other can be promoted by the therapist through the actions which are carried out by their verbal utterances and through the interactional sequences that these actions generate.

In this third and final part of this chapter, we will reflect, based on this analysis, on the particular contribution of CA to qualitative research of the psychotherapy process. We will take as a reference point another research in Latin America, which uses a different qualitative method to investigate a similar phenomenon. This is an interesting and valuable study on moments of meeting by Duarte et al. (2020) using the micro-phenomenological interview, which provides them access to subjective experiences of patients of moments of meeting in previous psychotherapy processes, as re-lived events they recall as moments of special emotional connection with their therapists. The researchers identified phases in such events, like the Syncopation Phase, which is described by the interviewees as a moment of misattunement with their therapists, and the Moment of Meeting Phase, described as a moment when this previous misattunement was resolved when the therapists did or said something which allowed them to reconnect and resynchronize with the patients.

If we compare this approach with our analysis applying CA to the interactional unfolding of the moments of meeting, it is difficult not to see in this illuminating account a description "from within" of what could have been the subjective experiences of the patients during these events. The different perspectives can be highlighted with a beautiful example of a moment of meeting provided by these researchers, in which the patient narrated a situation that made her furious, and about which first the therapist laughed, and then the patient laughed as well.

Applying some notions of CA, we will sketch a tentative analysis of the interactional sequence in that event, as it is reported by the patient in the micro-phenomenological interview. We write in italics the actions that the participants would carry out with their verbal utterances. First, the patient evokes that the laughter of the therapist first disoriented her and that noticing this, the therapist *apologized*: She noticed I was disoriented, and she said something like "I'm sorry, sorry for laughing." In her following turn, the patient seems to *accept this apology*: "and I said no, it's fine… it is actually very funny." The therapist then *repeats her apology* and *clarifies* that she was not laughing at the patient: she insisted, "Really, I'm sorry… I'm not laughing at you." The patient then explained that, due to this *clarification* from the therapist, she understood that she was not laughing at her but at the situation, which allowed her to recognize the funny element of that situation and to laugh about it as well: "so I started laughing too." It is at this point that the *shared laughter*, the "peak" of the moment of meeting, so to speak, emerges: "and we both laughed for a while" (Duarte et al., 2020, p. 62). From an interactional perspective, applying CA, we notice that this moment of meeting is brought about in and through a complex sequence involving both verbal and non-verbal actions by both participants.

In consequence, in addition to the more subjective "first person" account of the micro-phenomenological interview, CA provides us a "third person" account. If we had access to a detailed transcription of the audio and video recording of that segment of the session, we could examine step by step what actually occurs between patient and therapist and identify the interactional moves at the verbal and non-verbal level by which the moment of meeting is brought about. In that regard, we think that both perspectives can complement each other, with the common goal of contributing to the empirical research of a phenomenon which until now has mainly been theoretically described (Duarte et al., 2020).

Two additional findings of the application of CA to the interactional unfolding of the moments of meeting in our two examples are the following. First, it does not result from a single contribution by the therapist but emerges from an interaction to which both therapist and patient equally contribute. In that regard, it is co-created or co-constructed (Ugarte, 2019; Durand, 2023). Secondly, a noticeable feature of the sequence in our first example is the role of humor, laughter, and playfulness (Vásquez-Torres, 2021), which are significant ingredients and expressions of the transformation of relation that takes place in it (Herrera et al., 2023). Interestingly, both findings apply as well to the example by Duarte et al. (2020).

Finally, our analysis applying CA paves the way to a reappraisal of the role of language in intersubjective moments like moments of meeting. As we have pointed out in a previous publication (Herrera et al., 2023), Stern and the Boston Change Process Study Group (BCPSG) tend to assume that the relational moves that lead to a moment of meeting and the ensuing reorganization of the implicit relational knowing of the patient, changing their ways of being with others, take place mainly at an implicit level, which would be parallel to the exchange of language at the explicit level (Stern et al., 1998; Stern, 2004; Duarte et al., 2020, 2021). From that perspective, language is equated with the explicit, i.e., what is directly conveyed by the semantic content of the linguistic expressions, and therefore its role in psychotherapy is confined to conscious reflective work. Our results employing CA led to a more nuanced view of that issue because the sequences by which the two moments of meeting are brought about are made up of verbal utterances. Thus, in both examples:

> The moment of meeting (...) occurs not *in parallel* with the exchange of linguistic utterances between client and therapist. It occurs *through* the exchange of such linguistic utterances and *through* the sequence of actions carried out by that exchange. It does not result from a sequence of actions that takes place along with the words, but from a sequence of actions that are carried out through the words uttered by client and therapist in the exchange. (Herrera et al., 2023, p. 12)

As we have seen, sequences of actions carried out by the exchange of linguistic utterances also play a significant role in the beautiful example of a moment of meeting discussed in Duarte et al. (2020). Interestingly, these authors state in their article that:

> These emotions and sensations are produced by the therapist's move—something the therapist *says or does*—and have an impact that goes beyond words, as they feel these actions as bodily sensations. (Duarte et al., 2020, p. 62, our italics)

If we consider the key assumption of speech acts theory and CA that talk is acting, i.e., that every time a speaker produces a verbal utterance, they thereby perform an action, in describing the moves that lead to a moment of meeting, we should relativize the opposition between *saying* and *doing* because in some of these moves therapists and patients are *doing by saying*.

Finally, our study applying CA shows characteristic features of qualitative research of the psychotherapeutic process in Latin America, like the focus on relevant episodes and the practice of revealing microprocesses in the interaction between patient and therapist which can lead to change (Tomicic and Duarte, Book Preface) and can be relevant for practitioners in clinical settings, fostering a two-way dialogue between clinical practice and research (Altimir et al., 2022).

Appendix: Conversation Analysis Transcription Conventions (Jefferson, 2004; Raymond & Olguín, 2022; Herrera et al., 2023)

T, C:	Speaker identification. T: therapist, C: client.
re[mem]ber [word]	Onset and offset of overlapping talk
(.)	Pause less than 0.2 seconds
(2.6)	Timed pause
=	Latching: no gap between utterances
.	Falling final intonation

?	Rising final intonation
,	Slightly rising final intonation
_	Level final intonation
REMEMBER	Talk is louder than the surrounding talk
°remember°	Talk with lower volume than the surrounding talk
remember	stress or emphasis
>remember<	Faster-paced talk than the surrounding talk
<remember>	Slower-paced talk than the surrounding talk
reme:mber	Prolongation of the immediately preceding sound
remem-	abrupt cutoff
£remember£	smiley voice
#remember#	'creaky' voice
.hh	aspiration
hh	expiration
hehe, haha	laughter
((coughs))	non-verbal behavior

References

Altimir, C., Mantilla, C., & Serralta, F. (2022). Practice-based evidence: bridging the gap between research and routine clinical practice in diverse settings (Evidencia basada en la práctica: construyendo puentes entre la investigación y la clínica rutinaria en entornos diversos) *Studies in Psychology, 43*(3), 415–454. https://doi.org/10.1080/02109395.2022.2139998.

Antaki, C. (2008). Formulations in psychotherapy. In A. Peräkylä, C. Antaki, S. Vehviläinen, & I. Leudar (Eds.), *Conversation analysis and psychotherapy* (pp. 26–42). Cambridge University Press.

Austin, J. L. (1962). *How to do things with words*. University Press.

Bercelli, F., Rossano, F., & Viaro, M. (2008). Clients' responses to therapists' reinterpretations. In A. Peräkylä, C. Antaki, S. Vehviläinen, & I. Leudar (Eds.), *Conversation analysis and psychotherapy* (pp. 43–61). Cambridge University Press.

Buchholz, M. B. (2022). Strengthening the human bond: In psychotherapy, "doing We" is more important than intervention. In A. Dimitrijeviæ & M. B. Buchholz (Eds.), *From the abyss of loneliness to the bliss of solitude: Cultural, social and psychoanalytic perspectives*. Phoenix.

Buchholz, M. B., & Kächele, H. (2013). Conversation analysis: A powerful tool for psychoanalytic practice and psychotherapy research. *Language and Psychoanalysis, 2*(2), 4–30. https://doi.org/10.7565/landp.2013.004

Cantarutti, M. N. (2022). Co-Animation in troubles-talk. *Research on Language and Social Interaction, 55*(1), 37–58. https://doi.org/10.1080/08351813.2022.2026169

Deppermann, A. (1999). *Gespräche Analysieren: Eine Einführung in konversationsanalytische Methoden* [*Analyzing conversations: An introduction to conversation analysis methods.*]. Opladen: Leske + Budrich.

Duarte, J., Martínez, C., & Tomicic, A. (2020). Episodes of meeting in psychotherapy: An empirical exploration of patients' experiences of subjective change during their psychotherapy process. *Research in Psychotherapy: Psychopathology, Process and Outcome, 23*(1). https://doi.org/10.4081/ripppo.2020.440

Duarte, J., Martínez, C., & Tomicic, A. (2021). Sparks of psychotherapeutic change: How therapists understand moments of meetings' contribution to change in psychotherapy. *Psychotherapy Research*. https://doi.org/10.1080/10503307.2021.1948138

Durand, K. M. (2023). Desencuentros y reencuentros dialógicos: análisis de la conversación en dos sesiones de una psicoterapia psicoanalítica focal. Pontificia Universidad Católica del Perú. Unpublished.

Guxholli, A., Voutilainen, L., & Peräkylä, A. (2021). Safeguarding the therapeutic alliance: Managing disaffiliation in the course of work with psychotherapeutic projects. *Frontiers in Psychology, 11*, 139–157. https://doi.org/10.3389/fpsyg.2020.596972

Have, P. (2007). *Doing conversation analysis: A practical guide* (2nd ed.). Sage.

Herrera, M., Ugarte, A., Vásquez-Torres, G., Durand, K. M., & Sánchez, M. (2023). Doing-together with words: the sequential unfolding of a moment of meeting in a psychoanalytic therapy session. *Frontiers in Psychology, 14*, 1205500. https://doi.org/10.3389/fpsyg.2023.1205500

Hindelang, G. (1994). *Einführung in die Sprechakttheorie. [Introduction to speech act theory. Second edition]* (2nd ed.). Tübingen: Niemeyer.

Jefferson, G. (2004). Glossary of transcript symbols with an Introduction, in G. H. Lerner (ed.) *Conversation Analysis: Studies from the first generation*. Philadelphia: John Benjamins, 13–23.

Lakoff, G., & Johnson, M. (1980). *Metaphors we live by*. The University of Chicago Press.

Lakoff, G., & Johnson, M. (1999). *Philosophy in the flesh: The embodied mind and its challenge to western thought*. Basic Books.

Lindström, A., & Sorjonen, M. L. (2013). Affiliation in conversation. In J. Sidnell & T. Stivers (Eds.), *The handbook of conversation analysis* (pp. 350–369). Wiley-Blackwell.

Mitchell, S. (1997). *Influence and autonomy in psychoanalysis*. Routledge.

Muntigl, P. (2020). Managing distress over time in psychotherapy: Guiding the client in and through intense emotional work. *Frontiers in Psychology, 10*, 3052. https://doi.org/10.3389/fpsyg.2019.03052

Peräkylä, A. (2008). Conversation analysis and psychoanalysis: Interpretation, affect and intersubjectivity. In A. Peräkylä, C. Antaki, S. Vehviläinen, & I. Leudar (Eds.), *Conversation analysis and psychotherapy* (pp. 100–119). Cambridge University Press.

Peräkylä, A. (2013). Conversation analysis in Psychotherapy. In J. Sidnell & T. Stivers (Eds.), *The handbook of conversation analysis* (pp. 551–574). Wiley-Blackwell.

Peräkylä, A. (2019). Conversation analysis and psychotherapy: Identifying transformative sequences. *Research on Language and Social Interaction, 52*(3), 257–280. https://doi.org/10.1080/08351813.2019.1631044

Peräkylä, A., & Antaki, C. (2008). A review of the conversational practices of psychotherapy. In A. Peräkylä, C. Antaki, S. Vehviläinen, & I. Leudar (Eds.), *Conversation analysis and psychotherapy* (pp. 188–197). Cambridge University Press.

Peräkylä, A., & Buchholz, M. B. (2021). Editorial: Talking and cure – What's really going on in psychotherapy. *Frontiers in Psychology, 12*, 4–5. https://doi.org/10.3389/fpsyg.2021.693300

Raymond, C. W., & Olguín, L. M. (2022). *Análisis de la Conversación: fundamentos, metodología y alcances* [*Conversation Analysis: foundations, methodology and scope*]. Routledge.

Scarvaglieri, C. (2020). First encounters in psychotherapy: Relationship-building and the persuit of institutional goals. *Frontiers in Psychology, 11*, 585038. https://doi.org/10.3389/fpsyg.2020.585038

Schegloff, E. A. (2007). *Sequence organization in interaction: A primer in conversation analysis*. Cambridge University Press.

Stern, D. (2004). *The present moment in psychotherapy and everyday life*. W W Norton & Co.

Stern, D., Sander, L., Nahum, J., Harrison, A., Lyons-Ruth, K., Morgan, A., Bruschweiler-Stern, N., & Tronick, E. (1998). Non-interpretive mechanisms in psychoanalytic therapy: The 'something more' than interpretation. *The Process of Change Study Group. International Journal of Psycho-Analysis, 79*(5), 903–921.

Stivers, T. (2013). Sequence organization. In J. Sidnell & T. Stivers (Eds.), *The handbook of conversation analysis* (pp. 191–209). Wiley-Blackwell.

Ugarte, A. (2019). *La co-construcción de los momentos de cambio: una aplicación del análisis del diálogo a la sesión final de un proceso de psicoterapia psicoanalítica focal* [*The co-construction of moments of change: an application of dialogue analysis to the final session of a focal psychoanalytic psychotherapy process*]. Pontificia Universidad Católica del Perú. Unpublished.

Vásquez-Torres, G. (2021). *La risa en la interacción psicoterapéutica: un análisis de la risa en sesiones finales de procesos psicoterapia psicoanalítica focal desde la perspectiva del análisis de la conversación* [*Laughter in psychotherapeutic interaction: an analysis of laughter in final sessions of focal psychoanalytic psychotherapy processes from the perspective of conversation analysis*]. Pontificia Universidad Católica del Perú. Unpublished

Voutilainen, L., Peräkylä, A., & Ruusuvuori, J. (2011). Therapeutic change in interaction: Conversation analysis of a transforming sequence. *Psychotherapy Research, 21*, 348–365.

Willig, C., & Stainton-Rogers, W. (Eds.). (2008). *The sage handbook of qualitative research in psychology*. Sage Publications.

Chapter 9
Non-participant Observation as a Method of Data Collection Within Psychotherapeutic Sessions

Nelson Valdés Sánchez

Once the effectiveness of psychotherapy was demonstrated in terms of the nature, magnitude, and generalization of its effects, as well as the homogeneous effect among different therapeutic modalities in relation to said effectiveness, the need to develop more pertinent methodologies to more precisely estimate how psychotherapeutic change is constructed also became apparent. Taking on this challenge has led to the development of numerous studies that have emphasized the analysis of the interaction between patients and therapists, as well as the internal and external factors responsible for change, which are also transversal to the different therapeutic modalities.

Precisely this process perspective is what has allowed us to understand psychotherapeutic change as the result of a series of moments in which different meanings are transformed, placing it in the representational sphere. In other words, this change is related to the subjective view the patient has of themselves, their problems and symptoms, and how these relate to the environment in which they occur (Krause et al., 2007). This construction of new subjective theories is carried out through connections that are gradually co-constructed through associations facilitated during therapeutic conversation as a result of a successive process of resignification. During specific moments of the therapeutic process, it has been possible to identify sessions that, based on certain criteria, stand out as significant, striking, or relevant. These moments have been termed moments of insight (Elliott, 1984), of encounter (Stern, 2004; Stern et al., 1998), of empowerment (Timulak & Elliott, 2003), of innovation (Gonçalves et al., 2009; Gonçalves et al., 2012; Gonçalves & Peri, 2024; Magalhães et al., 2022), and of change (Krause et al., 2006).

N. V. Sánchez (✉)
Psychology Department, Universidad Santo Tomás, Santiago, Chile

Millennium Institute for the Study of Depression and Personality (MIDAP), Santiago, Chile
e-mail: nvaldes7@santotomas.cl

A. Tomicic, J. D. Soto (eds.), *Qualitative Research in Clinical Psychology and Psychotherapy in Latin America*, https://doi.org/10.1007/978-3-031-90782-1_9

Regardless of the terminology used, these moments mark the end of episodes within a single session or many sessions, in which changes that are clinically significant for the patient become evident (Bastine et al., 1989). Today it is known that this change, and the elements that facilitate it, can be micro-analytically observed in therapeutic communication during these episodes that serve as windows into the sessions and therapy (Boisvert & Faust, 2003; Elliott et al., 2001; Elliott & Shapiro, 1992; Krause et al., 2007; Llewelyn & Hardy, 2001; Orlinsky et al., 2004; Wallerstein, 2001). However, for a long time, this dimension received less attention compared to studies on the effectiveness of treatments (Asay & Lambert, 1999; Messer & Wampold, 2002; Wampold, 2005; Wampold et al., 2001) and studies about the therapeutic alliance (Baier et al., 2020; Horvath, 2018; Hubble et al., 1999; Krause, 2005; Krause et al., 2011; Maione & Chenail, 1999; Tschuschke et al., 2022; Wolf et al., 2022). Initially, it was premature to conclude that certain interventions associated with specific therapeutic models were not the main drivers of patient changes (Lambert & Barley, 2001; Wampold & Brown, 2005); however, evidence gradually demonstrated that the construction of a generic patient change occurred through therapeutic actions that are not specific to particular schools.

The above led to a growing interest in studying the process through which verbal interaction is configured during therapeutic conversation. Evidence suggests that successful therapies are distinguished by certain verbal and non-verbal exchanges between patients and therapists (Jones, 2000; Karlsson & Kermott, 2006; Pennebaker et al., 2003; Valdés, 2012), and that, during therapeutic activity, these verbal expressions take the form of communication patterns that allow coordination of communication with themselves and with the other during the conversation (Valdés et al., 2012). These patterns have allowed the characterization of verbalizations throughout the psychotherapeutic process, as well as the differentiation of the types of actions performed during certain episodes of the session (Valdés, 2012). It is known, for example, that the types of words used in conversation reflect the way in which some psychological processes are structured (Chung & Pennebaker, 2019; Lepore & Smyth, 2002; Niederhoffer & Pennebaker, 2002; Pennebaker, 1997; Stiles, 1992), which has even allowed the development of certain studies that correlate the above with a person's mental and/or physical health.

The main conclusions about the complexity of the entire series of processes involved in therapeutic interaction have made clear the need to study these processes using different levels of analysis that allow for a greater understanding of them, as well as the need for new research methodologies to systematically analyze what occurs within sessions (Hageman & Arrindell, 1999; Hill, 1990; Hill et al., 1992; Mahrer & Boulet, 1999; Stiles et al., 1990; Valdés, 2010; Valdés et al., 2005; Valdés et al., 2010; Valdés et al., 2011; Williams & Hill, 2001). For example, sessions have been analyzed to identify the main similarities and differences between the sessions considered by the dyad as clinically significant, in contrast to those less significant (Altimir et al., 2010), to describe the sequence of relevant segments throughout the process (Bastine et al., 1989; Fitzpatrick et al., 2006; Goldfried et al., 1998; Marmar, 1990; Vanaerschot & Lietaer, 2007), to determine the facilitators or obstacles to patient change (Russell et al., 2007), and to identify therapeutic cycles subject to a cyclical progression of emotional tone and level of abstraction in temporal sequences (Fontao & Mergenthaler, 2008; Mergenthaler, 1996, 2000). In that sense, therapeutic conversation is a scenario where a particular subjectivity occurs (Izard, 2002), which has increasingly sparked interest in observing the verbal and non-verbal interaction between patients and therapists during the session (Chatoor & Krupnick, 2001; Conte et al., 1990; Crits-Christoph & Gibbons, 2021; Hill, 1990; Hubble et al., 1999; Luborsky, 2000; Stiles et al., 2015; Valdés, 2010, 2012; Valdés et al., 2010; Valdés et al., 2011; Valdés et al., 2012; Valdés & Krause, 2015; Williams & Hill, 2001), generating new theoretical foundations that explain the structure of this type of interpersonal relationship.

Table 9.1 shows some of the classification systems developed up to the year 2010, which allowed for the description of different therapeutic interventions. Some focused solely on the verbalizations of therapists, while other systems also considered the verbalizations of patients. Moreover, some systems were constructed in light of specific therapeutic approaches or particular therapeutic issues. Over the years, some self-report instruments also emerged that allow for the evaluation of the use of different techniques during the session from the perspective of patients, therapists, and trained observers, such as: the Comparative Psychotherapy Process Scale (Hilsenroth et al., 2005), the Multitheoretical List of Therapeutic Interventions (McCarthy & Barber, 2009), and the Helping Skills Measure (Hill & Kellems, 2002). The main advantage of these instruments is the ability to collect a lot of information in less time; however, since they are retrospective evaluations of what happened during the session, the positive or negative inferences could be based on a general impression of the session, so the uncertainty is greater due to the lack of sufficient data for evaluation. Now, while all classification systems are useful for describing psychotherapeutic conversation, it was still necessary to have a single system that was also generic when describing the verbalizations of the dyad that facilitate psychotherapeutic change.

Therefore, it was necessary to develop new methodologies that would allow for the description, with maximum precision, of what occurs between patients and therapists, communicatively speaking. In that sense, this chapter does not seek to propose data production techniques different from those already known (interviews and observations), but to describe how some of these techniques were used within the framework of novel methodological designs.

Naturalistic Observation of Psychotherapeutic Sessions

Observation has been employed by social scientists over the last century as one of the techniques par excellence for data production (Madden, 2010; McKechnie, 2008). Its main utility lies in facilitating the understanding of situations that are complex to study, as human behavior, being both conscious and unconscious, is often susceptible to biases when attempting to study it through interviews or surveys that end up limiting the information to what can or wants to be shared. It is

Table 9.1 Therapeutic dialogue classification systems (Valdés et al., 2010)

Classification systems	Categories	Actor	Therapeutic model	Problematic
Counselor Verbal Response Category System (Hill, 1978, 2020)	Closed and open questions, information, guidance, reformulation, reflection, non-verbal reference, interpretation, self-disclosure, evaluation-reinforcement, confrontation, and encouragement	Therapists	–	–
Verbal Response Modes (Shaikh et al., 2001; Stiles, 1979; Stiles, 1992)	Disclosure, information, advice, confirmation, question, acknowledgment, interpretation, and reflection	Therapists	–	–
Friedlander (1982)	Approval, information, guidance, open questions, closed questions, paraphrasing, interpretation, confrontation, and free association	Therapists	–	–
Conversational Therapy Rating System (Goldberg et al., 1984)	Closed, open, and understanding questions; process definition; information-explanation; topic definition; general instructions; advice, re-expression; understanding hypotheses; and therapist-specific	Therapists	–	–
Elliott (1984)	Question, information, advice, reflection, interpretation, and self-disclosure	Therapists	–	–
Collaborative Study Psychotherapy Rating Scale (Evans et al., 1984)	Therapist actions to achieve treatment adherence, explicit directive actions, and facilitating methods and conditions	Therapists	–	Depression
Taxonomy of Procedures and Operations in Psychotherapy (Mahrer et al., 1988)	35 categories, for example: Simple clarifications, agreements or disagreements, general structuring, problem identification, reflection, patient explanation, and simple responses	Therapists	–	–

(continued)

Table 9.1 (continued)

Classification systems	Categories	Actor	Therapeutic model	Problematic
Psychotherapy Process Q-Set (Jones et al., 1991)	Attitudes, behaviors, and experiences of the patient; attitudes and therapist behaviors; and nature of the interaction	Therapists and patients	–	–
Wiser and Goldfried (1996)	Question, reflection, interpretation, and advice	Therapists	–	–
Cognitive Elaboration Rating Scale (Connolly et al., 1998)	Past or present experiences, emotions, or thoughts, and new or developing experiences, emotions, or thoughts	Therapists and patients	–	–
Comprehensive Psychotherapeutic Interventions Rating Scale (Trijsburg et al., 2004)	Facilitating interventions, experiential interventions, psychodynamic interventions, directive behavioral interventions, cognitive interventions, group psychodynamic interventions, and systemic interventions	Therapists	Generic/ integrative	–
Watzke et al. (2006)	Interpretation, confrontation, cognitive interventions, behavioral interventions, directive interventions, and focusing	Therapists	–	–
Etchebarne et al. (2008)	Specific interventions, non-specific interventions, and common interventions	Therapists	Psychodynamic, cognitive, and interpersonal	–

always complex to analyze only a part of reality due to the multifaceted nature of the different aspects of everyday life, from the most convenient initial delimitation of what is to be studied to the oral and/or written dissemination of the main findings, as well as considering a series of intermediate stages, such as: choosing the most suitable procedures for making observations that allow for the identification of as many elements as possible; organizing the data produced, recorded, and stored for subsequent analysis; ensuring quality procedures throughout the research; the different possibilities for data analysis and interpretation; and meeting the criteria of rigor. Therefore, the only way to efficiently use this technique is by taking the necessary actions to carry out observations that fully exploit all the capabilities required to make sense of that part of the social reality studied (Atkinson, 2015).

In general, it is known that qualitative observation has several key characteristics that distinguish it (Creswell, 2016; Taylor et al., 2016): (a) it places special emphasis on the subjective experience of people and on the subjective interpretation of the recorded information, recognizing the different perspectives when explaining a phenomenon; (b) it highlights the importance of contextual elements that explain or are associated with the behaviors studied; (c) it facilitates a holistic understanding of phenomena by studying the interrelationships between different emerging aspects; (d) it ensures greater flexibility of designs, adjusting methods and approaches based on the findings themselves; (e) it has an inductive logic that enables the generation of new hypotheses and theories from the findings, not only considering pre-existing information; and (f) it is often descriptive in attempting to capture the detailed richness of the data, but also in trying to explain the complexity of human behavior and social phenomena. Now, in an attempt to be more specific, the observation of therapeutic sessions is a partly naturalistic instance because it allows identifying certain verbal and non-verbal actions in the environment in which these actions typically occur. This type of observation conducted in real or natural settings would present the following advantages in practice: (a) it guarantees greater ecological validity since there are no major artificial interferences as appear in experimental situations, where patients and therapists gradually tend to behave more closely to real conditions; (b) it allows identifying much more information than could be produced through other methods, ensuring greater precision and depth in understanding; (c) it enables adaptation to changing situations in real-time by flexibly adjusting designs according to the needs of the observed environment; (d) it allows discovering novel and unexpected findings by not observing environments that are intentionally controlled; (e) it facilitates the production of data without affecting the well-being of the observed subjects, as the therapist will safeguard this principle at all times and there will be no intentional manipulation by the researcher, which is favorable from the ethical considerations' standpoint; and (f) it is possible to enrich the findings when complemented with other data production/collection strategies. At the same time, these naturalistic observations are also of a participant type (Fine, 2015), as both patients and therapists know they are being studied within the framework of a research study. Orlinsky and his collaborators (2015) clarified it that when observing, there are multiple perspectives of the same event, and therefore, when observing social interactions during psychotherapy sessions, it is always more convenient to consider the perspectives of the therapeutic dyad in their role as observer-participants, while the perspective of the researchers should be considered in their role as observer-non-participants. However, it is also true that these are observations in which researchers also implicitly participate in the studied situation (since they do not do so actively, but the observations are made from a distance), either from the videos of the sessions or through the one-way mirror (asynchronously or synchronously, respectively) (Corbetta, 2003). Both patients and therapists know they are being studied, not only because it is a requirement from a pragmatic and ethical standpoint to inform them that they are participating in a research study (Yager & Lee, 2023), but also because the success of the observation depends on the interactions occurring based on a social relationship marked by specific roles, which, in the case of those observing, implies presenting themselves as the research team in charge to communicate the research objectives, the procedures to follow, and the confidential use of the obtained information, among others. It is supremely important that the observed individuals can identify the researcher in their role as observer, regardless of whether they can perceive them during the observation, as occasionally the cameras are visible to the patients, and in other cases, they are not. On one hand, therapists and patients will be able to perceive firsthand the experience of the therapeutic activity carried out through verbal and non-verbal interaction, which implies that both will have greater or lesser awareness of their own and the other's thoughts, affects, and behaviors; and on the other hand, the observers will only be able to infer the internal states of the observed individuals without the possibility of interacting, thus respecting the inherent structure of the therapeutic situation (it will also be possible to watch the video of the observed situation as many times as necessary, pausing, rewinding, and/or fast-forwarding the video). Therefore, the result of the observation will always be the production of information with personal and social meaning (Moeran, 2009), in the sense that there are observers who will watch and listen to what happens during the session, while the dyad will interact during the session based on the degree of relationship between them, but also based on how much they feel interfered with by the implicit presence of those observing. From the positivist paradigm, this could be perceived as a methodological weakness due to discrepancies between the perspectives of the observed and the observers. However, these discrepancies are precisely a reflection of how complex it is to study and analyze social interactions, and as such, they must be recorded. As shown in Fig. 9.1, during the observation of therapeutic sessions, meanings circulate vertically (between patient and therapist) and horizontally (from the dyad to those observing). In this complex scenario, the important thing is that each one knows what their role implies: (a) patients and therapists must recognize themselves as informants, as they are the source of data that will be recorded, organized, coded, and interpreted later by the research team, and (b) the impossibility of the observers to interact communicatively with the dyad during the session is explicit, which marks a necessary epistemological distance between observers and those being studied as the object of study, since ethically it is not possible to conduct covert observations (Yager & Lee, 2023).

The production of information is carried out through the verbal interaction between the informants (patient and therapist), making it possible to access the internal states of both (subjectivity) and between both (intersubjectivity), by verbalizing contents that are part of the realm of ideas, affections, and behaviors worked on during therapy. And saying this already goes against the positivist principles related to the need for objectivity and epistemological distance between observers and their object of study, but it also breaks with the reductionist ideas that assume that said object of study is given in an absolute, concrete, and immediate form in reality. On the contrary, said object of study is the result of complex co-construction processes, in which the people who observe are also an important part, as they manage to holistically integrate the emerging theoretical foundations during the analyses. As Bourdieu (2001, 2012) states, the discursive skill of theory is useless if it is not applied to the specific reality from which it also arises, so it would end up being an empty theory without research or blind empirical research without theory.

It is expected that the observers can establish such an implicative relationship with their object of study that they manage to place themselves in the perspective of

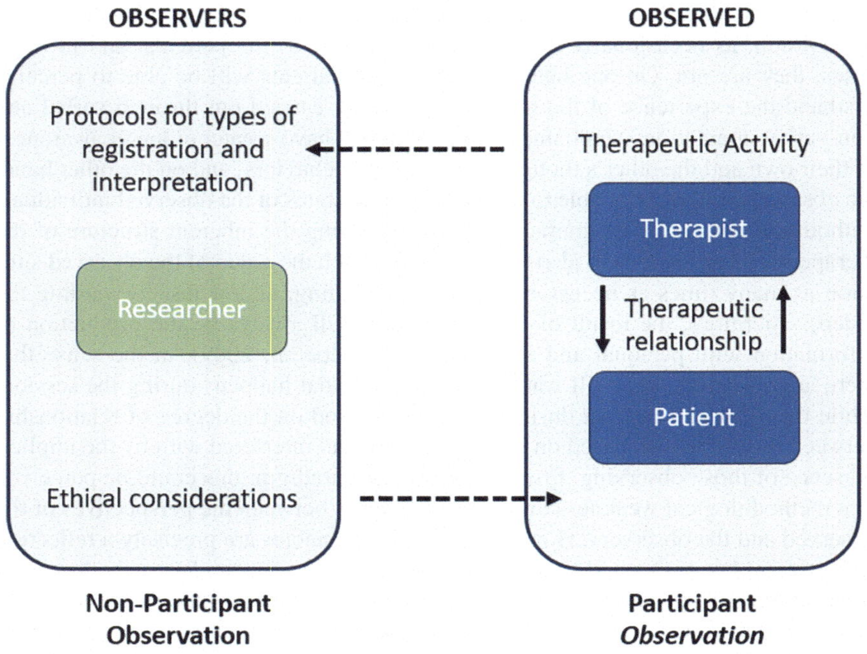

Fig. 9.1 Logical structure of the observed–observers situation

the observed; that is, the subjectivity of the observers is also implicated when interpreting the produced data. This position can be imagined as a continuum that ranges from the most open, warm, and personal in the case of the dyad (emic perspective) to a more neutral, closed, and impersonal position in the case of the observers (etic perspective), who are those who adhere to the rigorous and systematic procedures of research designs. There is evidence that having this dual perspective contributes to the development of a more integrated theory (Galperin et al., 2022; Woodside et al., 2012; Zhu & Hildebrandt, 2013) and compensates for some biases through the triangulation of the produced information.

The central point is to consider the observation of the session through the one-way mirror as a form of observation that starts as a participant but, as time goes by, *increasingly takes the form of a non-participant observation* (Blevins, 2017). In fact, one of the problems with this type of naturalistic observation is the *reactivity* of the observed people, as their behavior may be influenced by the explicit and/or implicit presence of the observers. It could happen that the dyad, knowing they are being observed and studied, initially acts somewhat differently than they would normally; however, it is also known that they end up getting used to or habituating to the situation, and over time they begin to show themselves more naturally to the eyes of the observers. Dahlberg (2006) also refers to the existence of a *surplus of meaning*, as observing simultaneously perceives a series of emotions, desires, and intentions through their verbal and non-verbal expressions, so the investigated phenomenon is never experienced in isolation, but in a much broader context. Therefore, the observation of therapeutic sessions is partially hybrid for the dyad, as it starts being very explicit about being studied, but gradually the social relationship with the observers becomes more implicit, natural, and habitual; while for the observers, it will always remain an explicit process adhering to the procedures established by the research. Thus, the degree to which an observation is more participant or non-participant will depend on the degree of rigidity or flexibility of the procedures that regulate the interaction between the observed and the observers.

It should not be forgotten that there is a power relationship for the therapist with their patient, and now both are also in a power relationship regarding the observers (Hockey & Forsey, 2020). The dyad could perceive themselves in a position of inferiority, activating a sense of alertness to possible risks to their safety or privacy. However, it is expected that this bias is susceptible to control through the interaction or familiarization of the dyad, as the therapist, in their emic position, is the one who defines and ensures the maintenance of the structure of the therapeutic relationship. The above implies being able to create the conditions that facilitate the deployment of verbal and non-verbal actions in their most natural form possible, meaning that there is no attempt to either please or sabotage the dense, deep, and emically valid production of information during observation.

Therefore, the observation of therapeutic sessions should be understood as a continuum that goes from a participant position to a non-participant one, and according to Seim (2024), there would be two forms of observation from the perspective of the observers:

(a) The first would be an *active observation* characterized by being a formal, impersonal, and distant relationship between the observed and the observers, in which there is no protocol for interaction beyond presenting themselves as researchers. This form of observation is closer to the non-participant type, as it places the observers in an external, passive, and limited position in front of the observed; however, the difference lies in the fact that all the protagonists explicitly and mutually recognize their respective roles. Additionally, this form of observation can be discreet or visible to the observed people (e.g., knowing that there is someone on the other side of the one-way mirror or having visible cameras within the session), or it can be indiscreet or invisible when neither the observers nor the recording conditions manage to be perceived by the observed. In this last case, it would be a full non-participant observation, which is not the case in observations of psychotherapeutic sessions, as there is from the first moment a social bond between observers and observed, no matter how minimal it may be.
(b) The second would be an *implicated observation* in which there is a relationship between the observed and the observers that varies in intensity depending on the degree of communicational involvement between both, which gives the observers a more active role within the scenario but with enough distance to avoid developing a personal relationship (e.g., observers who also apply instruments before or after each session, or at different moments of the therapy).

On the other hand, from the perspective of the therapeutic dyad, there are also two ways to observe during the therapeutic activity:

(c) An *observing-participation* by the therapist and the patient, which in the best case is characterized by being a relationship with a high level of involvement—reliable, close, and fluid—with full freedom to interact verbally and non-verbally during the session, respecting the structure of the therapy.
(d) A *permanent self-observation* carried out by each member of the dyad during the session, as both observe themselves at all times, in addition to observing the other present.

In this sense, it would be possible to obtain information from the observation of therapeutic sessions considering the following three sources: (a) verbal expressions of patients and therapists generally recorded in audio form; (b) non-verbal expressions of both recorded in audio form (e.g., rhythm, tone, volume, etc.) and video (e.g., facial expressions, posture, gaze, etc.); and (c) recording the context of the session (e.g., notes). This last point is very important, as regardless of whether the information is recorded in audio and/or video, the observers must note their theoretical or methodological reflections about the observed phenomenon, as well as their impressions and attitudes toward certain circumstances during the session, which will be basic data for subsequent analyses (Guest et al., 2013). It should not be forgotten that the interpretation of the data not only depends on the conditions in which the observation is made but also to a large extent on the characteristics of the observers. Therefore, it is necessary to integrate the record made by each of the observers to triangulate perspectives and reach an intersubjective consensus (Klinke & Fernandez, 2023).

The Challenge of Developing a New Classification System

As mentioned at the beginning of the chapter, despite the existence of some classification systems, it remained a challenge to have a unique and generic system to logically and in detail describe the verbal actions *of patients and therapists separately*, but also *between both*, to explain the process of constructing psychotherapeutic change. To face this complex task, the existence of a performative notion was made clear, which understands language as a constitutive element of reality and not merely a reflection of it. That is, when any member of the dyad *says* something, they are also *doing* something (Krause et al., 2006; Reyes et al., 2008; Searle, 1969, 1979; Valdés et al., 2010), which allows them to be permanently configuring new realities throughout the therapy. Thus, language is not only a vehicle for the communication of content by the speaker but also a means of performing actions that mutually influence each other during the therapeutic activity.

For the construction of a new classification system, it was decided to use a qualitative methodology based on an exploratory-descriptive design (Krause, 2005; Lutz & Knox, 2014), through procedures of review, discussion, and validation of the analyses by intersubjective agreements among the members of the research team. The sample unit was episodes of change, understood as being associated with successful outcomes (Hill, 1990, 2005; Krause, 2005; Krause et al., 2006; Mergenthaler, 2000), and which are also reliably identified by patients, therapists, and observers (Helmeke & Sprenkle, 2000; Hill, 1990).

Using episodes instead of the complete session already implied at least two methodological advantages: (a) relevant episodes were selected using an empirically validated procedure (Echávarri et al., 2009; Krause et al., 2006; Krause et al., 2007; Reyes et al., 2008; Valdés et al., 2005); and (b) by using relevant episodes, the problem of having an excess of information resulting from the microanalysis of verbal communication during the session was resolved. Therefore, a theoretical and practical sense was implicitly and simultaneously assigned to the procedure of sample selection through the decision to opt for the analysis of episodes of change (Elliot et al., 1987; Krause, 2005).

The system was developed from the analysis of 69 episodes of change identified in a total of five therapies of different approaches and modalities (see Table 9.2), which were conducted by five therapists (1 woman and 4 men) with experience ranging from 10 to 30 years of professional practice. Explicit authorization was obtained from patients and therapists to observe and videotape the sessions through one-way mirrors. Successful therapies were chosen based on the Reliable Change Index reported by patients in the OQ-45.2 questionnaire (Lambert et al., 1996), in its adapted and validated version for the Chilean population (from the de la Parra et al., 2002). The questionnaires were administered by the therapists at the beginning and at the end of the therapeutic process.

Observation of the sessions for the identification of change episodes was carried out in two successive stages:

(a) The sessions were observed by two therapists who were completing their Master's degree in Clinical Psychology, who presented themselves as researchers, explained the objectives and procedures of the observation, and requested the signing of the Informed Consent from patients and therapists, this being the only limited form of involvement (active observation). These observers were also responsible for videotaping each session through the one-way mirror and for preliminarily identifying the change episodes based on the established procedures (Chilean Program of Research in Psychotherapy and Change, 2012) to observe and delimit the change episodes (Echávarri et al., 2009; Krause et al., 2006). All sessions were transcribed following the norms of Mergenthaler and Stinson (1992), regardless of whether there were change episodes or not.
(b) The same sessions in which change episodes were identified were observed again, now by the entire research team, to reach a consensus that they met the required criteria. Videotapes and transcriptions were used, allowing the video to be paused, forwarded, or rewound as many times as necessary, along with reading the text (Guest et al., 2013). Another important result of this stage was the empirical delimitation of the episodes, tracing the interactions before the moments of change. For this, a thematic criterion was established so that the

Table 9.2 Characteristics of the therapeutic processes selected for analysis

Therapy no.	Therapeutic approach	Therapeutic modality	Gender	Age	Occupation	Marital status	Focus of therapy	Change episodes
I	Psychodynamic	Individual	F	29	Medical technologist	Married	Reduction of anxiety as a result of separation; strengthening of autonomy; and promoting the expression of emotional needs	10
II	Psychodynamic	Individual	F	38	Teacher	Separated	Grieving process for separation and recent losses	14
III	Social Constructionist	Family	F	38	Saleswoman	Separated	Conflict resolution between mother and son, and between the parents	12
IV	Cognitive-behavioral (substance abuse)	Group	M M M M M M	19 23 32 34 36 53	Student unemployed Doctor Salesman IT technician Professor	Single Single Single Married Married Married	Recognition of the existence of the addiction problem; strengthening the ability to set boundaries; identification of risk situations	9
V	Psychodynamic	Individual	F	43	School director	Married	Expression of needs; strengthening of autonomy; improving the quality of interpersonal relationships	

beginning of each episode was marked by the start of work on the theme present at the moment of change at the end of the episode (see Fig. 9.2). All sessions and respective identified change episodes were numbered in chronological order to not alter their real sequence at the time of analysis.

Once the episodes of the sample were identified and delimited, a Discovery-Oriented Content Analysis (Hill & O'Grady, 2001) was carried out, focusing the

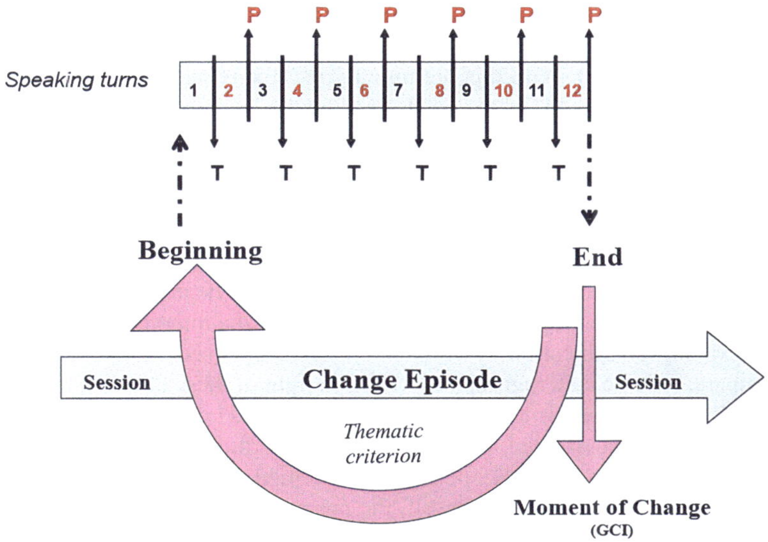

Fig. 9.2 Delimitation of change episodes and segmentation of speaking turns

qualitative analysis on the verbal expressions made by patients and therapists during the episodes. These verbal expressions were assigned codes that were called *Communicational Actions (AACC)*, that is, linguistic actions that the speaker performs at a given moment with the dual purpose of communicating specific information and influencing the other and the reality constructed by both (Valdés et al., 2010). To carry out this analysis of the AACC, each episode was subdivided into consecutive speaking turns so that each speaking turn began with the verbalization made by one of the speakers and ended with the start of the verbalization of the other speaker (Valdés et al., 2010). Thus, each speaking turn was ready to be coded separately, but always in the context of what was discussed by both speakers.

The analysis of the speaking turns was also carried out in two stages:

(a) Initially, the entire research team (researchers and therapists of different theoretical orientations in the role of researchers) coded all the speaking turns of patients and therapists included in the first five change episodes of each therapy ($n = 25$). For this, a strategy of intersubjective group validation of each of the codes assigned to each speaking turn was employed, considering that each turn generally had more than one code assigned simultaneously. As a result of this first stage, a list of *108 codes* was obtained, which, according to certain common denominators, were grouped into the following three categories: 4 codes that corresponded to AACC with very basic forms of language (agreeing, asserting, questioning, and denying); 9 codes that corresponded to AACC with an intentionality for the speaker (exploring, clarifying, focusing, tuning, providing feedback, re-signifying-constructing, re-signifying-consolidating, guiding behavior, and working on the affective); and 46 codes that corresponded to AACC with the presence of different types of techniques (Valdés et al., 2007; Valdés et al., 2010). With this preliminary list, the remaining change episodes of all therapies ($n = 44$) were coded, forming work subteams that again had the challenge of reaching a consensus on the assigned codes, leaving open the possibility for others not on the list to emerge.

(b) In a second moment, once all the episodes of the sample were coded, the list was refined to have a final version of the system. All the AACC contained in the previously mentioned categories were reviewed, following two simultaneous procedures: (1) only all the AACC that reached the degree of saturation were included and (2) a theoretical-empirical review of the interventions included in the existing classification systems was carried out (see Table 9.1) to check, compare, rename, and regroup the AACC in light of these other systems so that AACC identified empirically by other authors would not be excluded. A second dimension was also added, which includes two additional categories formed by codes that account for the Scope of the transmitted contents (ideas, emotions, or actions) and the Reference (oneself, the present other, another not present, the therapeutic relationship, the relationship with a third party not present, or a neutral reference). The result of this second stage was a definitive list of AACC that make up the classification system called the Therapeutic Activity Coding System (SCAT) (see Fig. 9.3). There is a manual for training in its use, which includes the criteria for segmenting speech turns, the procedures for completing the coding sheets, as well as the description and examples of the different AACC. For a deeper understanding of all these aspects, it is suggested to review the article by Valdés et al., 2010.

System Reliability: Statistically and Through Rigor Criteria

Once the system was developed, a reliability study was conducted in which two judges trained in its use participated. These two individuals were not part of the research team, nor did they participate in the previous stages. They were asked to code 3 relevant episodes ($n = 307$ turns): 2 change episodes ($n = 190$ turns) and 1 stagnation episode[1] to rule out any bias by episode type ($n = 117$ turns). These episodes were different from those used during the system generation process and were identified in sessions of the same therapy following the respective procedures. The reliability analysis for the five categories of the system was conducted by calculating the Kappa index (an agreement index used for categorical variable analysis)

[1] Stagnation episodes are characterized by a temporary halt in the patient's change process, with dysfunctional patterns reappearing during the therapeutic session, characterized by the persistence of some forms of understanding, behavior, and emotions related to the reason for consultation (Herrera et al., 2009).

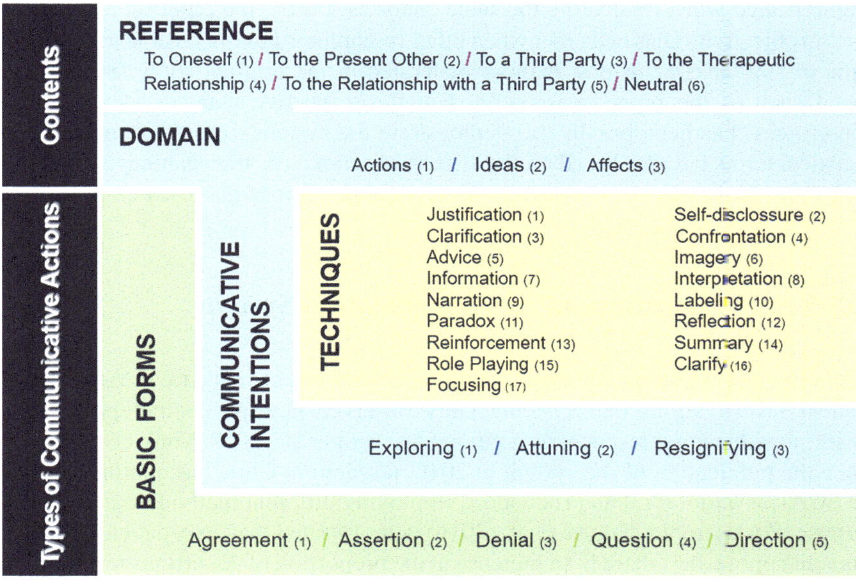

Fig. 9.3 Therapeutic Activity Coding System (SCAT)

(Hernández et al., 1991), using the statistical packages SPSS (version 14.0) and EPIDAT (version 3.1). The results showed an agreement between the judges from *substantial* (>0.61) to *perfect* (>0.81) when coding all categories (regardless of the episode type), *except for the Techniques category*, whose agreement was between *moderate* (>0.41) and *substantial* (>0.61). These differences were expected because: (a) it is the category with the most codes ($n = 14$ techniques); (b) there may be no technique in the speaker's verbalization; (c) there may be more than one technique in the same speech turn; and (d) there is an effect of the episode type, as therapeutic work in stagnation episodes is much less, and techniques are used less frequently (Fernández et al., 2012). Despite this, there were no statistically significant differences when overlapping the confidence intervals of each of the calculated kappa indices for the five categories.

In addition to the above, the system's reliability was, and continues to be, demonstrated through the fulfillment of rigor criteria (Angen, 2000; Hammersley, 2006; Lincoln & Guba, 1985; Shenton, 2004). The *credibility* of the system (internal validity) has been demonstrated to the extent that the findings are recognized by other therapists as a true approximation of what they therapeutically do during the session. The system has been presented to psychotherapists from different approaches, generating reflections that have led to the conclusion that the findings are true for people who are in permanent contact with the investigated phenomenon. There is also *transferability* (external validity) of the findings to other studies of therapeutic activity in other populations, showing an adequate fit to other contexts. Added to this is the criterion of *dependability* (reliability), since some results have been repeated when replicating the same analyses. Lastly, the criterion of *confirmability* (objectivity) has been met when other researchers have been able to reach the same or similar conclusions as those generated in the original study, as they followed each of the procedures outlined in the respective manuals step by step. Therefore, it has been possible to demonstrate the system's reliability not only in statistical terms but also based on the criteria of reflexivity, transparency, authenticity, and methodological systematicity, reflecting the rigor of the research processes.

Different Applications of the Classification System

The best way to demonstrate the system's reliability has been its use in various subsequent investigations that systematically observed new psychotherapeutic processes, now having a protocol as a guide (Anguera et al., 2018; Vonk et al., 2007). Since the publication of the system in 2010, research in Chile has continued using the SCAT as a tool for data production, employing different methodologies for this purpose. For example, Krause et al. (2016) demonstrated that, as a patient's change moment approaches, there is an increase in the proportion of Assertions made by the dyad and a decrease in Questions. Meanwhile, Fernández et al. (2012) demonstrated that in change episodes there is a more assertive for the therapist and more receptive in the patient, both actively involved in the construction of new meanings, while in episodes of stagnation, the conversation becomes rigid in a conversation that is less related to the patient. Likewise, they demonstrated that the Reference of the AACC in change episodes is usually strongly marked by the complementarity of roles in the therapeutic dialogue, while in stagnation episodes, it is usually referred to third parties who are not present in the session. Valdés et al. (2012) conducted analyses of temporal microsequences to detect the existence of sequences in the communicational coordination between patients and therapists during change episodes. They observed that when patients used Affective Explorations through argumentative emotional clarifications, this action by the patient was followed by Affective Tunings by the therapist as a way to show emotional empathy. Therapists did not add greater complexity to the therapeutic activity, which allowed patients to continue clarifying more emotional content argumentatively. It was also possible to demonstrate that there are moments in therapy when patients are satisfied with their therapists' interpretations and decide to participate in the construction of new meanings (Valdés, 2012). The SCAT was also used along with other analysis systems to deepen the description of the characteristics of therapeutic conversation. In this line, Valdés et al. (2010) used the Linguistic and Inquiry Word Count (LIWC) software to identify some associations between certain linguistic characteristics and the speaker's role. For example, it was observed that patients tend to use more personal pronouns in the first person singular, emotional content with a positive valence, and words that reflected cognitive subprocesses related to causality. Valdés et al. (2011) demonstrated that the manual coding of the AACC Domain was confirmed by the results found through the LIWC, as no significant differences were observed between patients and therapists at the communicational (SCAT) and linguistic (LIWC) levels in terms of the proportion of cognitive, affective, and behavioral content verbalized. Another study conducted by Valdés (2014) demonstrated that cognitive mechanisms play an important role in the change process and depend on the Communicational Pattern used by the speaker at a given moment. Therapy seeks to promote constructive reasoning, during which patients end up adopting some linguistic structures verbalized by their therapists during Affective Resignifications, being this a communicational indicator of the expansion of patients' knowledge about certain aspects of themselves. The SCAT has also been used to conduct process research in other Spanish-speaking countries. For example, Ruíz-Vásquez (2019) used the system to describe therapeutic interventions during a therapeutic process with a patient with dependent personality, while Carvajal-Mendoza (2023) used it to conduct a micro-analysis of change and stagnation episodes in a single case. Some studies have also been conducted in which only some SCAT categories were used, depending on the object of study, reaching similar conclusions to those obtained in the first studies conducted (Ceballos-Nava, 2022; DeSantiago-Sánchez, 2023; Figeac-Shillington, 2022; Gutierrez La Cruz, 2022; Roque, 2021). Likewise, the SCAT has also been considered an empirical antecedent for the development of instruments that evaluate therapists' interventions during the session: Gómez-Penedo et al. (2016) designed and validated the Comparative Scale of the Psychotherapeutic Process (CPPS), while Manubens et al. (2019) developed the Common Interventions Scale (EIC), both with adequate psychometric properties. However, in both cases, the focus is again placed on the actions performed by therapists, leaving aside what patients also say/do during the conversation. The SCAT has been used along with complex statistical analyses. For example, Valdés and Krause (2015) used a Hierarchical Linear Model (HLM) to analyze patients' AACC based on their personality organization (anaclitic and introjective), observing that patients with an anaclitic personality tend to make more verbalizations to Tune with their therapists, while those with an introjective personality do so more to Resignify, even during stagnation episodes. For their part, Masías et al. (2015) conducted Decision Tree analyses to demonstrate that Resignification is the most significant AACC when distinguishing a change episode from a stagnation one; however, it is a necessary but not sufficient variable, as it must occur in combination with other AACC. It is important to make clear that none of these results obtained from the use of the SCAT would have clinical significance if it were not possible to bring them to clinical practice and the training of psychotherapists. Observing sessions to identify what patients and therapists say/do during the conversation has allowed for a greater understanding of the mechanisms that prepare, interrupt, concretize, and/or consolidate psychotherapeutic change, which has improved learning processes during the training of future therapists. In this line, Valdés and Gómez (2024) developed a supervision proposal for psychology students that translates and applies some of the results in terms of feedback, along with the mechanisms that explain psychotherapeutic change. These authors propose the use of simulation experience as an effective pedagogical strategy to review, identify, reinforce, reflect, consolidate, and monitor the different psychotherapeutic competencies (personal, structural, attitudinal, theoretical, procedural, and communicational) in contexts that are as similar as possible to the real care context (Manolov & Losada, 2017). This model includes observation guidelines that facilitate the evaluation (Valdés te al., 2020), supervision, and monitoring of therapeutic competencies at the communicational level, which, together with the video feedback strategy, has allowed students to progressively transition from the experience of observing another person deploying these competencies (in the third person) to seeing themselves intervening (in the first person), in a space of joint reflective observation with their supervisors and peers, which facilitates the analysis of the different interactions as observer-spectators and protagonist-observed. Therefore, it is also being used today to conduct systematic observations based on relatively objective descriptive data and not on retrospective descriptions based on students' recollections (Cope et al., 2022).

Conclusion

Observation is one of the quintessential techniques when there are research questions that demand an in-depth understanding of certain practices in complex environments. It is a very useful technique but is underutilized in some contexts, which, for various reasons, are more difficult to access. This chapter offers a framework and a practical research example for the use of non-participant observation as a methodological option that allows access to verbal and non-verbal information present in the dialogue between patients and therapists during the session. A form of observation is proposed that places the observers in an indirect role of participation, in which, although they cannot provide a first-person description of the phenomenon as they are not explicitly within the session, it does allow them to perceive a large number of aspects from everything they see from the outside. Following the respective scientific rigor, this technique was used to develop a classification system that would allow the description of the conversation between patients and therapists, considering parallel dimensions of analysis that were not inclusive, being this one of the main differences with existing systems. It is a proposal for analysis that accounts for the complexity and multidimensionality of communicational interaction in the context of psychotherapy, enabling the identification, naming, comparison, and monitoring of the verbalizations of patients and therapists during the psychotherapeutic dialogue in episodes that, according to certain characteristics, end up being considered relevant for the change of patients throughout the psychotherapeutic process. The SCAT is a system that is based on a notion of psychotherapeutic change as a result of the co-construction of new meanings from the verbal actions of patients and therapists, which in itself speaks of a complementarity or symmetry of the therapeutic interaction. One of the main strengths of this system, besides its logical structure, is that it was developed from the qualitative analysis of therapies with different modalities and orientations, thus acquiring a generic character that allows the simultaneous analysis of therapeutic activity in terms of its specificity and in terms of its common character. But, above all, it is a system that was developed from the direct observation of the studied phenomenon and not from data obtained retrospectively. Although it is a method that requires a lot of time for the generation and analysis of data, there is also a reward at the end that translates into greater depth for developing knowledge with more solid foundations.

References

Altimir, C., Krause, M., de la Parra, G., Dagnino, P., Tomicic, A., Valdés, N., Perez, J. C., Echavarri, O., & Vilches, O. (2010). Clients', therapists' and observers' agreement on the amount, temporal location, and content in psychotherapeutic change and its relation to outcome. *Psychotherapy Research, 20*, 472–487. https://doi.org/10.1080/10503301003705871

Angen, M. J. (2000). Evaluating interpretative inquiry: Reviewing the validity debate and opening the dialogue. *Qualitative Health Research, 10*(3), 378–395. https://doi.org/10.1177/104973230001000308

Anguera, M. T., Portell, M., Chacón-Moscoso, S., & Sanduvete-Chaves, S. (2018). Indirect observation in everyday contexts: Concepts and methodological guidelines within a mixed methods framework. *Frontiers in Psychology, 9*, 13. https://doi.org/10.3389/fpsyg.2018.00013

Asay, T. P., & Lambert, M. J. (1999). The empirical case for the common factors in therapy: Quantitative findings. In M. A. Hubble, B. L. Duncan, & S. D. Miller (Eds.), *The heart & soul of change. What works in therapy* (pp. 23–55). American Psychological Association.

Atkinson, P. (2015). *For ethnography*. SAGE Publications.

Baier, A. L., Kline, A. C., & Feeny, N. C. (2020). Therapeutic alliance as a mediator of change: A systematic review and evaluation of research. *Clinical Psychology Review, 82*, 101921. https://doi.org/10.1016/j.cpr.2020.101921

Bastine, R., Fiedler, P., & Kommer, D. (1989). Was ist therapeutisch an der Psychotherapie?: Versuch einer Bestandsaufnahme und Systematisierung der Psychotherapeutischen Prozebforschung [What is therapeutic about psychotherapy?: Attempt to take stock and systematize psychotherapeutic process research]. *Zeitschrift für Klinische Psychologie, 18*, 3–22.

Blevins, M. D. (2017). Participant observation. In M. Allen (Ed.), *Encyclopedia of communication research methods* (pp. 1188–1190). Sage.

Boisvert, C. M., & Faust, D. (2003). Leading researchers' consensus on psychotherapy research findings: Implications for the teaching and conduct of psychotherapy. *Professional Psychology: Research and Practice, 34*(5), 508–513. https://doi.org/10.1037/0735-7028.34.5.508

Bourdieu, P. (2001). *Poder, derecho y clases sociales [Power, law and social classes]*. Desclée de Brower.

Bourdieu, P. (2012). *Bosquejo de una teoría de la práctica [Outline of a theory of practice]*. Prometeo Libros.

Carvajal-Mendoza, C.A. (2023). *Proceso de cambio y estancamiento en la atención de un consultante derivado por una institución de asistencia social [Process of change and stagnation in the care of a consultant referred by a social assistance institution]*. Master's Thesis in Psychotherapy, ITESO, Universidad Jesuita de Guadalajara. ITESO Institutional repository. https://hdl.handle.net/11117/9957

Ceballos-Nava. A. (2022). *Efecto de la intervención psicoterapéutica en una consultante perteneciente a la vida consagrada*. Un estudio de caso. *[Effect of psychotherapeutic intervention on a consultant belonging to consecrated life*. A case study]. Master's Thesis in Psychotherapy, ITESO, Universidad Jesuita de Guadalajara, ITESO Institutional repository. https://hdl.handle.net/11117/7853

Chatoor, I., & Krupnick, J. (2001). The role of non-specific factors in treatment outcome of psychotherapy studies. *European Child & Adolescent Psychiatry, 10*(1), 19–25. https://doi.org/10.1007/s007870170004

Chung, C. K., & Pennebaker, J. W. (2019). Textual analysis. In H. Blanton, J. M. LaCroix, & G. D. Webster (Eds.), *Measurement in social psychology* (pp. 153–173). Routledge/Taylor & Francis Group. https://doi.org/10.4324/9780429452925-7

Connolly, M. B., Chris-Cristoph, P., Shapell, S., Barber, J. P., & Luborsky, L. (1998). Therapist interventions in early sessions of brief supportive - Expressive psychotherapy for depression. *Journal of Psychotherapy Practice and Research, 7*, 290–300.

Conte, H. R., Plutchik, R., Jung, B. B., Picard, S., Karasu, T. B., & Lotterman, A. (1990). Psychological mindedness as a predictor of psychotherapy outcome: A preliminary report. *Comprehensive Psychiatry, 31*(5), 426–431. https://doi.org/10.1016/0010-440X(90)90027-P

Cope, E., Cushion, C. J., Harvey, S., & Partington, M. (2022). Re-visiting systematic observation: A pedagogical tool to support coach learning and development. *Frontiers in Sports and Active Living, 4*, 962690. https://doi.org/10.3389/fspor.2022.962690

Corbetta, P. (2003). Participant observation. In *Social research: Theory, methods, and techniques* (pp. 235–263). Sage.

Creswell, J. W. (2016). *30 essential skills for the qualitative researcher*. Sage Publications.

Crits-Christoph, P., & Gibbons, M. B. C. (2021). Psychotherapy process–outcome research: Advances in understanding causal connections. In M. Barkham, W. Lutz, & L. G. Castonguay (Eds.), *Bergin and Garfield's handbook of psychotherapy and behavior change: 50th anniversary edition* (7th ed., pp. 263–295). John Wiley & Sons, Inc.

Dahlberg, K. (2006). The individual in the world-the world in the individual: Towards a human science phenomenology that includes the social world. *Indo-Pacific Journal of Phenomenology, 6*(1), 1–9. https://doi.org/10.1080/20797222.2006.11433932

de la Parra, G., von Bergen, A., & del Río, M. (2002). Primeros hallazgos de la aplicación de un instrumento que mide resultados psicoterapéuticos en una muestra de pacientes y de población general [First findings from the application of an instrument that measures psychotherapeutic outcomes in a sample of patients and the general population]. *Revista Chilena de Neuropsiquiatría, 40*(3), 201–209. https://doi.org/10.4067/S0717-92272002000300003

DeSantiago-Sánchez, V.M. (2023). *Cambio terapéutico y estancamiento en pacientes con intento suicida: comparación de metodología de análisis de discurso. [Therapeutic change and stagnation in patients with a suicide attempt: comparison of discourse analysis methodology]*. Doctoral Thesis in Psychotherapy, ITESO, Universidad Jesuita de Guadalajara.

Echávarri, O., González, A., Krause, M., Tomicic, A., Pérez, C., Dagnino, P., de la Parra, G., Valdés, N., Altimir, C., Vilches, O., Strasser, K., Ramírez, I., & Reyes, L. (2009). *Cuatro terapias psicodinámicas breves exitosas estudiadas a través de los indicadores genéricos de cambio* [Four successful brief psychodynamic therapies studied through generic indicators of change]. *Revista Argentina de Clínica Psicológica, 18*, 5–19. http://www.redalyc.org/html/2819/281921800001/

Elliot, R., Hill, C. E., Stiles, W. B., Friedlander, M. L., Mahrer, A. R., & Margison, F. R. (1987). Primary therapist response modes: A comparison of six rating systems. *Journal of Consulting and Clinical Psychology, 55*, 218–223. https://doi.org/10.1037/0022-006X.55.2.218

Elliott, R. (1984). A discovery-oriented approach to significant change events in psychotherapy: Interpersonal process recall and comprehensive process analysis. In L. Rice & L. S. Greenberg (Eds.), *Patterns of change: Intensive analysis of psychotherapy process* (pp. 249–286). Guilford Press.

Elliott, R., & Shapiro, D. A. (1992). Client and therapist as analysts of significant events. In S. G. Toukmanian & D. L. Rennie (Eds.), *Psychotherapy process research: Paradigmatic and normative approaches* (pp. 163–186). Sage.

Elliott, R., Slatick, E., & Urman, M. (2001). Qualitative change process research on psychotherapy: Alternative strategies. In J. Frommer & D. L. Rennie (Eds.), *Qualitative psychotherapy research: Methods and methodology* (pp. 69–111). Pabst Science Publishers.

Etchebarne, I., Fernández, M., & Roussos, A. J. (2008). Un esquema clasificatorio para las intervenciones en terapia interpersonal [A classification scheme for interventions in interpersonal therapy]. *Anuario de Investigaciones, 15*, 15–30. https://www.redalyc.org/pdf/3691/369139944002.pdf

Evans, M. D., Piasecki, J. M., Kriss, M. R., & Hollon, S. D. (1984). *Raters' manual for the collaborative study psychotherapy rating scale—Fonn 6.* MN University of Minnesota and the St. Paul-Ramsey Medical Center.

Fernández, O., Herrera, P., Krause, M., Pérez, J. C., Valdés, N., Vilches, O., & Tomicic, A. (2012). Episodios de Cambio y Estancamiento en Psicoterapia: Características de la comunicación verbal entre pacientes y terapeutas [Episodes of change and stagnation in psychotherapy: Characteristics of verbal communication between patients and therapists.]. *Terapia psicológica, 30*(2), 5–22. https://doi.org/10.4067/S0718-48082012000200001

Figeac-Shillington, G. (2022). *Indicadores de cambio en psicoterapia de una consultante divorciada, un estudio de caso [Indicators of change in psychotherapy of a divorced client, a case study].* Master's Thesis in Psychotherapy, ITESO, Universidad Jesuita de Guadalajara. ITESO Institutional Repository https://hdl.handle.net/11117/8276

Fine, G. A. (2015). Participant observation. In *International encyclopedia of the social & behavioral sciences* (2nd ed., pp. 530–534). Elsevier.

Fitzpatrick, M. R., Janzen, J., Chamodraka, M., & Park, J. (2006). Client critical incidents in the process of early alliance development: A positive emotion-exploration spiral. *Psychotherapy Research, 16*(4), 486–498. https://doi.org/10.1080/10503300500485391

Fontao, M. I., & Mergenthaler, E. (2008). Therapeutic factors and language patterns in group therapy application of computer-assisted text analysis to the examination of microprocesses in group therapy: Preliminary findings. *Psychotherapy Research, 18*(3), 345–354. https://doi.org/10.1080/10503300701576352

Friedlander, M. L. (1982). Counseling discourse as a speech event: Revision and extension of the Hill Counselor Verbal Response Category System. *Journal of Counseling Psychology, 29*, 425–429. https://doi.org/10.1037/0022-0167.29.4.425

Galperin, B. L., Punnett, B. J., Ford, D., & Lituchy, T. R. (2022). An emic-etic-emic research cycle for understanding context in under-researched countries. *International Journal of Cross-Cultural Management, 22*(1), 7–35. https://doi.org/10.1177/14705958221075534

Goldberg, D. P., Hobson, R. F., Maguire, G. P., Margison, F. R., O'Dowd, T., Osborn, M., & Moss, S. (1984). The clarification and assessment of a method of psychotherapy. *British Journal of Psychiatry, 144*, 567–580. https://doi.org/10.1192/bjp.144.6.567

Goldfried, M. R., Raue, P. J., & Castonguay, L. G. (1998). The therapeutic focus in significant sessions of master therapists: A comparison of cognitive-behavioral and psychodynamic-interpersonal interventions. *Journal of Consulting and Clinical Psychology, 66*(5), 803–810. https://doi.org/10.1037/0022-006X.66.5.803

Gómez-Penedo, J. M., Barrientos, J. C., Martínez, A., & Roussos, A. (2016). Comparative Psychotherapy Process Scale (CPPS): Analysis of the validity and reliability of the Spanish adaptation/Escala Comparativa del Proceso Psicoterapéutico (CPPS): Análisis de la validez y confiabilidad de su adaptación al castellano. *Studies in Psychology, 37*(2–3), 656–677. https://doi.org/10.1080/02109395.2016.1189207

Gonçalves, M. M., Matos, M., & Santos, A. (2009). Narrative therapy and the nature of "innovative moments" in the construction of change. *Journal of Constructivist Psychology, 22*(1), 1–23. https://doi.org/10.1080/10720530802500748

Gonçalves, M. M., Mendes, I., Cruz, G., Ribeiro, A. P., Sousa, I., Angus, L., & Greenberg, L. S. (2012). Innovative moments and change in client-centered therapy. *Psychotherapy Research, 22*(4), 389–401. https://doi.org/10.1080/10503307.2012.662605

Gonçalves, M. M., & Peri, T. (2024). Innovative moments as markers of meaningful change: Introducing the special section. *Journal of Constructivist Psychology, 37*(1), 1–6. https://doi.org/10.1080/10720537.2023.2250483

Guest, G., Namey, E. E., & Mitchell, M. L. (2013). *Collecting qualitative data: A field manual for applied research.* Sage.

Gutierrez La Cruz, J. M. (2022). *Un análisis del ámbito y la referencia a partir de las funciones de las verbalizaciones en los Episodios de cambio de un proceso de psicoterapia psicoanalítica focal en una mujer víctima de violencia [An analysis of the scope and reference based on the functions of verbalizations in the Episodes of change of a focal psychoanalytic psychotherapy process in a woman victim of violence.]*. Master's Thesis in Psychoanalytic Clinical Intervention, Pontificia Universidad Católica del Perú. Pontificia Universidad Católica del Perú Institutional Repository http://hdl.handle.net/20.500.12404/21262

Hageman, W. J. J. M., & Arrindell, W. A. (1999). Establishing clinically significant change: Increment of precision and the distinction between individual and group level of analysis. *Behaviour Research and Therapy, 37*(12), 1169–1193. https://doi.org/10.1016/S0005-7967(99)00032-7

Hammersley, M. (2006). Ethnography: Problems and prospects. *Ethnography and Education, 1*(1), 3–14. https://doi.org/10.1080/17457820500512697

Helmeke, K. B., & Sprenkle, D. H. (2000). Clients' perceptions of pivotal moments in Couples Therapy: A qualitative study of change in therapy. *Journal of Marital and Family Therapy, 26*(4), 469–483. https://doi.org/10.1111/j.1752-0606.2000.tb00317.x

Hernández, R., Fernández, C., & Baptista, P. (1991). *Metodología de la investigación [Research methodology]*. McGraw-Hill.

Herrera, P., Fernández, O., Krause, M., Vilches, O., Valdés, N., & Dagnino, P. (2009). Revisión teórica y metodológica de las dificultades en Psicoterapia: Propuesta de un Modelo Ordenador [Theoretical and methodological review of difficulties in psychotherapy: Proposal of a computer model]. *Terapia Psicológica, 27*, 169–179. https://doi.org/10.4067/S0718-48082009000200003

Hill, C. E. (1978). Development of counselor verbal response category. *Journal of Counseling Psychology, 25*, 461–468. https://doi.org/10.1037/0022-0167.25.5.461

Hill, C. E. (1990). Exploratory in-session process research in individual psychotherapy: A review. *Journal of Consulting and Clinical Psychology, 58*, 288–294. https://doi.org/10.1037/0022-006X.58.3.288

Hill, C. E. (2005). Therapist techniques, client involvement, and the therapeutic relationship: Inextricably intertwined in the therapy process. *Psychotherapy: Theory Research, Practice, Training, 42*, 431–442. https://doi.org/10.1037/0033-3204.42.4.431

Hill, C. E. (2020). *Helping skills: Facilitating exploration, insight, and action* (5th ed.). American Psychological Association. https://doi.org/10.1037/0000147-000

Hill, C. E., Corbett, M. M., Kanitz, B., Rios, P., Lightsey, R., & Gomez, M. (1992). Client behavior in counseling and therapy sessions: Development of a pantheoretical measure. *Journal of Counseling Psychology, 39*, 539–549. https://doi.org/10.1037/0022-0167.39.4.539

Hill, C. E., & Kellems, I. S. (2002). Development and use of the helping skills measure to assess client perceptions of the effects of training and of helping skills in sessions. *Journal of Counseling Psychology, 49*(2), 264–272. https://doi.org/10.1037/0022-0167.49.2.264

Hill, C. E., & O'Grady, K. E. (2001). List of therapist intentions illustrated in a case study and with therapists of varying theoretical orientations. In C. E. Hill (Ed.), *Helping skills: The empirical foundation* (pp. 87–113). American Psychological Association.

Hilsenroth, M. J., Blagys, M. D., Ackerman, S. J., Bonge, D. R., & Blais, M. A. (2005). Measuring psychodynamic-interpersonal and cognitive-behavioral techniques: Development of the comparative psychotherapy process scale. *Psychotherapy: Theory, Research, Practice Training, 42*(3), 340–356. https://doi.org/10.1037/0033-3204.42.3.340

Hockey, J., & Forsey, M. (2020). Ethnography is not participant observation: Reflections on the interview as participatory qualitative research. In J. Skinner (Ed.), *The interview* (pp. 69–87). Routledge.

Horvath, A. O. (2018). Research on the alliance: Knowledge in search of a theory. *Psychotherapy Research, 28*(4), 499–516. https://doi.org/10.1080/10503307.2017.1373204

Hubble, M. A., Duncan, B. L., & Miller, S. D. (Eds.). (1999). *The heart & soul of change: What works in therapy*. American Psychological Association.

Izard, C. E. (2002). Translating emotion theory and research into preventive interventions. *Psychological Bulletin, 128*, 796824. https://doi.org/10.1037/0033-2909.128.5.796

Jones, E. E. (2000). *Therapeutic action: A guide to psychoanalytic therapy*. Jason Aronson.

Jones, E. E., Cumming, J. D., & Pulos, S. (1991). The psychotherapy process Q-set: Applications in single case research. In N. Miller, L. Luborsky, J. Barber, & J. Docherty (Eds.), *Handbook of psychodynamic research and treatment*.

Karlsson, R., & Kermott, A. (2006). Reflective functioning during the process in brief psychotherapies. *Psychotherapy, 43*, 65–84. https://doi.org/10.1037/0033-3204.43.1.65

Klinke, M. E., & Fernandez, A. V. (2023). Taking phenomenology beyond the first-person perspective: Conceptual grounding in the collection and analysis of observational evidence. *Phenomenology and Cognitive Sciences, 22*, 171–191. https://doi.org/10.1007/s11097-021-09796-1

Krause, M. (2005). *Psicoterapia y cambio: Una mirada desde la subjetividad [Psychotherapy and change: A view from subjectivity]*. Universidad Católica de Chile Editions.

Krause, M., Altimir, C., & Horvath, A. (2011). Deconstructing the therapeutic alliance: Reflections on the underlying dimensions of the concept. *Clínica y Salud, 22*(3), 267–283. https://doi.org/10.5093/cl2011v22n3a7

Krause, M., Altimir, C., Pérez, J. C., Echávarri, O., Valdés, N., & Strasser, K. (2016). Therapeutic verbal communication in change episodes: a comparative microanalysis of linguistic basic forms/Comunicación verbal terapéutica en episodios de cambio: un microanálisis comparativo de las formas lingüísticas básicas. *Estudios de Psicología, 37*, 513–546. https://doi.org/10.1080/02109395.2016.1227575

Krause, M., de la Parra, G., Arístegui, R., Dagnino, P., Tomicic, A., Valdés, N., Echávarri, O., Strasser, K., Reyes, L., Altimir, C., Ramírez, I., Vilches, O., & Ben-Dov, P. (2007). The evolution of therapeutic change studied through generic change indicators. *Psychotherapy Research, 17*, 673–689. https://doi.org/10.1080/10503300601158814

Krause, M., De la Parra, G., Arístegui, R., Tomicic, A., Dagnino, P., & Echávarri, O. (2006). Indicadores de cambio genéricos en la investigación psicoterapéutica [Generic change indicators in psychotherapeutic research]. *Revista Latinoamericana de Psicología, 38*, 299–325. https://www.psicoterapiaycambio.cl/wp-content/uploads/2014/04/Articulo_Rev_Latinoamericana_de_Psicologia.pdf

Lambert, M., & Barley, D. (2001). Research summary on the therapeutic relationship and psychotherapy outcome. *Psychotherapy: Theory, Research, Practice, Training, 38*(4), 357–361. https://doi.org/10.1037/0033-3204.38.4.357

Lambert, M. J., Hansen, N. B., Umpress, V., Lunnen, K., Okiishi, J., & Burlingame, G. M. (1996). *Administration and scoring manual for the OQ-45.2*. American Professional Credentialing Services.

Lepore, S. J., & Smyth, J. M. (2002). *The writing cure: How expressive writing promotes health and emotional well-being*. American Psychological Association.

Lincoln, Y. S., & Guba, E. (1985). *Naturalistic inquiry*. Sage.

Llewelyn, S. P., & Hardy, G. (2001). Process research in the practice of psychological therapy. *British Journal of Clinical Psychology, 40*, 1–21. https://doi.org/10.1348/014466501163436

Luborsky, L. (2000). A pattern-setting therapeutic alliance study revisited. *Psychotherapy Research, 1*, 17–29. https://doi.org/10.1093/ptr/10.1.17

Lutz, W., & Knox, S. (2014). *Quantitative and qualitative methods in psychotherapy research*. Routledge/Taylor & Francis Group.

Madden, R. (2010). *Being ethnographic. A guide to the theory and practice of ethnography*. Sage.

Magalhães, C., Pinheiro, P., Silva, J., & Gonçalves, M. M. (2022). Innovative moments and case formulation: Finding resources at the onset of the therapy. *Revista de Psicoterapia, 33*(123), 173–190. https://doi.org/10.33898/rdp.v33i123.35947

Mahrer, A. R., & Boulet, D. B. (1999). How to do discovery-oriented psychotherapy research. *Journal of Clinical Psychology, 55*(12), 1481–1493. https://doi.org/10.1002/(SICI)1097-4679(199912)55:12<1481::AID-JCLP6>3.0.CO;2-%23

Mahrer, A. R., Nadler, W. P., Stalikas, A., Schachter, H. M., & Sterner, I. (1988). Common and distinctive therapeutic change processes in client-centered, rational-emotive, and experiential psychotherapies. *Psychological Reports, 62*, 972–974. https://doi.org/10.2466/pr0.1988.62.3.972

Maione, P. V., & Chenail, R. J. (1999). Qualitative inquiry in psychotherapy: Research on the common factors. In M. Hubble, B. Duncan, & S. Miller (Eds.), *The heart and soul of change* (pp. 57–88). APA Press.

Manolov, R., & Losada, J. L. (2017). Simulation theory applied to direct systematic observation. *Frontiers in Psychology, 8*, 905. https://doi.org/10.3389/fpsyg.2017.00905

Manubens, R. T., Gómez Penedo, J. M., Juan, S., & Roussos, A. J. (2019). Propiedades psicométricas preliminares de la Escala de Intervenciones Comunes: un instrumento para estudiar las acciones de los terapeutas de distintos marcos teóricos [Preliminary psychometric properties of the Common Interventions Scale: An instrument to study the actions of therapists from different theoretical frameworks]. *Pensando Psicología, 15*(25), 1–24. https://doi.org/10.16925/2382-3984.2019.01.02

Marmar, C. R. (1990). Psychotherapy process research: Progress, dilemmas, and future directions. *Journal of Consulting and Clinical Psychology, 58*(3), 265–272. https://doi.org/10.1037/0022-006X.58.3.265

Masías, V. H., Krause, M., Valdés, N., Pérez, J. C., & Laengle, S. (2015). Using decision trees to characterize verbal communication during change and stuck episodes in the therapeutic process. *Frontiers in Psychology, 6*, 379. https://doi.org/10.3389/fpsyg.2015.00379

McCarthy, K. S., & Barber, J. P. (2009). The multitheoretical list of therapeutic interventions (MULTI): Initial report. *Psychotherapy Research, 19*(1), 96–113. https://doi.org/10.1080/10503300802524343

McKechnie, L. E. F. (2008). Observational research. In L. M. Given (Ed.), *The Sage encyclopedia of qualitative research methods* (pp. 573–577). Sage.

Mergenthaler, E. (1996). Emotion–abstraction patterns in verbatim protocols: A new way of describing psychotherapeutic processes. *Journal of Consulting and Clinical Psychology, 64*(6), 1306–1315. https://doi.org/10.1037/0022-006X.64.6.1306

Mergenthaler, E. (2000). The Therapeutic Cycle Model in psychotherapy research: Theory, measurement, and clinical application. *Ricerche sui Gruppi, 5*, 34–40.

Mergenthaler, E., & Stinson, C. (1992). Psychotherapy transcription standards. *Psychotherapy Research, 2*, 125–142. https://doi.org/10.1080/10503309212331332904

Messer, S., & Wampold, B. (2002). Let's face facts: Common factors are more potent than specific therapy ingredients. *Clinical Psychology: Science and Practice, 9*(1), 21–25. https://doi.org/10.1093/clipsy.9.1.21

Moeran, B. (2009). From participant observation to observant participation. In S. Ybema, D. Yanow, H. Wels, & F. Kamsteeg (Eds.), *Organizational ethnography: Studying the complexities of everyday life* (pp. 139–155). SAGE Publications.

Niederhoffer, K. G., & Pennebaker, J. W. (2002). Linguistic style matching in social interaction. *Journal of Language and Social Psychology, 21*, 337–360. https://doi.org/10.1177/026192702237953

Orlinsky, D., Heinonen, E., & Hartmann, A. (2015). Psychotherapy process research. In J. Wright (Ed.), *International encyclopedia of social and behavioral sciences* (Vol. 2, pp. 515–520) https://www.researchgate.net/publication/278304375_Psychotherapy_Process_Research

Orlinsky, D. E., Ronnestad, M. H., & Willutzki, U. (2004). Fifty years of psychotherapy process-outcome research: Continuity and change. In M. Lambert (Ed.), *Bergin and Garfield's handbook of psychotherapy and behavior change* (5th ed., pp. 307–393). Wiley.

Pennebaker, J. W. (1997). Writing about emotional experiences as a therapeutic process. *Psychological Science, 8*, 162–166. https://doi.org/10.1111/j.1467-9280.1997.tb00403.x

Pennebaker, J. W., Mehl, M. R., & Niederhoffer, K. G. (2003). Psychological aspects of natural language use: Our words, our selves. *Annual Review of Psychology, 54*, 547–577. https://doi.org/10.1146/annurev.psych.54.101601.145041

Programa Chileno de Investigación en Psicoterapia y Cambio. (2012). *Manual de observación, registro y codificación de episodios de cambio y estancamiento (versión 2.0) [Manual for observation, recording and coding of episodes of change and stagnation 2.0]*. Autor. http://midap.org/wpcontent/uploads/2015/06/manual_cambio_y_estancamiento.pdf

Reyes, L., Arístegui, R., Krause, M., Strasser, K., de la Parra, G., Tomicic, A., et al. (2008). Language and therapeutic change: A speech acts analysis. *Psychotherapy Research, 18*(3), 355–362. https://doi.org/10.1080/10503300701576360

Roque, B. E. (2021). La psicoterapia como función performativa: micro-análisis de una intervención de Minuchin [Psychotherapy as a performative function: Micro-analysis of an intervention by Minuchin]. *REDES, Revista de Psicoterapia Relacional e Intervenciones Sociales, 44*, 87–96. https://www.redesdigital.com/index.php/redes/article/view/191/148

Ruíz-Vásquez, A. (2019). *Modos de interacción psicoterapéuticos en el tratamiento de psicoterapia de una mujer con rasgos de personalidad dependiente. [Psychotherapeutic modes of interaction in the psychotherapy treatment of a woman with dependent personality traits]*. Master's Thesis in Psychotherapy, ITESO, Universidad Jesuita de Guadalajara. ITESO Institutional Repository http://hdl.handle.net/11117/6103

Russell, R. J., Jones, M. E., & Miller, S. A. (2007). Core process components in psychotherapy: A synthetic review of P-technique studies. *Psychotherapy Research, 17*, 273–291. https://doi.org/10.1080/10503300500529388

Searle, J. R. (1969). *Speech acts: An essay in the philosophy of language*. Cambridge University Press.

Searle, J. (1979). *Speech acts*. Cambridge University Press.

Seim, J. (2024). Participant observation, observant participation, and hybrid ethnography. *Sociological Methods & Research, 53*(1), 121–152. https://doi.org/10.1177/0049124120986209

Shaikh, A., Knobloch, L., & Stiles, W. (2001). The use of a verbal response mode coding system in determining patient and physician roles in medical. *Health Communication, 13*(1), 49–60. https://doi.org/10.1207/S15327027HC1301_05

Shenton, A. K. (2004). Strategies for ensuring trustworthiness in qualitative research projects. *Education for Information, 22*, 63–75. https://doi.org/10.3233/EFI-2004-22201

Stern, D. (2004). *The present moment in psychotherapy and everyday life*. Norton.

Stern, D., Sander, L., Nahum, J., Harrison, A., Lyons-Ruth, K., Morgan, A. C., Bruschweiler-Stern, N., & Tronik, E. (1998). Non interpretative mechanisms in psychoanalytic therapy. The "something more" than interpretation. *International Journal of Psycho-Analysis, 79*, 903–921.

Stiles, W. B. (1979). Verbal response modes and psychotherapeutic technique. *Psychiatry, 42*(1), 49–62. https://doi.org/10.1080/00332747.1979.11024006

Stiles, W. B. (1992). *Describing talk: A taxonomy of verbal response modes*. Sage.

Stiles, W. B., Hill, C. E., & Elliott, R. (2015). Looking both ways. *Psychotherapy Research, 25*, 282–293. https://doi.org/10.1080/10503307.2014.981681

Stiles, W. B., Shapiro, D. A., & Firth-Cozens, J. A. (1990). Correlations of session evaluations with treatment outcome. *British Journal of Clinical Psychology, 29*(1), 13–21. https://doi.org/10.1111/j.2044-8260.1990.tb00844.x

Taylor, S. J., Bogdan, R., & Devault, M. L. (2016). *Introduction to qualitative research methods. A guidebook and resource* (4th ed.). John Wiley & Sons, Inc.

Timulak, L., & Elliott, R. (2003). Empowerment events in process-experiential psychotherapy of depression: An exploratory qualitative analysis. *Psychotherapy Research, 13*, 443–460. https://doi.org/10.1093/ptr/kpg043

Trijsburg, R. W., Lietaer, G., Colijn, S., Abrahamse, R. M., Joosten, S., & Duivenvoorden, H. J. (2004). Construct validity of the comprehensive psychotherapeutic interventions rating scale. *Psychotherapy Research, 14*, 346–366. https://doi.org/10.1093/ptr/kph029

Tschuschke, V., Koemeda-Lutz, M., von Wyl, A., Crameri, A., & Schulthess, P. (2022). The impact of clients' and therapists' characteristics on therapeutic alliance and outcome. *Journal of Contemporary Psychotherapy: On the Cutting Edge of Modern Developments in Psychotherapy, 52*(2), 145–154. https://doi.org/10.1007/s10879-021-09527-2

Valdés, N. (2010). Análisis de los estilos lingüísticos de paciente y terapeuta durante la conversación terapéutica en episodios de cambio, utilizando el Buscador Lingüístico y Contador de Palabras (LIWC) [analysis of the linguistic styles of patient and therapist during the therapeutic conversation in episodes of change, using the Linguistic Finder and Word Count (LIWC)]. *Subjetividad y Procesos Cognitivos, 14*(2), 314–332. http://www.scielo.org.ar/pdf/spc/v14n2/v14n2a25.pdf

Valdés, N. (2012). Analysis of verbal emotional expression in change episodes and throughout the psychotherapeutic process: Main communicative patterns used to work on emotional contents. *Clínica y Salud, 23*(2), 153–179. https://doi.org/10.5093/cl2012a10

Valdés, N. (2014). Underlying cognitive mechanisms associated with the emotional work: Analysis of depressive patients' verbal expressions. *Psykhe, 23*(1), 1–17. https://doi.org/10.7764/psykhe.23.1.472

Valdés, N., & Gómez, D. (2024). *Supervisión Clínica para estudiantes de Psicología basado en el modelo de competencias psicoterapéuticas genéricas. [Clinical supervision for Psychology students based on the model of generic psychotherapeutic competencies].* [Manuscript submitted for publication]. RIL Editores: Editorial Iberoamericana.

Valdés, N., Gómez, D., Ocampo, D., & Espinosa, H.D. (2020). *Pauta de Observación para la Evaluación de Competencias Terapéuticas. [Observation Guideline for the Evaluation of Therapeutic Competencies].* [Unpublished manuscript].

Valdés, N., & Krause, M. (2015). Verbal expressions used by anaclitic and introjective patients with depressive symptomatology: Analysis of change and stuck episodes within therapeutic sessions. *Clínica y Salud, 26*(2), 103–119. https://doi.org/10.1016/j.clysa.2015.06.001

Valdés, N., Krause, M., & Álamo, N. (2011). ¿Qué dicen y cómo lo dicen?: análisis de la comunicación verbal de pacientes y terapeutas en episodios de cambio [What do they say and how do they say it?: Analysis of the verbal communication of patients and therapists in episodes of change]. *Revista Argentina de Clínica Psicológica, 20*, 15–28. Repositorio institucional Pontificia Universidad Católica de Chile https://repositorio.uc.cl/handle/11534/30742

Valdés, N., Krause, M., Tomicic, A., & Espinosa, D. (2012). *Expresión emocional verbal durante episodios de cambio: análisis de los patrones comunicacionales utilizados por pacientes y terapeutas para trabajar contenidos emocionales* [What do they say and how do they say it?: Analysis of the verbal communication of patients and therapists in episodes of change]. *Revista Argentina de Clínica Psicológica, 21*, 217–246. https://www.redalyc.org/pdf/2819/281929021004.pdf

Valdés, N., Krause, M., Vilches, O., Dagnino, P., Echavarri, O., Ben-Dov, P., Arístegui, R., & de la Parra, G. (2005). Proceso de cambio psicoterapéutico: análisis de episodios relevantes en una terapia grupal con pacientes adictos [Process of psychotherapeutic change: Analysis of relevant episodes in a group therapy with addicted patients]. *Psykhe, 14*(2), 3–18. https://doi.org/10.4067/S0718-22282005000200001

Valdés, N., Krause, M., Vilches, O., Dagnino, P., Echávarri, O., Ben-Dov, P., Arístegui, R., & de la Parra, G. (2007). Proceso de cambio psicoterapéutico: análisis de episodios relevantes en terapia grupal con pacientes adictos [Process of psychotherapeutic change: Analysis of relevant episodes in group therapy with addicted patients]. In D. Sharim, A. Machuca, & A. Reinoso (Eds.), *Salud Mental. Práctica clínica en un centro universitario [Mental health. Clinical practice in a university center]* (pp. 245–270). Ediciones Universidad Católica.

Valdés, N., Tomicic, A., Pérez, J. C., & Krause, M. (2010). Sistema de Codificación de la Actividad Terapéutica (SCAT-1.0): dimensiones y categorías de las acciones comunicacionales de pacientes y psicoterapeutas [Therapeutic Activity Coding System (SCAT-1.0): Dimensions and categories of communication actions of patients and psychotherapists]. *Revista Argentina de Clínica Psicológica, 19*, 117–130. https://www.redalyc.org/pdf/2819/281921801002.pdf

Vanaerschot, G., & Lietaer, G. (2007). Therapeutic ingredients in helping session episodes with observer-rated low and high empathic attunements: A content analysis of client and therapist postsession perceptions in three cases. *Psychotherapy Research, 17*(3), 338–352. https://doi.org/10.1080/10503300600650910

Vonk, M. E., Tripodi, T., & Epstein, I. (2007). Systematic observation. In *Research techniques for clinical social workers* (pp. 51–69). Columbia University Press.
Wallerstein, R. (2001). The generations of psychotherapy research: An overview. *Psychoanalytic Psychology, 18*, 243–267. https://doi.org/10.1037/0736-9735.18.2.243
Wampold, B. E. (2005). Establishing specificity in psychotherapy scientifically: Design and evidence issues. *Clinical Psychology: Science and Practice, 12*, 194–197. https://doi.org/10.1093/clipsy.bpi025
Wampold, B., Ahn, H., & Coleman, H. (2001). Medical model as metaphor: Old habits die hard. *Journal of Counseling Psychology, 48*(3), 268–273. https://doi.org/10.1037/0022-0167.48.3.268
Wampold, B. E., & Brown, G. S. (2005). Estimating therapist variability: A naturalistic study of outcomes in managed care. *Journal of Consulting and Clinical Psychology, 73*, 914–923. https://doi.org/10.1037/0022-006X.73.5.914
Watzke, B., Koch, U., & Schulz, H. (2006). Zur theoretischen und empirischen Unterschiedlichkeit von therapeutischen Interventionen, Inhalten und Stilen in psychoanalytisch und verhaltenstherapeutisch begründeten Psychotherapien [On the theoretical and empirical differences of therapeutic interventions, content and styles in psychoanalytic and behavioral therapy-based psychotherapies]. *Psychotherapie Psychosomatik Medizinische Psychologie, 56*(6), 234–248. https://doi.org/10.1055/s-2006-932576
Williams, E. N., & Hill, C. E. (2001). Evolving connections: Research that is relevant to clinical practice. *American Journal of Psychotherapy, 55*(3), 336–343. https://psychotherapy.psychiatryonline.org/doi/pdf/10.1176/appi.psychotherapy.2001.55.3.336
Wiser, S., & Goldfried, M. R. (1996). Verbal interventions in significant psychodynamic-interpersonal and cognitive-behavioral therapy sessions. *Psychotherapy Research, 6*, 309–319. https://doi.org/10.1080/10503309612331331828
Wolf, N., Oppen, P. V., Hoogendoorn, A. W., Balkom, A. J. L. M. V., & Visser, H. A. D. (2022). Therapeutic alliance and treatment outcome in cognitive behavior therapy for obsessive-compulsive disorder. *Frontiers in Psychiatry, 13*, 658693. https://doi.org/10.3389/fpsyt.2022.658693
Woodside, A. G., Ko, E., & Huan, T. C. (2012). The new logic in building isomorphic theory of management decision realities. *Management Decision, 50*(5), 765–777. https://doi.org/10.1108/00251741211227429
Yager, J., & Lee, J. S. (2023). Third-party observation in psychotherapy: Playing to the audience. *American Journal of Psychotherapy, 77*, 35–38. https://doi.org/10.1176/appi.psychotherapy.20230002
Zhu, Y., & Hildebrandt, H. W. (2013). Effective persuasion of international business sales letters: An emic-etic perspective. *Management International Review, 53*(3), 391–418. https://doi.org/10.1007/s11575-012-0154-z

Chapter 10
Model of Analysis of Discursive Positioning in Psychotherapy (MAPP) for the Study of the Reorganization of Subjectivity in Change Processes

Claudio Martínez, Alemka Tomicic, and Augusto Mellado

Introduction: Change in Psychotherapy from the Dialogic Theories of the Self

The dialogic perspective considers the self as decentralized and the mind as a set of discrete states of consciousness experienced by individuals as a unit from a healthy and adaptive illusion of having a unitary identity (Bromberg, 2011). As a result of the history of interpersonal experiences, these self-states could remain disconnected (dissociated) or be connected through dialogue between them. In this context, consciousness is conceived as an internal dialogue between these self-states or subjective positions (Bakhtin, 1986). The dynamics of the relationship between these subjective positions are part of the so-called positioning models, which, in turn, share some basic principles of the Dialogic Self Theory (TDS) (Hermans, 1996).

A subjective position is a way of living and being in the world. That is a particular way of perceiving, interpreting, thinking, and interacting with others and oneself. In addition, it involves specific verbal and non-verbal expressiveness. Verbally, a subjective position is expressed through identifiable discursive voices in the statements that the participants of the therapeutic dialogue express. A statement can

C. Martínez (✉) · A. Tomicic
Centre for Studies in Clinical Psychology and Psychotherapy (CEPPS), Faculty of Psychology, Diego Portales University, Santiago, Chile

Millennium Institute for Research in Depression and Personality (MIDAP), Santiago, Chile
e-mail: claudio.martinez@mail.udp.cl; alemka.tomicic@mail.udp.cl

A. Mellado
Millennium Institute for Research in Depression and Personality (MIDAP), Santiago, Chile

Faculty of Psychology, Central University of Chile, Santiago, Chile
e-mail: augusto.mellado@ucentral.cl

A. Tomicic, J. D. Soto (eds.), *Qualitative Research in Clinical Psychology and Psychotherapy in Latin America*, https://doi.org/10.1007/978-3-031-90782-1_10

contain multiple discursive voices, constituting its polyphonic aspect. These voices can be implicit in the text, but they can be made visible through various linguistic markers (Larraín & Medina, 2007; Martínez & Tomicic, 2019; Martínez et al., 2014).

Defensive Disconnection of Self-States: The Role of Dissociation

As we already mentioned, the multiplicity of positions or states of the self constitutes a person's identity, not only in dialogue with another person but also with other positions of their internal world. Some of these positions could take conscious control, temporary or permanent, and dominate internal and external dialogues (Dimaggio & Stiles, 2007). Occasionally, this excessive control prevents dialogue and the consideration of other voices of the individual when interpreting the environment, others, and oneself. Thus, at that moment, the psychological disposition of the subject becomes monologic and causes them to relate in a dissociated and rigid way with the world (Martínez & Tomicic, 2019).

This rigid dissociation, sometimes considered pathological in its effects, is defensive and, as can be assumed, undermines the person's reflective capacity, making certain narratives appear as the only description the person makes of their identity and alternative narratives seem unimaginable. It is about an unconscious rejection of specific unsaid meanings linked to unformulated experiences in early childhood interactions with other significant people (Stern, 2010).

In this way, dissociation allows specific experiences to be adaptively maintained in compartmentalized and separated self-states, with no connection between them, at least for some time. This period can be brief for some people but permanent for others. For the latter, dissociation is not only a mental process aimed at coping with daily stress but also a structure that organizes their life, reducing the range of experiences that can be lived. Therefore, this mechanism—capable of structuring a person's experience—guarantees the preservation of the continuity of the self but, at the same time, limits the ability to relate to others (Fonagy & Allison, 2014).

Function of Psychotherapy in the Dialogic Reorganization of Subjectivity

Psychotherapy can contribute to the restoration of dialogue among the multiple voices and positions of the patient, activating the relationship between them and favoring those less conscious—dissociated—to turn them into more conscious and integrated into the dialogue. In addition, it would allow the emergence of new voices that constitute a meta-position with novel meanings (Bromberg, 1998; Dimaggio & Stiles, 2007; Martínez et al., 2014).

From this perspective, therapeutic change can be considered a construction and a restoration of the dialogue between discursive voices and between subjective positions. This implies mutual recognition between different subjective positions and dissociated aspects of one's self, which can progressively reorganize relationships and establish new dialogues (Martínez & Tomicic, 2019). If dissociation decreases, a more significant presence of subjective positions can be expected, characterized by mental openness, reflectivity, and the ability to listen and critically look at other positions of the self. In therapeutic terms, the reciprocal process of active involvement with the states of mind of "the other" would allow a perception in the here and now of the patient's self to share the conscious experience of the previously dissociated and incompatible narratives of the self (Bromberg, 2004).

Dialogic Theories to Address the Subjectivity of Patients and Therapists in Psychotherapy

Within the framework of perspectives that address the subjectivity of patients and therapists in psychotherapy, dialogic approaches have emphasized subjectivity as a dynamic configuration in which social interactions are fundamental and transcend the distinction between the internal and external worlds. Dialogic approaches are distinguished from other perspectives in clinical psychology because they consider that the formation of subjectivity is constantly produced in a specific socio-historical scenario (Hermans, 2003; Valsiner, 2014), in which both the self and others interact and relate from different subjective positions that make indistinguishable the separation between internal consciousness and external reality (Konopka et al., 2019). Having as one of its references the Theory of the Dialogic Self, dialogic perspectives indicate that subjectivity is not then an unchanging internal state but a conglomerate or polyphony of subjective positions that can be activated depending on the intersubjective context in which an individual finds himself (Hermans, 2003, 2006). In addition, these different, even contradictory positions can be endowed with voices that express their particular perspective or situational constructions of reality (Georgaca & Avdi, 2019). That is, the interaction between the subjective positions of individuals, who converse from their specific voices, generates meanings and, in turn, transformations of those same meanings, depending on the culture they are part of and the type of specific interaction that is established. In subjectivity, dynamics can be found, such as "decentering movements," which lead to disorganization, crisis, and fragmentation in the self, although also allowing exploration and differentiation, and "centering movements" that facilitate coherence, continuity, and unity, and that are necessary to allow the organization in the self (Hermans, 2014).

In turn, the self can generate self-reflective processes accompanying the transition from monologic and rigid exchanges to dialogic and flexible discursive exchanges. These processes can be supported by positions called proposers and meta-positions. The proposers positions have the potential to generate and organize more specific and future-oriented positions and contribute to the reorganization of the self. On the other hand, meta-positions allow for maintaining a certain distance from other positions and provide an overall view that allows observing them simultaneously and identifying significant connections between them (Hermans & Gieser, 2013).

The research on change in psychotherapy, from this dialogic perspective, has shown that during the process, and in interaction with the psychotherapist, counter-positions and meta-positions emerge in the participants that favor dialogue and the negotiation of meanings, mediate between other positions of the self, including the previously dominant positions, and support the move toward better-organized self-narratives (Salvini et al., 2012). Meta-positions can unfold and enable reflexive processes in tune with an intersubjective space in which patient and therapist collaborate (Mellado et al., 2022a). On other occasions, it is a meta-perspective that helps to account for tensioning situations that occur even in moments of change (Cunha et al., 2011). Alternatively, there are innovative moments in the patients' narratives that support the constructions of the self that challenge problematic narratives, a dynamic process in the context of dialogic exchanges between therapist and patient (Ribeiro et al., 2010, 2011).

The Model of Analysis of Discursive Positions in Psychotherapy (MAPP)

Discursive Analysis in Psychotherapy Research

Discourse analyses in psychotherapy focus on constructing and reconstructing meaning in the psychotherapeutic dialogue process (Avdi & Georgaca, 2007). Martínez et al. (2014) argue that psychotherapy is a discursive genre, as it corresponds to a cultural practice and a tool of social exchange that follows specific rules and occurs under several restrictions (e.g., the framework). The fact that psychotherapy is a discursive genre also implies a particular form of expression and selection of linguistic resources that give rise to the expression and transformation of the subjectivities of its participants. Therefore, this approach of discursive analysis from research may be the one that best fits this object of study.

There are various methods of discursive analysis in this research field that approach the production and transformation process of patients' subjectivities. Among those who consider as a starting point the Dialogical Self Theories (DST; Hermans, 2008), there is the sequential analysis developed by Leiman (1992, 1997, 2002, 2006), the repertoire of personal positions (PPR) developed by Hermans (2001; Kluger, Nir, & Kluger, 2008), and the microgenetic analysis developed by Valsiner. Inspired by the same background of the mentioned methods, Larraín and Medina (2007) developed the dialogical analysis of discourse (ADD), which has been previously used in the field of psychotherapy research (see Martínez, 2011;

Martínez et al., 2012). The ADD is based on Bakhtin's theory of enunciation and integrates the models of Ducrot (Bakhtin, 1986) and Kerbrat-Orecchioni (1993) to offer a tool to make subjectivity visible in discourse. Specifically, the ADD aims to shed light on the various voices present in the statements, including the relationship between these voices and the actual "dialogue" between the participants. We developed a specific model from these works to analyze the positioning in discursive terms in the psychotherapeutic process, both for patients and their psychotherapists (Martínez & Tomicic, 2019).

Recognizing Voices and Subjective Positions: Model of Discursive Positioning Analysis in Psychotherapy (MAPP)

Based on the theoretical background mentioned, we have created a method that describes how the multiple subjectivities of patients and their therapists are organized in the discourse deployed in psychotherapy and participate in an active dynamic of mutual recognition (Martínez & Tomicic, 2019).

As we said above, several methods have been created in psychotherapeutic research to make multivocality visible and to reveal the relationship between the voices and their deployment throughout the process (Hermans, 2008). They all share the notion of multiple selves and address the subjective positioning through the participants' narratives. Although some of them consider both the self-states of the patient and the therapist (see Seikkula et al., 2012), most focus only on the patient's dialogical dynamics.

The Model of Discursive Positioning Analysis in Psychotherapy (MAPP) describes the discursive positions of both patient and therapist, considering them equivalent to a subjective position or self-position. This means a perspective or a way of being in the world that is expressed through statements that make up the discourse of an individual (Larraín & Medina, 2007; Martínez et al., 2012; Martínez & Tomicic, 2019).

Levels of Analysis in the MAPP: Voices, Positions, and General Taxonomy

The MAPP is a system of three levels of analysis (see Fig. 10.1). The *first level* is formed by the voices of an individual, patient, or therapist, constituting the most idiosyncratic—and therefore embodied—expression of subjectivity in the discourse. The *second level* is formed by the personal positions of a patient or therapist, which group repertoires of voices that express them. Finally, the *third level* of the MAPP is an abstract taxonomy that represents the typical organization of the

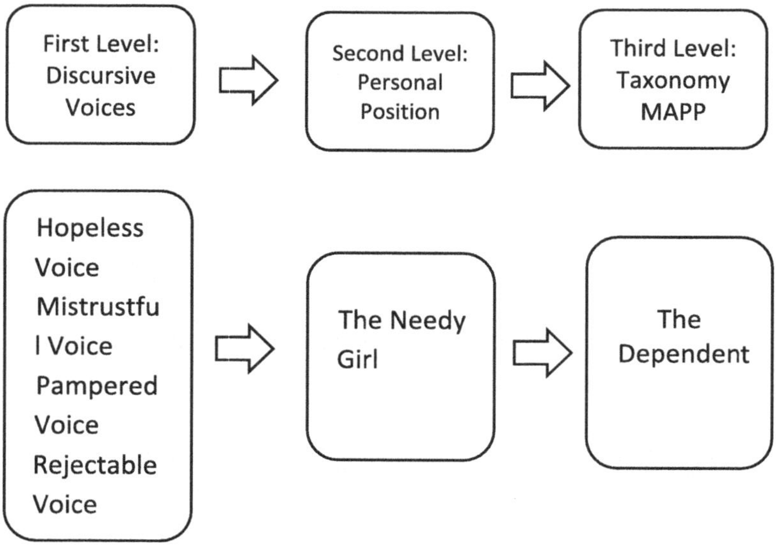

Fig. 10.1 Three levels of MAPP analysis

personal positions of patients and therapists, accounting for a level of social organization of these positions (Martínez & Tomicic, 2019).

Regarding the *first level* of the MAPP, we consider that patients and therapists can express different points of view in a statement through voices. Thus, a voice expresses spoken content and the perspective from which this context is addressed. Patients or therapists speak through a set or *repertoire of voices* that constitute the essential elements used by each of them to construct versions or interpretations of reality; these, when interwoven in the discourse, preserve the coherence of such interpretations (see Wetherell & Potter, 1988). The repertoire of voices tends to be diverse and unique in the case of patients; it represents how their subjectivity is organized. In the case of therapists, because their voices express their perspective within their professional role, they show less diversity, with inquiring, meta-analytical, confrontational, and assertive voices being frequent (see Morán et al., 2016).

In the *second level* of the MAPP, it is considered that, both for the case of patients and therapists, different repertoires of voices jointly express a recurring perspective called "personal position," a self-state. In other words, a specific repertoire of voices implies a shared subjectivity as part of the multiple self-states of the patient or the therapist. Again, there is a difference at this level when comparing the specificity and idiosyncratic traits of the patient and therapist positions. Based on the uniqueness of their voices, the positions of patients reveal the very idiosyncratic perspectives and ways of being of each of them. On the other hand, the positions of therapists are tied to their specific roles (Martínez, Tomicic, Medina, & Krause, 2014). In that sense, they reveal the perspectives they can adopt within their "social positions," such as a therapist, assistant, counselor, or psychologist (Hermans, 2001, 2004).

As mentioned earlier, the *third level* of the MAPP proposes a general and very abstract taxonomy that represents the configurations of positions typically adopted by the participants of the therapeutic encounter. This taxonomy emerged from categorizing the personal positions of patients and therapists, resulting from analyzing various psychotherapies (see Martínez & Tomicic, 2019). In the case of patients, three general positions represent the typical configuration: Reflective, Dependent, and Independent. As for therapists, they do so in two general positions: Proposers and Professor.

Therefore, in the case of patients, a triadic organization of positions has been described. Firstly, the general category of *Dependent* is characterized by positioning the patient's self as needy, weak, damaged, and/or vulnerable. On the contrary, the second general position—called *Independent*—is characterized by the positioning of the patient as someone strong and self-sufficient and/or someone who does not need help from others. These two general positions speak based on a single truth in a more monologic way (see Martínez et al., 2014).

Finally, the general positioning category *reflective* accounts for a subjective position in which the patient can have a distant perspective—but not disconnected—from emotional situations, listening to and critically looking at other positions while promoting dialogue between them in the manner of a meta-position (see Bertau and Gonçalves, 2007; Georgaca, 2001). This meta-position has been considered in the Dialogical Self Theory and has some qualities like the reflective positioning described here. For example, it allows taking distance from other positions, allowing a panoramic and simultaneous view of the different self-positions, thus providing a dialogical space for conversation between voices and opposing positions (Hermans, 2003).

On the other hand, the first general positioning of therapists is called The Proposers, in which the professional positions himself as someone who shows the patient what he observes and offers him a new perspective, thus generating a dialogical space between the patient's positions. On the other hand, the general positioning category called The Professor is more dominant and monologic, placing the therapist as someone possessing a truth or knowledge that can be presented, taught, or, sometimes, imposed on the patient as a single alternative.

In summary, the three levels of the MAPP reflect a vision of the self as a dialogical entity that encompasses the multiple expressions (i.e., voices) of the subjective positioning of the patient and the therapist (i.e., personal positions), which, in turn, reflect an organization of subjectivity determined socially and culturally (i.e., the MAPP Taxonomy). In the MAPP taxonomy, it is suggested that the multiplicity reflects certain aspects of personality and the development of individuals that constitute a supra-organization, a notion already proposed in other theoretical models to organize subjectivity (see the polarities of experience, introduced by Blatt et al., 2001, or the attachment categories such as avoidant and preoccupied, suggested by Main, 2000).

Example of Discursive Voices of Patients and Therapists, Personal Positions and MAPP Taxonomy: The Case of Patient B's Therapy

The Case of Patient B

Patient B was 29 years old at the start of therapy. She was of scarce resources and lived with her mother, brother, sister, and tiny niece. She had completed technical studies and worked in a call center as a supervisor. She received psychiatric treatment when she was 17 years old due to the death of her father. At 29, she was diagnosed with a personality disorder with dependent traits and a mixed adjustment disorder, for which pharmacological treatment and psychotherapy were indicated.

The patient began her treatment without knowing how psychotherapy worked; she was glad to have a space where she could talk about her difficulties and feel that someone was listening to her. During the first session, she reported that she had suffered sexual abuse when she was 5 years old. The aggressor was her father's brother, with whom, as a child, she occasionally stayed when her father was out of town due to his work obligations. When she started attending therapy, she was still suffering from memories of the abuse and felt that she needed to repair something about that experience. She tried to contact her uncle through Facebook but received no response. She also said she had problems at work, specifically with her superiors, who were very conflictive. In the realm of social relationships, she used to be mistreated and had problems with her partner or "friend with benefits," as she referred to him.

The psychotherapist, a 45-year-old woman, was a psychoanalyst with more than 20 years of experience. During therapy, she worked in her private practice and taught in a psychodynamic training program in a psychiatric hospital. She treated Mrs. B. in the context of this program. The psychotherapy was entirely recorded, and the therapist received feedback from the group that observed and listened to her on the other side of the mirror.

The discursive voices, personal positions, and discursive positions of applying the General MAPP Taxonomy (Martínez & Tomicic, 2019) for this case, described below, were analyzed using the first three psychotherapy sessions, which were fully transcribed.

Thus, the patient was identified as having three personal positions: "reflective adult," "needy child," and "empowered" (see Table 10.1).

From the reflective-adult position, the patient behaves, thinks, and feels like an adult, integrating and reflecting on different aspects of herself. From this position, she appears more autonomous and independent, but without ceasing to show her need for help. On the first level, this personal position is expressed through two discursive voices. One of them, the mentalizing one, is characterized by reflective expressions about herself and others, integrating thoughts and feelings. The other, the continuity voice, is characterized by providing therapeutic work material that allows the dialogue to continue, contributing ideas that are not necessarily reflective

Table 10.1 Example of patients' and therapists' discursive voices, personal positions, and MAPP taxonomy

Therapy	Patients' personal positions and discursive voices	Therapists' personal positions and discursive voices	Discursive positions according to MAPP taxonomy
Therapy B	Adult-reflective 1. Mentalizing voice 2. Continuity voice The needy girl 1. Hopeless voice 2. Mistrustful voice 3. Pampered voice 4. Rejectable voice 5. Abused voice Empowered 1. Assertive/executive voice 2. Defiant voice 3. Saving mother voice	The proposers 1. Inquires voice 2. Confrontational voice 3. Mentalizing voice 4. Self-revealing voice The imposer 1. Asserting voice 2. Mentalist voice	Patient 1. The reflective 2. The dependent 3. The independent Therapist 1. The proposers 2. The professor

Note: This data set comes from therapy analyzed within three research projects on the psychotherapeutic process (Regular Fondecyt Projects N° 1110361 and N° 1150639, and Postdoctoral Fondecyt Project N° 3150029). Some of the results, which include the MAPP, have been published by Tomicic et al. (2015) and Morán et al. (2016)

or mentalizing but imply a look at herself. Regarding the MAPP taxonomy, and on a third level, this personal position corresponds to the Reflective discursive position.

On the other hand, from the personal position of the needy child, the patient subjectively places herself in the place of a small and defenseless child, abused, damaged, rejectable, and unable to make decisions and think for herself. This position is expressed through five discursive voices. The first, the hopeless one, is characterized by expressions that present her in a life without exit and possibilities. The second, the Mistrustful voice, describes very dependent and symbiotic relationships, with demands for exclusivity for the other. With this voice, the patient sometimes expresses her doubts about therapy, either concerning its effectiveness or about the true intentionality of the therapeutic team. The third, the pampered voice, is characterized by a spoiled and sometimes "fussy" enunciative style: She does not want to work, does not want to think, and uses "I don't know" a lot. Sometimes, she tends to express idealizations of the other, especially when she feels protected by him. The last voices that express the position of the needy child are the rejectable and the abused. The nuclear enunciator of this voice refers to a situation of confirmed abuse in childhood, and that remains in the patient with discursive expressions of a damaged and defenseless child who can do nothing against abusive figures or acts in the present. This personal position corresponds to the Dependent discursive position regarding the MAPP taxonomy.

Finally, from the personal position called the empowered, the patient subjectively places herself as someone who does not need help but provides it with evident feelings of superiority, from where she can face difficulties with rationality and an active agency, but also with challenge, confrontation, and contempt. This position is expressed through three discursive voices. The first, assertive/executive, is a voice that underlines her capacity for agency, contrasting with others in which paralysis and passivity predominate. The second voice, the defiant one, is characterized by confrontational expressions and superiority over others. It expresses distrust, especially of the good intentions of others. The third, the saving mother, is a voice characterized by statements in which she underlines her strength and defensive capacity compared to others who are weaker. In this way, this voice describes others as defenseless and potentially harmful. This personal position corresponds to the Independent discursive position regarding the MAPP taxonomy.

On the other hand, the psychotherapist was identified as having two personal positions: the imposer and the proposers (see Table 10.1).

With the imposer position, the therapist places herself in front of the patient as someone who possesses the truth about her difficulties and can know what she thinks and feels about them. This position is expressed through two discursive voices. The first, the mentalist, is characterized by statements in the form of rhetorical questions and affirmations, in which the therapist impresses as reading the patient's mind. The second is asserting, a voice characterized by expressions that take the form of affirmations that seek to verify and/or reaffirm truths. It is also a voice that gives very sanctioning advice and opinions. This idiosyncratic position corresponds to the Professor's discursive position regarding the MAPP taxonomy.

From the proposer's position, the psychotherapist places herself in a subjective position from which she shows the patient what she observes and wishes to highlight, proposing it so that she can look at it again. This position is expressed through four discursive voices. The first is the confrontational voice, characterized by statements in which the therapist points out contradictory aspects of the patient's discourse or between the discourse and her gestures, tone of voice, etc. Likewise, with this voice, the therapist seems to express the intention of proposing to the patient the search for an explanation that allows her to understand or make sense of these contradictions. The second, inquires, is a voice with which the therapist performs interrogative actions, such as questions, points, or clarifications, that express a therapeutic intentionality. The third, mentalizing, is a voice characterized by expressions with which the therapist promotes the patient's reflection on herself and her relationship with others. This voice is manifested in enunciators that include propositions about mental states linked to emotions, feelings, bodily sensations, etc. Finally, the fourth is the self-revealing voice, with which the therapist reveals aspects of herself (thoughts, emotions, sensations, etc.) to propose an alternative perspective to the patient. Discursively and linguistically, this voice uses the first person singular and refers to the second person singular as an "I-with-you." This personal position corresponds to the Proposer's discursive position regarding the MAPP taxonomy.

Intersubjective Reliability Criteria in the Application of the MAPP

Both in the development of the coding system that allows describing the voices and positions as exemplified above, in the psychotherapy that is being analyzed, as well as in the subsequent codings of the selected material, it is suggested to use some intersubjective reliability procedure among coders.

From the analysis of the first three sessions, which allows for the development of an initial coding system for the voices of patients and therapists and which accounts for the most idiosyncratic expression of their subjectivities in discourse (Martínez & Tomicic, 2019), a search is established for those voices identified in chosen segments or the rest of the psychotherapy. The segments or complete sessions are coded considering each turn of speech, identifying the voices expressed in them.

This coding process is carried out, either individually or in pairs of coders, with the assistance of an expert judge who audits the work of the coding groups. The suggestion is that each coder independently analyzes and identifies the voices present in the turns of speech of patients and therapists using the initial system as a reference. It is important that this first coding is carried out before including all the selected material, even if the initial system was developed by the same coders who will do the rest of the task. Then, at a second moment, both coders meet and verify, comment on, and discuss the work done, seeking to reach a consensus on those codings in which they have not coincided until that moment. In case of not reaching an agreement regarding voices that are or are not present in a particular turn of speech, the presence of the expert judge will be required to help decide the coding.

The choice of a procedure that focuses on reaching a consensus, understanding it as the process by which researchers seek mutual agreement in their descriptions and interpretations of their data, seeking to strengthen the accuracy of the result (Levitt et al., 2021), lies in the particularity of the coding. Consensus aims for a common understanding regarding the interpretation of the data while maintaining different perspectives and openly considering disagreements and feelings in a scenario of listening and mutual respect (Hill et al., 2005). Within the framework of recognizing such diversity, the initial system and subsequent coding development require that the coders ideally have similar training in MAPP's conceptual and procedural foundations.

Additionally, being an analysis of discourse that determines categorical variables (that is, each voice can be categorized with a distinctive number or letter), the accuracy of the coding could be evaluated before the intersubjective discussion of the coders using inter-coder agreement measures such as Kappa coefficients (κ), Krippendorff's Alpha, etc. This type of measure can also be applied when an intersubjective agreement method is not intended to be pursued after developing the initial system. Although it is possible to make these measurements and report them, they do not openly consider a set of procedures to achieve reliable results in qualitative terms. Thus, using an intersubjective consensus procedure in applying MAPP, considering this coding exercise, does not intend to respond to the discussion about standards of objectivity or intersubjectivity for research. Instead, it focuses on the detailed description that refers to an intersubjective confirmation (Levitt et al., 2022), based on the experience and training of the coders, which is also supported by the robustness of the diversity of appreciation in front of the clinical material that is available.

Observing Change through MAPP

MAPP and Qualitative Designs

Given the nature and inductive coding procedure proposed by MAPP, it is qualitative and a model of analysis of subjective positioning in psychotherapy. Moreover, due to the intensity of work it requires and its performance in data production, observation of patterns, and saturation, MAPP can be used to design multiple cases and single cases. An example of the single case approach is the study by Martínez et al. (2012), using a preliminary version of MAPP called dialogic discourse analysis (DDA) at that time. In this work, rupture episodes from 60 videotaped sessions of long-term psychoanalytic therapy were analyzed. The dialogic discourse analysis was applied to both the therapist's and the patient's turns of speech, identifying linguistic markers, such as pronouns, proper names, and other elements that reflect the subjectivity of the participants. This allowed exploring how both participants constructed their subjectivity.

Among the main findings of the study by Martinez et al. (2012) on mutual regulation in psychotherapeutic dialogue, it is possible to point out four relevant results. First, the authors distinguished episodes of rupture of the therapeutic alliance, with and without repair. The episodes with the rupture repair showed a more frequent use by the patient and therapist of dialogic arguments and linguistic markers that restore the intersubjective field. In contrast, monologic arguments and markers that objectified—subtracted subjectivity—relationship were observed in the episodes without repair. Second, the analysis revealed that different discursive positions marked the dialogues between the participants. For example, when the patient described herself as a person who sacrificed herself for others, the predominant use of pronouns that reflected frustration and self-blame was observed, indicating a subjective position hidden behind self-demand. Third, regulating the tension between the therapist and the patient was crucial for repairing ruptures. It was observed that strategies oriented toward repair facilitated, in turn, psychotherapeutic change. Lastly, the authors (Martínez et al., 2012) developed a comprehensive model that describes the processes of mutual regulation in rupture episodes, differentiating between the processes of overcoming and repairing the ruptures. This model highlights the importance of discursive strategies in constructing and restoring the therapeutic relationship.

Taken together, the findings just described underscore the complexity of the therapeutic dialogue and the importance of subjectivity and intersubjectivity in the process of change in psychotherapy. Even when the authors suggest the need for more studies to strengthen or observe variations of the developed model, this approach allowed for collecting relevant data on the therapeutic dialogue and the micro-relationship between therapist and patient.

The study by Martinez et al. (2012) allows us to illustrate the use of MAPP with a single-case qualitative design. Also, it allows us to appreciate the value of this analysis model as a qualitative method for studying the subjective positions that psychotherapy participants can adopt at different relevant stages for the process and its outcomes. In this sense, the qualitative and micro-analytical nature of MAPP contributes to deep analysis and a detailed examination of the interactions between therapist and patient, and, at the same time, due to its multilevel approach—from voices to personal and subjective positions—it allows to explore how patients and therapists construct their subjectivity through discourse.

MAPP and Mixed Designs

Sometimes, mixed research designs are necessary for psychotherapy to distinguish different levels of the therapeutic process and encompass its complexity, especially when emphasizing patients' and therapists' subjectivity. In this context, a possible cross between qualitative and quantitative methodologies could be the evaluation of the different configurations of positions and voices obtained through applying MAPP over time.

So far, MAPP, before and after its most updated version (Martínez & Tomicic, 2019), has been used in single and multiple case studies, following exploratory sequential and concurrent nested designs (see the different types of mixed designs proposed for clinical psychology in Hanson et al., 2005).

Tomicic et al. (2015) examined the dynamics of discourse regulation strategies and voice—vocal qualities—during interactions between patients and therapists in psychotherapy. Using a preliminary version of MAPP, they analyzed the discourses of patients and therapists in episodes of change and ruptures of the psychotherapeutic alliance, integrating the application of the Model of Vocal Quality Patterns (Tomicic et al., 2011) to identify vocal qualities of the voice based on its self-regulatory and mutual regulatory capacity. This was a multiple case study with a concurrent nested mixed design, in which the episodes of five psychotherapies (of psychodynamic and cognitive-behavioral orientations) were studied, analyzing the data in an aggregated way for each group of patients and therapists. The synthesis of methods and analysis led them to identify and describe recurring discourse-voice regulatory strategies in patients and therapists, and specific groups of these strategies act as distinct regulatory configurations for the episodes of change and rupture of the alliance.

On the other hand, Mellado, Guastello, et al. (2022); Mellado et al., (2022a, 2022b) conducted a series of single case studies showing the subjective change of a patient diagnosed with Borderline Personality Disorder (BPD) in long-term psychotherapy. The first two studies used a convergent sequential design with a first qualitative stage and a second quantitative one. On the one hand, MAPP was applied to each of the 44 sessions of psychotherapy and each exchange or turn of speech between therapist and patient; this was complemented with a quantitative analysis with the State Space Grid (SSG, Hollenstein, 2013) technique to identify patterns in the interaction. The discursive voices used by the patient and therapist were transformed into categorical variables and treated as nominal time series, creating diagrams of their interaction session by session and calculating their characteristic patterns. This type of analysis allowed the synthesis of qualitative and quantitative information to describe the trajectory of the patient's subjective change based on the sessions that presented specific configurations defined theoretically and clinically in an intersubjective framework (Mellado et al., 2022a).

On the other hand, following the same design, another study performed similar analyses but in the change episodes that the patient manifested in her therapeutic process. This design incorporated the application of the qualitative methodology *Change Episodes Model* (Krause et al., 2015) to track and delimit each moment of achieved change. The results showed that different dynamic patterns of discursive voices between patient and therapist were formed in each group of the change episodes and coherent with the patient's change process (Mellado et al., 2022b).

Finally, a third study in the series described the degree of organization-disorganization that some psychotherapy sessions presented from how their interactive patterns of discursive voices of patient and therapist are constituted. In this study, the sequences of discursive voices of both participants were analyzed as nominal time series through the SSG and as frequency distributions of these time series using the quantitative technique *Orbital Decomposition* (ORBDE, Guastello, 2011). The analyses also integrated entropy calculations and non-parametric correlation tests to evaluate the relationship between the formation of specific sequences and the patient's therapeutic outcomes (Mellado et al., 2022). The advantage of using mixed methods to design case studies in psychotherapy is evident when considering the integration of different paradigms or worldviews. However, one of the main challenges is the inconsistency of quality standards (Tashakkori et al., 2012) that ensure the validity and reliability of the different methods used. This problem, at least when the application of MAPP has been involved, has been addressed by following the criteria specific to each methodological technique without trying to cross borders about a potential meta-criterion or the creation of new assumptions that aim to achieve a unified criterion for each technique or stage of the analysis process.

Conclusions

Throughout this chapter, we have shown one development in Latin America that offers a methodology for observing the micro-interactive and mutual regulation phenomena that sustain a psychotherapeutic process session by session. This methodology uses the notion of discourse and psychotherapeutic dialogue.

The Model of Analysis of Discursive Positioning in Psychotherapy (MAPP) (Martínez & Tomicic, 2019) focuses on key findings and their implications for clinical practice and future research.

Firstly, there is an emphasis on *intersubjective consensus* in the interpretation of data, where the diversity of voices and personal positions and their multiple reorganizations throughout the therapeutic process are recognized and respected. On the other hand, using mixed methods, when it comes to MAPP, stands out as an advantage. However, it presents challenges related to the validity and reliability of the different methods. Secondly, regarding the *subjective change in psychotherapy* (Krause, 2005), the case studies show how MAPP allows tracking and describing the subjective change of patients, showing dynamic patterns in the interaction between patient and therapist. Thirdly, and concerning *relevant episodes* during psychotherapy (Duarte et al., 2019), MAPP allows analyzing discursive voices and their relationship with the organization and disorganization of sessions, both in episodes of change as well as in those of alliance rupture, which provides a deep understanding of the therapeutic process. Fourthly and finally, regarding the construct of *mutual regulation*, what has been discussed throughout this chapter underscores the role of psychotherapeutic dialogue as an instance of regulation and self-regulation, where, for example, the ability to handle tension and ruptures in the therapeutic alliance is crucial to facilitate change.

Along with the above, MAPP is not only an analysis tool that offers a dialogic understanding of the psychotherapeutic process but also presents a valuable tool that allows therapists to understand, recognize, and work with the multiple voices and positions of the self of patients and therapists, promoting a dialogic reorganization of their subjectivity and a greater integration of their internal experiences. At the same time, he or she fine-tunes the listening toward the patient and with himself or herself as he or she gains experience. Thus, MAPP not only provides a theoretical framework to understand the complexity of the therapeutic dialogue but also offers practical tools to improve the effectiveness of psychotherapy, facilitating a space of recognition and appreciation of the various voices and positions that make up each treatment.

References

Avdi, E., & Georgaca, E. (2007). Discourse analysis and psychotherapy: A critical review. *European Journal of Psychotherapy and Counselling, 9*(2), 157–176. https://doi.org/10.1080/13642530701363445

Bakhtin, M. (1986). *Speech genres and other late essays*. University of Texas Press.

Bertau, M.-C., & Gonçalves, M. M. (2007). Looking at meaning as movement in development: Introductory reflections on the developmental origins of the dialogical self. *International Journal for Dialogical Science, 2*(1), 1–13.

Blatt, S. J., Shahar, G., & Zuroff, D. C. (2001). Anaclitic (sociotropic) and introjective (autonomous) dimensions. *Psychotherapy: Theory, Research, Practice, Training, 38*(4), 449–454. https://doi.org/10.1037/0033-3204.38.4.449

Bromberg, P. M. (1998). *Standing in the spaces: Essays on clinical process, trauma and dissociation*. The Analytic Press.
Bromberg, P. M. (2004). Standing in the spaces: The multiplicity of self and the psychoanalytic relationship. In H. J. Hermans & G. Dimaggio (Eds.), *The dialogical self in psychotherapy* (pp. 13–28). Brunner-Routledge.
Bromberg, P. M. (2011). *The shadow of the tsunami: And the growth of the relational mind*. Routledge.
Cunha, C. A. C., Gonçalves, M. M., & Valsiner, J. (2011). Transforming self-narratives in psychotherapy: Looking at different forms of ambivalence in the change process. In R. A. Jones & M. Morioka (Eds.), *Jungian and dialogical self perspectives* (pp. 43–66). Palgrave Macmillan.
Dimaggio, G., & Stiles, W. B. (2007). Psychotherapy in light of internal multiplicity. *Journal of Clinical Psychology, 63*, 119–127. https://doi.org/10.1002/JCLP20335
Duarte, J., Martínez, C., & Tomicic, A. (2019). Revisión teórica y metodológica de los eventos relevantes en psicoterapia para el estudio del cambio [Theoretical and methodological review of relevant events in psychotherapy for the study of change]. *Revista Argentina de Clínica Psicológica, 28*(3), 253–265. https://doi.org/10.24205/03276716.2019.1141
Fonagy, M. S. K., & Allison, L. (2014). The role of mentalizing and epistemic trust in the therapeutic relationship. *Psychotherapy, 51*(3), 372–380. https://doi.org/10.1037/a0036505
Georgaca, E., & Avdi, E. (2019). Developing a dialogical approach to analysing psychotherapy. In A. Konopka, H. J. M. Hermans, & M. M. Goncalves (Eds.), *Handbook of dialogical self theory and psychotherapy: Bridging psychotherapeutic and cultural traditions* (pp. 153–169). Routledge. https://doi.org/10.4324/9781315145693
Guastello, S. J. (2011). Orbital decomposition: Identification of dynamical patterns in categorical data. In S. J. Guastello & R. A. M. Gregson (Eds.), *Nonlinear dynamical systems analysis for the behavioral sciences using real data* (pp. 499–516). CRC Press/Taylor & Francis.
Georgaca, E. (2001). Voices of the self in psychotherapy: A qualitative analysis. *British Journal of Medical Psychology, 74*, 223–226.
Hanson, W. E., Creswell, J. W., Clark, V. L. P., Petska, K. S., & Creswell, J. D. (2005). Mixed methods research designs in counseling psychology. *Journal of Counseling Psychology, 52*(2), 224–235. https://doi.org/10.1037/0022-0167.52.2.224
Hermans, H. J. (1996). Voicing the self: From information processing to dialogical interchange. *Psychological Bulletin, 119*(1), 31–50.
Hermans, H. J. M. (2001). The dialogical self: Toward a theory of personal and cultural positioning. *Culture & Psychology, 7*, 243–281.
Hermans, H. J. M. (2003). The construction and reconstruction of a dialogical self. *Journal of Constructivist Psychology, 16*(2), 89–130. https://doi.org/10.1080/10720530390117902
Hermans, H. J. M. (2004). The dialogical: Between exchange and power. In H. J. M. Hermans & G. Dimaggio (Eds.), *The dialogical self in psychotherapy* (pp. 13–28). Brunner & Routledge.
Hermans, H. J. M. (2006). The self as a theater of voices: Disorganization and reorganization of a position repertoire. *Journal of Constructivist Psychology, 19*(2), 147–169. https://doi.org/10.1080/10720530500508779
Hermans, H. J. (2008). How to perform research on the basis of dialogical self theory? Introduction to the special issue. *Journal of Constructivist Psychology, 21*(3), 185–199. https://doi.org/10.1080/10720530802070684
Hermans, H. J. M. (2014). Self as a society of I-positions: A dialogical approach to counseling. *Journal of Humanistic Counseling, 53*(2), 134–159. https://doi.org/10.1002/j.2161-1939.2014.00054.x
Hermans, H. J. M., & Gieser, T. (2013). Introductory chapter: History, main tenets and core concepts of dialogical self theory. In H. J. M. Hermans & T. Gieser (Eds.), *Handbook of dialogical self theory* (pp. 1–22). Cambridge University Press.
Hill, C. E., Knox, S., Thompson, B. J., Williams, E. N., Hess, S. A., & Ladany, N. (2005). Consensual qualitative research: An update. *Journal of Counseling Psychology, 52*(2), 196–205. https://doi.org/10.1037/0022-0167.52.2.196

Hollenstein, T. (2013). *State space grids depicting dynamics across development*. Springer. https://doi.org/10.1007/978-1-4614-5007-8
Kerbrat-Orecchioni, C. (1993). *La enunciación. De la subjetividad en el lenguaje*. Edicial.
Kluger, A. N., Nir, D., & Kluger, Y. (2008). Personal Position Repertoire (PPR) from a bird's eye view. *Journal of Constructivist Psychology, 21*, 223–238.
Konopka, A., Hermans, H. J., & Gonçalves, M. M. (2019). The dialogical self as a landscape of mind populated by a society of I-positions. In A. Konopka, H. J. Hermans, & M. M. Gonçalves (Eds.), *Handbook of dialogical self theory and psychotherapy: Bridging psychotherapeutic and cultural traditions* (pp. 9–23). Routledge. https://doi.org/10.4324/9781315145693
Krause, M. (2005). *Psicoterapia y cambio: Una mirada desde la subjetividad [Psychotherapy and change: A view from subjectivity]*. Universidad Católica de Chile Editions.
Krause, M., Altimir, C., Pérez, J. C., & De la Parra, G. (2015). Generic change indicators in therapeutic processes with different outcomes. *Psychotherapy Research, 25*, 533–545. https://doi.org/10.1080/10503307.2014.935516
Larraín, A., & Medina, L. (2007). Utterance analysis: Operative distinctions for a dialogical discourse analysis. *Estudios de Psicología/ Studies in Psychology, 28*, 283–301. https://doi.org/10.1174/021093907782506443
Leiman, M. (1992). The concept of sign in the work of Vygotsky, Winnicott and Bakhtin: Further integration of object relations theory and activity theory. *British Journal of Medical Psychology, 65*, 209–221.
Leiman, M. (1997). Procedures as dialogical sequences: A revised version of the fundamental concept in cognitive analytic therapy. *British Journal of Medical Psychology, 70*, 193–207.
Leiman, M. (2002). Toward semiotic dialogism: The role of sign mediation in the dialogical self. *Theory & Psychology, 12*(2), 221–235S.
Leiman, M. (2006). The structure of subjectivity in utterances: Dialogical sequence analysis as a method of investigation. Paper presented at the 4th International Congress on the Dialogical Self. Braga, Portugal, 1–3 June, 2006.
Levitt, H. M., Ipekci, B., Morrill, Z., & Rizo, J. L. (2021). Intersubjective recognition as the methodological enactment of epistemic privilege: A critical basis for consensus and intersubjective confirmation procedures. *Qualitative Psychology, 8*(3), 407–427. https://doi.org/10.1037/qup0000206
Levitt, H. M., Surace, F. I., Wu, M. B., Chapin, B., Hargrove, J. G., Herbitter, C., Lu, E. C., Maroney, M. R., & Hochman, A. L. (2022). The meaning of scientific objectivity and subjectivity: From the perspective of methodologists. *Psychological Methods, 27*(4), 589–605. https://doi.org/10.1037/met0000363
Main, M. (2000). The organized categories of infant, child, and adult attachment: Flexible vs. inflexible attention under attachment-related stress. *Journal of the American Psychoanalytic Association, 48*(4), 1055–1096. https://doi.org/10.1177/00030651000480041801
Martínez, C. (2011). Regulación mutual yDialogicidad en Psicoterapia: Un Análisis Empírico de la Subjetividad e Intersubjetividad en el Discurso Terapéutico [Mutual Regulation and Dialogue in Psychotherapy: An Empirical Analysis of Subjectivity and Intersubjectivity in the therapeutic Discourse]. : EAE Publishing.
Martínez, C., Tomicic, A., & Medina, L. (2012). Dialogic discourse analysis of psychotherapeutic dialogue: Microanalysis of relevant psychotherapy episodes. *International Journal for Dialogical Science, 6*(1), 99–121.
Martínez, C., & Tomicic, A. (2019). From dissociation to dialogical reorganization of subjectivity in psychotherapy. In A. Konopka, H. J. Hermans, & M. M. Gonçalves (Eds.), *Handbook of dialogical self theory and psychotherapy: Bridging psychotherapeutic and cultural traditions* (pp. 170–185). Routledge. https://doi.org/10.4324/9781315145693
Martínez, C., Tomicic, A., & Medina, L. (2014). Psychotherapy as a discursive genre: A dialogic approach. *Culture & Psychology, 20*, 501–524. https://doi.org/10.1177/1354067X14551292
Martínez, C., Tomicic, A., Medina, L., & Krause, M. (2014). A microanalytical look at mutual regulation in psychotherapeutic dialogue: Dialogic discourse analysis (DDA) in episodes of

rupture of the alliance. *Journal Research in Psychotherapy: Psychopathology, Process and Outcome (RIPPPO), 17*(2), 73–92.
Mellado, A., Guastello, S. J., Martínez, C., Tomicic, A., & Krause, M. (2022). Self-organisation in dialogical patterns of a patient with borderline personality disorder and their therapist: A case study from nonlinear dynamics perspective. *Counselling and Psychotherapy Research, 23*, 577. https://doi.org/10.1002/capr.12527
Mellado, A., Martínez, C., Tomicic, A., & Krause, M. (2022a). Dynamic patterns in the voices of a patient diagnosed with borderline personality disorder, and the therapist throughout long-term psychotherapy. *Journal of Constructivist Psychology, 37*, 97. https://doi.org/10.1080/10720537.2022.2082606
Mellado, A., Martínez, C., Tomicic, A., & Krause, M. (2022b). Identification of dynamic patterns of personal positions in a patient diagnosed with borderline personality disorder and the therapist during change episodes of the psychotherapy. *Frontiers in Psychology, 13*, 716012. https://doi.org/10.3389/fpsyg.2022.716012
Morán, J., Martínez, M., Tomicic, A., Pérez, J. C., Krause, M., Guzmán, M., et al. (2016). *Verbal and nonverbal expressions of mutual regulation in relevant episodes of psychotherapy / Manifestaciones verbales y no verbales de la regulación mutua en episodios relevantes de psicoterapia*. Studies in Psychology. https://doi.org/10.1080/02109395.2016.1204784
Ribeiro, A., Bento, T., Gonçalves, M., & Salgado, J. (2010). Self-narrative reconstruction in psychotherapy: Looking at different levels of narrative development. *Culture & Psychology, 16*(2), 195–212. https://doi.org/10.1177/1354067X103614
Ribeiro, A. P., Bento, T., Salgado, J., Stiles, W. B., & Gonçalves, M. M. (2011). A dynamic look at narrative change in psychotherapy: A case study tracking innovative moments and protonarratives using state space grids. *Psychotherapy Research, 21*(1), 54–69. https://doi.org/10.1080/10503307.2010.504241
Salvini, A., Faccio, E., Mininni, G., Romaioli, D., Cipolletta, S., & Castelnuovo, G. (2012). Change in psychotherapy: A dialogical analysis single-case study of a patient with bulimia nervosa. *Frontiers in Psychology, 3*, 39246. https://doi.org/10.3389/fpsyg.2012.00546
Seikkula, J., Laitila, A., & Rober, P. (2012). Making sense of multi-actor dialogues in family therapy and network meetings. *Journal of Marital and Family Therapy, 38*(4), 667–687. https://doi.org/10.1111/j.1752-0606.2011.00238.x
Stern, D. B. (2010). *Partners in thought. Working with unformulated experience, dissociation, and enactment*. Routledge.
Tashakkori, A., Teddlie, C., & Sines, M. C. (2012). Utilizing mixed methods in psychological research. In I. B. Weiner, J. A. Schinka, & W. F. Velicer (Eds.), *Handbook of psychology, research methods in psychology* (Vol. 2, pp. 428–450). Wiley.
Tomicic, A., Martínez, C., Chacón, L., & Reinoso, A. (2011). Patrones de Cualidad Vocal en Psicoterapia: Desarrollo y Estudio de Confiabilidad de un Sistema de Codificación [Vocal quality patterns in psychotherapy: development and reliability study of a coding system]. *Psykhe, 20*, 77–93. https://doi.org/10.4067/S0718-22282011000100208
Tomicic, A., Martínez, C., Pérez, J. C., Hollenstein, T., Angulo, S., Gerstmann, A., et al. (2015). Discourse-voice regulatory strategies in the psychotherapeutic interaction: A state-space dynamics analysis. *Frontiers in Psychology, 6*, 97426. https://doi.org/10.3389/fpsyg.2015.00378
Valsiner, J. (2014). *An invitation to cultural psychology*. Sage.
Wetherell, M., & Potter, J. (1988). Discourse analysis and the identification of interpretative repertoires. In C. Antaki (Ed.), *Analyzing everyday explanation: A casebook of methods*. Sage.

Chapter 11
The Study of Mentalization in Process Studies in Psychotherapy with Adolescents: Development and Application of an Observation Scale

Javier Moran-Kneer, Camila Garay, and Juanpablo Betancourt

Investigating Mentalization in the Process of Psychotherapy with Adolescents

Process research in psychotherapy has advanced significantly in recent decades in Latin America (Paz et al., 2021). The development of real-time measures has greatly expanded qualitative psychotherapy research, enabling the study of previously inaccessible processes, such as verbal and non-verbal interactions (Morán et al., 2016), communication styles (Valdés, 2010), behavior (Zamignani & Meyer, 2017), and relational quality (Manubens et al., 2018), among other aspects. This progress has been pivotal in identifying dynamic interaction patterns essential to understanding therapeutic change (Barkham et al., 2021).

The study of mentalization in psychotherapy with adolescents exemplifies a field where the complexity of the phenomenon necessitates observation measures, without which research progress remains constrained.

Mentalization has experienced remarkable growth as a theoretical model for understanding the emergence of mental health problems and clinical change from an evolutionary perspective (Bateman & Fonagy, 2019). This relational psychological function, rooted in attachment experiences (Fonagy et al., 2002), enables understanding others' mental states ("seeing others from within") and recognizing the impact of one's behavior on others ("seeing ourselves from outside") (Bateman & Fonagy, 2006).

J. Moran-Kneer (✉) · C. Garay · J. Betancourt
School of Psychology, University of Valparaíso, Valparaíso, Chile

Millennium Institute for Research in Depression and Personality (MIDAP), Santiago, Chile
e-mail: javier.moran@uv.cl; ps.camilagaray@gmail.com; juanpablo.bettancourt@alumnos.uv.cl

A. Tomicic, J. D. Soto (eds.), *Qualitative Research in Clinical Psychology and Psychotherapy in Latin America*, https://doi.org/10.1007/978-3-031-90782-1_11

During adolescence, neurodevelopmental changes render mentalization more vulnerable to new social demands, linking these changes to the onset of mental health problems (Bak et al., 2015). Conversely, strengthening mentalization has been associated with symptom reduction in self-harm (Navarro et al., 2023), behavioral issues (Hauschild et al., 2023), borderline personality disorder (Gamarra, 2023), and eating disorders (Robinson et al., 2019). This evidence has led some authors to consider mentalization as a generic variable for change in psychotherapy (Luyten et al., 2024) and also as a common factor of psychopathology (Fonagy, Allison, & Campbell, 2019).

Evaluating mentalization in adolescent psychotherapy poses challenges due to its dynamic and relational nature.

One of the main challenges in researching mentalization in adolescent psychotherapy lies in its evaluation. Studies examining its association with the onset of mental health symptoms have predominantly relied on static measures that fail to capture its relational and interactive nature (Bevington et al., 2013). Similarly, studies addressing its promotion in psychotherapy have either not assessed it directly or relied on pre-post designs, which, once again, do not capture its dynamic nature (Lüdemann et al., 2021). In addition, evaluating adolescents' mentalization in psychotherapy presents unique challenges. Verbal communication, often central to the operationalization of mentalization (Guillén & Valls, 2023), is influenced by various factors in psychotherapy. Adolescents often communicate through silence (Gensler, 2015), use of jargon (Pinos, 2023), or demonstrate less fluency and spontaneity compared to adults. These characteristics necessitate considering paralinguistic aspects alongside verbal communication.

To address these challenges and advance the evaluation of mentalization as an interactive and dynamic phenomenon, while considering adolescents' unique characteristics—such as implicit responses and fluctuating capacities for self-reflection—we developed an observational measure for psychotherapy process studies (Moran-Kneer, 2019), called Observing Mentalization in Psychotherapy for Adolescents (OMP-A).

The scarcity of measures for studying mentalization in psychotherapy has significantly hindered process research in this field. Recent studies evaluating mentalization in psychotherapy have often adapted the Reflective Function Scale (RFS) (Fonagy et al., 1998) to analyze transcriptions of therapeutic interactions (Kornhas et al., 2020; Martínez Guzmán et al., 2017; Talia et al., 2019). While this scale is considered the gold standard for evaluating mentalization, transcription-based approaches have a critical limitation: they lack contextual cues, which are integral to the very nature of mentalization. For adolescents, this limitation is even more pronounced due to the prominence of non-verbal communication at this developmental stage and the frequent occurrence of silences and monosyllabic responses during verbal interactions. Consequently, exploring psychological phenomena in psychotherapy from a dynamic, real-time perspective—capturing moment-to-moment processes—is particularly important for advancing the study of mentalization in adolescents. In this context, observational measures of psychotherapy processes emerge as essential tools for investigating phenomena that require a detailed and specific focus on therapeutic interactions (Krause & Altimir, 2016).

In this chapter, we will describe the development and application of this observational scale, illustrating its use through clinical vignettes and presenting key research findings.

The OMP-A: Development Process and Structure

The development of a scale to evaluate mentalization in psychotherapy with adolescents arose as a response to a specific need. During a research project that sought to describe the deployment of mentalization in moments of rupture and resolution of the therapeutic alliance in individual psychotherapy with adolescents, we used the RFS adapted to psychotherapy by the team led by Martínez (2015). Martínez's team had already successfully applied this scale to psychotherapy processes with adults (see Martínez, 2021), based on the work of de la Cerda et al. (2019). The application of this scale to adolescents during episodes of rupture and resolution put us in real trouble when observing that a significant part of the clinical material during these moments was characterized by the presence of silences, monosyllables, or ideas that required the review of the videos more than the transcription to be coded. The clue for the development of an observation scale in the format of a rubric arose more from the collaboration with the team of Howard Steele and Miriam Steele at the New School for Social Research, who actively use observation guidelines to evaluate mother-baby interactions. Based on this experience, we sought to generate a scale similar to the one used by these researchers to train clinicians. This led to taking a step back and using the clinical material of ruptures and resolutions, originally intended to be evaluated with the RFS, to develop the scale through an inductive process.

For this purpose, ten moments of ruptures and ten moments of resolution were randomly selected from a total of 61 episodes, previously identified by a pair of evaluators trained in the 3RS (Eubanks-Carter et al., 2015). Each therapeutic interaction was described by two therapists trained in mentalization-based therapy for adolescents (MBT-A), using the mentalization-based therapy framework. In line with Braun and Clarke's (2006) guidelines, these analyses accounted for linguistic, paralinguistic, and contextual aspects. From the consensual descriptions of each segment, we sought to address the following questions: a) What actions of the therapists promote the patient's mentalization? b) What actions of the therapists do not promote the patient's mentalization? c) What responses from the patients to their therapists' interventions show a mentalizing stance? and d) What responses from the patients to their therapists' interventions show a non-mentalizing stance? The analysis of the answers to these questions was coded using grounded theory (Charmaz, 2024), emerging 42 indicators that were categorized for the emergence of the following scales:

Focus on Mental States (FMS)

This dimension refers to the ability of therapists and consultants to establish and maintain a consistent focus on the thoughts and emotions of the internal world—both their own and others'—while integrating descriptions of observable events and actions. Simply mentioning psychological aspects is not sufficient to determine that there is an active focus on mental states.

In therapists, this focus is observed through actions that encourage or demand mentalization from their patients, even in cases where patients initially resist. The following vignette illustrates such an interaction with a patient:

T: What don't you like about your classmates?
P: I'm not sure. **I couldn't really tell you.**
T: Can you help me understand what it is that bothers you about them?
P: **I just don't like going to school and seeing everyone in their own little world.** I don't connect with them. They act like they're better than everyone, but they don't even know anything. Okay, fine, maybe they know math, but **I'm good at it too, and I don't brag about it.**
T: So, it's their attitude that bothers you, then?
P: **Yeah, it's definitely their attitude.**

In patients, this dimension is observed when they adopt a reflective stance, either in response to the therapist's interventions or as a spontaneous expression. In some cases, this includes an intrinsic motivation to share and explain their experiences, connecting them to specific situations. The following vignette illustrates how the patient responds to the therapist's question by referring to their emotional states in relation to a particular situation:

T: Realizing that, what do you think?
P: **It really bothers me**, because… I don't know, I feel like I always have to ask for help to feel better. But in the end, **it just makes things worse,** and it keeps happening to me. Or, I mean… like, when I was arguing with my partner, I kept asking for more help.

Conversely, some therapeutic actions may lead patients to focus on describing events or observable aspects without fostering connections to their mental states. These actions may occur even in moments when adolescents spontaneously mentalize, thereby interrupting such processes and missing valuable opportunities to promote mentalization. Similarly, interventions where therapists consistently adopt a passive or silent stance in response to their patients may also hinder these opportunities.

Patients, in turn, can demonstrate a low focus on mental states in situations where, despite the therapists' efforts to guide them toward mentalization, they remain at a descriptive level, focusing on events and observable behaviors. The following vignette illustrates how, despite the therapist's question, the patient maintains a low FMS:

T: So your dad asked you to slow down. What did you do in that moment?
P: I told him, **"If you keep talking to me like this, I'm going to crash into a tree on purpose."**
T: How was he talking to you?
P: **I don't like it when he talks to me while I'm practicing.**
T: You know, listening to you, I wonder if, maybe, by asking you to slow down, **your dad was just trying to protect you from an accident.** Have you thought about that?
P: **No (laughs). Yeah, my dad always talks. He's good at talking.**

Opacity of Mental States (OMS)

This dimension corresponds to the level of uncertainty that both therapists and patients exhibit regarding the internal experiences and intentions of others, reflecting their ability to acknowledge the impossibility of directly and omnisciently accessing another's mind.

This can be observed by the way the story is structured, whether by the use of the first person singular, each time one's own point of view is made explicit and not "a reality" that is referred to; or by the use of expressions that evidence a quality of doubt about the internal experience of the other, such as: "maybe," "it is possible that," among others.

A high OMS is characterized by a curious disposition that encourages the formulation of questions to gather information, enabling a deeper and more precise, though not entirely certain, reflection on the minds of others. When the narrative includes certainty about others' intentions, explanations are typically provided to justify the reasons for that belief, as illustrated in the following vignette:

P: I think my mom is mad at me because I haven't been helping much around the house. **But I don't know; maybe she's got other things on her mind, and it's not about me.**
T: It sounds like part of you thinks her anger might be about you, but you also see that there could be other reasons. **Does that sound right?**
P: **Yeah, I feel like it's my fault,** but then I wonder if I'm just overthinking it and maybe she's just tired from other stuff.
T: It sounds like you're trying to figure out what's going on with her but you're not completely sure what she's feeling. **How does that uncertainty make you feel?**
P: **It's weird because I worry she's mad at me,** but at the same time, it's kind of a relief to think that not everything depends on me.

Its counterpart is observed through interactions that denote certainty about what goes on in the minds of others, without a basis in prior knowledge, or rather, "how things are or should be." During these moments, therapists and patients position themselves as experts on the experience of others, possibly assuming attitudes of control and showing little curiosity. In the following vignette, the patient's high level of certainty about the topics she is willing to discuss with the therapist and those she is not willing to discuss can be observed:

P: I don't want to talk about this with you. **It's none of your business,** so to speak, and I don't trust you enough to talk about it. It's like, **"Oh, not with you, no."**
T: **What do you think makes it that way?** So I can understand what part progressed and what didn't.
P: If you were my brother, I'd be here talking to you, because my brother saw what I went through back then. **But you can't understand if I just tell you.**
T: So, does it have to do with the people who were close to you at that time?
P: Yes, there are two or three people. **Only they understand.**

Contingent Communication (CC)

This dimension is based on the assumption that therapeutic exchange occurs within a dialogical context where the therapist and patient influence one another. Accordingly, both are expected to seek collaboration and maintain emotional attunement, enabling the construction of a shared narrative. Specifically, CC assesses the ability to sustain a sense of connection between one's proposal and the other's response in a fluid and contextualized manner.

In therapists, contingency is characterized by interventions that align verbally and non-verbally with the patient's behavior, emotions, and discourse. This is observed through attention to relevant aspects of the adolescent's experience and/or the explicit articulation of content that, while not directly stated, can be logically and plausibly inferred. Another indicator involves formulating interventions at a level of complexity appropriate for the adolescent, maintaining connections with previous interventions, and flexibly adapting to shifts in the conversation to follow their discourse.

In patients, CC is observed when they collaborate either actively—reflecting on the therapist's interventions—or passively but attentively, offering brief responses to express agreement or disagreement with the therapist's suggestions. The following vignette illustrates a therapeutic dialogue where the therapist and patient achieve a high level of contingent communication, resulting in a productive and connected exchange:

T: When you talk about feeling "caught in a mess," do you mean you're not really sure how to handle what's going on with your friends?
P: Yes, like, I don't know if **I'm the one doing something wrong, or if they're the ones exaggerating.** Everything just gets so confusing, and in the end, **I don't even know what to think.**
T: So, from what you're saying, it seems like there's a lot going on in your head, like their reactions make you doubt what you feel or how you're acting. **Does that sound right?**

P: Yes, because, I mean, sometimes I think I'm right, but other times I'm like, **"What if they're right?"** And then I just feel worse.

T: It sounds like these doubts make you feel really insecure. **Maybe what you're looking for is some clarity to figure out what's going on with you and them.** Does that sound right?

P: **That's right, because I feel like if I had a clear idea of what's happening, maybe I could fix things or at least feel calmer.**

Therapists engage in non-contingent actions when they disregard the adolescent's perspective, impose their points of view, or fail to incorporate the content conveyed by the patient. Examples of such actions include abrupt topic changes, interruptions, decontextualized interpretations, excessively theoretical interventions, irrelevant comments, critical remarks, and/or interventions with a level of complexity that is difficult for the patient to understand. In general, therapists engaging in these types of interventions can be described as emotionally out of sync with adolescents.

Conversely, patients demonstrate low CC when they appear not to follow or listen to the therapist. Their responses may range from a lack of alignment with the therapist's interventions to abrupt topic changes, evasions, or even overt attempts to control the interaction. Additionally, there is a type of response that can be described as pseudo-contingent: while it may exhibit a self-affirmative nature and constitute a clear example of mentalization, its monological positioning prevents it from contributing to the construction of a shared dialogical context.

The following vignette illustrates an interaction in which a therapist attempts to persuade a teenager of the need to talk with his parents. With evident frustration, the teenager responds, escalating the interaction into a discussion that culminates in a firm refusal to consider the therapist's insistently imposed position.

T: It's important that you talk to your parents about how you feel. They need to know in order to help you.

P: I don't know; **I feel like it's useless. They always get angry and do nothing.**

T: But if you don't tell them, how do you expect them to understand you?

P: **It's just that I've tried, and nothing changes. They still say that I complain about everything.**

T: **Well, but then, maybe, you should think about how you say it. Perhaps you do it in a way that doesn't reach them.** You could try to be clearer and calmer.

P: **Yeah, but I don't know; what if they still don't listen to me? I'd rather not waste my time.**

T: That's what I say: if you keep that "better not" attitude, you won't achieve anything.

P: **It reminded me of a reel I saw the other day. Can I show it to you? Do you use TikTok?**

Focus on the Present Moment (FPM)

This dimension refers to verbalizations aimed at focusing on the here and now or promoting the other's focus on the present moment. These verbalizations can be identified through participants' use of the present tense (e.g., "now that I think about it..." or "that makes me feel...") or through direct invitations to focus on the present—something more commonly associated with the therapist's role. While many interventions involve reviewing past experiences or future expectations, they are considered FPM when they maintain a connection to these events while anchoring the discussion in the immediate, present experience. Thus, merely mentioning the present is not sufficient to qualify as FPM.

Therapists' ability to regulate affect or safeguard this ability in the patient through actions such as actively interrupting reflections that keep adolescents stuck in the past or fixated on the future serves as a complementary, non-verbal criterion for this dimension. For patients, discourse focused on the here and now often conveys, as shown in the following vignette, a sense of being spontaneously and vividly connected with emotions and thoughts in the present.

T: Now, when we talk about this, what do you feel at this moment?
P: It's as if I were trapped. **I don't know how to get out of this situation.**
T: Trapped... **Is there any sensation that helps you understand more about that?**
P: **Yes, like a weight in my chest,** but at the same time, like I can't breathe well.
T: That sensation in your chest, **what does it tell you now that you notice it?**
P: Not really trapped. **Very tired, as if I were carrying everything,** and I don't know how to let it go.
T: And now that you say it, **how does it feel to share it here?**
P: **It relieves me a bit.**

Low FPM in therapists is evidenced through actions that contribute to the dysregulation of their patients' affect or when they become entrenched in non-mentalizing discourses about past or future situations. This includes interventions where therapists respond passively, allowing the patient to remain focused outside the here and now, or actively perpetuating the stagnation or dysregulation.

In adolescents, in addition to situations of emotional overwhelm or stagnation in past or future experiences, responses are observed that appear automatic. While these responses do not suggest emotional overwhelm, they give the observer the impression that the adolescent is rejecting the here and now, for instance, through the use of monosyllables. Another example of this type of response involves self-affirming discourses, where the adolescent seems to be convincing the therapist of a particular point of view or the validity of their experience.

The following vignette exemplifies a low level of FPM in both participants. Previously, the therapist delivered an extensive intervention analyzing the adolescent's reason for consultation. Initially, the adolescent appears attentive, but as the therapist delves deeper into the analysis, the adolescent becomes increasingly anxious and begins to withdraw from the interaction due to the high emotional intensity of the topic being addressed. This shift seems to go unnoticed by the therapist, who continues his intervention and attempts to explore further. By the end, it becomes evident that the patient was unable to engage with what the clinician proposed.

T: Now, when we talk about this, what do you feel in this moment?
P: It's as if I were trapped. **I don't know how to get out of this situation.**
T: Trapped... **Is there any sensation that helps you understand more about that?**
P: **Yes, like a weight in my chest,** but at the same time, like I can't breathe well.
T: That sensation in your chest, **what does it tell you now that you notice it?**
P: Not really trapped. **Very tired, as if I were carrying everything,** and I don't know how to let it go.
T: And now that you say it, **how does it feel to share it here?**
P: **It relieves me a bit.**

In addition to these four dimensions, the OMP includes the following, which are evaluated only when questions explicitly requiring mentalization are posed by the therapists:

Dynamic Nature of Mental States (DNMS)

This dimension characterizes interventions that demonstrate a recognition of the complexity of mental states, reflected in discourses that explicitly or implicitly acknowledge that there is not only one version of a particular mental state, or that mental states are not static. It is observed through interactions that discursively evidence: a) the existence of different points of view ("I felt sad, but I think they didn't notice anything was wrong with me"); b) the ability to recognize, tolerate, and integrate contradictions within mental states, including the recognition of mixed emotions ("On one hand, it seems like it doesn't worry you, but on the other hand, whenever that topic comes up, it seems like it does"); and c) the recognition of the changing nature of affects and cognitions, either through the passage of time ("When you first came in with this reason for consultation, do you remember how you were back then? You were like a different Sandra, much quieter than now, weren't you? How did you feel back then? How do you feel now?") or through the possibility of manipulating them at will, for instance, hiding or regulating them ("It's like... when I talk about my ex-girlfriend, it feels like something really big for me. Then I remember it, and it's like I see myself in a mirror and try to leave things out. I still say them, but when I do, it's like I'm forgetting").

The following vignette, set within the context of a session where a teenager is depicting emotions through a drawing, exemplifies the DNMS:

T: When you think about that friendship, **what else comes to mind?**
P: **There was a lot of happiness, but also a lot of sadness,** so it's a mix of those two.
T: **And with that happiness and sadness, are there other things? How did those emotions feel for you?**

P: **Frustration, not knowing how to handle things, not knowing how to carry all that.**
T: I remember that a while ago, you told me you worry a lot. **And you did things so people wouldn't notice.**
P: **Yes, I worry a lot about everything. I overthink things all the time**.

Low scores in this dimension are observed in therapists when they miss opportunities to promote its use in the patient, even when clear opportunities are present. This also occurs when the DNMS is expressed as a cliché (e.g., "Well, that's just how things are; there are always people who think differently") or when it is used to impose personal ideas rather than fostering the teenager's mentalization.

In patients, low scores are observed when this type of content is omitted in response to therapist interventions that encourage its use or when it is incorporated into discourse in a way that appears unnatural or emotionally inconsistent. These responses often give the impression of a utilitarian action, such as trying to convince the therapist, being condescending, or attempting to "get it over with." Such actions can be characterized as only superficially reflective, with the patient's discourse being irrelevant to the therapeutic process and/or having an exclusively self-affirmative purpose.

Causality of Mental States (CMS)

This is evidenced through verbalizations by therapists and patients that implicitly or explicitly consider, in a coherent and plausible manner, the multiple ways in which behaviors, affects, and cognitions—both of oneself and others—can mutually influence one another or be affected by relational dynamics. The following vignette exemplifies this latter aspect:

T: You told me that at the meeting with your colleagues, **you felt very uncomfortable. What do you think made you feel that way?**
P: I don't know… like **everyone was talking a lot,** and **I didn't know what to say.**
T: **How do you think that could have influenced how they behaved with you?**
P: **Maybe they thought I didn't want to be there because I didn't say anything.**
T: **Does it make sense to you that sometimes, when you don't participate, others might interpret that as disinterest?**
P: **Yes, it could be… but it still makes me nervous that they think that, because I actually do care, but I don't know how to make it show.**
T: So, on the one hand, it seems like you care about connecting with them, but, on the other hand, **the nervousness leads you to stay silent, and that could lead to misunderstandings. Is it something like that?**
P: **Yes, exactly that. It's like a circle, because the more I worry, the less I can speak.**

Low scores for both therapists and patients align with the same criteria as DNMS. In the case of therapists, this occurs when they do not promote the use of mental states in the patient despite clear opportunities to do so; when the causality of mental states is used in a clichéd manner; and/or when its use appears aimed at imposing personal ideas rather than fostering the adolescent's mentalization.

For patients, low scores are observed when the causality of mental states is omitted in response to therapists' demands or when it is incorporated into discourse in a way that appears unnatural, utilitarian, emotionally inconsistent, and/or driven by an exclusively self-affirmative objective.

Here, for example, we observe how a teenager provides a concrete response to a therapist's question that encourages reflection:

T: So, you said that talking about it helped you.
P: (Nods)
T: **Yeah? Why do you think talking about it helped you?**
P: **Because it did.**
T: **I mean, what was it about talking that made you feel good?**
P: **The conversation.**

As can be seen, the FMS, CMS, and DNMS dimensions mainly evaluate explicit aspects of the therapeutic interaction, while CC focuses on primarily paralinguistic elements. Finally, the OMS and FPM dimensions address both explicit and implicit aspects of mentalization in psychotherapy.

The original article detailing the development process of the instrument (see Moran-Kneer et al., 2020) provides further information on the methodological aspects related to its construction.

Applying the OMP-A to Psychotherapy Segments with Adolescents

The OMP-A is coded using videotaped therapeutic interactions, where the six dimensions of mentalization are evaluated and scored on a five-point scale for both patients and therapists. Table 11.1 illustrates the structure of the scale using one of the instrument's dimensions.

To illustrate the use of the OMP-A, the following example demonstrates its application through the coding of a therapeutic interaction (see Table 11.2). The episode corresponds to the transcription of an impasse with a teenage patient who enters the session room upset after having argued with the health center's secretary moments before the session. The interaction was segmented into two moments based on the patient's subjective positioning, showing greater openness to reflecting on distant and historical situations connected to the impasse.

The objective of segmenting the interaction in this way is exclusively didactic, as it serves to highlight the instrument's sensitivity to identifying differences in the

Table 11.1 The opacity of mental states dimension

	1	2	3	4	5
Therapist	The T exhibits a sense of total certainty regarding what occurs in the mind of the P (or others) or "how things really are" or "should be," adopting an expert attitude toward their internal world. There is an absence of curiosity about the p's personal experience, creating the impression of complete omniscience.	Despite adopting an expert attitude regarding the internal world of the P (or others), which creates the impression that the T knows with certainty what happens in their mind or "how things really are" or "should be," some interventions aim to consult the P about aspects still unknown or unclear to the T. In this case, the omniscience can be described as partial.	The T makes an effort to understand the experience of the P, demonstrating curiosity and adopting a collaborative role. The interventions are focused on exploring the p's experience rather than being strategically oriented toward a specific goal. In general, the recognition of the opacity of the EM can only be inferred from the attitude adopted by the T.	Most of the interventions reflect curiosity and an acknowledgment of uncertainty regarding the experience of the P (or others) or "how things really are." opacity is implicitly integrated into the discourse (e.g., "I wonder if...," "that makes me think that...," "I wonder what they might have thought..."), indicating that the intervention is grounded in the therapist's personal experience and/or perspective. Such interventions may also reveal something about the therapist's own mind (e.g., "do you remember that the other day we discussed this? That's why I ask you"). In general, the recognition of the opacity of the MS is considered and integrated into the intervention, although it is not its main focus.	The interventions denote curiosity and not certainty of the p's experience. The impossibility of directly accessing the internal world of others can be explicitly pointed out or implicitly integrated into the discourse ("I wonder if...," "that makes me think that...," "I wonder what they might have thought...") as a clear indicator that the intervention is based on their personal experience and/or own point of view, different and diverse. In general, the recognition of the opacity of the MS is a central aspect of the intervention.

(continued)

Table 11.1 (continued)

	1	2	3	4	5
Patient	The P seems to have total certainty of what occurs in the minds of others (including the T) or "how things are" or "should be," so their MS seems to be the only "truth." it is possible to appreciate an increase in arousal manifested as an overflowing affect and/or a non-integrated, imprecise, or even bizarre discourse. In global terms, there is a total omniscience.	While the p's attitude conveys a sense of certainty regarding the MS of others (including the T) and/or "how things truly are" or "should be," the P also acknowledges certain aspects of others that remain ambiguous or unknown to them. As such, the consultant can be described as demonstrating partial omniscience.	The P discusses the MS of others (including the T), providing additional information to substantiate the accuracy of their judgments about others' minds. However, the P does not adopt an expert stance regarding the internal world of others or "how things are" or "should be." while the recognition of the opacity of MS is not explicitly evident in their discourse, it can be inferred from their curiosity and/ or openness to explore and imagine the affects and cognitions of others or "how the world might be.'	The P talks about the MS of others (including the T), offering additional information that supports the accuracy of their judgments about the mind of others. In addition, they explicitly state through their discourse that their response is based on their personal experience and/or own point of view ("I believe...," "I think ...") and cannot be totally sure ("maybe...," "it's possible that..."). Most of the time they assume a curious attitude in relation to the MS of others.	The impossibility of fully knowing how others (including the T) experience reality is tolerated and seamlessly integrated into the discourse as a natural aspect of interaction. There is a complete and explicit acknowledgment that the experience is solely the p's and does not represent "how things really are." the P is characterized by openness and curiosity, along with a discourse that embodies a "maybe" quality.

Note: *T* therapist, *P* patient, *MS* mental state

deployment of mentalization during an interactive sequence that evidences two qualitatively distinct moments.

Finally, OMP-A indicators are assigned to each turn of speech, specifying whether they correspond to a low-level (↓), medium-level (→), or high-level (↑) performance.

Table 11.2 Example of coding, minutes 00:00:00 to 00:02:46

Dialogue	Coding observations	Indicator
T: What happened, Camila? I heard something about the secretary. What happened there?	T demonstrates awareness of a situation they are not fully familiar with and encourages P to express her frustration and expectation that her visit here should improve her mood rather than involve discussing such matters.	FPM ↓
T: But tell me a little about what happened. You went in, and she said that to you?	T insists on obtaining a clear description of what occurred.	FMS ↓
P: (still upset) yes, I went in, and she told me to be careful. It wasn't intentional! I accidentally bumped into a vase and almost knocked it over, but she had no reason to talk to me like that.	P remains upset and reluctantly provides details about the immediate situation.	FPM ↓
T: Hmm, I see. And you seemed to be in a bit of a hurry, right?	T introduces a contextual element that contingently focuses the intervention on the patient, suggesting a possible mental state.	FMS → OMS → CC ↑
P: Yeah, I was arguing with my boyfriend. I left him outside and came in quickly. But seriously, I think you should talk to her. She can't treat people like that, especially those coming here.	P redirects her focus to the immediate cause of her annoyance, this time adopting a position of control.	OMS ↓ FPM ↓
T: (pauses) okay, let's go back for a moment. She got upset about the vase, and when she said that to you, how did you respond?	T does not address the patient's request directly but instead seeks to calmly examine the sequence of events.	FMS ↓ FPM→
P: I told her to be careful about how she talks to people, that it was unintentional, that anyone can have an accident. And then she told me not to raise my voice… but she was the one who yelled at me first (continues to look upset).	P describes the events from a position of self-assertion.	FPM ↓ OMS ↓
T: Mmm… (pauses as if reflecting). So, it sounds like both of you got caught up in this argument.	T attempts to frame the situation from a neutral perspective, focusing on facts rather than motivations or subjective perceptions.	FMS ↓ CC ↑ OMS→
P: Yes, and the day was already bad. I'm supposed to come here to feel better, not to be dealing with things like this.	P challenges the therapeutic space, attributing some responsibility for her discomfort to the context of the therapy.	OMS ↓
T: When you say the day was already bad, are you thinking about the argument with your boyfriend?	T identifies a central aspect of p's discourse that is disconnected from the immediate event and subtly, yet curiously, invites her to refocus the intervention on this aspect.	CC ↑

(continued)

Table 11.2 (continued)

Dialogue	Coding observations	Indicator
P: Yes. We were arguing about something that happened at home with my mom.	P contingently follows the therapist's proposal.	CC→
T: It seems like a lot has happened today. It sounds like it may have started with something related to your mom.	T introduces a connection to a new event that may have influenced her emotional states and subsequent behavior.	CC ↑
P: Yeah, my mom… (her tone softens, appearing calmer).	P accepts this shift in the dialogue.	CC →
T: Would you like us to talk a bit about that?	T carefully considers the possibility of exploring this new event in greater depth.	FPM → CC →
P: The thing is, I had a deadline to pay the monthly fee for the dance school. My dad was helping me, but he couldn't. So I asked my mom for help, and she said yes, that I could count on that money. But then I found out that she gave it to my brother. She always does the same to me (voice rises, clearly angry).	P delves into the situation, focusing on describing facts. This time, her description is more general, avoiding judgments or positioning herself as knowing how things are or should be.	FMS ↓ CC →
T: And how did you find out?	T inquires with curiosity.	OMS →
P: From my mom. She always puts my brother as a priority. As if everyone else was more important than me (her tone softens as sadness begins to surface).	P connects with a new affect that aligns with her narrative.	CC →

Note: *T* therapist, *P* Patient

The segment is characterized by a low use of mental states by both the therapist and the patient. The therapist's reduced promotion of mental states is due to the need to regulate the patient's overflowing affect, which requires a high level of opacity. The therapist neither takes the events reported by the patient for granted nor dismisses them, instead focusing on carefully and non-judgmentally inquiring about the sequence of events as narrated.

This intervention is particularly attuned to the patient's affect, avoiding the reinforcement of value judgments or the patient's certainty about the intentions of others. The patient, for her part, while accepting the therapist's interventions, tends to maintain a stance centered on her own affect, which includes attempts to control the situation by demanding a resolution of the conflict with the secretary.

During the interaction, there were no questions explicitly demanding mentalization, nor was there any spontaneous use of mentalization in terms of causality or the dynamic nature of mental states. Therefore, the coding omits scores for these dimensions, as presented in Fig. 11.1.

The segment presented in Table 11.3 illustrates a significant shift in the patient's stance, demonstrating a greater willingness to reflect on what occurred and even acknowledge her own emotional states and potential responsibility.

In this second part of the interaction, it becomes evident how the therapist begins to incorporate and encourage the use of mental states, particularly by connecting

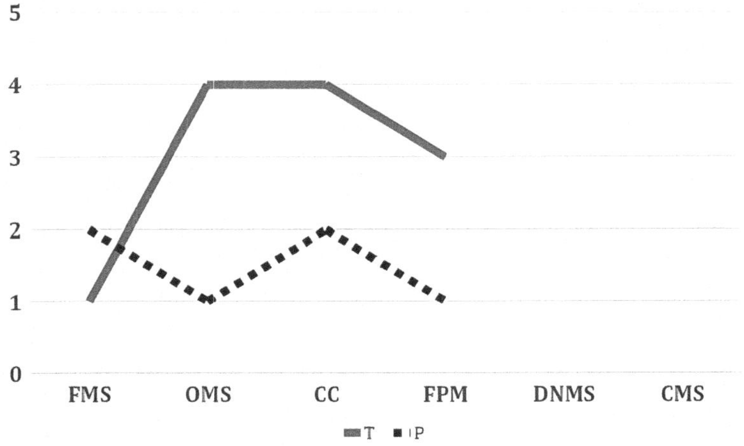

Fig. 11.1 Coding of interaction segment 1

experiences with their relative effects on emotions and thoughts. In this segment, the therapist shifts focus from regulating the patient's emotions to making the implicit aspects of the adolescent's discourse more explicit.

The combination of an intervention characterized by opacity and a high level of contingency allows the patient to feel neither threatened nor invalidated in her experience, which facilitates her emotional self-regulation. Although regulation is not the primary objective, this interaction enables the patient to achieve self-regulation, and only from that point can she begin reflecting, hastily, on the causality of her emotions while maintaining a focus centered on the here and now of the intervention. The coding of this segment according to the OMP-A is presented in Fig. 11.2.

Some Results of Studies through the Use of the OMP-A

The OMP-A has established itself as a versatile tool in psychotherapy process research, particularly for its ability to evaluate mentalization in specific segments or relevant episodes of psychotherapy sessions (Duarte et al., 2019). To illustrate its application, we provide examples from studies in which the OMP-A has been applied to clinical material.

Moran-Kneer (2019) conducted a study analyzing interactive rupture-resolution sequences in psychotherapeutic processes with adolescents. The study found that therapists' averages were significantly higher in both episodes for the dimensions of focus on mental states, opacity, dynamism, causality, and focus on the present moment. However, in the dimension of contingent communication, no significant differences were observed between actors. When comparing the overall averages

Table 11.3 Coding, minutes 00:02:46 to 00:05:37

Dialogue	Coding observations	Indicator
T: What's going on with what you're telling me?	T prompts the patient to engage with her emerging affect, creating an opportunity to explore emotional states for the first time.	CC → OMS→
P: It makes me angry because I'm always in second place for everyone (crying).	P connects with her affect, expressing a core belief about being "second place" to others.	OMS ↓ FMS ↓
T: That phrase catches my attention. It's quite harsh. It must not be easy to think or feel that, right?	T acknowledges the intensity of the patient's emotional expression, reflecting on its potential pain or complexity in the present moment.	OMS↑ CC ↑ FPM ↑
P: It's just that I'm not even asking for money for something extra; it's for my classes.	P explains to the therapist the reason for her frustration.	OMS →
T: Were you able to talk about this with your mom?	T inquires further to gather more context about the situation.	OMS →
P: Yes, but she told me that my brother is also important, that I'm not the center of the universe.	P is again able to describe the context, without assuming mental states.	OMS →
T: And was that when you left your house upset?	T seeks to connect events chronologically to better understand the sequence.	OMS →
P: Yes, upset… or sad, maybe both.	P recognizes the presence of contradictory emotions.	FMS → DNMS →
T: And when you were with your boyfriend on the way, did you tell him a little about what happened?	T tries to continue connecting the background to understand the sequence of events.	OMS →
P: Yes, I told him. He told me to calm down, that my mom would manage, that I shouldn't make such a big deal out of it. But of course, my brother always needs something.	P expresses her anger with a sense of certainty about her perspective.	OMS ↓
T: And how did you feel when he responded like that?	T seems to notice the lack of contingency between the patient's emotional needs and her partner's response. Asks about the emotional effect of her partner's action.	CC ↑ CMS →
P: I told him that I expected him to support me. not to side with my mom or my brother.	P responds with a focus on descriptive elements.	FMS ↓ CMS ↓
T: It seems like he didn't understand you much.	T proposes a mental state with a quality of opacity.	OMS → FMS →
P: No, it seems like he didn't.	P responds with a sense of ambiguity, aligning with the therapist's proposed mental state.	OMS →
T: Some time ago you had mentioned something similar, that you don't feel very understood at home. Is this a feeling that also accompanies you now?	T connects this situation with others in the past. Asks to confirm if the patient identifies this possible link.	OMS → FMS → CC ↑

(continued)

Table 11.3 (continued)

Dialogue	Coding observations	Indicator
P: Yes, it seems so.	Confirms the therapist's observation.	CC ↑
T: Do you think a bit of that also happened with the secretary? Maybe you came with so many things on your mind, and her saying something like that didn't help much.	T connects past themes with the recent situation, offering a hypothesis about how feeling misunderstood may have influenced the patient's emotional reaction.	OMS → CC ↑ CMS ↑
P: It could be… (thinks) but she also doesn't have to talk to me like that. It was the tone.	P seems to understand the link between her own past experiences and the automatic response. While her words reflect a self-affirming stance, her non-verbal cues suggest an emerging insight prompted by the intervention.	FPM ↑

Note: *T* therapist, *P* Patient

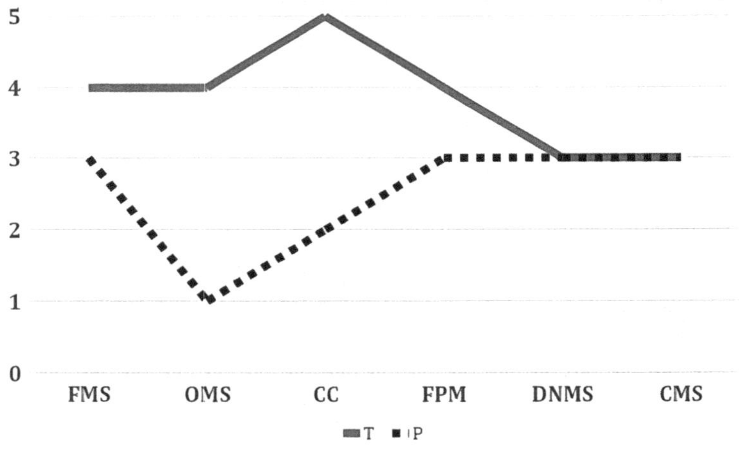

Fig. 11.2 Coding segment 2

between episodes, it was noted that the dimensions of opacity, contingent communication, causality, and focus on the present moment scored higher during the resolution episodes than during the rupture episodes, as expected. An interaction effect was identified between actor (therapist vs. patient) and episode (rupture vs. resolution) in the dimensions of focus on mental states, dynamism, and causality, where the differences observed between therapists and patients were only present during the rupture episodes. The tendency to demand explicit mentalization during ruptures may have been a key factor characterizing these episodes, where patients either withdraw or confront their therapists without being able to respond to the level of demand required. These findings further highlight how the deployment of mentalization varies depending on the interactive context, emphasizing its context-dependent nature.

In another study (Díaz & Moran-Kneer, 2019), the OMP-A was used to explore fluctuations in the mentalization abilities of both the therapist and the patient, as well as the dynamic relationships between these abilities and the therapeutic alliance during the first ten sessions of a psychodynamic psychotherapy process with a 19-year-old adolescent. The time series analysis revealed that the therapist's mentalization tended to be more consistent, while the patient demonstrated less integration across the dimensions of mentalization throughout the sessions. Additionally, it was noted that the ability to self-regulate and remain present (FPM) appeared to precede explicit mentalization (FMS, CMS, DNMS). Finally, the quality of the therapeutic alliance emerged as a critical factor associated with the deployment of mentalization. These findings further emphasize the importance of considering fluctuations and the complex interactive dynamics within the therapeutic process to better understand the progress of therapy.

On the other hand, the OMP-A has also proven to be a valuable tool for identifying interaction segments that meet specific characteristics of mentalization for subsequent analysis. For instance, in a study aimed at describing the therapeutic actions that promote adolescents' mentalization in MBT psychotherapy (Moran-Kneer et al., 2024), the OMP-A was used to identify segments of low mentalization in patients followed by moments of increased mentalization. With this sequence termed a "mentalizing interaction," 18 such configurations (low mentalization → high mentalization) were identified from a total of 21 sessions across 7 psychotherapy processes. In addition to suggesting that this pattern appears to be common in interventions with adolescents, the qualitative analysis of the low mentalization segments revealed two types of therapeutic actions: those aimed at supporting adolescents in organizing their experiences and another group of interventions focused specifically on empathic validation. The study provided a clinical description of how both groups of interventions facilitate moments of joint mentalization, during which patients are able to explicitly reflect on themselves and others.

Finally, regarding clinical analysis, the OMP-A also contributes to the description of therapeutic change. In the context of a feasibility study on the MBT model for adolescents and their families (Moran-Kneer & Duarte, 2023), an intensive analysis of a pilot case involving a patient with high adherence to the process was conducted.

Among the analytical strategies employed, two individual sessions were coded in 2-min segments—one from the initial phase and another from the intermediate phase of treatment—to describe the manifestation of mentalization in both actors and compare its deployment across these moments (see Fig. 11.3). As expected, the therapist's mentalization remained at higher levels most of the time. However, a comparison between the two moments revealed that the therapist's mentalization scores in session ten included low values, which were not present in session 3. The opposite pattern was observed in the patient.

A preliminary correlation analysis indicated an increase in the association between the mentalization scores of both actors, rising from $r = 0.14$ in session 3 to

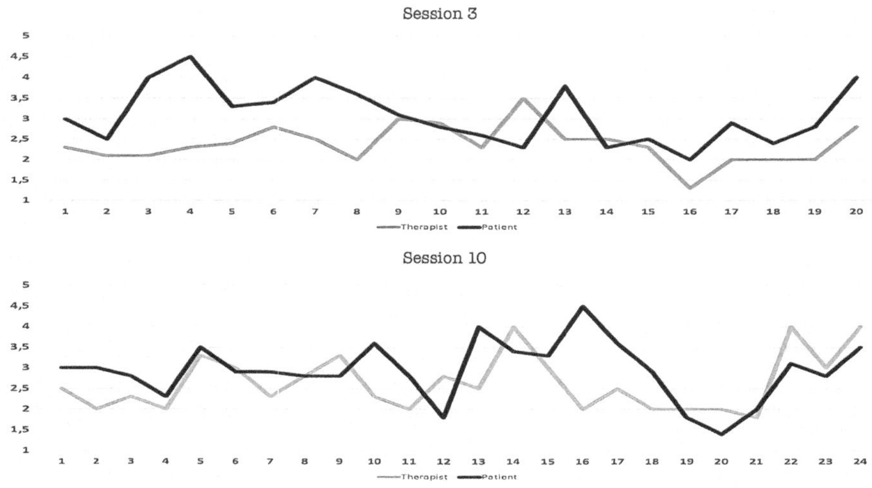

Fig. 11.3 Mentalization coding for sessions 3 and 10

$r = 0.29$ in session 10. Although these analyses are primarily descriptive, they allow for the hypothesis that the increase in the patient's mentalization may be linked to greater mentalizing coordination with their therapist. Theoretically, this idea aligns with the intersubjective nature of mentalization (Fonagy, Luyten, et al., 2019).

Final Reflections

This chapter has reviewed the process of constructing and applying the OMP-A to psychotherapy research with adolescents. The use of this scale exemplifies the contribution of observational measures to qualitative research in psychotherapy. In general, these measures have established themselves as essential tools in studying the psychotherapeutic process, particularly when aiming to understand the complexity of therapist-patient interactions.

The incorporation of such measures has expanded the scope of qualitative research in psychotherapy, enabling a deeper and more nuanced understanding of therapeutic processes. This includes identifying interaction dynamics that go beyond the discursive level and are fundamental to understanding how change occurs and how meaning is constructed in therapy (Cortés et al., 2018). A paradigmatic example is found in the study of the therapeutic alliance, where these measures have facilitated the transition from a monadic to a dyadic perspective, highlighting the value of therapeutic interaction (Gelo et al., 2015).

The OMP-A holds significant value as an observational tool specifically designed to evaluate the psychotherapy process while accounting for the mutual influence between therapist and patient. In the study of mentalization, this is an essential objective since, as reiterated throughout this chapter, mentalization is predominantly a relational phenomenon.

Process measures have additionally bridged qualitative and quantitative research, promoting the development of mixed-methods designs. Given the complexity of the phenomena studied, these designs have, in turn, proposed equally sophisticated strategies for identifying segments or moments of the process, as well as for their analysis. For instance, in a study analyzing 44 therapeutic sessions from five processes (de la Cerda et al., 2019), researchers coded the mentalization of therapists and patients in segments of change (Krause et al., 2007) and therapeutic alliance ruptures (Eubanks-Carter et al., 2015). This approach illustrates the use of a microanalytic strategy applied to segments derived from an equally microanalytic process.

Previous studies employing the OMP-A that follow this same structure for selecting and analyzing segments were described earlier. It is important to highlight that this instrument, like many process observation scales, offers significant versatility. It allows for tasks such as quantifying a set of interactions, providing criteria for the qualitative description of specific moments in psychotherapy, and even analyzing a particular interaction for purposes such as therapist training or therapeutic process evaluation.

In this sense, the OMP-A, like many other observation measures in psychotherapy, has the virtue of facilitating the transition between qualitative and quantitative methods, as well as their integration. It also holds potential not only for research purposes but also for clinical and training applications.

Finally, it is important to emphasize the value of this measure for advancing research with adolescents, a population often neglected compared to studies of change in adults (Weisz et al., 2013). Specifically, developing a line of research on mentalization in young people through observational measures in psychotherapy entails the significant challenge of generating evidence on the role of mentalization as a mechanism of change in psychotherapy for adolescents.

References

Bak, P., Midgley, N., Zhu, J., Wistoft, K., & Obei, C. (2015). The Resilience Program: Preliminary evaluation of a mentalization - Based education program. *Frontiers in Psychology, 6*, 753. https://doi.org/10.3389/fpsyg.2015.00753

Barkham, M., Lutz, W., & Castonguay, L. G. (Eds.). (2021). *Bergin and Garfield's handbook of psychotherapy and behavior change* (7th ed.). John Wiley & Sons.

Bateman, A., & Fonagy, P. (2006). *Mentalization-based treatment for Borderline Personality Disorder: A practical guide*. Oxford University Press.

Bateman, A., & Fonagy, P. (Eds.). (2019). *Handbook of mentalizing in mental health practice* (2nd ed.). American Psychiatric Association Publishing.

Bevington, D., Fuggle, P., Fonagy, P., Target, M., & Asen, E. (2013). Innovations in practice: Adolescent mentalization-based integrative therapy (AMBIT). *Child and Adolescent Mental Health, 18*(1), 46–51. https://doi.org/10.1111/j.1475-3588.2012.00666.x

Braun, V., & Clarke, V. (2006). Using thematic analysis in psychology. *Qualitative Research in Psychology, 3*(2), 77–101. https://doi.org/10.1191/1478088706qp063oa

Charmaz, K. (2024). *Constructing grounded theory* (3rd ed.). SAGE Publications Ltd..
Cortés, A. M., Fernández, O. M., Capella, C. M., Espinosa, H. D., & y Krause, M. (2018). ¿Qué es lo que cambia en la psicoterapia? La perspectiva de pacientes adolescentes con síntomas depresivos, sus terapeutas y observadores externos [What changes in psychotherapy? The perspective of adolescent patients with depressive symptoms, their therapists and external observers]. *Psykhe (Santiago), 27*(2), 1–15. https://doi.org/10.7764/psykhe.27.2.1134
de la Cerda, C., Tomicic, A., Pérez, J. C., Martínez, C., & Morán, J. (2019). Mentalizing in psychotherapy: Patients' and therapists' reflective functioning during the psychotherapeutic process. *Studies in Psychology, 40*(2), 396–418. https://doi.org/10.1080/02109395.2019.1583469
Díaz, R. A., & Moran-Kneer, J. (2019, July 3–6). *Mentalizing interactions: Modelling patient's and therapist's mentalizing capacities as a dyadic process* [Poster presentation]. SPR's 50th International Annual Meeting, Buenos Aires, Argentina. https://doi.org/10.13140/RG.2.2.26338.27843.
Duarte, J., Martínez, C. G., & Tomicic, A. (2019). Episodios relevantes y eventos para el estudio del cambio en psicoterapia [Relevant episodes and events for the study of change in psychotherapy]. *Revista Argentina de Clínica Psicológica, 28*(3), 253–265. https://doi.org/10.24205/03276716.2019.1141
Eubanks-Carter, C. F., Muran, J. C., & Safran, J. D. (2015). *Rupture resolution rating system (3RS): Manual*. https://doi.org/10.13140/2.1.1666.8488
Fonagy, P., Allison, E., & Campbell, C. (2019). Mentalizing, resilience, and epistemic trust. In A. Bateman & P. Fonagy (Eds.), *Handbook of mentalizing in mental health practice* (2nd ed., pp. 63–78). American Psychiatric Association Publishing.
Fonagy, P., Gergely, G., Jurist, E., & Target, M. (2002). *Affect regulation, mentalization, and the development of the self*. Other Press.
Fonagy, P., Luyten, P., Allison, E., & Campbell, C. (2019). Mentalizing, epistemic trust and the phenomenology of psychotherapy. *Psychopathology, 52*(2), 94–103. https://doi.org/10.1159/000501526
Fonagy, P., Target, M., Steele, H., & Steele, M. (1998). *Reflective-functioning manuel, version 5.0, for application to adult attachment interviews*. University College London.
Gamarra, P. (2023). *Terapia basada en la mentalización y el trastorno límite de la personalidad: una revisión aplicada [Mentalization and borderline personality disorder based therapy: an applied review]* [Professional sufficiency work to qualify for the Professional Degree in Psychology, Universidad de Lima] Universidad de Lima Institutional Repository. https://hdl.handle.net/20.500.12724/18262
Gelo, O. C. G., Pritz, A., & Rieken, B. (Eds.). (2015). *Psychotherapy research: Foundations, process, and outcome*. Springer-Verlag Publishing/Springer Nature. https://doi.org/10.1007/978-3-7091-1382-0
Gensler, D. (2015). Silence in adolescent psychotherapy. *Journal of Infant, Child & Adolescent Psychotherapy, 14*(2), 188–195. https://doi.org/10.1080/15289168.2015.1032635
Guillén, J., & Valls, J. (2023). Metacognición, mentalización y psicopatología [Metacognition, mentalization and psychopathology]. *Norte de Salud Mental, 18*(68), 32–40.
Hauschild, S., Kasper, L., Volkert, J., Sobanski, E., & Taubner, S. (2023). Mentalization-based treatment for adolescents with conduct disorder (mbt-cd): A feasibility study. *European Child & Adolescent Psychiatry., 32*, 2611–2622. https://doi.org/10.1007/s00787-022-02113-4
Kornhas, L. A., Schröder-Pfeifer, P., Georg, A., Zettl, M., & Taubner, S. (2020). Process of mentalization in a mentalization-based long-term therapy for borderline personality disorders: A case study. *Psychotherapeut, 65*, 357–365. https://doi.org/10.1007/s00278-020-00451-9
Krause, M., & Altimir, C. (2016). Introduction: Current developments in psychotherapy process research/Introducción: Desarrollos actuales en la investigación del proceso psicoterapéutico. *Estudios de Psicología, 37*(2–3), 201–225. https://doi.org/10.1080/02109395.2016.1227574
Krause, M., de la Parra, G., Arístegui, R., Dagnino, P., Tomicic, A., Valdés, N., Echávarri, O., Vilches, O., Ben-Dov, P., Strasser, K., Reyes, L., Altimir, C., & Ramírez, I. (2007). The evolu-

tion of therapeutic change studied through generic change indicators. *Psychotherapy Research, 17*(6), 673–689. https://doi.org/10.1080/10503300601158814
Lüdemann, J., Rabung, S., & Andreas, S. (2021). Systematic review on mentalization as key factor in psychotherapy. *International Journal of Environmental Research and Public Health, 18*(17), 9161. https://doi.org/10.3390/ijerph18179161
Luyten, P., Campbell, C., Moser, M., & Fonagy, P. (2024). The role of mentalizing in psychological interventions in adults: Systematic review and recommendations for future research. *Clinical Psychology Review, 108*(4), 102380. https://doi.org/10.1016/j.cpr.2024.102380
Manubens, R. T., Roussos, A. J., Olivera Ryberg, J. M., & Gómez Penedo, J. M. (2018). Rupturas en la alianza terapéutica y su asociación co*n cambio y abandonos tempranos en psicoterapia* [Ruptures in the therapeutic alliance and their association with change and early dropouts in psychotherapy]. *Academo, 5*(2), 143–158. Universidad Americana. https://doi.org/10.30545/academo.2018.jul-dic.7
Martínez, C. (Principal Researcher). (2015–2018). *Mentalización en procesos psicoterapéuticos con pacientes diagnosticados con trastornos de la personalidad: Su papel en la regulación mutua y su asociación con el cambio terapéutico* [Mentalization in psychotherapeutic processes with patients diagnosed with personality disorders: Its role in mutual regulation and its association with therapeutic change] (Proyecto FONDECYT Regular N° 1150639). Universidad Diego Portales. Financiado por la Agencia Nacional de Investigación y Desarrollo (ANID).
Martínez, C. (2021). Mentalización y Proceso Psicoterapéutico: Aproximaciones Empíricas Hacia el Cambio en Psicoterapia [Mentalization and psychotherapeutic process: Empirical approaches towards change in psychotherapy]. *Mentalización: revista de psicoanálisis y psicoterapia, 15*, 10–10.
Martínez Guzmán, C., Tomicic, A., de la Cerda, C., Rivera, M. J., & Salas, C. (2017). Función reflexiva en primeras entrevistas en psicoterapia: un estudio exploratorio sobre el papel de la mentalización en la interacción terapéutica [Reflective function in first interviews in psychotherapy: An exploratory study on the role of mentalization in therapeutic interaction]. *Revista Argentina de Clínica Psicológica, 26*(3), 274–282. https://doi.org/10.24205/03276716.2017.1026
Morán, J., Martínez, C., Tomicic, A., Pérez, J. C., Krause, M., Guzmán, M., et al. (2016). Verbal and nonverbal expressions of mutual regulation in relevant episodes of psychotherapy. *Estudios de Psicología, 37*(2–3), 548–579. https://doi.org/10.1080/02109395.2016.1204784
Moran-Kneer, J. (2019). *Regulatory function of mentalization in rupture-resolution sequence of the therapeutic alliance during psychotherapy processes with adolescents*. Tesis doctoral, Universidad de Chile y Pontificia Universidad Católica de Chile.
Moran-Kneer, J., & Duarte, J. (2023–2024). *Estudio de factibilidad y aceptabilidad de una intervención psicoterapéutica familiar breve informada por la mentalización para adolescentes entre 10 y 14 años con diagnóstico de depresión [Feasibility and acceptability study of a brief family psychotherapeutic intervention informed by mentalization for adolescents between 10 and 14 years old with a diagnosis of depression]* (Proyect SA22I0168). Financed by the National Research and Development Agency (ANID), within the framework of the XIX Health Research and Development Competition (FONIS).
Moran-Kneer, J., Martínez, C., Díaz, M. F., González, S., Arce, K., & Duarte, J. (2020). Observando la mentalización en psicoterapias con adolescentes: Diseño de un sistema de observación de la interacción terapéutica [Observing mentalization in psychotherapies with adolescents: Design of a therapeutic interaction observation system]. *Revista CES Psicologia, 13*(3), 51–75. https://doi.org/10.21615/cesp.13.3.4
Moran-Kneer, J., Pinilla, P., Celedón, A., Mundaca, V., & Sepúlveda, S. (2024, octubre). *Interacciones mentalizadoras en psicoterapia MBT con adolescentes [Mentalizing interactions in MBT psychotherapy with adolescents]* [Póster]. XVIII Congreso Chileno de Psicología, Universidad del Bío Bío, Chillán, Chile.
Navarro, M., Mozota, V., & García, A. (2023). Revisión de revisiones sobre la eficacia de los tratamientos psicológicos para adolescentes con trastorno de la personalidad límite [Review of reviews on the effectiveness of psychological treatments for adolescents with borderline

personality disorder]. *Revista de Psicología Clínica con Niños y Adolescentes, 10*(1), 91–98. https://doi.org/10.21134/rpcna.2023.10.1.8
Paz, C., Mascialino, G., Proaño, K., & Evans, C. (2021). Psychological intervention change measurement in Latin America: Where from? Where to? *Psychotherapy Research, 31*(1), 132–141. https://doi.org/10.1080/10503307.2020.1750728
Pinos, V. (2023). Actualidad del lazo social: la sexualidad, la ley y lo social en la jerga de los adolescentes [The social bond: Sexuality, the law and the social in the jargon of adolescents]. *Praxis der Psychotherapie, 24*(39), 54. https://doi.org/10.32995/praxispsy.v24i39.227
Robinson, P., Skarderud, F., & Sommerfeldt, B. (2019). Working with families: Systems in crisis. In *Hunger: Mentalization-based treatments for eating disorders* (pp. 145–154). Springer.
Talia, A., Miller-Bottome, M., Katznelson, H., Pedersen, S. H., Steele, H., Schröder, P., Origlieri, A., Scharff, F. B., Giovanardi, G., Andersson, M., Lingiardi, V., Safran, J. D., Lunn, S., Poulsen, S., & Taubner, S. (2019). Mentalizing in the presence of another: Measuring reflective functioning and attachment in the therapy process. *Psychotherapy Research, 29*(5), 652–665. https://doi.org/10.1080/10503307.2017.1417651
Valdés, N. (2010). Análisis de los estilos lingüísticos de paciente y terapeuta durante la conversación terapéutica en episodios de cambio, utilizando el Buscador Lingüístico y Contador de Palabras (LIWC)/Analysis of linguistic style in patient and therapist during therapeutic conversation in change episodes using the Linguistic Inquiry and Word Count (LIWC). *Subjetividad y Procesos Cognitivos, 14*, 314–332.
Weisz, J. R., Ng, M. Y., Rutt, C., Lau, N., & Masland, S. (2013). Psychotherapy for children and adolescents. In M. J. Lambert (Ed.), *Bergin and Garfield's handbook of psychotherapy and behavior change* (6th ed., pp. 541–586). John Wiley & Sons.
Zamignani, D., & Meyer, S. B. (2017). Comportamentos verbais do terapeuta no sistema multidimensional para a categorização de comportamentos na interação terapêutica (SiMCCIT) [Verbal behaviors of the therapist in the multidimensional system for the categorization of behaviors in therapeutic interaction (SiMCCIT)]. *Perspectivas em Análise do Comportamento, 2*(1), 25–45. https://doi.org/10.18761/perspectivas.v2i1.47

Chapter 12
Micro-Phenomenology Applied to Research in Psychotherapy: A First-Person Approach to the Study of the Subjective Experience of the Psychotherapy Process

Javiera Duarte Soto

Introduction to the Study of Processes in Psychotherapy

Psychotherapy process research, as Valdés has already mentioned in Chap. 9 of this same book, is characterized by its efforts to understand what happens throughout the psychotherapeutic process that makes it useful and, in the same vein, how psychotherapy works (Hardy & Llewelyn, 2015). This field of research has proven to be immensely valuable for psychotherapy research because, while studies of psychotherapy outcome have consistently and persistently demonstrated that psychotherapy works, the lack of answers to the questions of how and why it works is not only frustrating for clinicians but also hinders its reproducibility, teaching, and training.

In this context, process studies have increased substantially, and, in recent decades, different paths have been developed as attempts to answer these questions. The particular path that interests us for this chapter is the "Change Process Research" (Greenberg, 1986), which focuses on investigating what happens during psychotherapy in terms of its clinical meaningfulness and what those specific aspects of the therapeutic process through which patients change or improve are (Gelo & Manzo, 2015).

Change process research concentrates on identifying, describing, explaining, and predicting the processes that produce psychotherapeutic change (Greenberg, 1986). It emphasizes the importance of directing psychotherapy studies toward measuring change events within sessions and their effects on outcomes (Knobloch-Fedders

J. D. Soto (✉)
Centre for Studies in Clinical Psychology and Psychotherapy (CEPPS), Faculty of Psychology, Diego Portales University, Santiago, Chile

Millennium Institute for Research in Depression and Personality (MIDAP), Santiago, Chile
e-mail: javiera.duarte@mail.udp.cl

A. Tomicic, J. D. Soto (eds.), *Qualitative Research in Clinical Psychology and Psychotherapy in Latin America*, https://doi.org/10.1007/978-3-031-90782-1_12

et al., 2014). Change process research in psychotherapy, to a large extent, has been developed based on the identification and exhaustive description of events that, based on certain criteria, stand out significantly from the therapeutic process (Duarte et al., 2019). In this context, the interest in studying what are called relevant events or episodes in psychotherapy sessions has begun to gain importance, giving rise to many theoretical and empirical conceptualizations to account for the phenomenon in question (Duarte et al., 2019). For the most part, research on relevant episodes has been based on observation of therapy sessions, either live or videotaped, when looking to identify small segments or moments that may be clinically significant (Gonçalves et al., 2011; Krause, 2005; Safran et al., 2011), or on semi-structured interviews when seeking a general overview of what has been recognized as relevant, either from the patients' or the therapists' perspective, for example through follow-up interviews (Levitt et al., 2006; Levitt et al., 2016; Rhodes et al., 1994; Timulak, 2010). Some self-report instruments have also been developed, such as the Helpful Aspects of Therapy (HAT; Elliott et al., 2001), which has a version for patients and another for therapists. This brief questionnaire is applied once the session is over and seeks to identify and describe events or moments that benefited the process the most and those that hindered it.

All the measures for relevant episodes mentioned above have made an important contribution to advancing knowledge about what happens in psychotherapy that can be relevant for change; however, they present certain limitations. In the case of observational measures, those who interpret and make inferences about what is or is not meaningful are the observers. Even though these interpretations are based on previously established theoretical or empirical knowledge and use control measures such as observer triangulation or consensus to reach agreements (see Flick, 2002; Krause, 1995), the criterion is still in the hands of the observer, and as they are not an active participant in the session, there will always be the risk of losing important material or interpreting from a biased perspective. In the case of semi-structured interviews, we appeal to the patient's or therapist's memory, which is not always accurate and can be influenced by multiple aspects that may be difficult to isolate, especially when the interview is conducted several months after therapy has ended (between 2 months to a year: Levitt et al., 2006; Midgley et al., 2014). Something similar happens with the HAT (Elliott et al., 2001) because by applying the survey immediately after the session, the patient and the psychotherapist have not had much time to elaborate on what recently happened, possibly being left with general ideas of the session from specific aspects, making it difficult for researchers to access what really happened.

Thus, a little over 10 years ago, during the elaboration of my doctoral thesis, I began to search for a method that could narrow the gap between the researcher and the research object and provide access to the subjective experience of psychotherapy participants in a pre-reflective way, less mediated by recall or by third-party perceptions of what is relevant. In this search, I came across the micro-phenomenological approach, developed to understand the experience from a first-person perspective and access implicit experiences of the participants of the psychotherapeutic process that can be difficult to observe initially using videos or narratives of the session.

The Use of Micro-Phenomenology for the Study of the Subjective Experience

Micro-phenomenology, as a method of scientific research, is based on the fundamental principles of Husserlian phenomenology that emphasize the search for the original and pure experience of phenomena, highlighting the *how* instead of the *why*, focusing on the process of a given experience (Husserl, 1913/1983). From the micro-phenomenological perspective, cognition is understood as embodied, and experience is conceived as an action that arises from the interaction of the subject with the world, with a shared component that can be intersubjectively validated and not purely in the private domain. Thus, knowing is an active and embodied process in which the environment of the organisms is shaped by their actions (Valenzuela-Moguillansky, 2020). In this way, the assumption of an objective world preexisting before the subject and independent of him loses significance, and the structure of the organism, that is, its body, and its history of interactions with the environment acquire a central role in the configuration of his world (Varela et al. 1991).

Hence, the central notion underlying this approach is that all experience is based, at first, on the direct senses of the body and, only later, can it be brought to consciousness (Aron, 1998; Cozolino, 2002; Katz, 2011; Siegel, 2007; Wallace, 2006). This bodily sensation is the core of the subjective experience and, therefore, to truly understand it, it is essential to access the pre-reflective dimension of human experience. The felt bodily experience, however, often remains pre-reflective, as does the possibility of attributing meaning to it. This aspect of our experience, then, can remain hidden, out of our reach, unable to make sense of it (Duarte et al., 2020). Consequently, micro-phenomenology is an attempt to study experience from a first-person perspective systematically and rigorously (Valenzuela-Moguillansky & Vásquez-Rosati, 2019), accessing it to make it understandable.

The technique of micro-phenomenology was originally created by the French psychologist Pierre Vermersch during the 1970s in the context of experimental psychology, based on his research on learning and problem-solving. Until then, task resolution was studied mainly from quantitative variables with a focus on the result. However, for Vermersch, it was important to understand the cognitive processes and physical and mental actions that subjects carried out during these tasks. By directing people's attention to the how, instead of the why or the what, he realized that implicit dimensions of the experience were revealed, which allowed him to better understand the processes and strategies developed (Vermersch, 2012).

Later, Claire Petitmengin (1999, 2006) transferred Vermersch's learnings to cognitive science studies, and the Chilean biologist and philosopher Francisco Varela (1996) incorporated it into his neurophenomenological program to integrate the study of the experiential aspect of cognitive phenomena into his scientific study. Since then, this technique or approach has been used in a growing number of studies in cognitive (Lutz et al., 2002), clinical (Petitmengin et al., 2007), therapeutic (Katz, 2011), and management (Remillieux, 2009) fields.

The objective of micro-phenomenology is to obtain a detailed description of a unique experience, focusing on the procedural dimension from an embodied perspective (Petitmengin, 2006; Vermersch, 1994/2011). This approach allows implicit aspects of the experience that develop in a pre-reflective dimension and are not apprehensible through other methodologies to be revealed. Given that psychotherapy itself can be understood as a lived experience that unfolds both in an explicit dimension (through verbal cognition and reflective processes) as well as in an implicit dimension (through the regulation of affects and nonverbal communication), I considered that it would be consistent to apply micro-phenomenology to the psychotherapeutic process, specifically for the identification of a particularly significant moment associated with the process of change in psychotherapy, which I will detail in the last section of this chapter.

Micro-Phenomenology: A Tool for In-Depth Understanding of the Experience in Psychotherapy

If we consider that a significant fraction of what happens in the psychotherapeutic encounter, and the effect of change that it pursues, occurs outside the reflective plane and conscious attention (Aron, 1998; Siegel, 2007), phenomenologically speaking, we can assert that the embodied, pre-reflective, and intuitive experience is the privileged space where the cues to understand this complex phenomenon may be found. In this context, micro-phenomenology is a methodologically guided procedure to reflectively examine experience over meaning. In other words, as Leigh (2012) points out, being an embodied inquiry, it is part of a continuous process of reflexivity, exploration, attention, and unbiased awareness, both of one's own experience and that of others, of each movement and each moment. This procedure has its own data collection and analysis guidelines, which I will describe briefly, but for a more detailed explanation of both procedures, I suggest reviewing Vermersch (1994/2011) and Valenzuela-Moguillansky and Vásquez-Rosati (2019).

The Micro-Phenomenological Interview

The micro-phenomenological interview focuses on the *how* instead of the *why or what* of the lived experience, guiding the interviewee in a recall process through the evocation of a specific experience (Valenzuela-Moguillansky, 2020; Valenzuela-Moguillansky et al., 2013), to explore the temporal evolution of the experience (The diachronic dimension) and the qualitative aspects of a specific moment of the experience (the synchronic dimension).The micro-phenomenological interview is conducted in three steps (see Fig. 12.1).

The first step leads the interviewee to evoke an experience—evoking means recalling a specific experience as if it were being re-lived. This is achieved by asking the person to identify a single experience and then exploring the sensory atmosphere, facilitating a description from an "embodied position" (Vermersch, 1994/2011). The state of evocation can be recognized by the degree to which the person is "in contact" with the experience they are describing. A series of nonverbal, verbal, and paraverbal signs have been identified to indicate the level of the interviewee's connection with an experience (Hendricks, 2009; Petitmengin, 2006; Vermersch, 1994/2011).

Once the person is in a state of evocation, the actions (physical or mental) of the person throughout the evoked and specified situation are used as the axis of inquiry (Vermersch, 1994/2011; Petitmengin, 2006). Finally, in step three, we can ask about the temporal evolution of the actions and establish a scheme of their sequence, accessing what has been called the "diachronic dimension" of the experience. Depending on the research question, the diachronic dimension of the experience can be explored with different levels of detail. Thus, once a general sequence of events or actions is established, the interviewer can guide the interviewee into directing their attention to specific levels of the experience. Using the sequence of actions as an axis, the qualitative aspects of the experience at a given moment, or its "synchronic dimension," can be explored. Normally, interviewees tend to slide towards general descriptions of condensed situations that hinder the elaboration of precise descriptions. Therefore, it is important to constantly bring the interviewee back to the chosen situation (Valenzuela-Moguillansky et al., 2013).

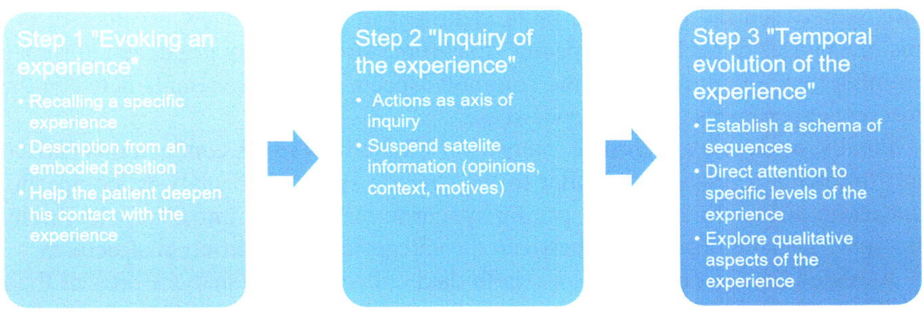

Fig. 12.1 The micro-phenomenological interview process

The Micro-Phenomenological Analysis

The micro-phenomenological interview analysis offers an individual and a group (generic) approach to both diachronic and synchronic aspects of the investigated experience. Both analyses are carried out in the following sequence: First, we begin with the preparation of the data, then the specific diachronic and synchronic analysis is carried out for each interview, followed by a generic diachronic and synchronic analysis of all the interviewees' experience (Valenzuela-Moguillansky & Vásquez-Rosati, 2019).

Once the interviews have been conducted in person or virtually and have been recorded in audio for later transcription, the data is prepared by performing a general reading of each interview. Then, data cleaning is carried out by selecting the fragments of the interviews that describe the procedural dimension of the experience (Valenzuela-Moguillansky & Vásquez-Rosati, 2019), leaving aside the general anecdotal descriptions and satellite information such as contexts, opinions, and undefined descriptions, such as "one" or "generally," which do not correspond to the experience of evocation. Next, a specific diachronic analysis is carried out for every interview, seeking to understand the temporal evolution of the evoked experience. At this stage, the selected fragments are organized according to the chronology of the experience into incipient diachronic units (DU), which will then be subjected to an iterative interrogation process to split and identify the units that characterize the temporal evolution, its phases, and subphases.

The following step corresponds to the specific synchronic analysis, aiming to gain insight into more detailed aspects of the subjective experience evoked by the participant. At this stage, an iterative interrogation process of the synchronic units is also carried out, which will then be grouped by thematic affinity, initiating a new iterative interrogation process to find stable aspects of the experience.

The fourth step is the generic diachronic analysis, which results from the comparison between the diachronic units identified in each interview conducted. For this, the phases of each of the specific diachronic structures are organized in such a way that they allow observing the common aspects and the invariants between the different experiences of the interviewees.

Finally, a generic synchronic analysis of all the interviews conducted is carried out, following a procedure similar to the specific synchronic analysis, comparing and reorganizing the result of specific synchronic structures into a new hierarchy that integrates the relationship between the categories of the different structures.

As the above description shows, both data collection and analysis present their challenges in terms of the level of detail and refinement with which they work. However, or perhaps because of this, the results obtained with this methodology, both in the interview and the analysis, contain a deep and rich description that few methods, even qualitative ones, can provide.

In a small study conducted by Cárdenas et al. (2019), ten researchers with different levels of training and experience in the use of micro-phenomenology were interviewed and asked about their own experience applying this methodology for the study of clinical and psychotherapeutic phenomena. The interviewees pointed out that micro-phenomenology is an appropriate device to explore all those study objects related to micro-processes, such as the psychotherapy process as the patients' and psychotherapists' individual processes. They also indicated that questions regarding experiences, such as the experience of a certain diagnosis or the experience of being in psychotherapy, which requires a detailed and fine description that prints a unique texture in the stories, can benefit from the use of this method. This is because both how the interview is conducted and the analysis carried out allow us to delve into the unique and individual experience of each participant and understand in greater depth the first-person human experience.

Cárdenas et al. (2019), also found that the researchers recognize certain advantages of this method, such as it's access the experience of evocation without interpretations, the high level of depth and detail, and the richness of the information obtained. In addition, they point out that micro-phenomenology allows awareness of a pre-reflective experience and deepening into different layers of the experience.

However, despite all the benefits micro-phenomenology has portrayed, the legitimacy of the method for its scientific use has also been questioned. I would like to briefly address this aspect before continuing, since I believe that in any field of study, especially in disciplines that study complex phenomena like the mind and psychotherapy, the methodological principles at base must ensure scientific rigor and validity, while maintaining a balance between respect for subjective experience and scientific research standards, be they quantitative or qualitative.

While the criticisms of micro-phenomenology are numerous, the majority are related to the possible error in terms of the observed stimulus, that is, what is being measured is really what is intended to be measured (this, in quantitative research, is known as validity); the impossibility of separating the action from the self-observation; and distortions in observation such as objectification and immobilization, the disruption of the course of experience, or the creation of experience (which, in quantitative research, is related to objectivity); and temporal distortion along with interpretation distortion that allude to verbal distortion, introspection blindness, and the non-verifiability of the results (which, in quantitative research, responds to the idea of reliability).

Regarding these criticisms, different authors have stated their positions, such as Petitmengin and Bitbol (2009), who point out that, to minimize these errors and biases, the most important issue is that the process of introspection must be correctly performed, and, for this, it is important to guide the interviewee appropriately during the evocation process. In addition, they propose that becoming aware of the pre-reflective aspects of an experience makes it more efficient, fluid, and meaningful. In this sense, rather than aiming for the evoked experience to be a replica of the original experience, the purpose of evocation is to connect the interviewee with the synchronic and diachronic aspects of that experience in the evocation itself. Likewise, they emphasize that the validation of scientific descriptions cannot be conditioned to their correspondence with the process itself, but must be carried out through performative consistency, that is, conformity between the perceptive interpretation of a phenomenon and the results of the actions guided by such perception. In other words, validity must be subject to the consistency of the procedure and not necessarily to the correspondence of verifiability and objectivity.

The prevailing idea for many years that the only way to produce data in science is through methods that are "reliable and objective" has slowly been challenged in some scientific communities (Guba & Lincoln, 1994). However, there is still much resistance and disbelief regarding alternative research methods, which seek to describe and deepen certain phenomena rather than measure them. From my experience as a researcher, I have been able to witness that the researcher is never neutral and is always permeated by their hypotheses, personal and professional interests, and other broader aspects such as socio-cultural and even political domains. So rather than a pretension to achieve objectivity in research, I consider it important to give transparency to our perspectives and points of view and use them as a control when analyzing our data and interpretations.

Examples of Applied Research in Psychotherapy with the Micro-Phenomenological Approach

To conclude this chapter, I will present some recent studies in which various authors and myself have used the micro-phenomenological approach to study different phenomena within the process of psychotherapy and clinical psychology. These examples show how the method has been adapted for the field and what results it has offered.

As I mentioned earlier, my interest in applying the micro-phenomenological approach to research in psychotherapy arose during the elaboration of my doctoral thesis as an attempt to study "moments of meeting in psychotherapy." A theoretical concept developed by the Boston group and Daniel Stern in 1998, but that had not managed to be studied empirically until that time. In this section, I will briefly explain the central ideas at the base of my research and how the use of micro-phenomenology allowed me to approach the research of this phenomenon. Subsequently, I will refer to other studies in clinical psychology and psychotherapy that have used this same methodology to investigate complex phenomena in clinical psychology.

The Study of Episodes of Meeting in Psychotherapy

Since the 2000s or maybe even earlier, interest in the relational and intersubjective aspects of psychotherapeutic processes began to acquire increasing relevance in the different theoretical approaches of postmodern psychotherapy (Mearns & Cooper, 2005; Safran & Muran, 2000). This is due, mainly, to the strong conviction of clinicians and researchers that it is through new experiences of relationship with the psychotherapist that the capacity for reflexive self-awareness of the patient increases, allowing the development of new internal representations, which would represent the essence of change (Orange et al., 1997). More precisely, there would be especially significant moments within psychotherapy, in which patient and psychotherapist connect emotionally with each other or, in other terms, generate deep feelings of connection and relationship. These moments would constitute for many psychotherapists the core of their clinical practice and the potential for psychotherapeutic change (for example, Friedman, 1985; Mearns & Cooper, 2005; Stern, 2004). This clinical intuition is supported by studies of relevant events or episodes (see above) that were being investigated as clinically significant moments in psychotherapy. In 2007, Ladislav Timulak conducted a meta-analysis of different types of significant events and concluded that they can be grouped into nine meta-categories: (1) Awareness/insight/self-understanding (2) Behavioral change/problem solution (3) Empowerment (4) Relief (5) Exploring feelings/emotional experiencing (6) Feeling understood (7) Client involvement (8) Reassurance/support/safety (9) Personal contact. Of these, four refer to the therapeutic relationship, indicating that a significant part of what patients point out and remember as significant is related to the therapeutic bond and actions of the therapist that make them feel seen and understood.

The work of Daniel Stern (1998, 2004) and the Boston Change Process Study Group (BCPSG, 2002, 2005, 2008, 2010) on moments of meeting in psychotherapy proposes that change, or at least part of it, is a relational and interactional phenomenon that takes place between patient and therapist. This notion is based on the concept of implicit relational knowledge coined by Karlen Lyons-Ruth et al. (1998) and defined as the knowledge that is procedurally acquired in relationships with others that operates outside the attentional focus and conscious verbal experience of the self. It also suggests that this knowledge of interpersonal events is recorded from early childhood (Stern et al., 1998). Thus, longitudinal research on attachment has also supported the idea that relational behaviors are based on relational history (Lyons-Ruth, 1999).

In psychotherapy, implicit relational knowledge is expressed through the process of subjective exchange that becomes shared implicit knowledge about the relationship. In this way, relational aspects and the emotional connection between patients and therapists would be fundamental for changes to occur during psychotherapy (Lyons-Ruth, 1999; Stern et al., 1998).

With this in mind, for Stern et al. (1998), change in psychotherapy resides precisely in the interaction, that is, in the moments of meeting between patient and therapist, as these moments of significant connection during the process would modify the relationship between both, allowing a transformation and reconfiguration of the patients' implicit relational knowledge and, as a result, of their sense of self and their way of "being with others."

Stern (1998, 2004) states that moments of meeting in psychotherapy are essentially intersubjective because they are jointly constructed by therapist and patient, with the contribution of something unique and particular from the subjectivity of each of them. In other words, the therapist-patient relationship facilitates change, specifically around the construction of new possibilities for adaptive regulation of intersubjective experiences. The therapist must then be able to deconstruct already established, but unsatisfactory, ways of "being with," while simultaneously helping the patient move towards new and satisfying ways (Lyons-Ruth, 1999); it would be through the significant connection provided by the moments of meeting in therapy that this process could partially take place.

With this conceptual framework, I decided to empirically study the moments of meeting in psychotherapy with micro-phenomenology as the method of choice to access the subjective experience of the patients. The objective of this work was to explore and understand the moments of meeting in psychotherapy as a lived experience by the patient and to identify its main characteristics, effects, and relevance both for the psychotherapeutic process itself and for its outcome.

Methodology: Towards the Meeting of Micro-Phenomenology

To carry out this study, I applied the micro-phenomenological interview to nine psychotherapy patients, as explained in the previous section, to explore and understand the moments of meeting in psychotherapy as a lived experience by the patient. The interviews focused on a specific relived event that the patient remembered that had the character of a special moment of connection or feeling met by their psychotherapist.

The ethical protocol of this research was approved by the Ethics Committee of the Faculty of Medicine of the University of Chile, and the informed consent forms were signed by all the participants of the study before conducting the interview, giving their permission for the use of the transcripts of the interviews for research purposes and related publications.

All interviews were audio recorded to be transcribed and lasted between 40 and 80 min each.

The interview began with the following initial question: *"If you agree, I would like to ask you to take your time and remember a moment of your psychotherapy process with (therapist's name) in which you felt a significant connection, a special moment of meeting... when you find it, please, let me know."*

Once the interviewee identified that specific moment, a general description of it was requested as if they were reliving or evoking it. To help the interviewee complete this task, I used different techniques offered by the micro-phenomenological interview to place the person in the time, space, and sensory memories of the event. Each time the interviewee interrupted the evocation, I gently led them back to the event.

Once the situation was described, I reviewed the event in detail to clearly understand the sequence of actions of that specific event and how it had occurred in terms of emotions, physical sensations, or thoughts. Every so often, I recapped the event to confirm that the sequences and sensations were being described correctly. Once the interview was completed, I corroborated the description with the interviewee.

I analyzed the interviews using the procedure described in the previous section, which I repeated for each of the nine interviews, allowing me to recognize nine individual representations of the structure (diachronic) of the experience of the moment of meeting. Next, I compared the individual structures of each interview, looking for invariants among the different experiences. From the invariants, I constructed a generic diachronic structure of the experience, and, in a second analysis, I grouped this structure into three subtypes according to their main characteristics. Once the generic diachronic structure was identified, I reviewed the experiential categories that characterize each phase, seeking to identify synchronic aspects of the interviewees' experience of meeting.

The analysis process was periodically discussed with researchers Claudio Martínez and Alemka Tomicic so that the identification of events, the interpretation of the data, and the generation of categories were validated by an intersubjective agreement process to ensure the quality of the results (strategies of triangulation of interpreters, Krause, 1995; Howe & Eisenhart, 1993; Patton, 1999).

Likewise, I used the criterion of dense description (Ponterotto, 2006) to understand and interpret each of the interviews in a contextualized way to plausibly describe the different elements that shaped the experience of moments of meeting.

Main Findings and Interpretations: Crossing the Bridge from the Implicit to the Reflective

From Moments of Meeting to Episodes of Meeting

The first finding of this research, which completely changed our way of studying moments of meeting, was that these moments were described by the interviewees as part of a broader event or episode of the psychotherapy session, in which the moments of meeting or feelings of connection were contained. This led us to think that the term "episode of meeting" describes better the patients' recall of the entirety of the event, while the moments of meeting seem to be specific instants, referring to that specific moment of "feeling found," "feeling met," or feeling connected with the therapist. This finding and the conceptualization of an "episode" instead of a "moment" have been used in further studies and have given us a better methodological grasp.

Generic Structure of "Episodes of Meeting": Diachronic Approach

The generic structure of the patient's experience of the moments of meeting was developed by integrating the diachronic structure, or temporal characterization of these moments, with the synchronic structure, or qualitative characterization of the different stages or phases.

Through the analysis of the interviews, we identified five phases that make up the diachronic structure of the episode of meeting (see Fig. 12.2). We also included an additional phase in the analysis that took place after the episode, due to the effect that this phase had on the patients. Some interviewees described some phases with more detail than others, while others focused on one or two of them.

The phases that describe the structure of the moments of meeting are described in detail in the article by Duarte et al. (2020) so I will give a brief explanation of the findings just for illustrative purposes and move on to the subtypes of episodes, which show the complexity of the phenomenon.

The first phase, called Phase 0 or "Preparatory Phase," contains the patients' descriptions of what they were experiencing before the episode of meeting took place and how they prepared to tell something to their therapists or to talk about an important topic.

The second phase, called Phase 1 or "Event Phase," describes the interaction that took place during the moment that the patient chose as a moment of meeting. This phase is present in all the interviews and tends to be very detailed and descriptive. This moment is described by all the interviewees as emotionally charged, due to the content of the event, the atmosphere of the session, or both. Although this phase turned out not to be the moment of meeting itself, it was very important because the "meeting" occurred around this specific interaction and, therefore, articulated the episode as such.

The third phase, called Phase 2 or "Syncopation Phase," is predominantly characterized by a therapist's action: this is when he did or said something that caught the patient by surprise or confused him. Something happened that the patient did not expect, a spontaneous gesture from the therapist like laughter or a nonverbal reaction like a pause, silence, or a supportive gesture. This unexpected action prompted a modification in the rhythm and synchrony of the session and an emotional impact on the patient, who did not seem to understand what was happening. The patients described this phase as a moment in which there seemed to be a mismatch or lack

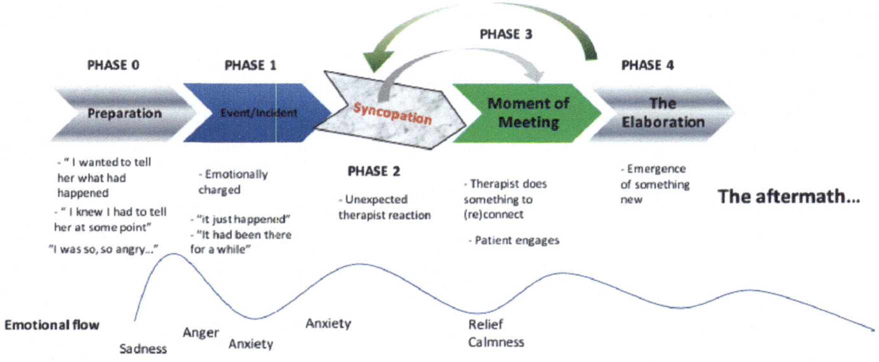

Fig. 12.2 Generic diachronic structure of "episodes of meeting". Taken from Duarte et al. (2020)

of attunement between them, and they did not know very well how to continue during the session.

The fourth phase, called Phase 3 or "Moment of Meeting," is the moment of meeting itself and was present in all the interviews. This phase was described as emotionally intense, associated with positive emotions, such as feeling found, met, supported, comforted, relieved, understood, or even feeling hugged—metaphorically—by their therapist. The patients also described with great precision certain actions and attitudes that the therapist had concerning the moment charged with emotions that made them feel that their psychotherapist really understood them and was connected with their emotions.

The fifth phase, called Phase 4 or "Elaboration or Consequence Phase," took place once the moment of meeting had passed and was experienced by patients in different ways. The main characteristic of this phase is that there is a subsequent reflection on what just happened, which helps patients understand something about themselves that they previously could not access. In other words, a new understanding arises, and new emotions about the event are produced.

Finally, the sixth phase, called Phase 5 or "Aftermath or Long-term Effects Phase," is relevant because it teaches us something about the framework or temporal boundaries of the moments of meeting. During the analysis of the interview material, we found a long-term effect, from a retrospective view of the described episode, in which the patient analyzes in the present how that episode could have affected their psychotherapy process. Most of the interviewees related these episodes to a change in the way the relationship with the psychotherapist was developing up to that point and/or as a catalyst for the development of a new perspective on how they related to others or themselves.

Subtypes of Episodes of Meeting: Refined Diachronic Analysis

In a more refined diachronic analysis, using the same previous data but paying special attention to the differentiating aspects of each case, we were able to categorize three types of episodes of meeting. The first category, called *Episode of Unexpected Meeting,* is an emerging, surprising, or unexpected moment, that takes place when the psychotherapist does or says something that the patient did not expect, which astonishes and confuses them. All the interviewees in this group include phase 2 ("The Syncopation Phase") in their description and describe it very vividly, almost anecdotally. However, this unexpected moment was followed, later, by a moment of meeting in which the psychotherapist repairs the previous lack of attunement. Apparently, the psychotherapist's intention to resolve and re-synchronize with the patient transforms what initially could be experienced as a negative event, into a moment of meeting. In other words, in this category, the encounter seems to be a consequence of the previous disconnection and can be felt as such because the psychotherapist can somehow notice the syncopation and is emotionally available to deal with it spontaneously and genuinely, even when a technical intervention is used.

The second type of episode, called *Episode of Feeling Met,* was described as less sudden or surprising than the previous one, mainly because it does not contain phase 2. In the category of feeling met, patients felt that the psychotherapist was so immersed in what was happening between them as a therapeutic couple, whether it was what the patient was telling them or what was happening in the session, that they felt met or connected with their psychotherapist. They described feeling in tune with the psychotherapist and profoundly understood by him or her, that the therapist knew exactly what he/she needed at that particular moment, with their actions being able to sustain this encounter and generate a space of deep intimacy.

This suggests that moments of meeting do not necessarily have to occur after an unexpected event or situation but can also take place as part of the regular rhythm of the session, where, due to different reasons, such as the topic being discussed or the high involvement of both participants in the session, the emotional intensity of the session increases, and the therapist can synchronize with the patient, making him feel seen.

The third type of episode we called *Episode of a Familiar Meeting*, and this was the most difficult to analyze; although the patients were able to identify a specific situation of feeling met, their feelings seemed to have to do with a certain familiarity or a certain relational understanding that had already been established between them and their psychotherapists, and not as a particular experience of emotional arousal. Apparently, in these cases, it was not a situation with a great emotional load, and the patients do not refer to feeling overwhelmed by the situations they narrate, but in a more cognitive way, the fact that the psychotherapist offers them exactly what they need seems to foster the feeling of being met in a way that is otherwise usual and typical in the interaction between them. This type of meeting was described by patients with long-term psychotherapy processes (at least over a year) and made us think that a new relational dynamic had in some way already been established.

Generic Structure of Episodes of Meeting: Synchronic Approach

Once the temporal analysis of the experience was finished, I proceeded to carry out an analysis that accounted in detail for the aspects and themes that compose this experience, a synchronic analysis. Although, as mentioned above, this analysis can be carried out for each phase, I decided to delve into phase 3 since it was one of the only ones described by the nine interviewees and seemed to be the moment of meeting or significant connection itself. The objective of this analysis was to comprehend its main components and identify experiential categories that would allow characterizing the experience in synchronic units of different levels of abstraction. In other words, the objective of this analysis was to represent the main components of the meeting experience.

As shown in Fig. 12.3, three main categories emerged from this analysis. All the interviewees described these categories as relevant aspects of feeling connected and met by their therapists.

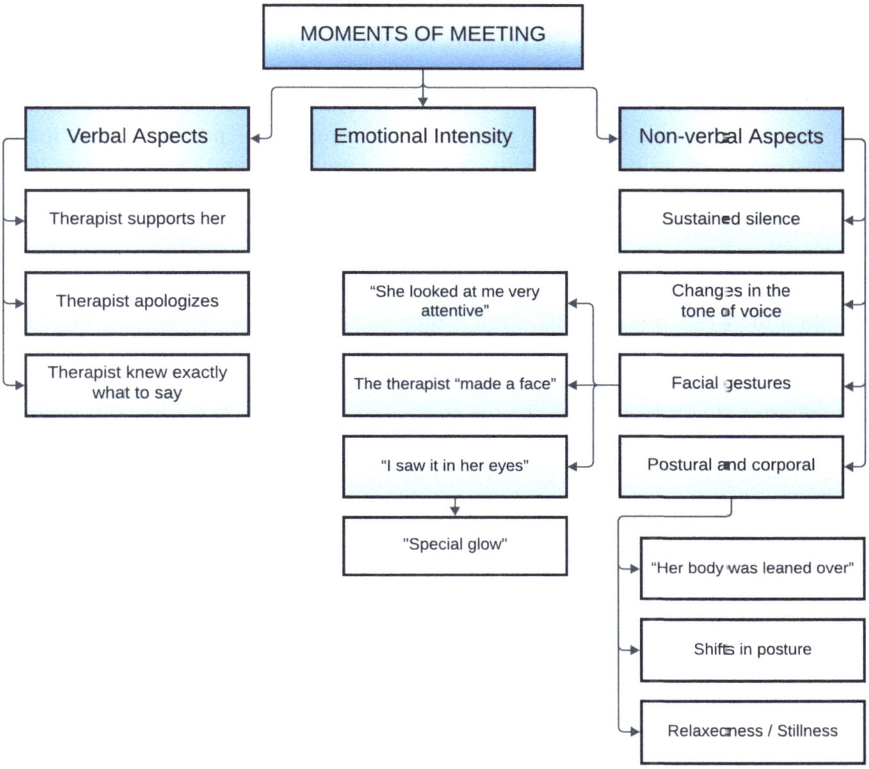

Fig. 12.3 Synchronic structure of phase 3: "moment of meeting"

The first category, called *verbal aspects*, describes all the verbal actions that psychotherapists perform to show their interest and commitment to their patients, which makes them feel genuinely seen and respected by the psychotherapist. The main themes found related to verbal support offered to the patient in some way, as in the case of a patient who says: *"She told me um, if you don't want to you don't have to tell me... at your own time, when you feel it's right... um... without rush... if you want to tell me now do it, if not, when you feel it's right and you want to talk about it (...) that made me feel confident and that I could tell her and that's why I did it" (PE5).*

These verbal actions also include the psychotherapist being able to apologize when he realizes that he has misdirected or has contributed to the patient's confusion, as in the case of an interviewee who remembers when her psychotherapist started to laugh and told her, *"I'm sorry, really, it's not that I'm laughing at you (...) but I understood that she was not laughing at me but at the situation" (PE1).* Or the idea that the therapist knows exactly what to say in moments when the patient feels helpless or needs to be reassured. As in the case of PE4 when her therapist tells her: *"You are not like your mother" (PE6).*

The category of *emotional intensity* was very variable in its appearance and described very differently by the patients, according to the moments they evoked or their personal characteristics. However, all the interviewees, when describing the phase of the moment of meeting, were able to recognize in themselves (and some in their psychotherapists) very strong emotions of connection and the substitution of negative emotions with more positive ones. As another patient says, *"It's as if we both knew it... I felt it... I thought it was not something to talk about because it was not going to do anything, but I felt her close" (PE9).*

Finally, the third category, *nonverbal aspects*, refers to the importance of nonverbal aspects at that moment to identify or interpret what was happening between them and their psychotherapists, even if they were very small or initially insignificant. The main nonverbal aspects described were changes in the tone of their psychotherapist's voice. One of the interviewed patients remembers *"Her tone of voice was different, it was like naive, like she was very interested... that's how I remember it... and that's how I received it" (PE5).* They also identify their gestures or facial expressions; *"Like her facial gestures... I don't know, smiling, interested... um....I don't know... yes... well she is always sitting in front of me... um... she doesn't move much, but yet sometimes I can feel her curiosity" (PE3).* Posture and general bodily cues are also relevant in this category, as in the case of another interviewee, *"I realized that she was connected by her physical way of being, relaxed, paying attention, she didn't move her hand, she didn't do anything that could distract me, she was serene, sitting... um... listening to me and looking at me. Her whole body was connected and available for what I was talking about" (PE5).*

Thus, moments of meeting seem to be characterized not only by explicit signs of meeting, such as the psychotherapist expressing verbally that he understands or is present for his patients, but they are also more fully felt moments that have an emotional impact on the patient and can also be recognized in the nonverbal signals that create a special atmosphere of connection.

Another research that also used micro-phenomenology to access and better understand its object of study was carried out by Danilo Rodríguez for his master's thesis in clinical psychology. Rodríguez (2020) studied the concept of self-appropriation by Paul Ricoeur applied to psychotherapy, in order to understand how patients can develop an understanding of the subjective foundations of their suffering throughout psychotherapy and how this occurs. In his study, he interviewed ten patients who underwent constructivist psychotherapy and analyzed the interviews with the procedure proposed by Valenzuela-Moguillansky & Vazquez-Rossati (2019). The results showed that the phenomenon of self-appropriation is a process that is characterized by a transformation in the way the patient comprehensibly accesses his own suffering, which would allow a new way of positioning himself about it, generating ownership of his circumstances. This, in turn, would be what guides the renewing action and opens new possibilities through personal transformation.

In a similar line but focusing not on the experience of psychotherapy but on the experience of diagnosis, Serrano (2021) also carried out qualitative research with micro-phenomenological methodology, aiming to understand from an embodied position the experience of being diagnosed with depression. She interviewed nine patients with this diagnosis, seeking to access the sensory, cognitive, and emotional dimensions of the memory. The results of her analysis allowed an understanding of the construction of a narrative identity in the dynamic evolution of the construction of the diagnosis of depression. In this study, she concluded that patients slowly move from an external label towards a comprehensive integration of their suffering beyond the symptoms. This research provides insight into how the experience of being diagnosed with depression has a significant impact not only on how patients perceive their symptoms but also on how they perceive themselves. It also contributes to clinical psychology and therapists, granting them valuable information to face psychotherapy processes with people with this diagnosis.

Conclusions and Future Perspectives for Micro-Phenomenological Research

The micro-phenomenological approach has proven to be a valuable tool for exploring subjective experience in psychotherapy, allowing unique access to implicit and pre-reflective dimensions that cannot be captured with other methods. This chapter has presented its potential to enrich the understanding of complex phenomena, such as episodes of meeting in psychotherapy, underlining how these episodes significantly contribute to therapeutic change and the strengthening of the relationship between patient and therapist. From the findings presented as a result of the application of the interview and the micro-phenomenological analysis, it is clear that moments of meeting not only represent a key relational core in the psychotherapeutic process but also highlight the importance of exploring the diachronic and synchronic aspects of these experiences. These detailed descriptions, along with their classification into subtypes, provide a solid basis for continuing to deepen our knowledge of therapeutic processes from the patient's perspective.

Implications for Clinical Practice

In the clinical field, micro-phenomenology has multiple implications. First, it accounts for the relevance of therapists developing a greater sensitivity towards their patients' subjective processes, especially at emotionally significant moments. Second, the findings invite therapists to reflect on the importance of repairing moments of disconnection in therapy, using these events as opportunities to strengthen the therapeutic relationship.

In addition, micro-phenomenology can be integrated as a reflective tool in daily practice, helping therapists identify relational patterns and adapt their interventions to the individual needs of their patients. Likewise, its application can enrich the training of new professionals, fostering skills to work with implicit and relational aspects of therapy. Along with this, its use to explore the experience of diagnosis or similar processes can provide valuable information for designing more personalized and humane interventions, promoting a practice centered on the patient's subjectivity.

Implications for Future Research

Micro-phenomenology opens multiple directions for research. Its application could extend to contexts such as group or community therapy, exploring how moments of meeting emerge and are configured in more complex dynamics. In addition, it would be valuable to conduct longitudinal studies that analyze the impact of these episodes on the therapeutic process over time.

Integration with disciplines such as neuroscience also offers promising possibilities, particularly for studying how subjective processes relate to changes in brain activity to better understand the associated neurobiological concomitants. Likewise, mixed-qualitative studies could establish designs that combine micro-phenomenology and other qualitative approaches (see the chapter by Tomicic et al., in this same book), which could help to establish denser understandings about episodes relevant to change in psychotherapy. On the other hand, future research should also focus on designing specific tools based on this approach, which may allow observing and analyzing subjective experiences related to psychotherapy systematically, integrating research and practice.

All in all, it can be said that micro-phenomenology offers an innovative and deeply enriching perspective for research and clinical practice in psychotherapy, which has been developed with enthusiasm in our region. By focusing on the first-person experience and exploring the implicit dynamics of psychotherapeutic processes, this approach not only expands our understanding of human phenomena but also contributes to imagining the design of more effective, ethical, and personalized interventions informed by different sources of evidence.

References

Aron, L. (1998). The clinical body and the reflexive mind. In L. Aron & F. S. Anderson (Eds.), *Relational perspectives on the body* (pp. 3–38). The Analytic Press.

Boston Change Process Study Group. (2002). Explicating the implicit: The local level and the micro process of change in the analytic situation. *The International Journal of Psycho-Analysis, 83*, 1051–1062.

Boston Change Process Study Group. (2005). The "something more" than interpretation revisited: Sloppiness and co-creativity in the psychoanalytic encounter. *Japa*, 693–729.

Boston Change Process Study Group. (2008). Forms of relational meaning: Issues in the relations between the implicit and reflective-verbal domains. *Psychoanal Dialog, 18*, 125–148. https://doi.org/10.1080/10481880801909351
Boston Change Process Study Group. (2010). *Change in psychotherapy: A unifying paradigm*. Norton.
Cárdenas, C., Rodriguez, D., & Duarte, J. (2019). The micro-phenomenological interview applied to research in psychotherapy: A first-person approach. In *50th international annual meeting*. Society for Psychotherapy Research.
Cozolino, L. J. (2002). *The neuroscience of psychotherapy: Building and rebuilding the human brain*. W.W. Norton and Company.
Duarte, J., Martínez, C., & Tomicic, A. (2019). Revisión teórica y metodológica de los eventos relevantes en psicoterapia para el estudio del cambio [Theoretical and methodological review of relevant events in psychotherapy for the study of change]. *Revista Argentina de Clínica Psicológica, 28*(3), 253–265. https://doi.org/10.24205/03276716.2019.1141
Duarte, J., Martinez, C., & Tomicic, A. (2020). Episodes of meeting in psychotherapy: An empirical exploration of patients' experiences of subjective change during their psychotherapy process. *Research in Psychotherapy: Psychopathology, Process and Outcome, 23*(1), 56–66. https://doi.org/10.4081/ripppo.2020.440
Elliott, R., Slatick, E., & Urman, M. (2001). Qualitative change process research on psychotherapy: Alternative strategies. In J. Frommer & D. L. Rennie (Eds.), *Qualitative psychotherapy research: Methods and methodology* (pp. 69–111). Pabst Science.
Flick, U. (2002). *An introduction to qualitative research* (2nd ed.). Sage.
Friedman, M. S. (1985). *The healing dialogue in psychotherapy*. Jason Aronson.
Gelo, O.C.G., & Manzo, S. (2015) Quantitative approaches to treatment process, change process, and process-outcome research. In O.C.G. Gelo, A. Pritz & Rieken B. (eds.), Psychotherapy research. Foundations, process and outcome (247–277). Springer. DOI https://doi.org/10.1007/978-3-7091-1382-0_13.
Gonçalves, M. M., Ribeiro, P. A., Mendes, I., Matos, M., & Santos, A. (2011). Tracking novelties in psychotherapy process research: The innovative moments coding system. *Psychotherapy Research, 21*(5), 497–509. https://doi.org/10.1080/10503307.2011.560207
Greenberg, L. S. (1986). Change process research. *Journal of Consulting and Clinical Psychology, 54*(1), 4–9. https://doi.org/10.1037/0022-006X.54.1.4
Guba, E. G., & Lincoln, Y. S. (1994). Competing paradigms in qualitative research. In N. K. Denzin & Y. S. Lincoln (Eds.), *Handbook of qualitative research* (pp. 105–117). Sage Publications, Inc.
Hardy, G. E., & Llewelyn, S. (2015). Introduction to psychotherapy process research. In O. C. G. Gelo, A. Pritz, & B. Rieken (Eds.), *Psychotherapy research. Foundations, process and outcome* (pp. 183–194). Springer. https://doi.org/10.1007/978-3-7091-1382-0_9
Hendricks, M. (2009). Experiencing level: An instance of developing a variable from a first-person process so it can be reliably measured and taught. *Journal of Consciousness Studies, 16* (10–12), 129–155.
Howe, K., & Eisenhart, M. (1993). Criterios de investigación cualitativa (y cuantitativa) [Qualitative (and quantitative) research criteria]. *Prolegómenos. Revista de Educación, 300*, 173–189.
Husserl, E. (1913/1983). *Ideas pertaining to a pure phenomenology and to a phenomenological philosophy. First book: General introduction to a pure phenemenology*. Martinus Nijhoff Publishers.
Katz, E. (2011). *Attending to clinical practice: A phenomenological study exploring the structure of clinical attention and its relationship with holistic competence*. PhD thesis, University of Toronto.
Knobloch-Fedders, L., Elkin, I., & Kiesler, D. (2014). Looking back, looking forward: A historical reflection on psychotherapy process research. *Psychotherapy Research, 25*, 1–13. https://doi.org/10.1080/10503307.2014.906764

Krause, M. (1995). La investigación cualitativa: Un campo de posibilidades y desafíos [Qualitative research: A field of possibilities and challenges]. *Revista Temas de Educación, 7*, 19–40.

Krause, M. (2005). *Qualitative (and quantitative) research criteria [Qualitative (and quantitative) research criteria]*. Ediciones Universidad Católica.

Leigh, J. (2012). *Somatic movement and education: A phenomenological study of young children's perceptions, expressions, and reflections of embodiment through movement*. s.l., Ph.D. Thesis, University of Birmingham.

Levitt, H. M., Butler, M., & Hill, T. (2006). What clients find helpful in psychotherapy: Principles for facilitating change. *Journal of Counseling Psychology, 53*, 314–324. https://doi.org/10.1037/0022-0167.53.3.314

Levitt, H. M., Pomerville, A., & Surace, F. I. (2016). A qualitative meta-analysis examining clients' experiences of psychotherapy: A new agenda. *Psychological Bulletin, 142*, 801. https://doi.org/10.1037/bul0000057

Lutz A., Lachaux J.-P., Mar6nerie J. & Varela F. J. (2002). Guiding the study of brain dynamics by using first-person data: Synchrony patterns correlate with ongoing conscious states during a simple visual task. *Proceedings of the National Academy of Sciences of the United States of America 99*(3) 1586–1591.

Lyons-Ruth, K. (1999). The two-person unconscious: Intersubjective dialogue, enactive relational representation, and the emergence of new forms of relational organization. *Psychoanalytic Inquiry, 19*, 576–617.

Lyons-Ruth, K., Bruschweiler-Stern, N., Harrison, A. M., Morgan, A. C., Nahum, J. P., Sander, L., Stern, D. N., & Tronick, E. Z. (1998). Implicit relational knowing: Its role in development and psychoanalytic treatment. *Infant Mental Health Journal, 19*(3), 282–289. https://doi.org/10.1002/(SICI)1097-0355(199823)19:3<282::AID-IMHJ3>3.0.CO;2-O

Mearns, D., & Cooper, M. (2005). *Working at relational depth in counselling and psychotherapy*. Sage.

Midgley, N., Ansaldo, F., & Target, M. (2014). The meaningful assessment of therapy outcomes: Incorporating a qualitative study into a randomized controlled trial evaluating the treatment of adolescent depression. *Psychotherapy, 51*, 128. https://doi.org/10.1037/a0034179

Orange, D. M., Atwood, G. E., & Stolorow, R. D. (1997). *Working intersubjectively: Contextualism in psychoanalytic practice*. The Analytic Press.

Patton, M. Q. (1999). Enhancing the quality and credibility of qualitative analysis. *Health Service Research, 5*, 1189–1208.

Petitmengin, C. (1999). The intuitive experience. *Journal of Consciousness Studies, 6*(2–3), 43–47. https://cepa.info/2411

Petitmengin, C. (2006). Describing one's subjective experience in the second person. An interview method for the science of consciousness. *Phenomenol Cognitive Sci, 5*, 229–269.

Petitmengin, C., & Bitbol, M. (2009). The validity of first-person descriptions as authenticity and coherence. *Journal of Consciousness Studies, 16*(10–12), 363–404.

Petitmengin, C., Navarro, V., & Le Van Quyen, M. (2007). Anticipating seizure: Pre-reflective experience at the center of neurophenomenology. *Consciousness and Cognition, 16*, 746–764.

Ponterotto, J. G. (2006). Brief note on the origins, evolution, and meaning of the qualitative research concept "thick description". *The Qualitative Report, 11*, 538–549. Available from: http://www.nova.edu/ssss/QR/QR11-3/ponterotto.pdf

Remillieux, A. (2009). *Explicitation et modélisation des connaissances de conduite dechangement à la SNCF: Vers une gestion des connaissances pré-réfléchies*. Doctoral Thesis. Institut national des telecommunications d'Evry. (Manuscript in French).

Rhodes, R., Hill, C., Thompson, B., & Elliott, R. (1994). Client retrospective recall of resolved and unresolved misunderstanding events. *Journal of Counseling Psychology, 41*(4), 473–483.

Rodríguez, D. (2020). *Psicoterapia como una experiencia hermenéutica. Abordaje experiencial de la apropiación de sí [Psychotherapy as a hermeneutical experience. Experiential approach to self-appropriation]*. Thesis to qualify for the degree of Master in Adult Clinical Psychology, Universidad de Chile, Chile. https://repositorio.uchile.cl/handle/2250/186845

Safran, J. D., & Muran, J. C. (2000). *Negotiating the therapeutic alliance*. Guilford Press.
Safran, J. D., Muran, J. C., & Eubanks-Carter, C. (2011). Repairing alliance ruptures. *Psychotherapy, 48*(1), 80–87. https://doi.org/10.1037/a0022140
Serrano, M. R. (2021). *Hacia una comprensión de la construcción de la identidad narrativa a partir de la experiencia de diagnóstico en depresión [Towards an understanding of the construction of narrative identity based on the experience of diagnosis in depression]*. Thesis to qualify for the degree of Master in Adult Clinical Psychology, Universidad de Chile. https://repositorio.uchile.cl/handle/2250/200198
Siegel, D. J. (2007). *The mindful brain: Reflection and attunement in the cultivation of well-being*. W.W. Norton & Company.
Stern, D. (2004). *The present moment in psychotherapy and everyday life*. Norton.
Stern, D., Sander, L., Nahum, J., Harrison, A., Lyons-Ruth, K., Morgan, B., Stern, N., & Tronik, E. (1998). Non-interpretative mechanisms in psychoanalytic therapy. The "something more" than interpretation. *The International Journal of Psycho-Analysis, 79*, 903–921.
Timulak, L. (2010). Significant events in psychotherapy: An update of research findings. *Psychology and Psychotherapy: Theory, Research and Practice, 83*(4), 421–447.
Valenzuela-Moguillansky, C., & Vásquez-Rosati, A. (2019). An analysis procedure for the micro-phenomenological interview. *Constructivist Foundations, 14*(2), 123–145. https://constructvist.info/14/2/123
Valenzuela-Moguillansky, C. (2020) Microfenomenología: Una nueva herramienta para el estudio de la experiencia. Módulo 1: Conducción de la entrevista. Material de clases.
Valenzuela-Moguillansky, C., O'Regan, J. K., & Petitmengin, C. (2013). Exploring the subjective experience of the rubber hand illusion. *Frontiers in Human Neuroscience, 7*, 00659. https://doi.org/10.3389/fnhum.2013.00659
Varela, F. J. (1996). Neurophenomenology: A methodological remedy for the hard problem. *Journal of Consciousness Studies, 3*(4), 330–349.
Varela, F. J., Thompson, E., & Rosch, E. (1991/2016). *The embodied mind: Cognitive science and human experience* (Revised ed.). MIT Press.
Vermersch, P. (1994/2011). *L'entretien d'explicitation. The elicitation interview* (7th ed.). ESF Editeur. [Book in French].
Vermersch, P. (2012). *ExplicitaDon et phénomé-nologie: vers une psychophénoménologie*. Presses universitaires de France.
Wallace, B. A. (2006). *The attention revolution: Unlocking the power of the focused mind*. Wisdom Press.

Chapter 13
Qualitative Research in Dyadic Interventions Using Video-Feedback

Catalina Sieverson, Marcia Olhaberry, and María José León

Research on the effectiveness of interventions in early childhood has demonstrated their impact through changes in the child's symptoms and difficulties in the child, caregiver, and the dyad, such as reduced anxiety, improved emotional regulation, and enhanced caregiver-child interactions. However, there is a growing need to explore the mechanisms within psychotherapy that contribute to these changes and to clarify how specific therapeutic processes relate to the observed post-intervention outcomes.

The development of qualitative and process research in child psychotherapy is still pioneering and scarce compared to studies focused on adult and adolescent psychotherapy (Midgley, 2007; Kazdin, 2009). Some have taken place in Chile and have shown the feasibility of using existing research methodologies in adult and adolescent populations. They have also highlighted the challenges for their use and the need to develop specific procedures and methods when it comes to relational interventions and with young children (e.g., Capella et al., 2022; Nuñez et al., 2022; Sieverson et al., 2022).

Psychotherapy with children and their caregivers has particularities that make its study challenging and complex, especially psychotherapy process research.

First, at least one of the participants presents developing reflective skills, such as recognizing and responding to others' emotions or engaging in basic problem-solving behaviors. These skills often manifest in non-verbal ways, as young

C. Sieverson (✉) · M. J. León
Millennium Institute for Research in Depression and Personality (MIDAP), Santiago, Chile
e-mail: Csievers@uc.cl; mjoseleon@fundacionmasmentes.com

M. Olhaberry
Millennium Institute for Research in Depression and Personality (MIDAP), Santiago, Chile

School of Psychology, Pontifical Catholic University of Chile, Santiago, Chile
e-mail: mpolhabe@uc.cl

A. Tomicic, J. D. Soto (eds.), *Qualitative Research in Clinical Psychology and Psychotherapy in Latin America*, https://doi.org/10.1007/978-3-031-90782-1_13

children cannot typically articulate their experiences through speech. This necessitates therapeutic approaches that account for and interpret these developmental characteristics. Along with this, young children are highly dependent and influenced by the relationship with their caregiver but are still active subjects in the intervention (Stern, 2009, p. 72).

Second, the research on psychotherapeutic processes with young children and caregiver-infant dyads implies additional challenges and the need to access and gather a large amount of clinical data (Wallin, 2007; p. 12; Nuñez et al., 2022). Therapists must work with several patients at the same time (the child, their caregivers, and the relationship between them), at different levels and times (behavioral and representational; individual, dyadic, and triadic), and establish differentiated relationships with each one (Allamo, 2019; Shirk et al., 2011; Karver et al., 2018; Stern et al., 1998).

Third, the challenge is given by the understanding of therapeutic change in this evolutionary period, given that when we ask ourselves what changes when it changes, we must look at all those dimensions mentioned before.

That is why it is essential to study psychotherapy's inner processes and understand how bonds improve and become healthier, such as by observing increased mutual responsiveness, reduced conflict, and enhanced emotional attunement between caregivers and children. This kind of research enriches our understanding of psychotherapy, thus improving the training of therapists and clinical supervision spaces, and thus enhancing clinical results.

This chapter aims to account for the experience and implications of (1) process research in psychotherapy in dyadic interventions in early childhood that use a relational intervention strategy with a model developed in Chile (Olhaberry, 2024; Olhaberry et al., 2025) and (2) the results of research on this topic, which has also become a very valuable source of learning for the training and development of therapists and reflective supervision models.

Process Research and Therapeutic Change in Psychotherapy with Young Children and Their Caregivers

The scientific literature that accounts for the effectiveness of psychotherapeutic interventions with babies and young children is numerous, and in some reviews, certain intervention strategies with better observed post-intervention results are highlighted (O'Hara et al., 2019; Newton et al., 2022). However, there is very little evidence that accounts for the processes that underlie their effectiveness, the processes of change, and their content ("what changes when it changes") (Midgley, 2007; Capella et al., 2015).

To ask ourselves what changes when it changes and why it changes, it becomes necessary to provide a definition of therapeutic change working with young children and early relationships. Therapeutic change has been defined as a "moment that stands out within the intervention process as significant, striking or relevant for change" (Fiedler & Rogge, 1989, p. 46), that enables "windows into the process of change in psychotherapy" (Elliott & Shapiro, 1992, p. 164). From an integrative and transtheoretical model of therapeutic change developed in Latin America, it is proposed that therapeutic change implies a transformation in the subjective theories of each patient (Krause & de La Parra, 2006). In this sense, the patient's reality would gradually transform through psychotherapy, and their ability to elaborate would increase, including these changes in cognitive, affective, and evaluative processes that are implicitly expressed in the patient's behavior during or outside the session (Krause & Altimir, 2018).

Implicit Relational Knowledge as a Dimension to Observe Therapeutic Change in Children

Often language is not enough to capture the emotional experience in children, as their developmental stage limits their ability to articulate emotions verbally. Nonverbal methods, such as observing behavior, play, and interactions, compensate for this by providing insights into their emotional and relational worlds that words cannot convey. Given that "words are not enough" to access therapeutic change (Bick, 1968; Winnicott, 1971), a language-centered change model may not be suitable, and it becomes necessary to incorporate other elements related to experience (Stern, 2002). Thus, when we think about the definition of therapeutic change in young children, we must consider the evolutionary characteristics, the different patients who participate in the same process (the child, their caregivers, and the relationship between them), and their levels and dimensions (behavioral and representational; individual, dyadic, and triadic) (Allamo, 2019; Shirk et al., 2011; Karver et al., 2018; Stern et al., 1998).

Ester Bick (1968), known for the Method of Infant Observation, explores how children develop ways of relating and expressing security and change through what she calls "emotional membranes." She refers to the use of bodily sensations and behaviors instead of words to communicate inner states, suggesting that the therapist should attend to these manifestations in child therapy. Winnicott (1971), on his part, refers to a series of clinical cases showing therapeutic change in children (2 to 12 years) through their behavior, play, and their ability to relate and to manage anxiety.

Winnicott establishes parallels between the caregiver-child relationship and the therapist-child relationship, highlighting the importance of certain elements that allow the child to re-experience and heal fundamental emotional aspects (1971). In this sense, it is worth noting the Implicit Relational Knowing (IRK), which refers to the information that we build on how we relate to others and is stored in our implicit memory, which is automatic and non-reflective (Polanyi, 1958). The IRK, in Mitchell's (2000) words, is a "window" for understanding what changes in psychotherapy; that is, what is internalized is a "relational offer" and a way of "being together."

The IRK is the earliest evolutionary example of mutual co-regulation between two people who have a significant bond. This process becomes a function that is updated throughout life in moments of need for co-regulation, occurring in parenting, friendships, and partnerships, as well as in the patient-therapist relationship.

In the therapeutic work with dyads, the "relational offer" that the therapist makes to the caregiver is a way of being together considering the needs of the baby as central. According to Lyons-Ruth et al. (1998), the IRK cannot be transformed into conscious verbal knowledge, but it can be integrated into verbal knowledge. Thus, the relational offer that the therapist makes could modify the caregiver's IRK, laying the basis for a therapeutic change. This change, in turn, could manifest in a new narrative in the caregiver and new ways of relating in the caregiver-baby dyad. This has been well described by Murphy et al. (2012), explaining that the therapist behaves in a way that makes a relational offer that responds to the caregiver's needs and, in turn, to the baby's needs, forming a series of nested systems of relationships that influence each other and amplify their ways of relating.

In our opinion, the article "Ghosts in the Nursery," developed by Selma Fraiberg et al. (1975), contributed to the foundations of Psychotherapy Process Research with young children and their caregivers and is an example of what is explained before related to the IRK. Fraiberg et al. (1975) highlight the intergenerational transmission of trauma, focusing on the series of nested systems of relationships during the processes, on what happens within the process of psychotherapy in caregiver-child dyads, as well as on the therapists. This pioneering study not only illustrates the observation of behaviors of mothers and their babies but also emphasizes the relational offer between therapist and mother-baby dyad as a key mechanism of therapeutic change. Furthermore, it set the groundwork for later methodologies by demonstrating how therapists guide caregivers to confront and understand their ghosts (e.g., adverse experiences and childhood trauma), thereby gradually freeing themselves from dysfunctional interaction patterns. The therapist-caregiver relationship was highlighted as a transformative space, inspiring subsequent research to further explore the intricate dynamics of therapeutic change within relational contexts.

More recently, Paris et al. (2009), from the therapists' perspective, describe elements of the clinical process that are related to therapeutic change, observable improvements in the mother-baby relationship, and therapeutic alliance.

The authors highlight that, despite evidence of the effectiveness of the intervention, there are questions about what clinicians actually do in psychotherapy and how this relates to improvements in the mother-baby relationship and even in maternal mental health. The results point out the observational strategies present in the psychotherapy processes of intervention, the use of intervention techniques related to the focus on the mother-baby relationship, the pleasure in this relationship, and the normalization of maternal concerns. They explicitly highlight the presence of the baby as a key element, emphasizing that the processes involved in therapeutic change are observable, naming them as "turning points" in mothers and in the mother-baby relationship. For example, when referring to "What came to mind was what the mother considered significant, what were the turning points for her... It was a moment when the baby seemed to recognize her, seemed to care about her, or followed her... The mother changed when she said, 'My baby recognized me, my baby turned around when I left the room'." In this work, the author interprets the processes of change based on the notion of the IRK and the principle that the power of therapy is derived from processes that are implicit and non-verbal. They propose the concept of "now moments" by D. Stern (1998) as a common "port" of entry in mother-baby psychotherapies, referring to moments of attunement that lead to moments of encounter that are transformative and are related to change (e.g., moments in which the therapist alerts a depressed mother about a smile from her baby towards her, leading to a moment of shared smile).

A recent study by Avdi et al. (2020) shows the results of an observational research of caregiver-infant psychotherapy through a brief interactional episode in a psychoanalytic therapy with a mother and her baby (20 weeks) aimed at working with relational trauma (Lieberman & van Horn, 2008). The authors describe an episode of "enactment" of a potentially traumatogenic interaction (generated by trauma) in which the dynamic of dysregulation between the caregiver and her baby is observed. Initially, the therapist gets "entangled" in this dynamic and then interrupts it, gradually leading it to a verbal and reflective domain. This study develops an observational methodology *ad hoc* from a relevant episode, based on a series of clinical observation instruments. As in previous studies, it is concluded that this type of research contributes to the understanding of the psychotherapeutic process, incorporating both the verbal domain and the implicit interactional processes in clinical practice, especially when it comes to interventions with babies.

The use of the principles of microanalysis for the study of psychotherapy has been widely extended in process research in psychotherapy. Besides, the training of researchers and therapists in the use of different observational instruments benefits the development of methods that become a rich source of information from which Psychotherapy Process Research nourishes (Boston Change Process Study Group (BCPSG) ,2002, 2007). The richness of the data that can be obtained from the observation of behavior, facial expression, rhythm, interactions, and representations is immense (Beebe & Steele, 2016). In fact, the study of dyads with small babies and related psychotherapies usually evaluates the level of effectiveness of interventions also based on these instruments.

The study by Avdi et al. (2020) and Baradon et al. (2023) bases their research methodologies on the clinical training and observational instruments of therapists and researchers. Baradon et al. (2023) describe a layered analysis methodology that combines the report of the therapists' countertransference and microanalytic research approaches. In this study, they conclude that countertransference and the use of observational instruments are complementary perspectives that allow studying conscious and unconscious elements in the patient-therapist relationship. In addition, they describe that patients and therapists interact in therapy with complex and subtle patterns, where ruptures and resolutions are not always obvious to both members of the dyad but have a significant impact on the course of therapy.

Chilean Experience in Process Research in Psychotherapy with Young Children and Their Caregivers

The Psychotherapy Process Research carried out in Chile on child psychotherapy constitutes a pioneering area of scientific development. In this field, the studies have used specific research strategies that were originally developed to study psychotherapy with adult populations and have a rich trajectory in their understanding of therapeutic change, its development, and its application as a research methodology. The results of these studies have highlighted that the study of relevant episodes constitutes privileged access to comprehend what happens within the psychotherapeutic process, the therapeutic change, and its content, as well as the need to consider various perspectives on it at the same time (Capella et al., 2022; Nuñez et al., 2022; Sieverson et al., 2022).

The possibility of accessing relevant episodes within psychotherapy opens a window toward the understanding and strengthening of opportunities for change during the intervention process itself. About this, Capella et al. (2018, 2022) and Capella and Boddy (2021) studied therapeutic change in psychotherapy with school-aged children and adolescents who were victims of child sexual abuse. They conducted multiperspective research through narrative and drawing analysis, as well as case analysis. The results allowed us to comprehend the process and evolution of subjective therapeutic change in patients. Therapeutic change was defined as a dynamic and gradual process that increases its level over psychotherapy. This is similar to the progression of therapeutic change studied with adults. By its part, Nuñez et al. (2022) conclude that the therapeutic relationship is a facilitating element of change both for children and their caregivers, showing a progressive increase throughout the psychotherapy process, and the caregiver-therapist relationship is highlighted as a key element in the child's therapeutic change. The results of this study also allow us to conclude a series of implications for clinical practice, difficult to observe and describe without the use of methodologies that allow access to the depth of the experience and what happens inside psychotherapy.

The local evidence generated from Psychotherapy Process Research in caregiver-young children dyads is scarce; however, a case study published in 2022 analyzed the therapeutic change process in a brief psychological intervention with babies and their mothers with postpartum depressive symptoms (Sieverson et al., 2022). The authors conclude that a qualitative research approach allows understanding the therapeutic change, and its results are further commented on.

Strategies and Research Procedures in Psychotherapy with Young Children and Their Caregivers

As already mentioned, the tendency to use observational instruments in the therapeutic work with young children and their caregivers is an answer to the specific developmental characteristics and needs at this age and to the needs of psychotherapy itself. Psychotherapy with young children demands maintaining simultaneous focuses related between them: the caregiver-baby/infant relationship, the individual characteristics of each of the patients, and specific developmental characteristics.

An observational and psychotherapy strategy widely used with young children is video-feedback. The use of it has been highly recommended and promoted as a cost-effective and focused therapeutic strategy (Juffer et al., 2017; Olhaberry et al., 2017; Bakermans-Kranenburg et al., 2003). This method is particularly effective because it highlights subtle interactions and allows for direct observation of relational dynamics, offering a unique opportunity to identify and reflect on the meaning of behaviors (Juffer & Steele, 2014; Beebe & Steele, 2016). Compared to other therapeutic strategies, video-feedback combines observation with guided reflection, fostering a deeper comprehension of relational dynamics within the dyad.

Some research groups that use this strategy have explored the mechanisms and contents underlying the therapeutic change. Results of these studies point out interrelated elements of the psychotherapy: (a) the therapist helps the adult to translate what is happening at a procedural level to then describe in words what is happening in the video and explore what he/she is thinking and feeling at that moment, which becomes a springboard to reflect on the meaning of the observed behaviors (Beebe, 2003; Beebe, 2010); (b) seeing oneself in a video activates meta-cognitive processes that allow one to see oneself from a new, more benevolent perspective that implies a shared construction of reality with the support and collaboration of the therapist (Doria et al., 2013; Paris et al., 2009); (c) the therapist promotes reflective functioning in the adult, the exploration of the internal world and relational experiences, and provides calm and containment in moments of stress (Doria et al., 2013; Steele et al., 2014; Juffer & Steele, 2014); (d) observing oneself accompanied by the therapist provides a more comprehensive and reflective perspective (Juffer & Steele, 2014;) (e) seeing oneself moment-to-moment allows for precise observations of subtle behaviors in the adult and the child, enabling him/her to subtitle the behaviors, emotions, and expressions observed in the video (Juffer & Bakermans-Kranenburg, 2018; Olhaberry et al., 2015).

The study conducted by Sieverson et al. (2022) aimed to test the research methodology of change and its Generic Change Indicators (GCI) developed by Krause and de La Parra (2006), which have been widely used in studies of psychotherapeutic processes in adults and adolescents. This study is the first to use the GCI model to determine therapeutic change in dyadic psychotherapy in early childhood. Namely, the GCI model is designed to identify specific moments of change within the therapeutic process, such as shifts in emotional expression, cognitive reframing, or relational dynamics. Unlike other methodologies, the GCI focuses mostly on verbal expressions but also on non-verbal cues as an additional element to determine the therapeutic change. The study of Sieverson et al. (2022) demonstrated that these indicators are applicable and useful for identifying and analyzing therapeutic change in a brief psychological intervention for mother-baby dyads that uses video-feedback as the main therapeutic strategy.

Thus, this model provides a framework to observe and understand the nuances of therapeutic change, making it a valuable tool for therapist training and supervision, as it bridges the gap between theoretical constructs and practical application in early childhood interventions. In addition, the study concluded that the GCI model allows identifying "windows" that, in turn, permit access, observation, and understanding of the processes and contents of therapeutic change. This model defines the therapeutic change as individual and subjective in the patient, but the episodes are triggered by therapist interventions, allowing observation of aspects related to therapeutic skills.

The results found by Sieverson et al. (2022) and further research using the same model of the GCI have reported that the content of the therapeutic change is commonly related to deepening the understanding of the relationship with the baby, her self-perception as a mother, and identifying the influence of one's own history in current motherhood.

Given the fact that often "language is not enough" working with young children, a deeper comprehension of the content of therapeutic change is needed. Although incipient and still mostly based on the mother's narratives, the content of the therapeutic change was analyzed by looking into the non-verbal cues of change.

For example:

> In the fourth video-feedback intervention session, a mother discovers a behavior that she did not remember from the video recording the previous week. In the recorded interaction, her approximately 10-month-old baby makes a gesture that the mother then imitates. The gesture the baby makes refers to "little" or "small" with the thumb and index finger, which in this case is related to food and the feeling of satiety. When the mother responds: "don't you want more?" the baby responds with a gesture that non-verbally indicates "little," and the mother imitates this gesture of the baby accompanied by pertinent verbalization. The mother was surprised at how her baby understands everything that the adults express and respond with their personal style. The therapist asks her: "What else does it make you feel? Or what else does it make you think?" The mother states that "She understands what I tell her; she understands what I'm asking her; she understands what we're doing. So, obviously, that gives me joy because, uhh, I see that, for her, uhh, even though I don't realize it, she's learning things day by day, things that I don't even notice." "Yes. I think you live life so fast and you're always in such a hurry and you're always doing everything… I think when you watch videos like this, so carefully, uhh, there are really a lot of things happening around you that you don't realize."
>
> The mother stops insisting that the baby finish all the food on the plate. Then, the therapist asked the mother why she didn't insist on more food. The mother expressed awareness that some of her behaviors and attitudes could be related to her own childhood experiences. In this way, she links her childhood experiences with her subsequent development into adulthood and her role as a mother with her baby and the baby's development: "Yes, of course, for me it's like this… forcing them affects everything, their personality, it holds them back, children start to inhibit themselves. I, also, say this based on my own experience, maybe, too. I was very shy…," "Yes, because when I was a child, I was very shy, and well, maybe

when I was a child nobody listened to my opinion… for many years I let others think for me," "With my mother, with everyone, I think. Until I was an adult, then I realized or well, that's what I'm thinking now, because at that precise moment, one doesn't realize that, well, all these things come from when one is very young" (Sieverson et al., 2022).

This kind of research provides specifically a new approach to identify and understand therapeutic change in interventions with video-feedback with young children. The results have shown that therapeutic change is a reflection of the transformations in the narratives and understandings of the mothers about themselves, their babies, and their relationships, with different levels of complexity.

Considering the therapeutic actions in the use of video-feedback, it is possible to think that in the relationship with the therapist, mothers experience a secure base from which to explore and reflect on what happens in the relationship with their babies and in their inner world, contributing to the understanding not only of her individually but in relation to her daughter and others. Therefore, seeing oneself from the outside and the baby from the inside allows "unlocking" new ways of seeing, thinking, feeling, and understanding the challenges of everyday life with a small baby and with mental health difficulties.

In this sense, the concept of "embodied mentalization" was developed by Dana Shai (Shai & Belsky, 2017) and defined as the ability of parents to recognize, understand, and extrapolate infant mental states from the child's body expression, adjusting their movement in tune with the infant's need, could also provide elements to enrich the understanding of change, including dyads with young children. This way of understanding the reflective function of parents highlights the relevance of going beyond the verbal and declarative capacities of parents, capturing the subjective experience of the child expressed in the quality of movement, rhythms, space, time, sensations, and touch. It also emphasizes the parental ability to modify their own behavior based on a mental state expressed by the child in a non-verbal way, recognizing that the mental states of parents and children can be in conflict. It also implies recognizing that parents are able to repair the ruptures that occur in the interaction based on a change in what they do and express non-verbally.

On the other hand, the kind of research mentioned in this chapter is a contribution to the investigative challenges associated with conceptual definitions and data collection and analysis procedures. For example, where and what to observe in these types of interventions? How do we understand change and its processes when we talk about young children and caregiver-baby dyads? Are the procedures that we have useful, and do they account for therapeutic change?

In our experience, and in relation to the contents of change in therapies with young children, elements appear that are evident in theoretical terms but complex in data analysis and coding procedures. Therapeutic change is understood as a transformation of subjective theories, but in the case of mothers in the postpartum period and their babies, there is a kind of shared identity in the process of differentiation that prevents defining changes individually. It is such that it is not possible to understand the baby without knowing her mother, going from dependence and interrelation that goes from the physiological, advancing in development towards psychological aspects (Feldman & Greenbaum, 1997).

This may be given by the focus of dyadic interventions, but at the same time, it does not rule out the need to adjust coding and analysis procedures in view of incorporating elements such as the IRK, of the baby and the evolutionary period. In fact, the fact that IRK has been described as being evidenced in the narratives of the mothers allows to supposition of changes in the IRK that preceded the GCI. In turn, it allows thinking about the mechanisms of therapeutic change based on therapeutic skills and intervention strategies used.

The results and learnings of this type of research for clinical practice highlight the importance of the therapist's stance and ability to narrate and process an observed experience in the dyad, to connect the past with the present, and to make a relational offer. This allows, in turn, the caregiver to have an affective experience with her baby more loaded with pleasure and enjoyment in that relationship. In this line, they highlight the focus placed on the development of the relationship between the therapist and the mother that allows observation and reflection on what is observed from everyday moments between the mother and her baby. They also highlight supervision groups for therapists as a space where they reflect on their work while building capacities for observation and openness. affective.

Learnings from the Chilean Experience

What has been done so far in research on microprocesses in psychotherapy with babies and caregiver-baby dyads is still incipient and pioneering, specifically in terms of the definition and observation of therapeutic change. In this sense, there is still a great challenge in terms of the development of further research and the dissemination and publication of results.

So far, the procedures used for the research of dyadic interventions have allowed us to learn and understand aspects that are relevant and unique to this type of intervention. Among them, the training and attitude of the coder during observation, the consideration of the baby as an active subject in the session or in the mother's mind, and the need to adapt methodologies developed for the adult population in individual therapies stand out.

Another point that has been relevant and not without challenges is the process of triangulation and agreement between coders. In this sense, the training of coders becomes key not only in observational tools but also in the themes and evolutionary periods addressed in therapies. Thus, it is essential that researchers and those who work with the material have knowledge and a level of clinical understanding of the case (which we call a "3D" view).

Another relevant aspect associated with the skills necessary for coding is related to the learning process for the teams of coders, especially when they do not have the experience or training in relational psychotherapies, in which the patients are the caregiver, the baby, and the relationship between them. Since the relationship is composed of at least two people, we work with several individuals at different levels, all these elements being observed when studying micro-processes of psychotherapy.

References

Allamo, N. A. (2019). *Contenido y evolución del cambio en la psicoterapia con niños y niñas: propuesta de un modelo genérico y de proceso [Content and evolution of change in psychotherapy with boys and girls: proposal of a generic and process model]* (Unpublished doctoral thesis). Faculty of Social Sciences, School of Psychology] Pontificia Universidad Católica de Chile.

Avdi, E., Amiran, K., Baradon, T., Broughton, C., Sleed, M., Spencer, R., & Shai, D. (2020). Studying the process of psychoanalytic parent–infant psychotherapy: Embodied and discursive aspects. *Infant Mental Health Journal, 41*(5), 589–602. https://doi.org/10.1002/imhj.21901

Bakermans-Kranenburg, M. J., van IJzendoorn, M. H., & Juffer, F. (2003). Less is more: Meta-analyses of sensitivity and attachment interventions in early childhood. *Psychological Bulletin, 129*(2), 195–215. https://doi.org/10.1037/0033-2909.129.2.195

Baradon, T., Avdi, E., Sleed, M., Salomonsson, B., & Amiran, K. (2023). Observing and interpreting clinical process: Methods and findings from 'Layered analysis' of parent–infant psychotherapy. *Infant Mental Health Journal.*

Beebe, B. (2003). Brief mother-infant treatment: Psychoanalytically informed video feedback. *Infant Mental Health Journal, 24*(1), 24–52. https://doi.org/10.1002/imhj.10041

Beebe, B. (2010). Mother-infant research informs mother-infant treatment. *Clinical Social Work Journal, 38*(1), 17–36. https://doi.org/10.1007/s10615-009-0216-x

Beebe, B., & Steele, M. (2016). How does microanalysis of mother–infant communication inform maternal sensitivity and infant attachment? In *Maternal Sensitivity* (pp. 141–160). Routledge.

Bick, E. (1968). The experience of the skin in early object relations. *The International Journal of Psychoanalysis, 49*(2-3), 484–486.

Boston Change Process Study Group. (2002). Explicating the implicit: The local level and the microprocess of change in the analytic situation. *The International Journal of Psychoanalysis, 83*(5), 1051–1062. https://doi.org/10.1516/00207570260338746

Capella, C., Gutiérrez, C., Rodríguez, L., & Gómez, C. (2018). Change during pshychotherapy: The perspective of children and adolescents who have been sexualy abused. *Research in Psychotherapy: Psychopathology, Process and Outcome, 21*(1), 24–39. https://doi.org/hbzv

Capella, C., & Boddy, J. (2021). Listening to the opinista? Relational understandings of voice and silence in a multiperspective narrative study of child psychotherapy. *Children & Society, 35*(6), 835–849.

Capella, C., Rodrìguez, L., Águila, D., Dussert, D., Lama, X., Gutierrez, C., et al. (2015). Storied images of psychotherapeutic change: Approaching children's voices through drawings. *Research in Psychotherapy: Psychopathology, Process and Outcome, 18*(2). https://doi.org/10.4081/ripppo.2015.156

Capella, C., Rodríguez, L., Azócar, E., Lama, X., Núñez, L., Águila, D., et al. (2022). Psychotherapeutic change in children and adolescents who have been sexually abused: A model from participants' perspectives. *Research in Psychotherapy: Psychopathology, Process, and Outcome, 25*(1). https://doi.org/10.4081/ripppo.2022.508

Doria, M. V., Kennedy, H., Strathie, C., & Strathie, S. (2013). Explanations for the success of video interaction guidance (VIG): An emerging method in family psychotherapy. *The Family Journal, 22*(1), 78–87. https://doi.org/10.1177/1066480713505072

Elliott, R., & Shapiro, D. A. (1992). *Client and therapist as analysts of significant events.* Sage Publications, Inc.

Feldman, R., & Greenbaum, C. W. (1997). Affect regulation and synchrony in mother—infant play as precursors to the development of symbolic competence. *Infant Mental Health Journal, 18*(1), 4–23. https://doi.org/10.1111/j.1467-8721.2007.00532.x

Fiedler, P., & Rogge, K. E. (1989). Zur Prozess Untersuchung psychotherapeutischer Episoden. Ausgewählte Beispiele und Perspektiven [On the investigation process of psychotherapeutic episodes. Selected examples and perspectives]. *Zeitschrift für Klinische Psychologie, 18*, 45–54.

Fraiberg, S., Adelson, E., & Shapiro, V. (1975). Ghosts in the nursery: A psychoanalytic approach to the problems of impaired infant-mother relationships. *Journal of the American Academy of Child Psychiatry, 14*(3), 387–421. https://doi.org/10.1016/S0002-7138(09)61442-4

Juffer, F., Bakermans-Kranenburg, M., & van Ijzendoorn, M. (2017). Video-feedback intervention to promote positive parenting and sensitive discipline: Development and metaanalytic evidence for its effectiveness. In H. Steele & M. Steele (Eds.), *Handbook of attachment-based interventions* (pp. 1–26). The Guilford Press.

Juffer, F., & Bakermans-Kranenburg, M. J. (2018). Working with Video-feedback intervention to promote positive parenting and sensitive discipline (VIPP-SD): A case study. *Journal of Clinical Psychology, 74*(8), 1346–1357. https://doi.org/10.1002/jclp.22654

Juffer, F., & Steele, M. (2014). What words cannot say: The telling story of video in attachment-based interventions. *Attachment and Human Development, 16*(4). https://doi.org/10.1080/14616734.2014.982231

Karver, M. S., de Nadai, A. S., Monahan, M., & Shirk, S. R. (2018). Meta-analysis of the prospective relation between alliance and outcome in child and adolescent psychotherapy. *Psychotherapy (Chic), 55*(4), 341–355. https://doi.org/10.1037/pst0000179

Kazdin, A. E. (2009). Understanding how and why psychotherapy leads to change. *Psychotherapy Research, 19*(4–5), 418–428. https://doi.org/10.1080/10503300902808325

Krause, M., & Altimir, C. (2018). *El Programa Chileno de Investigación del Cambio en Psicoterapia* [The Chilean Program for Research on Change in Psychotherapy]. *Revista Brasileira de Psicoterapia, 20*(3).

Krause, M., & de La Parra, G. (2006). Indicadores genéricos de cambio en el proceso psicoterapéutico [Generic indicators of change in the psychotherapeutic process]. *Revista Latinoamericana de Psicología, 38*(2), 299–325. https://doi.org/10.14349/rlp.v38i2.3097

Lieberman, A., & van Horn, P. (2008). *Psychotherapy with infants and young children: Repairing the effects of stress and trauma on early attachment*. The Guilford Press.

Lyons-Ruth, K., Bruschweiler-Stern, N., Harrison, A. M., Morgan, A. C., Nahum, J. P., Sander, L., et al. (1998). Implicit relational knowing: Its role in development and psychoanalytic treatment. *Infant Mental Health Journal: Official Publication of The World Association for Infant Mental Health, 19*(3), 282–289.

Midgley, N. (2007). Researching the process of psychoanalytic child psychotherapy. In E. Kennedy & N. Midgley (Eds.), *Process and outcome research in child and parent-infant psychotherapy: A thematic review* (pp. 8–53). NHS.

Mitchell, S. A. (2000). *Relationality: From attachment to intersubjectivity*. Routledge. https://doi.org/10.4324/9780203753639

Murphy, A., Steele, M., & Steele, H. (2012). From out of sight, out of mind to in sight and in mind: Enhancing reflective capacities in a group attachment-based intervention. In J. E. Bettmann & D. D. Friedman (Eds.), *Attachment-based clinical work with children and adolescents* (pp. 237–255). Springer Science & Business Media.

Newton, K., Taylor Buck, E., Weich, S., & Uttley, L. (2022). A review and analysis of the components of potentially effective perinatal mental health interventions for infant development and mother-infant relationship outcomes. *Development and Psychopathology, 34*, 37–54. https://doi.org/10.1017/S0954579422000292

Nuñez, L., Fernández, S., Alamo, N., Midgley, N., Capella, C., & Krause, M. (2022). The therapeutic relationship and change processes in child psychotherapy: A qualitative, longitudinal study of the views of children, parents, and therapists. Research. *Psychotherapy, 25*(1). https://doi.org/10.4081/ripppo.2022.508

O'Hara, L., Smith, E. R., Barlow, J., Livingstone, N., Herath, N. I. N. S., Wei, Y., et al. (2019). Video feedback for parental sensitivity and attachment security in children under five years. *Cochrane Database of Systematic Reviews, 2019*(1). https://doi.org/10.1002/14651858.CD010534.pub2

Olhaberry, M., León, M. J., Escobar, M., Iribarren, D., Morales-Reyes, I., & Álvarez, K. (2017). Video-feedback intervention to improve parental sensitivity and the quality of interactions in mother-father-infant triads. *Mental Health in Family Medicine, 13*(1).

Olhaberry, M., Mena, C., Zapata, J., Miranda, Á., Romero, M., & Sieverson, C. (2015). *Terapia de Interacción Guiada en díadas madre-bebé con sintomatología depresiva materna en el embarazo: Un estudio piloto.* [Guided Interaction Therapy in mother-infant dyads with maternal depressive symptoms in pregnancy: A pilot study.]. *Summa Psicológica UST, 12*(1), 63–74.

Olhaberry, M. (2024). From dyad to triad in early childhood: Mentalization-informed interventions developed in Chile. *Journal of Infant, Child, and Adolescent Psychotherapy.* https://doi.org/10.1080/15289168.2024.2314419

Olhaberry, M., Morán-Kneer, J., Sieverson, C., Costa-Cordella, S., Muzard, A., Honorato, C., León, M. J., & Leyton, F. (2025). Impact of strength-based video-feedback intervention on maternal sensitivity in mother–infant dyads with maternal depressive symptoms. *Infant Mental Health Journal, 46*(2), 160–180.

Paris, R., Spielman, E., & Bolton, R. E. (2009). Mother–infant psychotherapy: Examining the therapeutic process of change. *Infant Mental Health Journal, 30*(3), 301–319. https://doi.org/10.1002/imhj.20209

Polanyi, M. (1958). *Personal knowledge: Towards a post-critical philosophy.* University of Chicago Press.

Shai, D., & Belsky, J. (2017). Parental embodied mentalizing: How the nonverbal dance between parents and infants predicts children's socio-emotional functioning. *Attachment & Human Development, 19*(2), 191–219. https://doi.org/10.1080/14616734.2016.1255653

Shirk, S. R., Karver, M. S., & Brown, R. (2011). The alliance in child and adolescent psychotherapy. *Psychotherapy, 48*(1), 17–24. doi:https://doi.org/10.1037/a0022159

Sieverson, C., Olhaberry, M., Duarte, J., Morán-Kneer, J., Costa, S., León, M. J., et al. (2022). Beyond the outcomes: Generic change indicators in a video-feedback intervention with a depressed mother and her baby: A single case study. *Research in Psychotherapy: Psychopathology, Process, and Outcome, 25*(1).

Steele, M., Steele, H., Bate, J., Knafo, H., Kinsey, M., Bonuck, K., et al. (2014). Looking from the outside in: The use of video in attachment-based interventions. *Attachment and Human Development, 16*(4), 402–415. https://doi.org/10.1080/14616734.2014.982233

Stern, D. N., Bruschweiler-Stern, N., Harrison, A. M., Lyons-Ruth, K., Morgan, A. C., Nahum, J. P., et al. (1998). The process of therapeutic change involving implicit knowledge: Some implications of developmental observations for adult psychotherapy. *Infant Mental Health Journal, 19*(3), 300–308. https://doi.org/10.1002/(SICI)1097-0355(199823)19:3<300::AID-IMHJ6>3.0.CO;2-U

Stern, M. (2002). *Child friendly therapy. Biopsychosocial innovations for children and families.* W.W Norton & Company.

Stern, D. N. (2009). *The first relationship.* Harvard University Press.

Wallin, D. J. (2007). *Attachment in psychotherapy.* Guilford Press.

Winnicott, D. W. (1971). *Therapeutic consultations in child psychiatry.* Basic Books.

Part III
Innovative Qualitative Methods for Studying Complex Phenomena in Clinical Psychology and Psychotherapy

Chapter 14
Discovery-Oriented Biographical Analysis (DOBA) as a Qualitative Method for the Study of Mental Health Experience as a Complex Process

Alemka Tomicic, Javiera Duarte Soto, and Martina Fischersworring

Introduction: A Small Amount of History

When we learn about the logic of qualitative research, it is often evident, in contrast with quantitative research, that the former is characterized by paradigmatic principles that guide methodological decision-making. At the same time, the latter follows prescriptions that allow compliance or approach to the regulatory ideals of objectivity, reproducibility, and generalization. When conceiving the construction and production of knowledge, we qualify as scientific by these different principles and procedures. However, both must respond to ad hoc criteria *of rigor and quality* (Levitt et al., 2018). In the case of quantitative research in psychotherapy, we know, for example, the prescriptions or protocols for conducting Randomized Clinical Trials (RCT), whose objective is to evaluate the efficacy of a specific treatment or a clinical intervention modality, which, moreover, is usually the gold standard of outcome research. Other methods, such as routine outcome monitoring (ROM), systematically evaluate the consultants' progress to improve results, and practice-oriented research (POR) seeks to understand and improve mental health care as it is delivered in practice. All of these, in terms of the history and types of psychotherapy research, are part of outcome research (Barkham et al., 2010).

A. Tomicic (✉) · J. D. Soto
Centre for Studies in Clinical Psychology and Psychotherapy (CEPPS), Faculty of Psychology, Diego Portales University, Santiago, Chile

Millennium Institute for Research in Depression and Personality (MIDAP), Santiago, Chile
e-mail: alemka.tomicic@mail.udp.cl

M. Fischersworring
Millennium Institute for Research in Depression and Personality (MIDAP), Santiago, Chile

Body Phenomenology Laboratory (LAFEC), Santiago, Chile

A. Tomicic, J. D. Soto (eds.), *Qualitative Research in Clinical Psychology and Psychotherapy in Latin America*, https://doi.org/10.1007/978-3-031-90782-1_14

According to the quantitative research criteria, each research that deviates from this protocol loses rigor and quality and increases the probability of error in its observations and conclusions (see PRISMA, 2020). Given the above, it is possible to state that quantitative research emphasizes quantity and extensiveness, aiming to collect significant and numerous samples to ensure representativeness and legitimacy, as well as comprehensive databases. However, this can imply, at times, a superficial and less nuanced understanding of the object of study.

At the risk of simplifying our argument, although only initially, we can state that in qualitative research, precisely the opposite occurs. In this case, as we already mentioned, the technical-methodological decisions respond to orientations or principles, and this is because the relationship between theory, method, and object of study is one of mutual determination (Maxwell, 2013). So much so that, even when we find the same qualitative methodological approaches in different studies, we can see at first glance their variations in implementation in response to the specificities and particularities of the defined study object. It is important to add that these variations, unlike quantitative protocols, constitute a closer approach to the principles of qualitative research, because the method is subordinated to the requirements of the object of study and its context, and not the other way around. For example, in psychotherapy research, there has been a tradition for years of studies of the subjective experiences of patients and therapists about the processes and the psychotherapeutic change trajectories (Levitt, 2014). However, unlike the case of RCTs, there is no single protocol for their study, but rather, multiple approaches that, even in this relationship between theory, object, and method, conceive the subjective dimension differently and privilege different points of view or access to what we call subjectivity (see, for example, Altimir et al., 2010; Duarte et al., 2020, 2022).

Well, the story of the Discovery-Oriented Biographical Analysis (DOBA) is not very different from the variations of studies of subjective experience in psychotherapy (e.g., Krause et al., 2018), nor from those of the studies of subjective experiences of health problems and mental disorders (e.g., Martínez, et al., 2014). As such, it has faced the same challenge of combining creativity with the principles of consistency, relevance, generativity, and communicability of all qualitative research that, as we have said, consistently exhibits variations (Krause, 1995; Levitt, 2014).

However, what was the object of study that required creating a variation from two existing qualitative analysis approaches? That is, combining grounded theory analysis with a model of autobiographical narrative analysis. In the context of a broader research project on experiences of success and failure in psychotherapy (Krause, 2017), we set out to explore the process of change in the case of psychotherapy with a patient with borderline personality disorder, whose psychotherapist worked from a psychoanalytic orientation. The agenda determined that the psychotherapy was part of a research, which implied that the entire process was video recorded and transcribed. We also had follow-up interviews with the patient and the psychotherapist, who agreed to positively evaluate the psychotherapy process and results. We organized the material, and in weekly meetings, we analyzed it using Constructing Grounded Theory (Charmaz, 2014) with the purpose of understanding and explaining, in qualitative terms, what could contribute, in this case, and possibly in others, to the achievement of such good and consistent results. Initially, we developed, very enthusiastically, emerging categories, concepts, and properties; we immersed ourselves in the material and oriented ourselves to discovery. However, we could not arrive at a plausible relationship scheme when reviewing our notes and memos and starting to relate the categories to develop a comprehensive explanation to answer our research question. We had the intuition and, at times, the certainty that there was a procedural element that we could not capture with the model of axial coding and the progressive orientation to abstraction and construction of an emerging model of Constructing Grounded Theory (Charmaz, 2014). How did we get from this point to the following Biographical Analysis? It is difficult to reconstruct. It had something of luck and opportunism, which, in turn, is associated with the creative character of qualitative research and, probably, of all investigative practice (Energici et al., 2025). The point is that one of us had used, years ago, The Construction of the Self in the Autobiographical Narrative model of Carlos Piña (1998, 1999) and thought it might be a good idea to examine if this model permitted us to apprehend the object we were trying to understand and explain. Moreover, well, this chapter is the evidence that this creative leap, this variation, yielded results for this and other studies (see Duarte et al., 2017; Fischersworring, 2018; Martínez et al., 2025; Tomicic, Martínez, Pérez, et al., 2020).

In what follows, we will present the DOBA, exposing its two dimensions separately: the orientation to discovery, variation of Grounded Theory (Charmaz, 2014), and the biographical analysis, variation of the analysis of The Construction of the Self in the Autobiographical Narrative (Piña, 1998, 1999). We will also review two technical-methodological aspects that we were pouring off DOBA: a case approximation in qualitative analysis and text production through narrative interviews. With this, we will present the DOBA in an integrated way, that is, as a model, and illustrate some applications with their respective variations.

Orientation to Discovery: DOBA and Grounded Theory

Grounded Theory already has the denomination of a qualitative research approach and, even though it stands out for offering a well-systematized analysis model and is easy to communicate, incorporates, like any qualitative methodology that prides itself as such, mentions regarding participant selection procedures or observations and those of information collection. The above pays special attention to the reciprocal relationship between selection, recollection, and analysis that allows the development of an inductive theory—"emergent"—its ultimate goal (Krause, 1995; Corbin & Strauss, 2015).

The Grounded Theory method has been widely used in psychotherapy research in our region and globally (e.g., Dourdouma & Mörtl, 2013). However, its initial development is a product of the work of two sociologists at the "Chicago School"—Barney Glaser and Anselm Strauss—who, in the late 1960s, published their inaugural work on this method, titled "*The Discovery of Grounded Theory: Strategies for Qualitative Research*" (Glaser & Strauss, 1967). As John McLeod (2010) points out, just through the title of this first publication, it is possible to identify three central aspects that guide this method and that, from its origin, except for one of them, have not been modified in substance. These three aspects are that (a) the main task of the researcher is that of "discovery," (b) the main goal is to develop a "theory," and (c) this theory must be "grounded" (founded) in the data. The orientation to discovery, in the logic of the "blank page," refraining the researcher from the use of previous referential theoretical frameworks and proposing a radical inductive approach, placed Grounded Theory under the post-positivist paradigm (Guba & Lincoln, 1994; Krause, 1995). That is, it placed Grounded Theory as a method that operates on the assumption that (a) social reality exists and occurs independently of the researcher; (b) the relationship of knowledge of this reality is governed by the regulatory framework of objectivity, which, in other words, seeks to prevent the interference of the researcher's subjectivity in what is studied, and that, given the two previous assumptions, (c) inductive methodologies and triangulation techniques make sense for the development of emerging provisional theories that can subsequently be verified with quantitative methodologies (Glaser & Strauss, 1967; Guba & Lincoln, 1994).

Over time, the original proposal of Glaser and Strauss (1967) started showing variations as this approach became part of the work of new researchers (for example, Charmaz, 2006; Corbin & Strauss, 2015; Levitt, 2021; Strauss & Corbin, 2002), who applied the model to different fields and study objects. Nevertheless, they also began developing and publishing their learnings and methodological reflections, which, along with global paradigmatic transformations in the field of social sciences (e.g., the crisis of representation and the crisis of legitimation, Denzin & Lincoln, 2005), led to Grounded Theory to inhabit a new paradigmatic place in research: Constructivism.

In the 1990s, along with Anselm Strauss, Juliet Corbin, also a sociologist, wrote a key book, and probably one of the most read on Grounded Theory, titled "*Basics of Qualitative Research*." This publication, in addition to introducing axial analysis—an "operationalization" of the emerging theory—emphasized the importance of the researcher's reflexivity, pointing out the impossibility of obtaining researchers' neutrality in the analysis process since it will always be influenced by their perceptions and worldviews (Corbin & Strauss, 2015; Strauss & Corbin, 2002). We do not have space, nor is it the purpose of this chapter to delve into the rupture that these assumptions meant with Glaser's original model (2007). However, it is essential to indicate that this, which might seem like a slight variation of the method, opened the door for later developments that gave rise to the Constructivist Grounded Theory (e.g., Charmaz, 2006; Levitt, 2021). In research in clinical psychology and psychotherapy at a global level, particularly in Latin America and Chile, there are exponents of the method who have moved from the classic Grounded Theory—in its version closest to postpositivism—to the Constructivist Grounded Theory.

Kathy Charmaz, also a sociologist by training, published in the year 2006 the first edition of "*The Construction of Grounded Theory*," making explicit mention of the original publication of the method by Glaser and Strauss (1967), "*The Discovering of Grounded Theory*." As it can be read in her book, the change she introduced had to do with the distinction between an orientation to discovery and one that recognizes the social and intersubjectively constructed character of the concepts and interpretations that are part of grounded theories (Charmaz, 2006). This constructivist turn recognizes, then, the presence of subjectivity and the implication of the researchers in the construction and interpretation of the data in flexible processes and mutual determination between the previous theories they carry and those that emerge during the research process (Charmaz, 2006, 2014). In clinical psychology and psychotherapy research, Heidi Levitt (2021) has been one of the most significant exponents and promoters of Grounded Theory in its constructivist version. Among others, she has shown that the incorporation of the researchers' subjectivity as a vehicle of interpretation not only does not jeopardize the quality and credibility of the findings of qualitative research but, on the contrary, enriches the quality of the results.

As we have pointed out, the constructivist aspect of Grounded Theory emphasizes that emerging theories have a socially constructed character based on the production of interactions between researchers and participants. Instead of objective truth, it proposes that the incorporation of subjectivity—the perspective of the researcher and the perspective of the participant—is not only inevitable but, above all, a fundamental condition for constructing interpretations about the data that are contextualized, relevant, and generative. Why, then, do we maintain the orientation to discovery in the DOBA? The answer is, apparently, complex. However, in simple terms, we understand that the orientation to discovery can still be interpreted from a constructivist epistemological approach. Thus, theories emerge from the data—discovery—but, in turn, they become theories through the interpretive lens of the researcher—constructivism. While discovery implies an inductive approach, constructivism recognizes that the researcher actively contributes to creating knowledge, influenced by their context and interactions with the participants. Ultimately, the discovered theory does not constitute an objective reality but is a contextualized and co-constructed interpretation of the studied phenomenon.

The Contribution to DOBA of the Biographical Analysis Model in the Construction of the Self

Carlos Piña is a Chilean anthropologist, researcher, and academic renowned for his work in autobiographical studies. In 1998, he published his method of autobiographical narrative analysis. At that time, he pointed out that this type of narrative should not be analyzed in terms of an "objective truth" but as a type of narration that organizes and attributes meaning to life events from the perspective of the narrator and whose function and effect is to sustain, with each narrative, the construction of the self.

The nature of the autobiographical narrative is, then, that of an interpretive text generated by one or more speakers who narrate their own life or an aspect of it (Piña, 1998, 1999). It is a narrative not limited to a simple sum of facts. Still, it seeks to articulate a narrative with a general sense, in which the past is reinterpreted from the present, becoming intelligible and meaningful. Through memory, the narrator or narrators elaborate and give meaning to their past, creating a textual product that reflects their identity and continuity over time. In addition, Carlos Piña (1998, 1999) says that the autobiographical narrative is produced in a specific context—which can include, for example, that of a psychotherapeutic process or that of an investigation. This context is known as a "biographical situation," which, among others, includes the material and symbolic conditions in which this can occur. This also implies that the narrator is not the only author of the narrative, as others can intervene in its elaboration by becoming co-authors through roles such as psychotherapists or interviewers.

On the other hand, the "self" in the context of the autobiographical narrative is equivalent, in a certain sense, to the identity of the speaker who narrates his life or part of it. However, we know that the notions of self and identity are problematic and not permanently fixed in psychology (see Chap. 9, Martinez et al.). The self and identity, in the narrative, are understood as linguistic productions that are expressed with a proper name and become the mechanism that allows the relationship between the whole (the narrator's life) and its parts (the events and narrated episodes). Hence, the autobiographical narrative enables the speaker to decompose and recompose his biographical experience, articulating his story so that the continuity and development of his identity (Piña, 1998, 1999) is perceived. Thus, the autobiographical narrative not only reflects the past but also contributes to the construction of the "self" in the present, allowing the narrator to understand himself and his life trajectory, or a period of it, in a more precise and more meaningful way, as well as being able to project an identity perceived by others.

Taking into consideration the conceptual aspects mentioned above, the analysis of the Construction of the Self in the Autobiographical Narrative offers a narrative analysis structure that, similar to the case of Grounded Theory and axial analysis (see Corbin & Strauss, 2015), enables the identification of different elements or parts that make up the narrated life—synchronic approach—and the relationships between these, on a temporal or processual axis —diachronic approach. With this, it is possible, then, to analyze one or several narratives by the biographical situation that summons them: a psychotherapeutic process (e.g., Duarte et al., 2017), a mental health process (e.g., Martínez et al., 2025; Tomicic et al. 2020; Valenzuela, 2024), or a professional trajectory in the field of mental health (e.g. Fischersworring, 2018). To carry out this analysis, the author (Piña, 1998) describes a series of events that an autobiographical narrative can contain, according not only to a synchronic approach—for example, open coding in Grounded Theory—but also based on their value and meaning to compose the narrative given the construction of the self. These elements distinguish the narrative, milestones, attributions of causality and motivations, contexts, and references to moral orders, which offer the analysis's diachronic or processual dimension.

Regarding the first element, in Western culture, people usually organize narratives, mainly biographical narratives, in stages. In these, the narrator makes distinctions of extensive periods that can be anchored in geographic locations, specific periods of their life span, personal or family events (e.g., Martínez et al., 2025), certain activities or psychological experiences (e.g., Duarte et al., 2017), among others. The stages can vary from one narrative to another and constitute a simple way the narrator organizes his story towards his destination (for example, towards the current situation or expected future). On the other hand, and in the opposite way, the milestones are events that usually occur in short or limited periods and are underlined by the narrator because they imply an inflection in the narrative. They typically mark the beginning of a chain of events, being, therefore, of a very diverse nature. Some coincide with conventionally essential events, such as, for example, the deaths of loved ones, the birth of children, the search for or loss of a job, etc. Others may be linked to the idiosyncrasy of the narrator, and in that sense, could be pointed out as milestones, a failure in a central subject in psychology training, or a significant moment for the own psychotherapy process (e.g., Duarte et al., 2020, 2022).

On the other hand, attributions of causality and motivations are arguments in the narrative that implicitly or explicitly explain the occurrence of the events or actions that are narrated. On the one hand, the attributions of causality can be very varied: a milestone, like an impasse with the psychotherapist, could be narrated as the cause of having abandoned psychotherapy (Martinez et al. 2014), but we could also find causes based on beliefs, like "I do not deserve to be helped," that prevent the patient from attending psychotherapy (Tomicic et al., 2021). Thus, the causes can be "properly causal," like the exemplified, or teleological, like "this had to happen for that other thing to happen." On the other hand, motivations are characterized by accounting in the narrative of the purposes, longings, or desires that "move" the narrator and the others who are part of his story to perform or not specific actions to fulfill those ends, like, for example, getting out of a suicidal process (Martinez et al., 2014), or follow a professional career path as a psychotherapist (Fischersworring, 2018).

Regarding the context, Piña (1998) points out that most of the narratives, particularly those of an autobiographical nature, are carried out from a particular narrative position while arguing the state of things from that same position (for example, having survived a suicidal process, Martínez et al., 2025; Tomicic et al. 2020). This is how the context accounts for that narrative position performed and explained by the narration, as it provides the basis by which events, places, and characters have been selected and articulated in a meaningful temporal structure. Lastly, at various moments in a narrative, references are made to moral orders or conventions that offer models for the behaviors and thoughts of a group, community, or person. For example, direct references can be found to the rule of confidentiality in psychotherapy through the fear that recordings of the sessions will be published on YouTube (Duarte et al., 2017), or the presence in the stories of cultural models of the hopeless fate in the stories of young gay survivors of a suicidal process (Film "*The Secret of the Mountain*," Tomicic et al. 2020).

DOBA: Design and Integrated Analysis Procedures

As mentioned above, we constructed the DOBA to expand the descriptive and relational scope proposed by Grounded Theory in its constructivist version (Charmaz, 2006, 2014; Levitt, 2021). Incorporating, in turn, the historical temporality of a biographical analysis method and understanding that stories about experiences related to psychotherapeutic and clinical phenomena constitute per se biographical situations associated with the constitution of the self, the DOBA could address this central aspect when delving into the study of the subjective experience regarding these study objects.

In summary, the DOBA method combines the principles of Grounded Theory (Charmaz, 2006, 2014; Levitt, 2021) with the technique of Biographical Analysis in the Construction of the Self (Piña, 1998, 1999). The first, through open coding, allows us to develop concepts, categories, and properties from the data, considering their descriptive scope. In contrast, the second, through the inquiry into the narrative organization of the concepts and categories developed, allows us to reconstruct shared narratives, thus contributing to an interpretive scope. Along with the above, the combination of these two approaches provides richness and density to the processual understanding of phenomena that involve, in their nature, a biographical situation—as is the case of psychotherapy and clinical phenomena—providing an opportunity to delve into the cultural and contextual characteristics of the subjective experience.

An Approach Based on Case Studies

The DOBA method has shown its applicability in research with qualitative case methods, whether single case type (Duarte et al., 2017) or multiple (Fischersworring, 2018; Martínez et al., 2025; Tomicic et al. 2020; Alomar, 2020; Valenzuela, 2024).

All qualitative research is a case study since each participant, situation, or event incorporated as part of its design represents a particular aspect we pursue from the phenomenon or study object. This means that, in a qualitative research design, our purpose is not to account for the way a phenomenon is distributed in a population in terms, for example, of its frequency. On the contrary, we are interested in understanding the nature of that phenomenon by incorporating cases that enrich the range of possible expressions (Levitt, 2021).

Having clarified the sense of the case in qualitative research and, consequently, for the DOBA, there are multiple strategies and criteria for selecting cases that exclude random selection. The above is because choosing one or more cases to enrich the understanding of a phenomenon requires intentional selection (McLeod, 2010). Hence, for example, we characterize the cases as typical cases (when the case is known to be usual and helps to strengthen the "generalization" towards the phenomenon), extreme cases (when the case is known not to be similar to other cases, which reinforces its heuristic value), deviant cases (when there are attributes of the case that deviate from what is expected, which can strengthen the construction of theory), influential cases (when the case has received much attention, contributing to its theoretical value, through the comparison of previous analyses), and innovative cases (when the cases are selected, for example, to represent an innovative intervention/therapy).

In some applications of DOBA, the cases represent such heuristic value that they have been presented with brief descriptions that carry the sense of the situation and the biographical narrative. For example, in the study by Martínez et al. (2025), the researchers represent each of the cases of young trans survivors of a suicide process through titles, many of them extracted from the participants' own stories. Each title, which operates as a synthesis of cases, accounts for the central conflict and biographical situation that organizes the participants' narration.

Data Collection for the DOBA with Narrative Interviews

As we have already pointed out, regarding the type and form of production of the stories it analyzes, the DOBA method is applicable in qualitative designs to generate a greater understanding of study objects with a processual character. Due to the above, the techniques used to collect the participants' stories are qualitative interviews of a narrative or biographical type, whether open or semi-structured (Kvale & Brinkmann, 2009). Now, whether using an open interview script or a semi-structured one, the presence of an opening question or an initial assignment and start-up is necessary to allow the deployment of a biographical narrative. For example, in the study carried out by Duarte et al. (2017) about a psychotherapy process, the initial question for the patient and the psychotherapist was: "*Tell me about your experience during the psychotherapeutic treatment. I would like to collect your general impressions, whatever comes to mind*," and "*I would like to ask you about the therapy process with your patient, how was that experience for you?*" In Fischersworring's study (2018), participants were asked the following open question to explore the narratives about their professional trajectories as psychotherapists: "*Tell me, how did you become the therapist that you are today?*" On the other hand, in the study of Martínez et al. (2025), about a clinical phenomenon such as the experience of having survived a suicide process, the starting was "*You can start from wherever you wish.*"

Sometimes, the initial question can be preceded by one that contextualizes their interest in participating in the research, which could also be understood as biographical. This allows, in relevant cases, to understand the context and the *self* that will be sustained by the biographical narrative that will help produce the interview. For example, the question "*What motivated you to participate in this research?*" was the one that started the interviews of the study by Tomicic et al. (2020) about the subjective experience of having survived a suicide process of young lesbians and gays. This question allowed the researchers to identify "the testimonial position," which accounted for the context and biographical situation from which the interviewees produced their stories.

Interviews need to be audio-recorded and transcribed for their subsequent analysis with DOBA. The possibility of having the stories of the participants transcribed textually is fundamental for the application of the analytical operations of DOBA, which, to some extent, can be classified as microanalytical. Even though it is possible to imagine a biographical analysis applied to the notes of a psychotherapist from a psychotherapy process (example, Martínez & Tomicic, 2023), the analysis can significantly reduce its richness, as we lose linguistic and semantic information present in the production of the narrative, not mediated or selected by a third party.

DOBA Analysis Model

The first of the two analytical operations of DOBA is linked with its discovery-oriented dimension, the open coding procedure of Grounded Theory (Charmaz, 2014) (see Fig. 14.1). This procedure consists of developing concepts and categories based on the narratives collected through the interviews. To perform this analytical operation, we approach the interpretation of the interviews that have been transcribed, selecting units of meaning. These correspond to fragments of narratives that contain one or more meanings that can be interpreted and developed in terms of concepts and their properties.

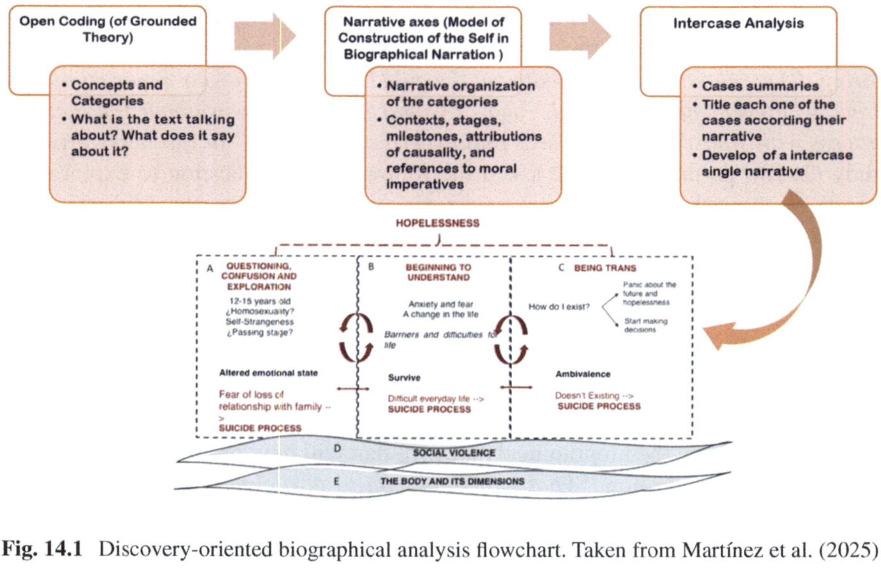

Fig. 14.1 Discovery-oriented biographical analysis flowchart. Taken from Martínez et al. (2025)

To accomplish the above, we use two analysis questions proposed for open coding in Grounded Theory: What does this narrative fragment talk about? And What does it tell us about what it is talking about? The answer to the first analytical question gives rise to the development of one or more concepts and the second to the properties of these concepts. Once the ideas are developed, for example, in analyzing one or more interviews, the categorization procedure is carried out, answering whether two or more concepts suggest and can be grouped into a higher-order category. By applying the coding and categorization processes iteratively, we can move towards developing hierarchical classification schemes, which allow us to identify concepts and categories with more excellent saturation that will then be processed with the second analytical operation of DOBA.

In this first phase of analysis, the research team must hold regular meetings to triangulate the analysis and reach intersubjective agreements regarding the categories, concepts, and properties developed (Flick, 2004).

The second analytical operation of DOBA corresponds to the narrative organization of the categories and concepts developed during the open coding procedure. This is where the model of Construction of the Self in the Autobiographical Narrative (Piña, 1998, 1999) provides axes that contribute to a flexible structure for such an organization. It is essential to remember that this analysis model considers the narrative as a product of the *subjective self*, which organizes, interprets, and signifies the explored life situations in the research framework. As we detailed previously, to reconstruct the stories of a case or a group of cases, the autobiographical analysis recommends identifying contexts, stages, milestones, attributions of causality and motivations, and references to moral orders and their subsequent organization in a narrative structure (see Fig. 14.1).

When using DOBA, each interview or case needs to be analyzed on its merit, parallel to the inter-case analysis carried out with the first analytical operation. As we mentioned, case syntheses can be made, and titles that represent central aspects of the studied experience or specific stages of the narrative can be given. The analyses of a case or each interview organize and articulate a common and unique narrative structure that reflects a shared or frequent narrative.

The organization and presentation of the analysis and results in qualitative research usually present a creative challenge, and DOBA is no exception. DOBA demands presenting results that account for trajectories involving synchronic and diachronic aspects, where process and temporality are not linear and do not always coincide with chronological time. Figures 14.2 and 14.3 illustrate different creative efforts to communicate the results of DOBA's application graphically

Illustrations of DOBA Applications

As we mentioned at the beginning of this chapter, the work titled "*I couldn't change the past; the answer wasn't there*" (Duarte et al., 2017) was the first analysis we carried out integrating two methods—one oriented to discovery and another of

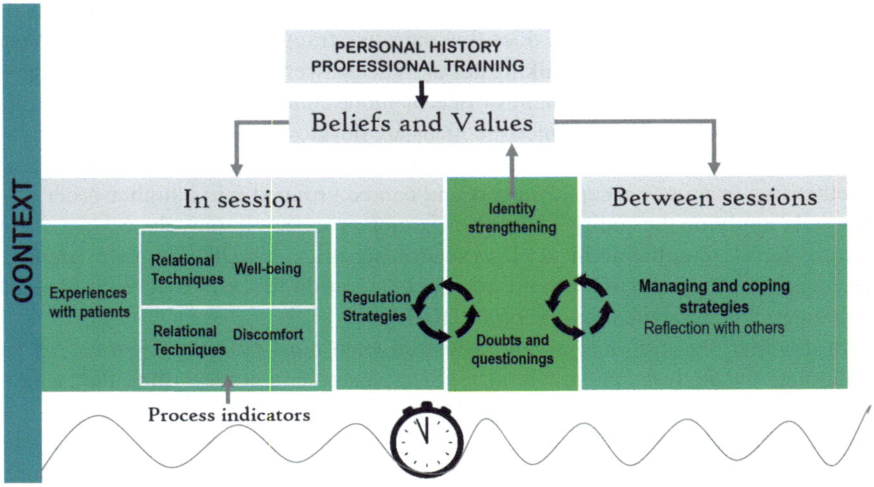

Fig. 14.2 The development of a professional identity as a psychotherapist. Taken from Fischersworring (2018)

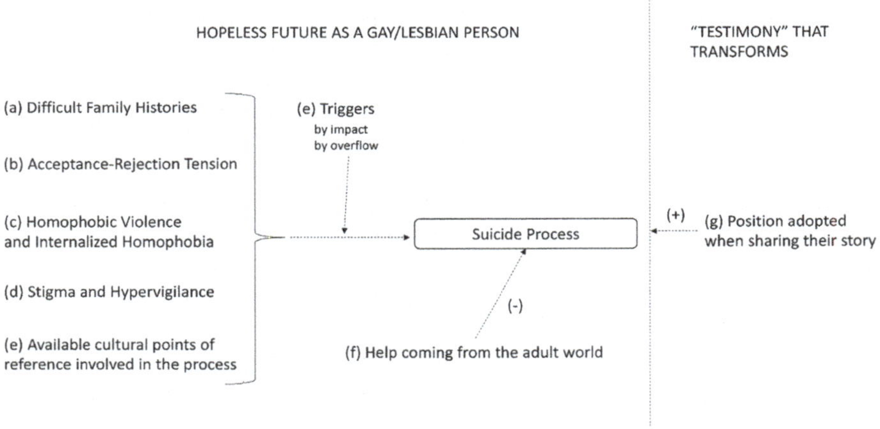

Fig. 14.3 Subjective construction of the suicidal process in young gay and lesbian. Taken from Tomicic et al. (2020)

biographical analysis—which gave rise to DOBA. We carried it out in the context of the project we mentioned previously (Krause, 2017), in which we conducted follow-up interviews with therapists and patients to collect their experiences in psychotherapy processes that had already ended. More specifically, we wanted to systematically and in-depth explore the subjective construction of the psychotherapeutic change process from the participants' perspectives (McLeod, 2011, McLeod et al., 2021).

In the work of Duarte et al. (2017), we selected a case from a series of cases for an in-depth analysis according to the criterion of a "good result" in terms of objective measures (OQ-45.2, Jacobson & Truax, 1991; Lambert et al., 1996) and based on the positive global subjective evaluation of the process, carried out both by the patient and the psychotherapist. The chosen case was also an influential case within the context of psychotherapy in Chile (McLeod, 2010), as it has received special attention for research purposes and training, given its usefulness for understanding the change processes observable in Chilean public health institutions in patients with borderline personality disorder.

The result of the application of DOBA was the reconstruction of a two-voiced narrative —the patient's and the psychotherapist's— about the patient's change process and the formation of the therapeutic bond between them. In this analysis and its presentation, the most salient analytical category was that of stages and milestones, so we organized the shared narrative into four "chapters" titled 'YouTube," "I Couldn't Change the Past," "The Baby," and "WhatsApp." For example, this last chapter, which refers to the closure of the psychotherapy process, examines in the participants' narration the continuity of the therapeutic relationship beyond the end of formal therapy; it analyzes how communication and mutual support are symbolically maintained through platforms like WhatsApp, which reflects the lasting impact of treatment, particularly in the patient's life.

Another work in which DOBA was applied is the research conducted by Fischersworring (2018), focusing on how psychotherapists construct their professional identities and the subjective impact of therapeutic success and failure on their experiences of well-being/discomfort. The design of this study included conducting two complementary studies, following the triangulation strategy of methods proposed by Patton (1999). The first study focused on the salient experiences in the biographical narratives regarding work and professional trajectories. This study granted a broad perspective of the phenomenon of professional development of psychotherapists. It was complemented by a second study where recent or situated experiences in the context of specific psychotherapy were analyzed.

By applying DOBA to this study, the author extracted, from the narratives of the psychotherapists, concepts and categories related to a) the experiences of success and failure of their psychotherapeutic processes, b) how they appraised their subjective well-being, and c) the relationship between both experiences On the other hand, the organization of these categories into a biographical analysis that included context, stages, milestones, attributions of causality, motivations, and the reference to moral orders enabled the generation of different trajectories (see Fig. 14.2), which offer an understanding of the professional growth of psychotherapists and of processes of professional burnout and stagnation. Additionally, an attempt was made to understand and interpret each case in its context, socio-historical, socio-political, and institutional, to describe in depth each of the elements that shaped their narratives, applying the criterion of the quality of dense description (Geertz, 2003).

Two other investigations in which the DOBA method was used are those of Tomicic et al., (2020) and Martínez et al. (2025), both under the umbrella of a project from the Health Research Fund, FONIS, of Chile (Martínez, Tomicic, et al.,

2014). The general objective was to characterize the subjective experience of LGBT youth who had survived a suicidal process. In this study, a multiple-case design was used, and semi-structured qualitative interviews of a narrative type were conducted with all the participants. The study was based on the assumption that stories of suicidal processes convey meanings in themselves, as narratives function as a fundamental human means for organizing and communicating life experiences (McLeod, 2010). This approach allowed the researchers to focus on how participants who had had experiences of ideation or suicidal behavior interpreted themselves, their actions, and their environments (Hjelmeland & Loa Knizek, 2011).

In the study by Tomicic et al., (2020), when applying DOBA to the narratives of a subgroup of eight participants, lesbians, and gays, the researchers were able to reconstruct what they concluded seems to be a recurrent experience of members of sexual minorities when they face and survive a suicidal process. They organized this recurrent experience by describing multiple aspects of it, which are combined temporally, diachronically, and synchronically to account for the motives and intentions associated with suicidal behavior, synthesized in the subjective experience of a "hopeless future as a gay/lesbian person." Then, they described aspects that organize the narration in this case and that offer an explanation of the biographically studied situation: (a) Difficult family histories, (b) Acceptance-rejection tension (c) Homophobic violence and internalized homophobia, (d) Stigma and hypervigilance, (e) Available cultural reference points that intervene in the process, (f) Triggers of the suicidal process, (g) Help from the adult world, and finally (h) Position adopted when sharing their story (see Fig. 14.3).

Martínez et al. (2025) used DOBA to analyze seven narrative interviews with trans youth who had survived a suicide process; the researchers reconstructed a shared and constant experience in which the emergence of one's own gender identity is intertwined with the processes of going through and surviving a suicidal experience. To organize this recurrent experience, a descriptive model of three stages or moments was developed. Within each of them, the participants described situations and milestones in which they had the idea of committing suicide. These stages or moments were named as: (a) questioning, confusion, and exploration; (b) beginning to understand; and (c) being trans. The researchers identified two aspects that cut across the narratives: (d) social violence and (e) the body and its dimensions. All in all, these results allowed the researchers to account for the relationship between the emergence of the trans identity and the suicidal process.

The DOBA method has also been applied in two other Chilean studies to understand aspects related to the configuration and reconfiguration of narrative identity in mental health.

The research by Alomar (2020) sought to characterize the configuration of the personal identity of adult women sexually assaulted in childhood or adolescence. This study conducted in-depth interviews with eight adult women users of a psychiatry unit of a public hospital in the Biobío region of Chile. The application of DOBA as a method of analysis allowed the identification of five main themes that compose two central axes of the experience of abuse in childhood.

The first axis, called the phenomenology of sexual aggression, is composed of three significant themes. The first theme refers to the secret (of abuse) and includes both its creation, self-defense strategies, and unveiling, as well as its rupture. The second theme alludes to the revictimization throughout life, including this experience in the workplace. As a third theme, the participants refer to the way they have coped with sexual aggression in their lives, with the identification of triggering events of psychological symptoms, suicide attempts, and the meaning given to sexual aggression. The second axis refers to the personal identity of women sexually assaulted in childhood or adolescence and contains two associated themes. A central theme covers the subjectivity characterized by the impossibility of being loved, loneliness, "being a woman"—making particular reference to the role of women in society—distrust in relationships, fear of life, and protection—referring to the overprotection of others, but the lack of protection towards themselves. The last theme accounts for characteristics of their life trajectory, identifying milestones such as childhood, the formation of couple relationships, motherhood, work, and self-perception in the present.

The results obtained by Alomar (2020), applying the DOBA method, contribute to understanding the phenomenology of sexual aggression and how it impacts the development and maintenance of personal identity. It understands aggression as an autobiographical milestone and, simultaneously, as a process throughout their lifespan, difficult but possible to integrate into personal identity. It also highlights psychotherapy as a space that supports reworking and incorporating one's experience.

On the other hand, the study *What Is this, What's Happening to Me: Is It Me or the Bipolar Disorder?* developed by María José Valenzuela (2024) aimed to describe and understand how the subjective experience of living with bipolar disorder (BD) reshapes the narrative identity. This study used a qualitative methodological design with a descriptive-interpretative scope, based on a combination of a narrative biographical approach with a phenomenological-hermeneutic ontological approach. In-depth interviews were conducted, aiming to explore mood changes throughout life, the diagnosis of BD, and the medical-psychiatric treatment associated with the disorder. Ten adults with a previous diagnosis of BD participated in a phase of euthymia and underwent pharmacological and psychological therapy.

The analysis of the interviews using the DOBA method yielded five categories that characterize the subjective experience of BD: (a) experiences of vulnerability, which refer to external discomfort throughout the life course; (b) experiences of instability, which allude to internal discomfort throughout the life course; (c) the impact of BD on life; (d) experiences and perception of treatment; and, finally, (e) euthymia, which is related to experiences and practices of self-care.

In the second analysis stage, four recurring trajectories were described, accounting for narrative identities in which the identified categories intertwine and characterize the subjective experience of BD. For example, one of these trajectories illustrates the development of a strong sense of duty and moral obligation, given childhood circumstances and its connection with emotional symptomatology. The importance of setting boundaries appears as an expression of personal growth and determination to protect one's well-being. This action of self-affirmation and the creation of boundaries emerges as a crucial aspect of the trajectory toward recovery and stability. In addition, these trajectories show that narrative identity seems to be dynamically reconfigured about symptoms, diagnosis, and treatment. Within these, the tension between being bipolar or having bipolar disorder gives way to a conception where the disorder is integrated with personal identity, "for better or worse," becoming an inseparable component of the self.

Final Reflections

The Discovery-Oriented Biographical Analysis (DOBA) model offers an approach where the analytical operations allow, based on the narratives of the clinical psychology and psychotherapy study participants, to identify stages that organize their stories and recognize milestones that mark their changes and inflections. Thus, it also contributes to analyzing their contents regarding contexts, intentionality, and social prescriptions. In addition, DOBA, akin to the practices of analysis and communication of the results of qualitative research, proposes to graph the narratives based on their movements, which can help identify a typical trajectory in the stories or different possibilities of trajectories. These graphical representations offer a global understanding of the "narrative arc" and its key moments. From this, the graphical representation that DOBA allows for the analytical work of the narratives and their communication provides a visual method that, eventually, can facilitate the design of observation or self-report guidelines. These can be imagined to eventually contribute to monitoring trajectories and processes linked to psychotherapy, which could be part of intervention programs oriented to different biographical objects previously of investigative interest.

On the other hand, DOBA allows integrating into the analysis the sociocultural determinants present in the narratives, offering a reading in which contexts and milestones reflect a set of facts or events that acquire individual meaning and the influences of family, community, and cultural dynamics. Thus, in biographical situations that appear to be intimate or individual, such as the process of psychotherapy or professional development as a psychotherapist, it is possible and desirable to identify the presence of social and cultural aspects that participate in them. These aspects provide meaning and understanding to the narratives, which, in addition to being explained as a relevant biographical situation, are found to support the construction of the self. Hence, the identification in the narratives of references to moral orders allows for studying the ethical and normative dimensions that frame personal experiences. We believe that this is one of the valuable aspects of DOBA and its applications so far, that is, the possibility of understanding how these social and symbolic norms change and affect narratives between genders or sociocultural groups, as well as over time.

DOBA is a proper qualitative research method for the study of psychotherapy and clinical psychology with populations with complex mental health problems or whose problems are linked to experiences of discrimination and stigma. Narrative analysis can help understand, in a systematic and rooted way, through their own stories, how people understand in their lives the experience of a psychotherapy process, the development of their mental health problems, and experiences of victimization.

In this sense, it is possible to affirm, as many of the interviewees point out, that mere participation in this type of study in a testimonial way facilitates the process of reorganizing their experience and grants a better understanding of themselves. In addition, the results obtained enable the design of contextualized interventions, which balance individual experiences with aspects that can be interpreted as common or shared in a more abstract dimension.

Also, when we analyze the motivations and the evaluation of past stages that the participants make, DOBA offers us a vision of how people reinterpret difficult experiences and how they construct what we could call a narrative of resilience (for example, "The testimonial position," Tomicic et al., 2020; "The answer wasn't there," (Duarte et al., 2017). We think that this perspective can also be applied shortly in studies of narratives about addictions, grieving processes, and experiences of psychotherapies in traumas, among others.

In summary, it is our conviction that DOBA not only supports the analysis and deep understanding of individual narratives in the context of psychotherapy and clinical psychology research but also opens the possibility of a variety of practical applications in a diversity of fields where personal narratives reflect both the unique experience of the person and the social and cultural structures in which they are immersed.

References

Alomar, F. (2020). *¿Quién soy hoy? Una mirada integral de las agresiones sexuales en la infancia o adolescencia en la identidad personal de mujeres adultas. [Who am I today? A comprehensive look at sexual assaults in childhood or adolescence in the personal identity of adult women].* Master's Thesis. https://repositorio.uchile.cl/bitstream/handle/2250/187724/Qui%C3%A9n-soy-hoy.pdf?sequence=1

Altimir, C., Krause, M., de la Parra, G., Dagnino, P., Tomicic, A., Valdés, N., & Vilches, O. (2010). Clients', therapists', and observers' agreement on the amount, temporal location, and content of psychotherapeutic change and its relation to outcome. *Psychotherapy Research, 20*(4), 472–487. https://doi.org/10.1080/10503301003705871

Barkham, M., Hardy, G. E., & Mellor-Clark, J. (2010). *Developing and delivering practice-based evidence: A guide for the psychological therapies.* John Wiley & Sons.

Charmaz, K. (2006). *Constructing grounded theory: A practical guide through qualitative analysis.* SAGE Publications Ltd..

Charmaz, K. (2014). *Constructing grounded theory* (2nd ed.). SAGE Publications Ltd..

Corbin, J., & Strauss, A. (2015). *Basics of qualitative research: Techniques and procedures for developing grounded theory* (4th ed.). SAGE Publications.

Denzin, N. K., & Lincoln, Y. S. (2005). *The Sage handbook of qualitative research* (3rd ed.). SAGE Publications.

Dourdouma, A., & Mörtl, K. (2013). The creative journey of grounded theory analysis: A guide to its principles and applications. *Research in Psychotherapy: Psychopathology, Process and Outcome, 15*(2), 96–106. https://doi.org/10.4081/ripppo.2012.108

Duarte, J., Fischersworring, M., Martínez, C., & Tomicic, A. (2017). "I couldn't change the past; the answer wasn't there": A case study on the subjective construction of psychotherapeutic change of a patient with a borderline personality disorder diagnosis and her therapist. *Psychotherapy Research*. https://doi.org/10.1080/10503307.2017.1359426

Duarte, J., Martinez, C., & Tomicic, A. (2020). Episodes of meeting in psychotherapy: An empirical exploration of patients' experiences of subjective change during their psychotherapy process. *Research in Psychotherapy, 23*(1), 440. https://doi.org/10.4081/ripppo.2020.440

Duarte, J., Martinez, C., & Tomicic, A. (2022). Sparks of psychotherapeutic change: How therapists understand moments of meetings' contribution to change in psychotherapy. *Psychotherapy Research, 32*(4), 511–524. https://doi.org/10.1080/10503307.2021.1948138

Energici, A., Tomicic, A., & Schöngut-Grollmus, N. (2025). Qualitative research quality in Latin American vulnerable and precarious contexts. In U. Flick (Ed.), *The SAGE handbook of qualitative research design*. Sage Ed.

Fischersworring, M. (2018). *Impacto subjetivo del éxito y fracaso terapéutico sobre las vivencias de bienestar/malestar del terapeuta [Subjective impact of therapeutic success and failure on the therapist's experiences of well-being/discomfort]* [Doctoral thesis]. Universidad de Chile.

Flick, U. (2004). *Introducción a la Investigación Cualitativa [Introduction to Qualitative Research]*. Ediciones Morata.

Geertz, C. (2003). *La interpretación de las culturas [The interpretation of cultures]*. Gedisa. (Original work published 1973)

Glaser, B., & Strauss, A. (1967). *The discovery of grounded theory. Strategies for qualitative research*. Aldine Publishing Company.

Glaser, B. G. (2007). Constructivist grounded theory? *Historical Social Research/Historische Sozialforschung. Supplement, 19*, 93–105. http://www.jstor.org/stable/40981071

Guba, E. G., & Lincoln, Y. S. (1994). Competing paradigms in qualitative research. In N. K. Denzin & Y. S. Lincoln (Eds.), *Handbook of qualitative research* (pp. 105–117). SAGE Publications.

Hjelmeland, H., & Loa Knizek, B. (2011). Methodology in suicidological research – Contribution to the debate. *Suicidology Online, 2*, 8–10.

Jacobson, N. S., & Truax, P. (1991). Clinical significance: A statistical approach to defining meaningful change in psychotherapy-research. *Journal of Consulting and Clinical Psychology, 59*, 12–19.

Krause, M. (1995). *La investigación cualitativa: Un campo de posibilidades y desafíos* [Qualitative research: A field of possibilities and challenges.]. *Revista Temas de Educación, 7*, 19–39.

Krause, M. (2017). *Final Report: PROYECTO FONDECYT°1141179: "Experiencias de Éxito y Fracaso en Psicoterapia – Construcción de un Modelo Comprehensivo Multidimensional" ["Experiences of Success and Failure in Psychotherapy – Construction of a Comprehensive Multidimensional Model"].*

Krause, M., Espinosa, H. D., Tomicic, A., Córdoba, A. C., & Vásquez, D. (2018). Psychotherapy for depression from the point of view of economically disadvantaged individuals in Chile and Colombia. *Counselling and Psychotherapy Research*.

Kvale, S., & Brinkmann, S. (2009). *Interviews: Learning the craft of qualitative research interviewing* (2nd ed.). Sage Publications, Inc.

Lambert, M. J., Burlingame, G. M., Umphress, V., Hansen, N. B., Vermeersch, D. A., Yanchar, S. C., & Clouse, G. C. (1996). The reliability and validity of the outcome questionnaire. *Clinical Psychology and Psychotherapy, 3*, 249–258.

Levitt, H. M. (2014). Qualitative psychotherapy research: The journey so far and future directions. *Psychotherapy*. Advanced online publication. https://doi.org/10.1037/a0037076

Levitt, H. (2021). *Essentials of Critical-Constructivist Grounded Theory Research*. APA.

Levitt, H. M., Motulsky, S. L., Wertz, F. J., Morrow, J. A., & Ponterotto, J. G. (2018). Journal article reporting standards for qualitative research (JARS–Qual). *American Psychologist, 73*(1), 26–46. https://doi.org/10.1037/amp0000151

Martínez, C., Gálvez, C., Quiroz, C., Vicencio, B., & Tomicic, A. (2014). He decidido vivir: Factores que disuaden a una persona de cometer suicidio [I have decided to live: Factors that deter a person to commit suicide]. *Revista Argentina de Clínica Psicológica, 23*(3), 267–280.

Martínez, C., & Tomicic, A. (2023). *"Salir del closet" no es lo mismo que sentirse orgulloso de ser quien se es: Proceso de psicoterapia y estigma sexual internalizado* [*"Salir del closet" no es lo mismo que sentirse orgulloso de ser quien se es: Proceso de psicoterapia y estigma sexual internalizado*]. En C. Martínez, A. Tomicic, A. Brandelli, & M. Ruedas (Editores/a), *Psicoterapia y salud mental en personas de la diversidad sexual y de género (LGBT+): Investigación y práctica en Iberoamérica [Psychotherapy and mental health in people of sexual and gender diversity (LGBT+): Research and practice in Latin America.].* RIL Editorial.

Martínez, C., Tomicic, A., Medina, L., & Krause, M. A (2014). Microanalytical look at mutual regulation in psychotherapeutic dialogue: Dialogic discourse analysis (DDA) in episodes of rupture of the alliance. *Journal of Research in Psychotherapy: Psychopathology, Process and Outcome (RIPPPO), 17*(2):73–92. https://doi.org/10.7411/RP.2014.021

Martínez, C., Tomicic, A., Rodríguez, J., Galvez, C. & Aguayo, F. (2025). *"El trauma nuestro de cada día": Construcción subjetiva sobre procesos suicidas de jóvenes trans* que viven en Chile ["Our everyday trauma": subjective construction of suicidal processes of trans* young people living in Chile]. Psykhe,* first online.

Maxwell, J. A. (2013). *Qualitative research design: An interactive approach* (3rd ed.). SAGE Publications.

McLeod, J. (2010). *Case study research in counselling and psychotherapy.* SAGE Publications.

McLeod, J. (2011). *Qualitative research in counselling and psychotherapy.* SAGE Publications Ltd.

McLeod, J., Stiles, W. B., & Levitt, H. M. (2021). Qualitative research: Contributions to psychotherapy practice, theory, and policy. In M. Barkham, W. Lutz, & L. G. Castonguay (Eds.), *Bergin and Garfield's handbook of psychotherapy and behavior change* (pp. 351–384). John Wiley & Sons.

Patton, M. (1999). Enhancing the quality and credibility of qualitative analysis. *Health Service Research, 34*(5, part II), 1189–1208.

Piña, C. (1998). *La construcción del "sí mismo" en el relato autobiográfico [The construction of the "self" in the autobiographical story]* (Working Document 383)]. Programa FLACSO-Chile.

Piña, C. (1999). *Tiempo y memoria: Sobre los artificios del relato autobiográfico* [Time and memory: On the artifices of the autobiographical story]. *Proposiciones, 29,* 1–5.

PRISMA Group. (2020). PRISMA 2020 statement: Updated guidelines for reporting systematic reviews. Available at: https://www.prisma-statement.org/

Strauss, A., & Corbin, J. (2002). *Bases de la investigación cualitativa: Técnicas y procedimientos para desarrollar la teoría fundamentada [Basis of qualitative research: Techniques and procedures for developing grounded theory]* (2nd ed.). CONTUS-Editorial Universidad de Antioquia.

Tomicic, A., Immel, N., & Martínez, C. (2021) Experiences of psychological and psychotherapeutic support for LGBT youth who have survived a suicide process. *Revista Interamericana De Psicología/Interamerican Journal of Psychology, 55*(1), e1453. https://doi.org/10.30849/ripijp.v55i1.1453

Tomicic, A., Martínez, C., Pérez, J. C., Hollenstein, T., Angulo, S., Gerstman, A., Barroux, I., & Krause, M. (2020) Discourse-voice regulatory strategies in the psychotherapeutic interaction: a state-space dynamics analysis. *Frontiers in Psychology, 6*:378, 1–17. https://doi.org/10.3389/fpsyg.2015.00378

Tomicic, A., Martínez, C., Rosenbaum, C., Aguayo, F., Leyton, F., Rodríguez, J., Galvez, C., & Lagazzi, I. (2020). Adolescence and suicide: Subjective construction of the suicidal process in young gay and lesbian chileans. *Journal of Homosexuality.* https://doi.org/10.1080/00918369.2020.1804253

Valenzuela, M. J. (2024). *Qué es esto, que me pasa: ¿soy yo o el trastorno bipolar?* [What is this, what's wrong with me: Is it me or bipolar disorder?] Master's Thesis. Available in the online repository of the University of Chile.

Chapter 15
Body Map for a Phenomenological Exploration of the Bodily Experience of Trans* People (TGNC)

María Isabel Gaete, Mariana Castillo-Hermosilla, Claudio Martínez, and Francisca Avilés

The traumatic effects of the stigmatization and discrimination suffered by TGNC people have been widely studied (Coleman et al., 2022; Meyer, 2003; Puckett et al., 2023; Testa et al., 2015), but not those related to the experience of *bodily discordance* that have marked their life trajectories and are embodied in their gender identities. We understand by *experience of bodily discordance* that lived moment in which the body that the person *has* (objective body) does not agree with the body that *is* (subjective body). Without being synonymous, the term bodily discordance is related to the concept of bodily dysphoria. This latter, in the context of gender identity, is a term that is used to describe a significant discomfort or uneasiness that a person experiences with their own body, especially concerning the discrepancy between the gender that a person feels internally and the physical characteristics associated with the sex assigned at birth (Bockting, 2014; Coleman et al., 2022). This experience of bodily discordance is part of everyday life, permeating it with moments that we could consider "micro-traumatic," in which the body itself is both the territory where trauma unfolds and the place where it is registered (Martínez et al., 2024/2025; Peterson et al., 2017). This sedimented traumatic embodied

The authors recognize the immense variety of sexual and gender identities that exist, but in this chapter, to refer to transgender or transsexual people, we will use the acronym TGNC, which refers to "trans and gender non-conforming" people, or just trans* with an asterisk, which underlines the openness of what the category may contain.

M. I. Gaete (✉)
Body Phenomenology Laboratory, Santiago, Chile

M. Castillo-Hermosilla
Osnabrück University, Osnabrück, Germany

C. Martínez · F. Avilés
Diego Portales University, Santiago, Chile

A. Tomicic, J. D. Soto (eds.), *Qualitative Research in Clinical Psychology and Psychotherapy in Latin America*, https://doi.org/10.1007/978-3-031-90782-1_15

register becomes the daily emotional-affective background, difficult to articulate with words, which hinders the affirmation of a core aspect of the felt identity in TGNC people and which is of great relevance for its effects on mental health and psychological well-being.

This chapter seeks to illustrate an original methodological proposal on the application of the Body Mapping (BM) technique in the trans* population, aimed at exploring the implicit and pre-reflective embodied cues of the experience of discordance between the felt body "the body that I am" and the object body "the body that I have".

First, we introduce the theoretical-methodological framework that supports it, then we present a review of the Body Mapping technique, and then we detail the complete process of data collection and analysis through two cases of trans masculine people extracted from the study: "*The dreamed body: research on the bodily experience of trans* and non-conforming gender people (TGNC)*" (Martínez, 2023). Finally, we analyze the potential use of this qualitative-phenomenological method of art-based research to account for the particularities of the bodily experience in a given group and, specifically, in the TGNC population, as well as its possible clinical and psychotherapeutic applications.

Giving Voice to the Lived Body: Theoretical and Methodological Foundations

Trying to give voice to the bodily register of the experience is a complex challenge that, during the last decades, has convened different disciplines such as psychology, philosophy, cognitive sciences, health sciences, neuroscience, and neurophenomenology, among others, grouped around what has been called "embodied approaches" to experience (e.g., Fuchs et al., 2018; Gallagher, 2006). On the other hand, giving voice to the complexity of the trans* bodily experience has been pointed out as a contribution to the process of individual transition (Langer, 2016) and to a better social understanding of this experience, both individual and collective.

The concept of bodily experience refers to the experience of sensory-motor processes that, through a dynamic flow of consciousness (between pre-reflective and reflective bodily consciousness), shape an organization of a sense of embodied self (Gaete & Fuchs, 2016). Understanding the experience from the lived body implies assuming that to access it, one must distinguish in its structure at least two levels: a *pre-reflective level* and a *reflective level*. This is what Fuchs (2012) calls the double structure, in which the flow of experience runs in a dynamic movement between the implicit emotional bodily register from moment to moment, corresponding to the pre-reflective level, and the explicit material available for the subject's narrative about their own experience, the reflective level. Thus, the experience of our body acts fundamentally in a pre-conscious or pre-reflective way; we continuously scan our body, obtaining an update of its somatic-emotional state moment by moment, and when we detect that "something happens" (a discomfort, pain, emotion, intense sensation, etc.), that pre-reflective consciousness moves to a reflective level, where the object of attention is our body.

The relevance of embodied experience in mental health is increasingly recognized (Drayson, 2009; Nielsen, 2020; Fuchs et al., 2018; Fuchs & Schlimme, 2009; Gaete & Fuchs, 2016), resulting in the search and development of new research methodologies oriented to the study of that which is bodily registered and cannot be accessed through words (Barone & Eisner, 2011; Gaete et al., 2023; Leavy, 2017; McNiff, 1998; Smrdu & Jereb, 2023; Valenzuela-Moguillansky & Demšar, 2023).

Associated with this embodied approach to the study of experience, what has been called "first-person research" emerges, a methodological proposal for a rigorous and systematic examination of the lived experience about a certain object of study (Varela & Shear, 1999; Varela et al., 2016). This approach considers that its object of study cannot exclude the subject owner of the experience, which enriches and validates the results.

Body Mapping: An Art-Based Research Tool

The technique of *Body Mapping (BM)* is a plastic-expressive tool, initially developed at the University of Cape Town for psychotherapeutic purposes for a group of South African women living with HIV/AIDS (Devine, 2008), adapted by Jane Solomon as an art therapy technique.

BM has been gaining space as a tool for *art-based research*, highlighting among its qualities the horizontality in the relationship with the participants, who are an active part of the data collection, thus making it possible to give voice to minority groups of the population through their artistic creations (Furman et al., 2019; Solomon, 2002; Gastaldo et al., 2012; Gitau et al., 2022; Skop, 2016).

Regarding the contexts of the use of BM, a review by Jager et al. (2016) points out that it has been used as a visual form of storytelling to advocate for people at a political level, to communicate and examine the embodied experience in physical spaces, also as a method focused on children and adolescents, and as a therapeutic and educational tool. On the other hand, the review by Murray et al. (2023) focuses on mental health studies that apply BM. They highlight that this technique allows exploring the *embodied experience* of self-perceived stressors, or self-identified coping strategies, and that it has shown potential to explore emotions and experiences difficult to access otherwise. They also highlight its usefulness in exploring the strengths and resilience of the participants, especially in the child and adolescent population.

For the aims of this proposal, we have found inspiration in this technique to involve participants creatively in complex topics regarding their verbal articulation, such as pain, anger, or frustration, or experiences of trauma, creating this way stories that become collective experiences that potentially represent the experience of a group or community (Gitau et al., 2022; Maina et al., 2014; Murray et al., 2023; Senior et al., 2014; Skop, 2016; Sweet and Escalante, 2015). We also highlight its usefulness in directing attention to the body to promote awareness and reflection on the bodily experience, visually capturing the bodily dimensions of gender diversity, and helping to examine thoughts and emotions by drawing the physical outline of the body (Gastaldo et al., 2012; Lys et al., 2018; Solomon, 2002).

While most available studies have used BM from a *representational approach* to experience, that is, as a "representation" of the body, or of its life stories, recently BM has begun to be applied from a phenomenological approach, allowing us to take advantage of the eminently non-verbal and expressive quality of this technique. In this line, the study by Tarr and Thomas (2011) stands out, framed in an embodied and phenomenological approach to the experience of pain and a study developed in Chile with women recovered from fibromyalgia, which combines BM with a qualitative-narrative interview and a micro-phenomenological interview to account for the recovery process of symptoms (Valenzuela-Moguillansky et al., 2021). Inspired by this last study, Smrdu and Jereb (2023) in Slovenia, also with women with fibromyalgia, mainly focused on the BM technique in combination with the micro-phenomenological interview as a tool for evoking experience and a method of image analysis that presents some similarities with the proposal in this chapter.

Next, we detail the main concepts and tools that ensure a respectful stance of the phenomenological framework that underpins this proposal:

1. ***Enactive Quality of Artistic Creation*** (Gaete, 2022). The author's body is part of his artwork corresponding to the *enactive quality* of the creative process. We understand BM as a tool to access the embodied experience not only because it involves an attentional focus toward the body but also because of the inherent qualities of every type of artistic creation in which the body is actively involved through the sensory-motor processes that participate in it. As we will see, the latter plays an important role in our proposal in terms of observation and analysis of the procedural-enactive aspects of the creative process.
2. ***Emotional Bodily Experience*** (Gaete & Fuchs, 2016). It is the relationship that we as living organisms have with our environment in terms of being affected or moved in a sense both affectively and emotionally. It is a dynamic and multidimensional experience in which we move between an *implicit* or *pre-reflective level* (the body acts as the background music in terms of an affective background tone) and an *explicit or reflective level* (some novel or relevant stimulus, internal or external, causes the body to become the object of attention). This flow of emotional bodily experience is what gives us a sense of embodied identity.
3. ***Bodily Resonance*** (Fuchs, 2013a, 2013b). Defined as the capacity of our organism to resonate in our interaction with the environment. Every lived experience requires a body that *resonates* with the stimuli that surround it, since from this bodily resonance it is possible to construct a narrative of the experience and deploy an adaptive and consistent course of action. The face, the gut, and the chest are relevant areas of great richness in emotional bodily resonance. This includes both the autonomic nervous system and the endocrine and

musculoskeletal systems, which inform us that *something is happening* emotionally and affectively. This concept, taken to the aesthetic realm, is conceptualized as ***aesthetic bodily resonance*** which, according to Vittorio Gallese, arises in the aesthetic experience as a multisensory affective-emotional state in which vision, touch, and movement participate (Falvo, 2018; Gallese, 2017a, 2017b; Gallese et al., 2022). Thus, to resonate with an artistic work is to resonate with another; we resonate with an object loaded with intentional content on the part of its author.

4. ***Phenomenological Reduction*** (Butler, 2016; Morley, 2010; Quail & Peavy, 1994; Wertz, 2023). Method of exploration of experience based on the premise that our primary experience is hidden behind assumptions and beliefs that make up our *natural attitude* (Husserl, 2006). We assume that promoting the creative and spontaneous gesture as *an expressive form of experience* is at the same time a way of promoting a form of *phenomenological reduction,* in which immersion in the creative-expressive process is a way of postponing reflections or judgments about what is spontaneously deployed through impulses and sensorimotor patterns. Therefore, figurative expression is avoided as much as possible, closer to a symbolic or verbal representation, and the spontaneous creative gesture is stimulated. We consider that plastic-expressive creation, as is the case with BM, constitutes a form of *phenomenological reduction applied to the very conditions in which research data are produced*, which, together with data analysis, would constitute a form of *double phenomenological reduction* of the research process (Gaete, 2022; Gaete et al., 2023).
5. ***Atmosphere*** (Fuchs, 2013a, 2013b). An emergent phenomenon of the intersubjective encounter, defined by the emotional and affective peculiarities of the shared experiential space that form a dynamic gestalt unit, is possible to be identified through bodily and intercorporeal resonance.

Application and Analysis Protocols of Body Mapping

To illustrate our application and analysis protocol of BM of the bodily experience of trans* people, we will describe two cases from our research project: "*The dreamed body: research on the bodily experience of trans* and gender non-conforming (TGNC) people*"[1] (Martínez, 2023). It is in the context of this study, aimed at exploring the reflective and pre-reflective dimensions of the experience of discordance between the felt body and the object body in trans* people, that the procedures and methodologies presented here arise.

[1]The use of this material has been authorized by the Scientific Ethics Committee of the Diego Portales University, and the participants have consented to its use for academic and research purposes.

Participants

The first participant, M3, is a 19-year-old trans male, with university studies, who resides in the city of Santiago in the Metropolitan Region of Chile and who, at the time of his participation in the study, had been on hormone treatment for 12 months. The second participant, M4, is a 21-year-old trans male, also with university studies and living in the city of Santiago in the Metropolitan Region of Chile. At the time of his participation in the study, he had been on hormone treatment for 18 months, and, in addition, as part of his gender affirmation, he had undergone surgery to perform a bilateral mastectomy. Both participants declare to use male pronouns.

Application Protocol

The application of this πrotocol requires a space with enough amplitude for the person to be able to lie down on the floor to outline their figure on the paper, good lighting conditions, noise isolation, and privacy are also required. The art supplies that are made available should be varied enough to stimulate the subject's creativity and provide different options of textures, colors, and materiality. Once established, they must remain stable during the research to offer the same conditions to all participants. The researcher will remain silent, attentive, and available as a facilitator of the process, taking notes of it on the registration template (Fig. 15.3).

The application of the four-step protocol we propose (see Fig. 15.1) is framed in the context of the aforementioned study and the proposal published by the authors (Gaete et al., 2023; Martínez, 2023) and first involves the *evocation of a moment of bodily discordance* through the conduction of the micro-phenomenological interview (Petitmengin, 2017). This first step can be approached with different techniques to bring to the present an embodied experience that one wishes to explore,

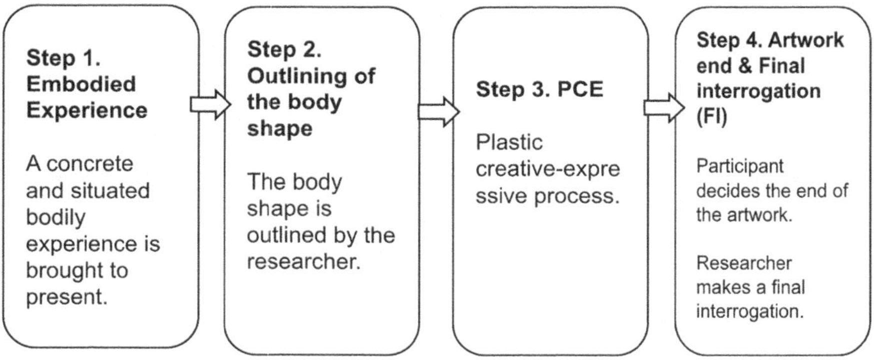

Fig. 15.1 Four-step protocol for the application of Body Mapping. PCE: Plastic creative-expressive process. Taken from Gaete et al. (2023)

for example, the technique of *imagery* (Pearson et al., 2015), *the felt sense* (Gendlin, 1969), or contemplative practices such as the *body scan* (Gan et al., 2022).

After this first step, the evoked experience is expressed non-verbally through BM (Steps 2 and 3, Fig. 15.1). At the end, a brief inquiry is made that collects the description that the author makes of his work (Step 4, Fig. 15.1). The approximate total duration of this process is two hours.

Step 1. Micro-phenomenological Interview (Estimated Duration Between 30 and 50 Minutes)

The evocation is a state of consciousness that the interviewer promotes and observes through concrete signals, both bodily and in the form of verbal expression, which indicate whether the participant is vividly evoking or only narratively or rationally explaining what is desired to evoke. The interviewer makes an initial effort together with the interviewee to delimit a specific and concrete moment of a given experience. In this case, the subject is guided to *choose and evoke a moment of bodily discordance,* ensuring that their level of discomfort is not greater than seven on a scale of one to ten. Once the specific moment to work on is delimited and agreed upon, the process of evoking the experience that will be subsequently expressed through the Body Mapping method is deployed.

Participant M3 chooses the moment to explore a situation in which he sees himself without the binder[2] he uses to cover his chest:

> [...] last Monday, that...as if...I didn't like the image I gave in the mirror eh...and I was getting ready to go to university, so I took a long time to know what to put on to not feel so bad and I ended up wearing the sweatshirt all day.

On the other hand, M4 chooses the discomfort with his genitals when he takes off his clothes for the first time in front of his partner in the context of a sexual encounter:

> I was with my partner, we had already had sexual relations so to speak, and I had never taken off my boxer shorts. And I had never taken off my shirt either. [...] when I took them off [the boxer] I wanted to cover myself discreetly. So, on that occasion she didn't pressure me much, she wasn't invasive, but after that, I was able to relax. But during the whole moment I was very nervous, I'm feeling more comfortable as more time passes, but I still felt [...].

---

[2] Binder is a compression garment designed specifically to flatten the chest area made with elastic materials that distribute pressure evenly, preventing injuries. It requires precautions such as limiting the time of use and avoiding inappropriate sizes that generate respiratory, skin, or musculoskeletal problems.

Steps 2 and 3. Outlining of the Body Shape and Unfolding of the *Plastic Creative-Expressive* Process (PCE) (Approximate Duration of 30 Minutes)

After the interview, the participant is invited to lie down on a sheet of paper that has been previously stretched out on the floor and is asked *to find the position that best expresses the moment just evoked*, giving time to reconnect with that moment. Once he finds that position, the researcher outlines his contour on the paper. Once his figure is outlined, he is asked to stand up and observe his contour. He is shown all the available art supplies (i.e., pastel and graphite-colored pencils, colored papers, solid tempera, scissors, glue, markers, etc.) and is invited to express all the sensations of discordance present at that moment.

Instruction: *"Now you can get up and I invite you to observe the figure of your body on the paper and go expressing the colors and shapes that account for the sensations of your body at that moment. There are no rules, you can use the materials you want with total freedom. The only important thing is that IT IS YOUR SPONTANEOUS EXPRESSION of what your body feels at that moment you remembered just now. It is not necessary to think about it too much either, just let yourself be carried away by what your body guides you to express on paper"... "I will be here at your disposal; you can ask me anything and ask for help if you need it for your creative process."*

The researcher can give suggestions during the process, especially at the beginning, such as *insisting that it is not about an artwork that requires knowledge or artistic skills*, but it is expected to be genuine and authentic regarding their lived experience. The process is considered finished when the participant says so.

Step 4. Final Interrogation (FI) (Approximate Duration 15 Minutes)

When the participant finishes their work, the researcher initiates a final interrogation about the expressive creative process (ECP) and the resulting final image, using the following instruction

Instruction: "*Now I would like you to tell me how you made your body map. Tell me how the different images that you were creating emerged, how your creation process was.*"

Here the researcher maintains a role of attentive listening instead of intervening. In case the participant was not aware of the order of appearance of the images, the researcher can intervene and help in reconstructing the process and formulating clarifying questions about it, avoiding stimulating a reflective position regarding the process. If the participant does not explicitly refer to the body posture, then they are asked to comment on how they chose that posture and what it expresses.

To finish, they are invited to observe their work and describe what they see and everything that appears new or that catches their attention from this other perspective:

Instruction: *"Now, before finishing, I invite you to look at your work from 'outside'. Take some distance, observe, and tell me how you see it now. What does the image express to you, what does the image tell you seeing it from the outside? Take your time and tell me if new things arise that you want to comment on when looking at it this way"*

Analysis Protocol and Preliminary Results

Body Mapping Analysis

Figure 15.2 shows the two sources of information to analyze: *process and result information*. From these two analysis instruments were developed: the *TEMA registration form* (process information) and the *Beholders Observation Guideline for external judges and strangers to the process* (result information) *(Gaete et al.,* 2023*)*. The participant's description of their own process and their narrative of the resulting image or result in the *final interrogation* (Step 4. IF in Fig. 15.2) is also obtained. This last information is analyzed through a thematic analysis, which, since its report exceeds the scope of this chapter, will be the subject of further publications.

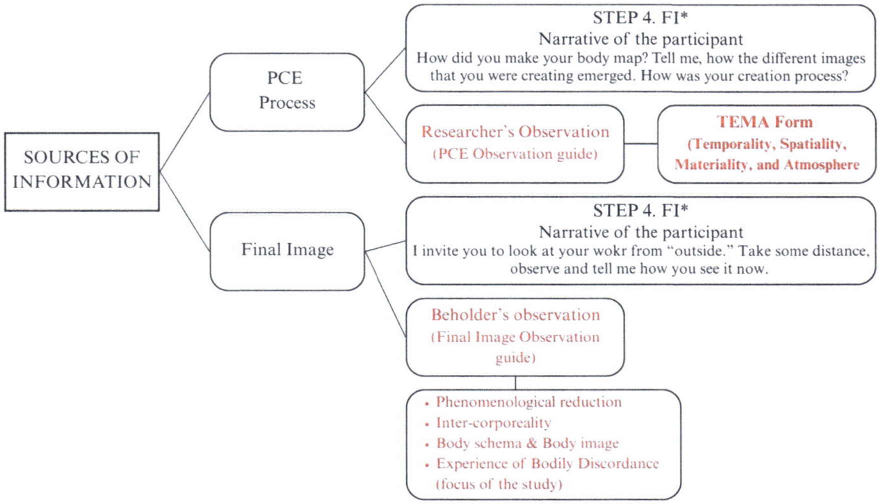

Fig. 15.2 Sources of information for the analysis of Body Mapping (Gaete et al., 2023). *FI= Final Interrogation, step 4 of the 4 steps application protocol

Next, using the example of cases M3 and M4, we present our protocol for analyzing the information obtained from the application of BM.

First, we detail the analyses carried out about the observation of the expressive-creative process and define how we conceptualized and operationalized this process in the TEMA registration form (Fig. 15.2).

Second, we present the analyses carried out about the result or resulting image. We define how we conceptualized and operationalized the role of the spectator of an artistic work and present our *observation guideline of the resulting image* by external judges as a tool for this analysis.

(1) Expressive-Creative Process (ECP) This dynamic process fluctuates between immersion in creative work (the pre-reflective aspect of experience) and taking perspective or distance, which occurs when making decisions such as changing material, changing color, or ending work (a first-order reflective aspect of experience). The movement toward reflection through perspective-taking during the process is different from a "representation or explanation" about it; although there is a certain distance, there is a closeness with the direct experience, which we understand as first-order reflection or *perspective observational or contemplative* (Gaete, 2022). During the ECP, which mainly takes place in silence with the creator immersed in their creative deployment, the researcher applies a registration template to collect relevant procedural details (see Fig. 15.3), which are then organized into categories

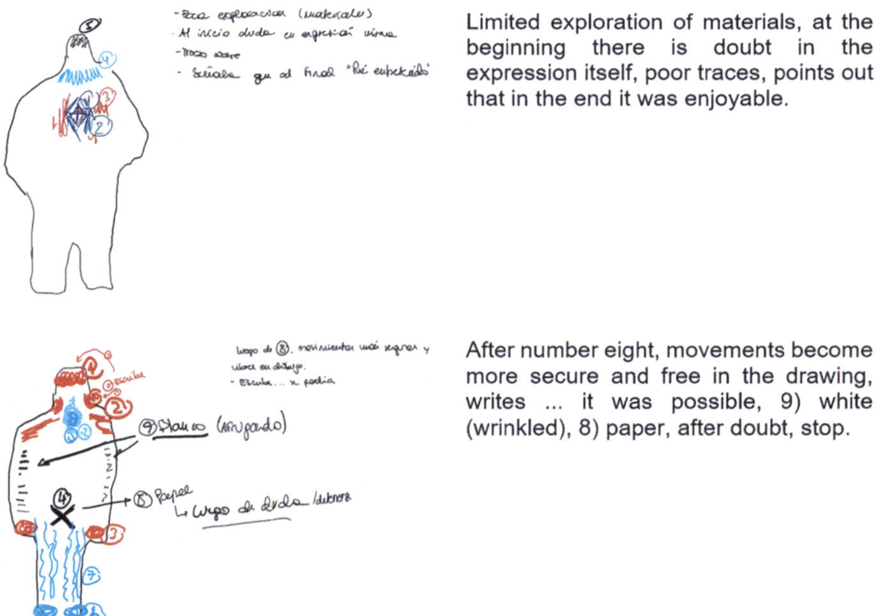

Fig. 15.3 Registration template of the expressive-creative process of Body Mapping, M3 and M4

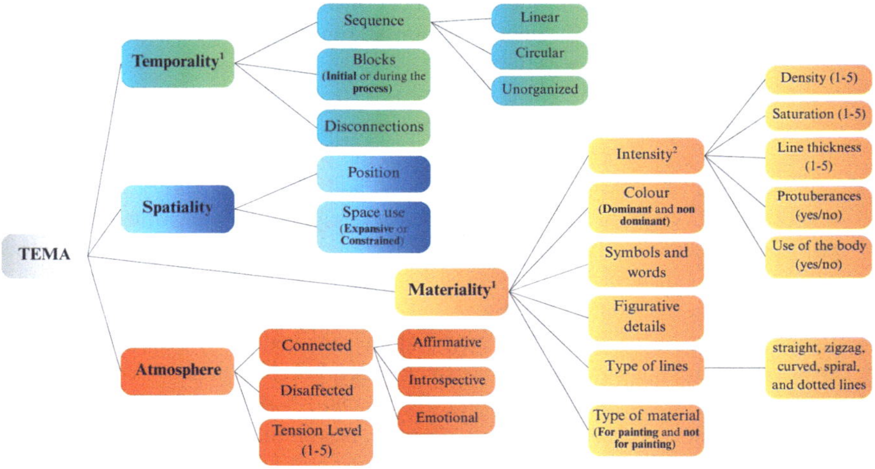

Fig. 15.4 TEMA Form with the categories and subcategories that comprise each of the dimensions. 1. Both temporality and materiality are registered by each of the zones of the human figure (head, neck, shoulders, etc.). 2. Global score of Intensity is calculated here by the Saturation and Line Thickness mean scores only. Note that Density, Saturation, Line Thickness and Level of Tension are scored from 1–5 (1 minimum and 5 maximum). The use of protuberances, use of the body, use of symbols, and use of figurative details are registered 'Yes or No' if they are present or not in each zone of the human figure

in the TEMA registration form developed for this purpose (Fig. 15.4) (Gaete et al., 2023).

TEMA Registration Form

From the field information recorded by the researcher (see Fig. 14.3), two researchers from our team with experience in plastic arts and art therapy developed a *second-order registration form,* which was peer-reviewed by a group of three external art therapists. They evaluated the form in terms of its relevance and pertinence, being able to confirm a large part of its categories and dimensions, as well as modify, add, and delete others. This TEMA form addresses four dimensions of analysis: ***Temporality*****,** ***Spatiality*****,** ***Materiality*****, and** ***Atmosphere***, whose Spanish acronym gives the name to this registration form (see Fig. 14.4).

- **Temporality:** Rhythms in which the creative process develops, accounting for the fluidity and sequence in which the elements of the BM appear.

- **Spatiality:** Use of space on the paper sheet during the creative process: expansive or restricted, inside or outside the human figure, body position in which the participant lies on the paper sheet.
- **Materiality:** The way the work materialized. It includes six categories that are recorded for each area of the body from the head to the feet, both inside the human figure and outside of it: ***Intensity***[3] in the way of using the material (color saturation and line thickness, density, relief, and use of the body), ***Color*** of the material used, ***Type of lines*** (straight, wavy, zigzag, spirals, dotted) ***Type of material*** (*painting material*: graphite pencils, markers, tempera, papers, or other materials and *material that is not paint*: cardboards, masking tape, papers, etc.). It also records the ***Use of Symbols or Words*** and if it adds ***Figurative Details*** (facial features, clothing, organs, etc.; that are not used for symbolic purposes).
- **Atmosphere** refers to the intersubjective/intercorporeal aspect of the PCE that is perceived by the researcher through the *emotional bodily resonance and empathy*. That is, the expressive, gestural, postural, respiratory, and sensory-motor set deployed during the creative process transmits an atmosphere that goes beyond what is being created in his plastic work.

To illustrate this way of organizing information, we present the BM of participants M3 and M4 along with the final story about their work and their respective TEMA forms (those categories that were not observed are not presented) "Figs. 15.5, 15.6, 15.7, and 15.8".

The ECP results obtained from M3 and M4 show differences that seem relevant to point out. Firstly, regarding the ***temporality***, M3 shows a creative linear sequence with an initial blockage and another in the head area, understanding by blockage the difficulty to enter or continue with the ECP, that is, he wants to continue but does not know how; he stays blank. The total duration of his creative process was 11 minutes. M4 shows a creative circular sequence with a disconnection in his genital area, understanding by "disconnection" when we observe that the person gets distracted or leaves the ECP, bringing attention to externalities, interrupting his work (i.e., talking with the researcher about unrelated topics). The total duration of his creative process was 18 minutes. Regarding ***spatiality,*** although both choose a frontal position and work within the human figure, M3 had a *restricted use of space*, focusing on the area of the head, neck, hands, and chest; and M4 used the space in an *expansive way* leaving only the torso area (abdomen and chest) unworked. The ***materiality*** shows in M3 a low intensity of creative work. That is, although he showed a moderate color saturation level (he energetically shaded), he only used one type of material throughout his work (colored graphite pencils) with the main colors being red (the most predominant of all), black, and light blue. M4 shows a

[3] Both ***saturation*** in the use of colors and ***thickness of lines*** are used here for getting a ***global score of intensity*** in the way of using materials while they are more robust indicators of it. *Density* (use of more than one art supply or color in a zone of the human figure) is also scored but kept apart for the moment because further analyses are required, as it seems to depend more on other aspects such as previous artistic knowledge or experience.

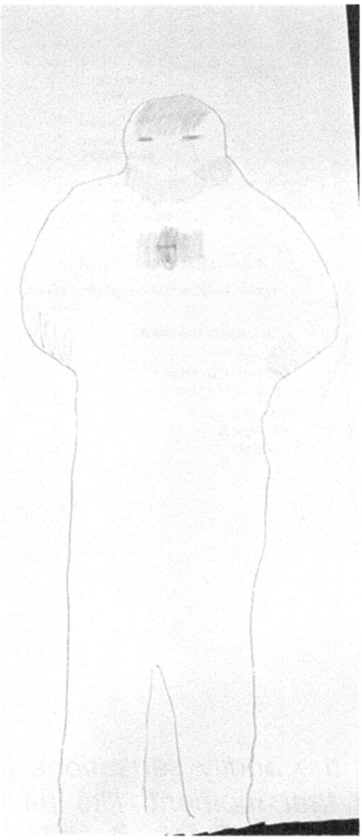

"...I mean, this is like the mental image I have of my anxiety... although anxiety is like the sensation of anxiety, I think of it as an, I mean...I get the idea of a little purple thing, like ...so it's like the representation of how eh...of the constant anxiety that I feel in the chest...eh...this was because besides the anxiety I was with anger...this red part...and this is, as if, because of the sorrow that provoked me to think as, remembering the little support I have from my family...what is in the neck represents the family...eh...the red in the eyes because it makes me angry like that...it made me angry to see myself in the mirror and the black from above is because there were many things at once, like everything mixed".

Fig. 15.5 Body Mapping participant M3 and story about his work

work of high intensity with protuberances on the arms, that is, he used more than one material in various parts of the body, and the level of color saturation was mostly "very saturated" predominating first the colors red and light blue, and second black and white. Regarding the ***atmosphere,*** the researcher refers that in the case of M3 a ***connected introspective*** atmosphere of *insecurity, doubt, and rage* was perceived with *very high tension*, and in M4, a ***connected emotional non-aggressive*** atmosphere of *pain and of a high level of tension.*

According to the TEMA registration guideline, we understand by **connected atmosphere** *when we observe the subject emotionally and affectively connected, involved, and immersed in his creative process. The work may have pauses, but these are active: he observes, meditates, explores the materials, makes decisions, and resumes the work in a creative continuum despite the pauses. There may also be no pauses, and the work is continuous and fluid as if it were driven by a very consistent internal script. He is observed in a continuous internal dialogue oriented to the creative process. It is further subdivided into five subcategories:* ***affirmative,***

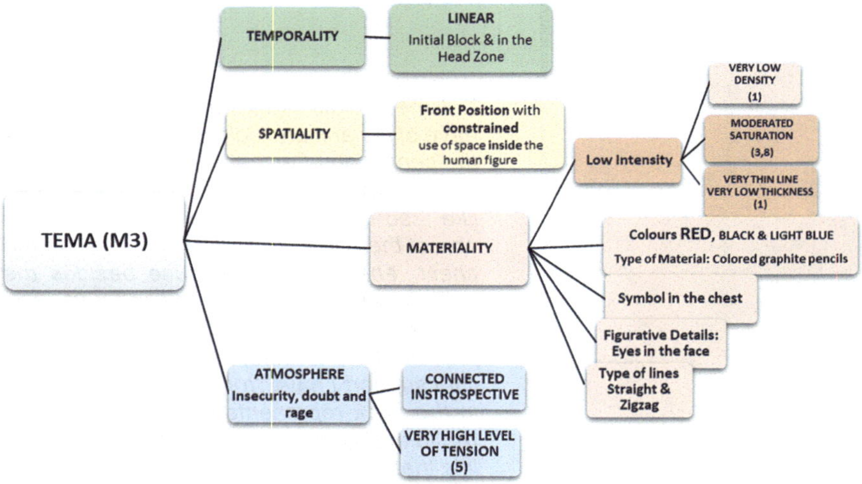

Fig. 15.6 Expressive creative process (ECP) TEMA, M3

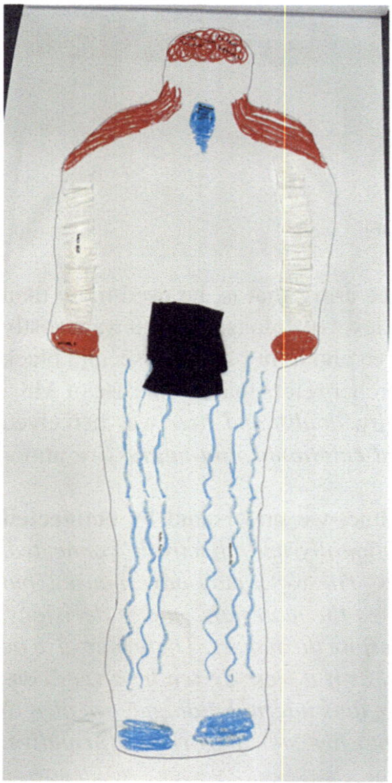

"It's all the bodily sensations I had at that moment: like this end upwards I felt a lot of tension, like a heat, but not that rich heat, but that tense heat."
"It's about the trunk upwards, because in my head were only thoughts and it was all very scrambled and I also had heat, but from here downwards it was as if I was asleep, I was tense, but in another way, like I felt like when a foot goes numb, like tense but very tense with shivering."

Fig. 15.7 Body map of participant M4 and the story about his work

introspective, and emotional (non-aggressive, aggressive, constrained) (see Table 15.1).

In our example cases, the ***introspective connected atmosphere*** of M3 corresponds to a silent work, fluid but with active, reflective pauses of internal dialogue. Interacts little with the researcher. Concentrated and driven by his internal motivations and emotions that unfold fluidly in the choice of materials and expressive forms. The emotional tone is moderate; emotions are perceived, but at a medium intensity level. The atmosphere is fluid, light despite the concentration that shows in his work. The ***non-aggressive emotionally connected atmosphere*** of M4 is of high emotional intensity (of any type that is not identifiable as aggressive), expressed in gestures and in the intensity of strokes and movements. Work rhythms are identified that accompany the expressed contents as well as the choice of materials, which configures a work consistent with well-defined and observable emotional qualities for the researcher. A clear and intense emotional tone (different from anger) is identified throughout the PCE, both in the gestures of the subject himself, his body posture, breathing rhythm, and movements, as well as in the contents that he is unfolding in his creative work.

(2) Resulting Image Considering that the encounter with any type of work of art is an intersubjective and intercorporeal encounter between the observer and the author of the work (e.g., Falvo, 2018; Gallese, 2011, 2017a, 2017b), we wanted to give "voice" to the impact that images have by themselves on the observer.

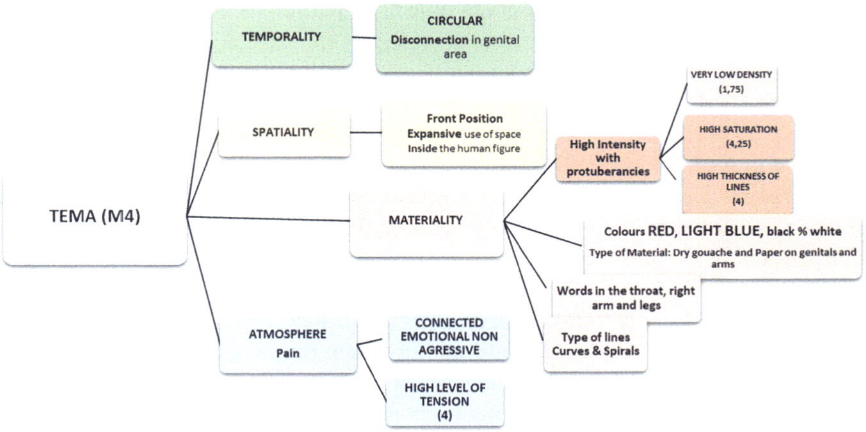

Fig. 15.8 Expressive creative process (ECP) TEMA, M4

Table 15.1 Categories comprising the atmosphere dimension of the TEMA registration form

	Connected Atmosphere				
Disaffected Atmosphere	Affirmative	Introspective	Emotionally expressive	Emotional aggressive	Emotionally constrained
Emotionally or affectively disconnected, distant, or indifferent.	Security and fluidity in the stroke express an affirmative certainty of the contents that are being expressed. The gestures and strokes are defined and quick, without doubt.	Works in silence, in a fluid manner, but with active, reflective pauses of internal dialogue.	A clear and intense emotional tone (different from rage) is expressed both in gestures, body posture, breathing rhythm, and movements, as in the contents that unfold in the creative work.	Use materials that break with hands, crush, or hit hard. Use of paint that drips or spreads over the sheet prioritizes aggressive emotional expressions over the care or neatness of the work.	Very intense emotional tone, but as 'drowned'. The process unfolds more slowly even if this is a subjective perception. There is a certain density in the atmosphere that feels charged with feelings.

Resulting Image Observation Guide

This guide was developed **from** the concept of *embodied simulation* (Gallese, 2011, 2017a), in which the different sensory-motor systems of an observer are functionally involved at the moment of observing what is relevant to account for the intersubjective dimension of the bodily experience to explore. We consider the observer as a creator at the same time as the observer. Therefore, he is not a passive encoder, but in the interaction with the observed object, he participates in what he is observing through his sensory-motor systems.

A group of four researchers from our team, who did not participate in the application of the BM, completed this guide aimed at exploring the aesthetic bodily resonance experience that the observation of the MC produced in them. This guide is organized in four levels of information:

Perceptual Level corresponds to a phenomenological reduction in which the observer is guided to obtain a purely sensory description of the image: *Describe what you see in the most detailed way possible as if you were telling someone who is not seeing the image. Take care to stay at a descriptive level and not interpretative. Describe colors, textures, volume, type of strokes, etc.* This aims to lead the observer to "suspend" the natural attitude in which our observations are confused with our representations, judgments, or explanations about what is observed. Therefore, it is considered a "perceptual accommodation exercise" and is not part of the material to be analyzed, but of the way to obtain the information we are looking for.

Intercorporeal Level you are invited to describe how the image resonates both physically and emotionally: *Describe and express what resonates bodily and*

emotionally in you when observing the image. What emotions does this image awaken in me? Do you identify any impulse of movement or action in your body when observing the image? Do bodily sensations appear when observing the image? Do you feel that the image touches or affects you in some way?

Body Schema and Image Level You are asked to describe the position of the person on the sheet of paper *What bodily emotional sensations does that position express for you? Observe the areas of asymmetry: with more or less plastic work in the image, greater or lesser intensity in the saturation of color, use of space, etc.: What do these asymmetries in the intensity of the plastic work convey to you in terms of movement, rigidity, tensions, distensions, etc.? How do you think* ***the person feels, sees, and thinks*** *about his body?*

Level of Bodily Experience Corresponds to the focus of the study. In this case, you are invited to account for how and in what aspects of the final image they perceive that the experience of bodily discordance is present. *They are also asked to describe in one sentence or in one word what the bodily experience of this person.*

The results of the intercorporeal body schema and image and bodily experience levels to be studied are presented below.

M3 and M4 Observers Pattern Results[4]

M3: "Snowman with Ornament on the Chest" (O2)

- **Intercorporeality.** The observers agree that this image awakens in their ***feelings*** of coldness, oppression, isolation (in the image's author), threat, attack, fright (toward the observer), or defense (in the image's author to some threat). The ***sensations*** they refer to coincide with devitalization, snow, cold, numbness, tight chest, and heaviness. This image awakens contradictory movement impulses; two of our observers are moved to approach (to comfort or socialize), and another is moved to run away, feeling it as someone who lurks with resentment. The observers refer that this image touches or arrives as someone with whom it is difficult to connect, self-absorbed, and exhausting.
- **Body Schema and Image.** The observers agree in referring to a ***body schema*** characterized by rigidity and immobility with contradictory impulses of mobility vs. stillness, apparent relaxation vs. inner tension, firmness or distrust vs. the need to be cared for: upper half of the body active with the presence of movement-still and lower half inactive, absent, upper half as a barrier, tense posture. ***Body image*** is diffuse, negative, and with anger. The lower half of the body does not see it, does not feel it, nor thinks about it.
- **Bodily Discordance.** The observers refer that the discordance is perceived in the experience of not inhabiting the body, rejecting it, and disgust toward it: "*The*

[4] We identify each of our four observers numerically: O1, O2, O3 and O4.

discordance for me is represented in the little involvement with the drawing. As if the body were not a place for in-depth exploration" (O3). *"The lack of dedication in making the strokes shows me neglect"* (O4). Discordance is also observed in the contradiction between the upper and lower half of the body and in the disconnection both with his own body and with the external environment, which is described as a "*disintegrated presence*" (O1) or "*difficulty integrating the experience*" (O4).

M4: "In Flames and Frozen" (O3)

- **Intercorporeality.** This image awakens the observer's **feelings** of tension and concentrated anger in the shoulders, head, and hands. Physical and emotional pain. The **sensations** they refer to coincide with great muscular tension in shoulders and fists, in contrast with weak or devitalized arms and legs. They also refer to a sensation of a lump in the throat and sensations in the genital area of discomfort, pain, blockage, or weight. Contradictory sensations of heat, energy (upper half), and cold, immobility (limbs). It moves the observer to squeeze, close, and hit with the fists; to move with energy; to touch his shoulders and bring him to the present (the image's author); curiosity to touch the image.
- **Body Schema and Image.** They refer to observing a ***body schema*** characterized by rigidity, paralysis, and tension, with asymmetry or contradiction in the bodily experience of the upper half (strong) compared to the lower half (weak not available): "It *makes me think about the lack of grounding*" (O3), the impulse to hit with the fists and crushed genitals. Throat is not available. It is observed that he feels his ***body image*** with anger, shame, and fear of rejection; it overwhelms and paralyzes him. Genital area annulled, he feels it with modesty, an attentional effort to reject it, and tension. Paradox: "*Omnipresent genital absence*" (O1).
- **Bodily Discordance.** The bodily discordance resonates in the observers as contradictory experiences between the upper and lower half of the body and in the contradiction of wanting to "cover" the genitals and the omnipresence it acquires in the image with a black square. It also resonates as a contradiction between an intense negative emotion that is contained and not expressed corporally (rage and contained tension), which results in rigidity and paralysis.

Conclusions

The use of a non-verbal research tool based on art seems promising for studies aimed at exploring embodied experiences and revealing aspects that are psychologically dissociated due to their traumatic content or a high level of emotional intensity. The plastic expression of a lived experience allows access to the underlying content that is, at least, complementary, if not different from the narrative we construct about the same experience.

The protocol we propose allows us to account for the ECP in terms of its procedural and content details, which represents a novelty in what has been reported so far regarding the application of the BM. The richness of its results is part of the possibilities of both clinical and scientific use of this technique.

We also highlight the impact that the resulting image has on "naive" observers of the creation process. In this sense, the phenomenological reduction that we promote to access observation allows a *perceptual adjustment* in favor of obtaining information free of prejudices or interpretations. It is surprising in this sense the ***consistency between observers and between the observers and the account of the participants of their own work***, both regarding their experience of discordance, their EPC, and the resulting image itself. On the other hand, the use of well-detailed prompts has been rigorous work to obtain a true *phenomenological method* in the application of this technique that is possible to be replicated in other studies.

TGNC people tend to dissociate the primary experience with their body (especially the one lived during their early childhood) from the narrative about it. Thus, the trans* child develops throughout his life a narrative that distances him from the original meaning that the experience had for him. Therefore, in adulthood, by not being able to access this original sense or meaning, the person suffers or presents symptoms that usually "distract" even more from the original embodied experience, becoming more complex in a narrative increasingly dissociated. That's why words are not enough or do not serve to heal that traumatic history. In this way, an embodied contact with the experience, using non-verbal tools like the BM, would facilitate the exchange with the history of those bodies through creativity and the pre-reflective dimension of the experience.

In this chapter, we wanted to share the experience of creating a research context and original methodologies to apply the BM tool to access that embodied record that has remained silenced for the same subjects throughout their history.

So far, such tools have allowed us—as we illustrate with participants M3 and M4—to access the experience of living and socially coexisting with bodies that are felt at times as objects to hide, dissociate, or suffer. They have allowed us to imagine and understand the daily experience of those micro-moments of discordance/dislocation, which leave painful embodied traces.

Finally, this tool, presented here as a qualitative methodological technique, could also be combined with traditional psychotherapeutic interventions to restore the dynamic flow between the reflective and pre-reflective experience, which is usually experienced as dislocated (contracted or marked by contradictions and asymmetries) in TGNC people.

Acknowledgment This chapter was written with the support of the National Agency for Research and Development (ANID) through the FONDECYT project n° 1230262

References

Barone, T., & Eisner, E. W. (2011). *Arts based research*. Sage.

Bockting, W. (2014). Transgender identity development. In D. Tolman, L. Diamond, J. Bauermeister, W. George, J. Pfaus, & M. Ward (Eds.), *APA handbook of sexuality and psychology* (pp. 739–758). American Psychological Association.

Butler, J. L. (2016). Rediscovering Husserl: Perspectives on the epoché and the reductions. *The Qualitative Report, 21*(11), 2033.

Coleman, E., Radix, A. E., Bouman, W. P., Brown, G. R., de Vries, A., Deutsch, M. B., Ettner, R., Fraser, L., Goodman, M., Green, J., Hancock, A. B., Johnson, T. W., Karasic, D. H., Knudson, G. A., Leibowitz, S. F., Meyer-Bahlburg, H. F. L., Monstrey, S. J., Motmans, J., Nahata, L., Nieder, T. O., et al. (2022). Standards of care for the health of transgender and gender diverse people, Version 8. *International Journal of Transgender Health, 6*(23, Suppl 1), S1–S259. https://doi.org/10.1080/26895269.2022.2100644

Devine, C. (2008). The moon, the stars, and a scar: body mapping stories of women living with HIV/AIDS. *Border Crossings, 27*(1), 58–65.

Drayson, Z. (2009). Embodied cognitive science and its implications for psychopathology. *Philosophy, Psychiatry, & Psychology, 16*(4), 329–340.

Falvo, P. G. (2018). Conversation with Vittorio Gallese about empathy and aesthetic experience. *Studies in Digital Heritage, 2*(1), XXX–XLVII.

Fuchs, T. (2012). The phenomenology of body memory. In S. F. Koch, Thomas, M. Summa, & C. Müller (Eds.), *Body memory, metaphor and movement* (Vol. 84, pp. 9–22). John Benjamins Publishing Co..

Fuchs, T. (2013a). Depression, intercorporeality, and interaffectivity. *Journal of Consciousness studies, 20*(7-8), 219–238.

Fuchs, T. (2013b). The phenomenology of affectivity. In K. W. M. Fulford, M. Davies, R. Gipps, G. Graham, J. Sadler, G. Stanghellini, & T. Thornton (Eds.), *The Oxford handbook of philosophy and psychiatry* (pp. 612–631). Oxford University.

Fuchs, T., Sattel, H., & Henningsen, P. (2018). *The embodied self: Dimensions, coherence and disorders*. Klett-Cotta.

Fuchs, T., & Schlimme, J. E. (2009). Embodiment and psychopathology: A phenomenological perspective. *Current Opinion in Psychiatry, 22*(6), 570–575.

Furman, E., Singh, A. K., Wilson, C., D'Alessandro, F., & Miller, Z. (2019). "A space where people get it": A methodological reflection of arts-informed community-based participatory research with nonbinary youth. *International Journal of Qualitative Methods, 18*, 1–12. https://doi.org/10.1177/1609406919858530

Gaete, M. I. (2022). Creative-expressive artwork as a phenomenological exploration of experience. *GMS Journal of Arts Therapies, 4*, 1–15.

Gaete, M. I., Castillo-Hermosilla, M., Martínez, C., Concha, F., Paiva-Mack, I., & Tomicic, A. (2023). Protocol of application and phenomenological exploration of body mapping in transgender population: An art-based research method. *International Journal of Qualitative Methods, 22*. https://doi.org/10.1177/16094069221150108

Gaete, M. I., & Fuchs, T. (2016). From body image to emotional bodily experience in eating disorders. *Journal of Phenomenological Psychology, 47*(1), 17–40.

Gallagher, S. (2006). *How the body shapes the mind*. Clarendon Press.

Gallese, V. (2011). Embodied simulation theory: Imagination and narrative. *Neuropsychoanalysis, 13*(2), 196–200.

Gallese, V. (2017a). The empathic body in experimental aesthetics–embodied simulation and art. In V. Lux & S. Weigel (Eds.), *Empathy: Epistemic problems and cultural-historical perspectives of a cross-disciplinary concept* (pp. 181–199). Palgrave Macmillan.

Gallese, V. (2017b). Visions of the body. Embodied simulation and aesthetic experience. *Aisthesis. Pratiche, linguaggi e saperi dell'estetico, 10*(1), 41–50.

Gallese, V., Freedberg, D., & Umiltà, M. A. (2022). Embodiment and the aesthetic experience of images. In A. Chatterjee, & E. Cardilo (Eds.), Brain, Beauty, and Art (pp. 88–92).

Gan, R., Zhang, L., & Chen, S. (2022). The effects of body scan meditation: A systematic review and meta-analysis. *Applied Psychology: Health and Well-Being, 14*(3), 1062–1080.

Gastaldo, D., Magalhaes, L., Carrasco, C., & Davy, C. (2012). Body-map storytelling as research: Methodological considerations for telling the stories of undocumented workers through body mapping. http://www.migrationhealth.ca/sites/default/files/Body-map_storytelling_as_reseach_HQ.pdf

Gendlin, E. T. (1969). Focusing. *Psychotherapy: Theory, Research & Practice, 6*(1), 4.

Gitau, L., Kenning, G., Burgess, S., Bennett, J., Kuchelmeister, V., Neidorf, M., & Ginnivan, N. (2022). Pre-Engagement as method: An EmbodiMapTM VR experience to explore lived experience of people from south Sudanese refugee background. *International Journal of Qualitative Methods, 21*, 1–12. https://doi.org/10.1177/16094069221123167

Husserl, E. (2006). The natural attitude and the "Natural Concept of the World". The Basic Problems of Phenomenology: From the Lectures, Winter Semester, 1910–1911 From the German "Aus den Vorlesungen, Grundprobleme der Phänomenologie, Wintersemester 1910/1911" in Zur Phänomenologie der Intersubjektivität, Husserliana XIII, edited by Iso Kern, 1–28.

Jager, A., Tewson, A., Ludlow, B., & Boydell, K. (2016). Embodied ways of storying the self: A systematic review of body-mapping. *Forum Qualitative Social Research, 17*(2). https://doi.org/10.17169/fqs-17.2.2526

Langer, S. J. (2016). Transbodies and the failure of mirrors. *Studies on Gender and Sexuality, 17*(4), 306–316. https://doi.org/10.1080/15240657.2016.1236553

Leavy, P. (2017). *Handbook of arts-based research*. Guilford Publications.

Lys, C., Gesink, D., Strike, C., & Larkin, J. (2018). Body mapping as a youth sexual health intervention and data collection tool. *Qualitative Health Research, 28*(7), 1185–1198. https://doi.org/10.1177/1049732317750862

Maina, G., Sutankayo, L., Chorney, R., & Caine, V. (2014). Living with and teaching about HIV: Engaging nursing students through body mapping. *Nurse Education Today, 34*(4), 643–647. https://doi.org/10.1016/j.nedt.2013.05.004

Martínez, C. (2023). *FONDECYT: "El cuerpo soñado: investigación sobre la experiencia corporal de las personas trans* y de género no conforme (TGNC)"*. ANID.

Martínez, C., Tomicic, A., Rodríguez, J., Gálvez, C., Leyton, F., Aguayo, F., & Rosenbaum, C. (2024/2025). *Our daily trauma: Subjective construction of suicide experiences of young trans people*.

McNiff, S. (1998). *Art-based research*. Jessica Kingsley Publishers.

Meyer, I. (2003). Prejudice, social stress and mental health in lesbian, gay and bisexual population: Conceptual issues and research evidence. *Psychological Bulletin, 129*(5), 674–697. https://doi.org/10.1037/0033-2909.129.5.674

Morley, J. (2010). It's always about the epoché. *Les Collectifs du Cirp, 1*(1), 223–232.

Murray, A., Steffen, M., Keiller, E., Turri, M. G., & Lau, J. Y. F. (2023). Body mapping for arts-based inquiry in mental health research: A scoping review. *Lancet Psychiatry, 10*, 896–908. https://doi.org/10.1016/S2215-0366(23)00224-9

Nielsen, K. (2020). *What is mental disorder? Developing an embodied, embedded, and enactive psychopathology*. Open Access Te Herenga Waka-Victoria University of Wellington.

Pearson, J., Naselaris, T., Holmes, E. A., & Kosslyn, S. M. (2015). Mental imagery: Functional mechanisms and clinical applications. *Trends Cogn Sci, 19*(10), 590–602. https://doi.org/10.1016/j.tics.2015.08.003

Peterson, C., Matthews, A., Copps-Smith, E., & Conard, L. A. (2017). Suicidality, self-harm, and body dissatisfaction in transgender adolescents and emerging adults with gender dysphoria. *Suicide and Life-Threatening Behavior, 47*(4), 475–482. https://doi.org/10.1111/sltb.12289

Petitmengin, C. (2017). *Uncovering the dynamics of lived experience through micro-phenomenology*. Seminar of the Cognition Institute, University of Plymouth.

Puckett, J. A., Dyar, C., Maroney, M. R., Mustanski, B., & Newcomb, M. E. (2023). Daily experiences of minority stress and mental health in transgender and gender-diverse individuals. *Journal of Psychopathology and Clinical Science, 132*(3), 340–350. https://doi.org/10.1037/abn0000814

Quail, J. M., & Peavy, R. V. (1994). A phenomenologic research study of a client's experience in art therapy. *The Arts in Psychotherapy*.

Senior, K., Helmer, J., Chenhall, R., & Burbank, V. (2014). 'Young clean and safe?' Young people's perceptions of risk from sexually transmitted infections in regional, rural and remote Australia. *Culture, Health & Sexuality: An International Journal for Research, Intervention and Care, 16*(4), 453–466. https://doi.org/10.1080/13691058.2014.888096

Skop, M. (2016). The art of body mapping: A methodological guide for social work researchers. *Aotearoa New Zealand Social Work, 28*(4), 29–43. https://doi.org/10.11157/anzswj-vol28iss4id295

Smrdu, M., & Jereb, L. (2023). Body-mapping the experience of Fibromyalgia syndrome. In *The Routledge international handbook of innovative qualitative psychological research* (pp. 173–188). Routledge.

Solomon, J. (2002). *"Living with X": A body mapping journey in time of HIV and AIDS*. Facilitator's Guide. REPSSI.

Sweet, E. L., & Escalante, S. O. (2015). Bringing bodies into planning: Visceral methods, fear and gender violence. *Urban Studies, 52*(10), 1826–1845. https://doi.org/10.1177/0042098014541157

Tarr, J., & Thomas, H. (2011). Mapping embodiment: Methodologies for representing pain and injury. *Qualitative Research, 11*(2), 141–157. https://doi.org/10.1177/1468794110394067

Testa, R. J., Habarth, J., Peta, J., Balsam, J., & Bockting, W. O. (2015). Development of the gender minority stress and resilience measure. *Psychology of Sexual Orientation and Gender Diversity, 2*, 65–77. https://doi.org/10.1037/sgd0000081

Valenzuela-Moguillansky, C., & Demšar, E. (2023). Toward a science of experience: Outlining some challenges and future directions. *Adaptive Behavior, 31*(5), 449–466.

Valenzuela-Moguillansky, C., Díaz, D., Vásquez-Rosati, A., & Duarte, J. (2021). Inhabiting one's body or being haunted by it: a first-person study of the recovery process of women with fibromyalgia. *GMS Journal of Art Therapies, 3*, 1–18. https://doi.org/10.3205/jat000013

Varela, F. J., & Shear, J. (1999). First-person methodologies: What, why, how. *Journal of Consciousness Studies, 6*(2-3), 1–14.

Varela, F. J., Thompson, E., & Rosch, E. (2016). *The embodied mind: Cognitive science and human experience*. MIT Press.

Wertz, F. J. (2023). The relevance of the phenomenological method of epoché and reduction for psychology. *Journal of Phenomenological Psychology, 54*(1), 37–75.

Chapter 16
Mixed Research Models for the Evaluation of Clinical Change in Psychotherapy

Andrés Roussos

This paper is derived from a talk in 2023 at the CEPPS, Center for Studies in Clinical Psychology and Psychotherapy, with the Latin American Chapter of the Society for Psychotherapy Research and the doctoral program in Psychology at the Diego Portales University.

Using mixed models concerning the study of processes and outcomes in psychotherapy is a methodological strategy that combines quantitative and qualitative methods consistently and with a holistic vision.

Throughout psychotherapy research, there have been and still are researchers and methodologies who consider qualitative and quantitative methodologies as mutually exclusive. They argue that both methods respond to opposing epistemological positions and that, ultimately, they address different objects of study, so their integration results in methodological and conceptual error. However, many researchers and methodologists have proposed alternative visions, seeking to articulate both methods coherently and respectfully, integrating their epistemological and methodological principles to enrich knowledge in the field, in this case, psychotherapy.

Carrying out research following the premises of both models is not easy, as it is not simply a matter of superimposing work methodologies and data collection or analysis techniques from both positions but also articulating them coherently without either overwhelming or distorting the vision of the other. This is the challenge that anyone who intends to use mixed research models must face: not only understanding the form of methodological integration but also the fundamental limits of integration and understanding of the information that is made from the confluence of these two methods.

A. Roussos (✉)
Universidad de Belgrano, Ipehcs/CONICET, Buenos Aires, Argentina
e-mail: andres.roussos@comunidad.ub.edu.ar

A. Tomicic, J. D. Soto (eds.), *Qualitative Research in Clinical Psychology and Psychotherapy in Latin America*, https://doi.org/10.1007/978-3-031-90782-1_16

Integration Strategies in Mixed Research Models

There are different strategies for the integration of qualitative and quantitative methods. In this chapter, we will examine five possible types of integration for mixed models, which are as follows:

i. Mixed exploratory designs: which orient their work from qualitative to quantitative,
ii. Post-explanatory designs: which orient their work from quantitative to qualitative,
iii. Triangulation designs: which seek a constant interaction between qualitative and quantitative,
iv. Nested designs: in which a research device contains a differentiated section with differentiated methodologies and, finally,
v. Hybrid designs are borderline designs, both for their instrumentation and for their data analysis modality.

To exemplify how each of these types of integration of qualitative and quantitative methodologies operates, research in psychotherapy will be presented that allows us to understand how these types of studies with mixed designs are carried out and detail how their methods operate.

By combining these two approaches to research, mixed models provide a more comprehensive view when studying psychotherapeutic processes and changes in psychotherapy. This is particularly valuable because it generates the possibility to include dimensions such as the socio-historical context and the subjective and lived experience, among others, and to make them interact with descriptive and explanatory orders, enhancing both approaches.

The Territory and the Methods: The Dispute? In Psychotherapy Research

Research in psychotherapy has faced a historical tension between qualitative and quantitative methodological approaches. This is due to the complex and rich nature of its object of study, which not only invites but also obliges one to observe and evaluate this object through different questions and, therefore, with other methodologies. Hence, different epistemological positions, often presented as irreconcilable, strive to occupy and retain spaces of action, like someone trying to win territory for themselves, preventing another from approaching and arguing why this is impossible and/or desirable.

Some actors in this dispute have come to distribute areas of study, like someone dividing territories. For example, quantitative approaches have focused on the so-called "objective" measurement and appropriating the notion of explanation. They argue that only their predetermined procedures can definitively establish the "cause" of phenomena and the generalization of results. On the other hand, qualitative approaches have emphasized the in-depth understanding of patients' subjective experiences in their treatments, claiming the power to address the human and to be a flexible methodology that transcends reductionist notions. Although the arguments from both sides regarding these positions are serious and based on fascinating debates, it is not the purpose of this chapter to discuss them but to point out that none of the arguments so far allow for the division of knowledge and the non-integration of both visions. This false dichotomy has led many researchers to view these two approaches as mutually exclusive, when in fact, they can complement and enrich each other.

The premise of this chapter is apparent on this point: psychotherapy is a single territory in which both methodological approaches for research can and should interact to generate more and better knowledge. As McBeath et al. (2023) point out, combining qualitative and quantitative methods offers a depth and breadth of data that cannot be achieved with a single approach, thus promoting a greater understanding of complex phenomena such as change in psychotherapy.

In this integration stance, there is nothing new; numerous studies have highlighted the need to complement quantitative research with qualitative approaches and vice versa. In this way, the aim is to deepen the subjective experience of the work of patients and psychotherapists and their relationship with change in psychotherapy, with nomothetic notions that enable the generalization of criteria and results, the generalization of theories, and the demonstration of their postulates and practices. That is the demonstration of the truth of their theories (or not) and the effectiveness of their practice (or not).

From this perspective, qualitative research allows researchers to capture the richness of patients' experiences, which contributes to improving the quality of psychotherapeutic care. For example, Winkler et al. (1993) emphasize the importance of addressing relevant aspects of treatments from the patient's perspective, which provides information about the patient's experience and enriches studies on the effectiveness of therapeutic interventions. Exploring how patients perceive and value their therapists' interventions is crucial for adjusting and improving clinical practices.

The use of mixed models in psychotherapy research represents a response to this need for complementarity. By integrating qualitative and quantitative methods, mixed designs allow researchers to capture objective data and understand the subjective experiences underlying those data. This methodological approach does not simply imply the superposition of collection or analysis techniques but requires a coherent articulation of both perspectives, which presents a significant challenge for researchers.

However, despite the potential of using mixed methods in psychotherapy, there are still clear obstacles, such as, for example, the lack of adequate training in qualitative and quantitative methodologies. This is the case for many researchers in psychology, who either do not see one of the two approaches to research or study them in a dissociated way, which limits their coherent and synergistic implementation. Another obstacle is the unequal access to funds for research with mixed designs, as even today, as Bartholomew and Lockard (2018) point out, qualitative components are perceived as secondary or "tokenized", that is, as an accessory element to simulate a proper mixture of procedures. This contributes to some readers underestimating the value of the full integration of qualitative and quantitative data, finding mixed models as trivial and/or overloaded, depending on the reader's stance.

Implementing mixed methods in evaluating clinical change in psychotherapy must be carried out systematically and strategically, respecting the fundamental principles of both qualitative and quantitative approaches. This integration should not be treated as a simple juxtaposition of methods but as a carefully designed process where each technique is applied in its logical times and according to its epistemological structures of support and meaning.

In addition, the evolution of psychotherapy in a global context, where social and cultural realities are constantly changing, requires researchers to maintain a critical and reflective stance on the concepts they handle and the methodologies associated with their studies. Integrating mixed approaches enriches the research process and contributes to the formation of a more holistic knowledge about change in psychotherapy. By simultaneously considering qualitative and quantitative dimensions, mixed models offer a platform to explore and understand the complexity of the psychotherapeutic experience, which allows clinicians to adapt their approaches to the specific needs of their patients.

In this sense, research in psychotherapy cannot be considered as a mere accumulation of data but as a dynamic process that involves multiple perspectives and approaches, which enables the construction of theories that allow the interpretation of data, a process that in turn results in more prosperous and more comprehensive theories (Stiles, 2014). Hence, mixed models represent a way to achieve this complexity and richness in the study of clinical phenomena, facilitating the exploration of how different variables interact in psychotherapy. Thus, a path is opened for researchers and clinicians to collaborate in the search for more effective and meaningful practices for the processes of change and well-being of patients while advancing the theoretical understanding of psychotherapy.

Rennie and Frommer (2015) point out the need for a coherent integration that respects the specific purpose of each methodological technique to capture both the complexity of clinical phenomena and participants' subjective experiences. This implies that the researcher must consider the appropriate temporal sequence and the descriptive, interpretative, explanatory, or predictive depth of each approach. The value of mixed methods lies in leveraging the strengths of both techniques, maintaining their integrity and meaning while minimizing their weaknesses through their interaction, that is, making one complete the other.

Multiple texts enable the learning of mixed research models, as well as specialized journals in this type of design, being a perfect example of the "Journal of Mixed Methods Research".

As mentioned before, in this chapter, I will focus on presenting different integration strategies between qualitative and quantitative methods for clinical change in psychotherapy. Table 16.1 shows five main typologies of mixed designs: mixed

Table 16.1 Typology of mixed designs

Types of mixed designs	Texts to exemplify
Mixed exploratory designs: oriented from the qualitative to the quantitative, it allows the generation of hypotheses from patients' subjective experiences.	– A classification scheme for interventions in Cognitive and Psychoanalytic psychotherapy. Roussos, Etchebarne, Waizmann (2006) – The cadence in the presentation of interpretations in a patient–therapist dyad. Roussos (2008)
Post-explanatory mixed designs: originates in results of quantitative studies and uses qualitative approaches to explore their implications, providing a deeper interpretation context.	– A time-series analysis of therapeutic alliance, interventions, and client's clinical status in an evidence-based single-case study: Evidence for establishing change mechanisms in psychotherapy. Roussos et al. (2018) – Therapeutic interventions from the patient's perspective: a qualitative approach. Olivera, (2017)
Triangulation designs: simultaneously combines qualitative and quantitative methods, allowing continuous feedback between both types of data.	– The importance of the theoretical framework in the formulation of clinical inferences in psychotherapy. Roussos et al. (2007)
Nested designs: one methodological approach is subordinate to another, using qualitative data to complement a broader quantitative analysis.	– The Meaningful Assessment of Therapy Outcomes: Incorporating a Qualitative Study Into a Randomized Controlled Trial Evaluating the Treatment of Adolescent Depression. Midgley et al. (2014)
Hybrid designs: These are border research designs, both in their conceptualization, their instrumentation, and their data analysis modality.	– Identifying core categories of client-identified impact of helpful events in psychotherapy: A qualitative meta-analysis. Timulak (2007)

exploratory designs, post-explanatory mixed designs, triangulation designs, nested designs and hybrid designs.

Each of these types of research not only illustrates how qualitative and quantitative approaches can be integrated, but it is also possible to highlight the importance of methodological creativity in psychotherapy research. As the discipline faces new challenges, such as incorporating emerging technologies and analyzing large volumes of data (big data), the flexibility and adaptability of mixed designs become even more crucial. This allows researchers to answer complex questions that require a profound understanding of both objective data and patients' subjective experiences.

Mixed Designs in Psychotherapy Research

Next, the five types of mixed designs mentioned above are examined, illustrating how each design can be applicable in psychotherapy research through different studies.

1. Exploratory Mixed Design

The exploratory mixed design organizes the integration of methods in temporal terms. It begins with a qualitative approach that seeks to generate hypotheses or comprehensive categories inductively from data collection. These hypotheses and categories will then be validated through quantitative analysis. This type of mixed design is ideal when there is not enough previous theory or an initial detailed exploration is required.

Representative Example The study by Roussos et al. (2006) on cognitive and psychoanalytic psychotherapy interventions stands out as a clear example of an exploratory mixed design. In this study, a qualitative analysis was carried out from transcripts of therapeutic sessions. The researchers identified patterns and categories in the therapists' interventions, which allowed a more in-depth understanding of how different techniques were applied in therapy.

The qualitative collection and analysis approach allowed the researchers to discover significant aspects that may not have been considered in purely quantitative studies. For example, identifying categories such as "directive interventions" versus "receptive interventions" offered a new perspective on how therapists interact with their patients. Subsequently, the qualitative findings were validated through quantitative analysis. These analyses showed that the categories were consistent in terms of their potential for grouping and differentiation; that is, the interventions were consistent in their category and different from the other categories generated through quantitative models, which allowed for verifying the robustness of the identified categories and their applicability to a broader group (see Fig. 16.1).

Reasoning This design of the study by Roussos et al. (2006) is an example of an exploratory mixed design because it begins with a deep immersion in a qualitative analysis through the examination of material from clinical sessions and then expands its findings through a quantitative study that allows establishing patterns of sequences of interaction between patient and therapist. Integrating the subjective with the objective allowed us to achieve greater validity and generalization and, in turn, generated a basis for developing theories on the use of therapeutic interventions.

This approach is especially relevant in psychotherapy, where understanding the patient's subjective experience can guide clinical practice and contribute to developing new intervention strategies. By using a mixed exploratory design, researchers can uncover dimensions of the therapeutic process that would not be evident through research designs with quantitative methods alone.

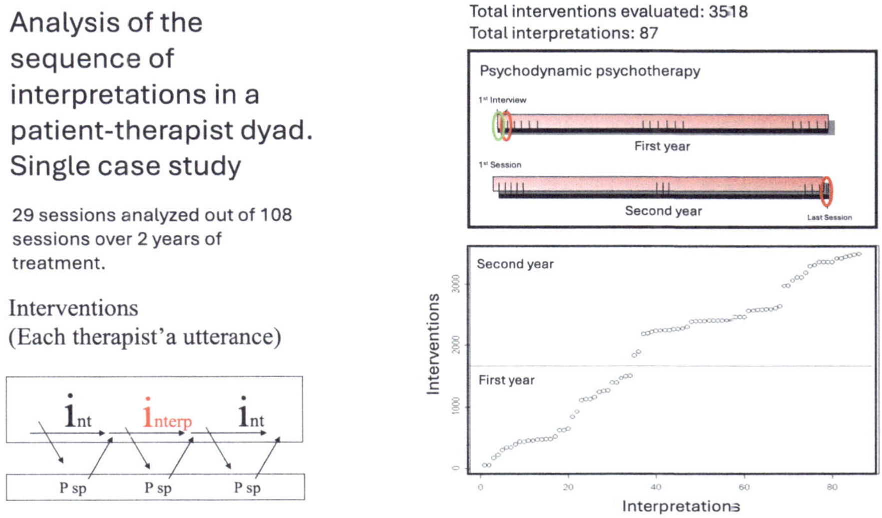

Fig. 16.1 Validation process of qualitative categories in the exploratory design

2. *Post-explanatory Mixed Design*

The post-explanatory mixed design also organizes the integration of methods in temporal terms, although in reverse order to the previous one. It focuses on collecting quantitative data that provide preliminary results, followed by qualitative analyses to explore the implications of those results in greater depth. This type of mixed design is proper when quantitative data require a more detailed contextual understanding to make sense of the findings.

Representative Example Olivera et al. (2013, 2017) conducted a study combining quantitative results on therapeutic interventions with qualitative interviews with patients (see Fig. 16.2). In this research, quantitative data was initially collected to identify the most common interventions performed by therapists, thus establishing a context for subsequent analysis.

From these findings, qualitative interviews allowed patients to express how they perceived and evaluated these interventions. This dual approach allowed the researchers to gain more insight into the relationship between the therapeutic intervention and the patient's subjective experience. For example, although a specific intervention had been identified as frequent at the quantitative level, the interviews revealed significant variations in how patients experienced and valued it, depending on their contexts and expectations.

Reasoning This study exemplifies the post-explanatory mixed design because it starts from a solid quantitative analysis that identifies frequent interventions but then adds a qualitative reading that enriches the interpretation of the data. This inter-

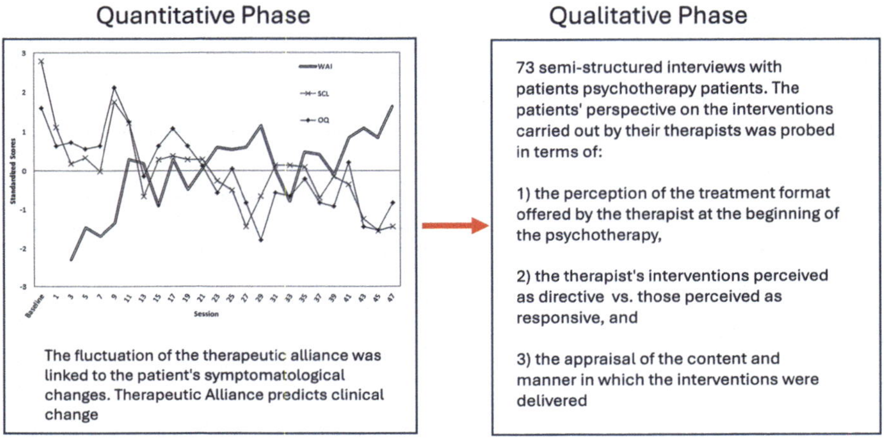

Fig. 16.2 Integration scheme of qualitative interviews after quantitative results

action between approaches provides a complete understanding of the patient's experiences, highlighting how interventions can be received differently depending on contextual and subjective factors.

The post-explanatory mixed design is particularly valuable in psychotherapy research, where the patient's experience is fundamental to the success of the treatment. By combining quantitative and qualitative methodologies, researchers can develop a narrative that measures and describes objective observations and explores the depth and meaning of therapeutic experiences.

3. *Triangulation Mixed Design*

Triangulation mixed designs, unlike the other two (mixed exploratory design and post-explanatory mixed design), instead of integrating linearly and sequentially, simultaneously combine qualitative and quantitative methods, allowing constant feedback between both types of data. This approach is fundamental for a more complete and rich understanding of the clinical phenomenon. While quantitative data can offer objective, measurable, and generalizable information about the phenomenon studied, qualitative data provide a level of depth and context that allows interpreting those figures within the experiential framework of the patients.

By integrating both methods simultaneously, the possible limitations of each approach separately are reduced. For example, a quantitative study could identify trends in patient improvement. Still, without the qualitative component, it would be difficult to understand why certain interventions work better than others in specific contexts. Conversely, a purely qualitative approach can capture subjective nuances of the therapeutic process but lacks the statistical rigor to validate these findings in larger populations.

Representative Example The study by Roussos et al. (2007) on clinical inferences is a clear example of a mixed triangulation design (see Fig. 16.3). This study collected qualitative and quantitative data simultaneously to evaluate clinical interventions. The quantitative data provided information on the effectiveness of the interventions, while the qualitative data offered insights into how therapists arrived at their conclusions and how patients perceived these interventions.

Reasoning The mixed triangulation design is characteristic because there is no primary or secondary approach; both qualitative and quantitative methods are interrelated and continuously feed back into each other. This interaction allows researchers to gain a more prosperous and in-depth understanding of the clinical phenomenon as multiple perspectives are considered. Roussos, et al. (2007).

Triangulation in this context offers a robust way to evaluate therapeutic interventions, as it combines the external validity of quantitative data with the depth and richness of qualitative information. This design is handy for research in psychotherapy, where subjective and contextual factors are critical to understanding the intervention's dynamics and the change process. Along with the above, it offers more excellent data collection and analysis flexibility, allowing the study to be adjusted in real time as new findings emerge. This simultaneous integration and triangulation of qualitative and quantitative data improves the observations' validity and facilitates their practical application in complex clinical settings.

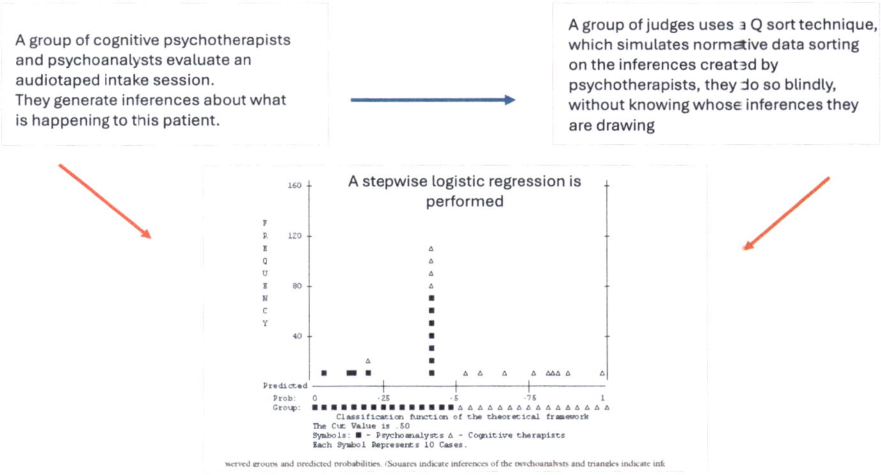

Fig. 16.3 Diagram illustrating the interrelation between qualitative and quantitative data in triangulation

Thus, by integrating both methods, mixed triangulation designs allow researchers to address the complexity of psychotherapy and the patient experience in a way that is impossible through single methods. Thus, this methodology encourages a dialogue between quantitative and qualitative data, leading to a more complete interpretation of the results related to the study of psychotherapy.

4. Nested Mixed Design

Nested mixed designs, as their name suggests, integrate qualitative and quantitative methods in a hierarchical relationship and, thus, imply that one methodological approach is subordinate to another to provide additional context or detail. In this type of design, the qualitative data usually complements a broader quantitative analysis.

Representative Example The study by Midgley et al. (2014) on adolescent depression is a clear example of a nested design. In this randomized controlled trial, qualitative data on patient experiences were embedded within the quantitative analysis. This approach enabled the researchers to enrich the interpretative context of the clinical results derived from the quantitative data (see Fig. 16.4).

Reasoning This research design exemplifies nesting because the qualitative data do not alter the quantitative study but complement it by offering additional context that enriches the interpretation. This approach is crucial in psychotherapy research, where patients' experiences can significantly influence treatment outcomes and therefore explain unexpected results from Randomized Clinical Trials.

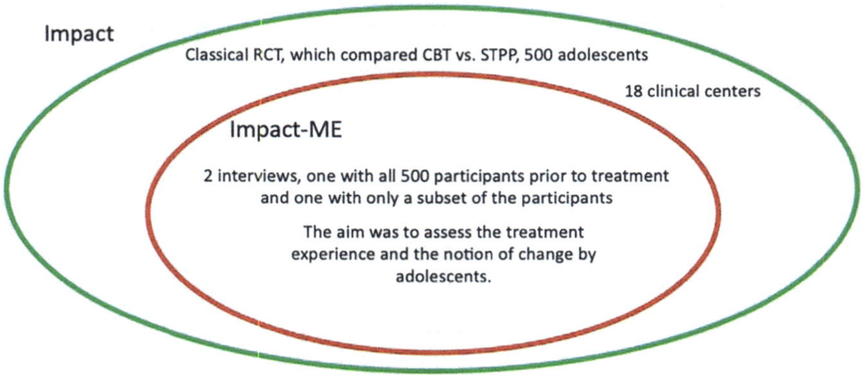

Fig. 16.4 Comparison of nested qualitative data in the main quantitative trial, showing how both approaches are integrated

The nested mixed design allows researchers to obtain a more complete view of therapeutic processes by considering measurable outcomes and individual narratives. This type of integration is vital, for example, for understanding the factors contributing to interventions' success or failure.

5. *Hybrid Mixed Designs*

Hybrid mixed designs in research are situated on a frontier in terms of conceptualization, instrumentation, and data analysis modalities. These designs combine qualitative and quantitative aspects in a deeply integrated way, allowing the researcher to exploit the methodological advantages of both approaches without the limitations of rigidly following the traditional rules of each one. A clear example of this methodological hybridization is qualitative meta-analyses, where the findings of qualitative studies are synthesized using techniques that allow quantifying certain aspects or recurring themes while maintaining an interpretative perspective. This type of design enables the creation of new knowledge through complex synthesis, making it an ideal approach for studies seeking to explore complex phenomena such as clinical change in psychotherapy.

Representative Example Marren et al. (2022) present an example of a hybrid design in their work on a qualitative meta-analysis on patients' experiences in emotion-focused therapies. In this study, one can observe an example of a hybrid design in research, where approaches that at times act qualitatively and quantitatively are integrated simultaneously to address a complex phenomenon, such as the experience of clients in emotion-focused therapy (EFT). The study starts from the analysis of 11 different works, all qualitative, examining the clients' experiences through interviews and other forms of narrative data collection; the methodology goes beyond the traditional boundaries of the qualitative approach. By conducting a qualitative meta-analysis of existing studies, the researchers employ data synthesis techniques that allow quantifying recurring themes, such as the frequency with which clients report helpful or challenging aspects of therapy. This hybrid approach allows for identifying quantifiable patterns within the diversity of subjective experiences, achieving a deep integration between the qualitative and the quantitative without losing the interpretative richness of individual experiences.

In addition, the study reflects methodological hybridism in how the results are interpreted and presented. Identifying common elements (such as intense emotional work in EFT) perceived as valuable or difficult by clients and quantifying how many studies or clients report these experiences show how the primary quantitative analysis is applied to summarize the qualitative findings comprehensibly. This hybrid approach allows a more complete understanding of complex phenomena by maintaining an interpretative perspective but quantifying certain aspects of the study. This is the case of the dynamics of clinical change in psychotherapy, which would be difficult to compare using exclusively a qualitative approach or a quantitative approach, losing the different forms of interpretation.

Reasoning This approach is characterized by its ability to synthesize the results of multiple qualitative studies, offering a deep integration of the data through systematic procedures that identify frequent patterns and central themes. Inspired by quantitative meta-analyses, this method takes the rigorous structure and systematic approach of quantitative meta-analyses but adapts it to treat qualitative data. Unlike traditional meta-analyses, which focus on numerical data, this method combines interpretative qualitative tools with a structure that allows quantifying certain key aspects. The value of this border modality lies in its methodological flexibility, where qualitative approaches are not only exploratory but also analytical, providing a detailed and rigorous understanding of the phenomenon of clinical change in psychotherapy, maintaining the integrity of both approaches without diluting their essence.

Discussion

The examples presented only show some of how mixed designs can be implemented in psychotherapy research. However, researchers should be aware that these typologies are not fixed formulas, and creativity is key to developing new forms of methodological integration.

For many years, the international scientific community has emphasized the importance of integrating diverse research approaches in psychotherapy, yet this remains a pressing issue today. Recently, Levitt et al. (2024) revisited this long-standing concern through a collaborative effort that brought together experts from various parts of the world representing multiple traditions and methodologies in research. They provided recommendations for incorporating qualitative methods into the development of clinical guidelines. Their conclusions highlighted that while mixed methods have been widely promoted for clinical and psychotherapy research, qualitative research still faces significant biases and challenges, particularly in obtaining government or academic funding. Nonetheless, as underscored in this chapter, researchers advocate for integrating mixed methods, emphasizing that combining qualitative and quantitative approaches can yield a more comprehensive understanding of therapeutic processes.

In addition, given the current context of rapid evolution and emerging challenges—such as integrating *big data* and *small data*, or incorporating artificial intelligence (AI) into research—new methodological approaches are needed. For instance, *big data* enables the identification of patterns across vast datasets, while *small data* (qualitative data) offers contextual depth. These approaches can be effectively combined through mixed-methods designs.

Conversely, AI presents itself as a disruptive tool that allows complex quantitative analysis but also raises questions about interpreting the results from a qualitative perspective. Mixed designs can address this disruption by integrating AI findings with qualitative interpretations, allowing a more holistic understanding of the impact of technologies on the psychotherapeutic process.

Conclusion

The evolution of mixed models in psychotherapy research reflects a significant advance in breaking the traditional dichotomies that separate qualitative and quantitative as opposing and irreconcilable methodological approaches. Historically, these divisions have been supported by epistemological positions that argue that qualitative methodologies, focused on the deep exploration of human experience, and quantitative ones, oriented towards objective measurement, cannot coexist coherently. However, the works presented in this article directly challenge this idea, demonstrating that not only is the coexistence of these approaches possible, but their integration is crucial to obtaining a richer and more complete understanding of clinical phenomena and psychotherapy.

Mixed designs, such as exploratory, post-explanatory, triangulated, nested, and hybrid, testify to how both methodological perspectives can fruitfully complement each other. These designs allow for capturing both the subjectivity of the patient and the nuances of clinical interactions, as well as measurable patterns that can be generalized and used to validate theories (Stiles, 2014). Instead of creating tension, the interaction between qualitative and quantitative enriches research by generating a dialogue between data that capture lived experience and those that measure observable effects.

One of the most significant contributions of mixed designs is the creation of shared spaces, where qualitative and quantitative not only coexist but collaborate to address joint needs. For example, in the mixed exploratory design, the qualitative approach generates the hypotheses that are then evaluated quantitatively, creating a logical sequence of research that reinforces the validity of the findings. In the post-explanatory design, the initial quantitative results find their whole meaning through subsequent qualitative analysis, which contextualizes and deepens the understanding of the data.

Beyond their methodological integration, mixed models reveal a joint need to leverage the strengths of both approaches to address the complexity of clinical phenomena. Psychotherapy, in its multifaceted nature, presents challenges that no single approach could exhaustively address. The measurement of therapeutic outcomes must be complemented with an understanding of patients' subjective experiences, and clinical interventions cannot be thoroughly evaluated without considering patients' personal and social context, which can only be captured through qualitative methodologies.

As psychotherapy research faces new realities, such as the incorporation of emerging technologies and the massive analysis of data (*big data* and *small data*), the need for integrative approaches becomes even more evident. These new methodological tools cannot be fully understood from a solely quantitative or qualitative perspective. Artificial intelligence, for example, generates large volumes of data that must be interpreted through human experience. It is at this point where mixed models prove to be the ideal strategy, by allowing technological advances to integrate with the interpretive richness of qualitative approaches, creating a research space that is both rigorous and deeply human.

In summary, mixed designs allow for breaking with traditional divisions and dichotomies and create a common methodological ground where the qualitative and quantitative complement each other. Through this collaboration, new opportunities open up to address the challenges of contemporary research in psychotherapy, where a profound understanding of human experience must be combined with the precision and validity of measurable data. The key to advancing in this direction lies in the continuous creativity and adaptation of researchers, who must continue exploring new ways to integrate these methodologies to answer the complex questions that the field of psychotherapy research poses.

References

Bartholomew, T. T., & Lockard, A. J. (2018). Mixed methods in psychotherapy research: A review of methodology integration in psychotherapy science. *Journal of Clinical Psychology, 74*(10), 1687–1709.

Levitt, H. M., Hamburger, A., Hill, C. E., McLeod, J., Pascual-Leone, A., Timulak, L., et al. (2024). Broadening the evidentiary basis for clinical practice guidelines: Recommendations from qualitative psychotherapy researchers. *American Psychologist.*

Marren, C., Mikoška, P., O'Brien, S., & Timulak, L. (2022). A qualitative meta-analysis of the clients' experiences of emotion-focused therapy. *Clinical Psychology & Psychotherapy, 29*(5), 1611–1625. https://doi.org/10.1002/cpp.2745

McBeath, A., Bager-Charleson, S., & Finlay, L. (2023). Views about mixed methods research from counseling and psychotherapy research students and supervisors. *European Journal for Qualitative Research in Psychotherapy, 13.*

Midgley, N., Ansaldo, F., & y Target, M. (2014). The meaningful assessment of therapy outcomes: Incorporating a qualitative study into a randomized controlled trial evaluating the treatment of adolescent depression. *Psychotherapy, 51*(1), 128.

Olivera, J., Braun, M., Gómez Penedo, M., & y Roussos, A. (2013). A qualitative investigation of former clients' perception of change, reasons for consultation, therapeutic relationship, and termination. *Psychotherapy: Theory, Research, Practice, Training. American Psychological Association., 50*(4), 505–516.

Olivera, J., Juan, S., & Roussos, A. J. (2017). *Las intervenciones terapéuticas desde la perspectiva del paciente: una aproximación cualitativa.* [Therapeutic interventions from the patient's perspective: a qualitative approach.]. *Anuario de investigaciones, 23*(1), 43–51.

Rennie, D. L., & Frommer, J. (2015). Applications of qualitative and mixed-methods counseling and psychotherapy research. *Psychotherapy research: Foundations, process, and outcome,* 429–454.

Roussos, A. (2008). *La cadencia en la presentación de interpretaciones en una díada paciente-terapeuta* [The cadence in the presentation of interpretations in a patient-therapist dyad.]. *Revista de la Sociedad Argentina de Psicoanálisis, 11*(12), 193–216.

Roussos, A., Etchebarne, I., & Waizmann, V. (2006). *Un esquema clasificatorio para las intervenciones en psicoterapia cognitiva y psicoanalítica* [A classification scheme for interventions in cognitive and psychoanalytic psychotherapy]. *Anuario de investigaciones. Facultad de psicología – UBA. Secretaría de investigaciones, XIII*, 51–61.
Roussos, A. J., Gomez Penedo, J. M., & y Muiños, R. (2018). A time-series analysis of therapeutic alliance, interventions, and client's clinical status in an evidence-based single-case study: Evidence for establishing change mechanisms in psychotherapy. *Psychotherapy Research, 28*(1), 137–149.
Roussos, A. J., Lissin, L. B., & De Duarte, A. L. (2007). The importance of the theoretical framework in the formulation of clinical inferences in psychotherapy. *Psychotherapy Research, 17*(5), 535–543.
Stiles, W. B. (2014). Theory building, enriching, and fact gathering: Alternative purposes of psychotherapy research. In *Psychotherapy research: Foundations, process, and outcome* (pp. 159–179). Springer Vienna.
Timulak, L. (2007). Identifying core categories of client-identified impact of helpful events in psychotherapy: A qualitative meta-analysis. *Psychotherapy Research, 17*(3), 305–314.
Winkler, M. I., Avendaño, C., Krause, M., & Soto, Á. (1993). *El Cambio Psicológico desde la Perspectiva de los Consultantes* [Psychological Change from the Consultants' Perspective]. *Revista Terapia Psicológica, 20*, 7–19.

Chapter 17
Researching Bipolar Disorder: The Case of an Incubator with Qualitative Methodologies

Alemka Tomicic

Research Project, Research Program, and Incubator

I typically use the film "Finding Nemo"[1] to explain the difference between a project and a research program. The film presents the East Australian Current (EAC), a powerful ocean current, which carries the characters, the clownfish Marlin and the adorable blue surgeonfish, Dory, to their destination efficiently and quickly. In the movie, the EAC is a natural highway that facilitates long-distance travel, leading fish and other marine animals to the point where they must arrive without significant deviations. Let's take this oceanic highway and its users as a metaphor or analogy to explain the difference between a project and a research program. It is possible to indicate that the former is a more limited and specific effort, with a particular objective in a bounded temporal framework. Thus, in "Finding Nemo," a research project is similar to a particular section within the current that its users travel; Marlin and Dory enter the current with a specific objective, to get to Sydney, seeking to answer a particular question: where is Nemo? The current facilitates their arrival, but the journey is limited to that concrete goal.

On the other hand, a research program is much broader and continuous; it encompasses a series of interrelated projects that can evolve. It is about the Australian current, a highway that remains over time, regardless of who enters or leaves it. A

[1] Stanton, A. (Director). (2003). *Finding Nemo* [Film]. Pixar Animation Studios; Walt Disney Pictures.

A. Tomicic (✉)
Centre for Studies in Clinical Psychology and Psychotherapy (CEPPS), Faculty of Psychology, Diego Portales University, Santiago, Chile

Millennium Institute for Research in Depression and Personality (MIDAP), Santiago, Chile
e-mail: alemka.tomicic@mail.udp.cl

A. Tomicic, J. D. Soto (eds.), *Qualitative Research in Clinical Psychology and Psychotherapy in Latin America*, https://doi.org/10.1007/978-3-031-90782-1_17

research program, then, deals with a broader set of research questions, encompassing multiple and diverse individual projects, each of which contributes to the advancement of the program as a whole. As can be assumed, research projects must show methodological consistency, while research programs can exhibit, within certain borders, paradigmatic pluralism (Guba & Lincoln, 1994).

With all this, this analogy shows how individual projects are part of a greater effort that exceeds them—that is to say, the program. Every time we formulate a research project, we become part of a research program, while the program gives meaning and ensures this new study's disciplinary and social relevance. Between the research program and the research project, it is possible to establish and review the idea of the research incubator in detail. Of course, a research incubator is a metaphor or analogy, just as the ocean current is. We can also talk about a laboratory. However, I favor incubating because it refers to an image akin to qualitative research's processes and naturalistic character (e.g., Flick, 2004).

A research incubator is an environment or space deliberately or emergently designed to support and foster the creation, development, and execution of research projects with aspirations to shape a program, especially in the early stages. Its main objective is to provide resources, guidance, and collaboration for researchers, research teams, and undergraduate and postgraduate students who seek to explore new ideas or areas of study. When I mention early stages, I refer to individuals just taking their first steps in research or the initial stage of a research question, defining its object and field of study. Therefore, a research incubator's purpose is to provide resources, guidance, and collaboration among researchers at various stages of their academic career development. Above all, they constitute collaborative spaces and network formation, which are housed and occur in research centers under the wing of an academic unit such as a research center or faculty of psychology.[2]

Research incubators provide support regarding access to infrastructure, technology, funding, and expert advice on research methodology and project development. They are, in turn, spaces for mentoring and training in research, academic writing, and communication of results. They also promote interdisciplinary and network creation in the scientific ecosystem and foster a creative and flexible environment for the exploration and development of new ideas, with a focus on generating new knowledge. Finally, but no less importantly, they provide access to essential resources for the implementation of research. In this way, incubators stimulate early and frontier research and strengthen the development of research skills and competencies in undergraduate and graduate students. Incubators facilitate knowledge transfer through the practical application of the knowledge produced and generate an ecosystem characterized by creation and innovation.

---

[2] The example of a qualitative research incubator presented in this chapter is mainly organized around the School of Psychology and the Center for Studies in Clinical Psychology and Psychotherapy (CEPPS), both from the Faculty of Psychology of the Diego Portales University (https://cepps.udp.cl/).

Incubating a Research Problem, Bipolar Disorder

Bipolar Disorder (BD) is a potentially severe mental illness characterized by recurrent mood variations and also has a chronic nature (Grande et al., 2016; Vieta et al., 2018). It is estimated that the prevalence of this disorder in Latin America is between 1% and 2% of the population and that there are no substantive differences by sex (Lopez-Jaramillo et al., 2015; WHO, 2017). Chile's prevalence is 2.2% in the population over 15 years old (MINSAL, 2017). There is no evidence to suggest that people who carry this diagnosis present any form of remission (Vieta et al., 2018). In addition, BD is one of the mental pathologies with the highest disease burden—associated with a higher risk of suicide, abusive consumption of alcohol and drugs, psychiatric and somatic comorbidity, and difficulties in the family and social sphere, among others (Grande et al., 2016).

Since 2018, in Chile, BD has been incorporated as one of the priority pathologies of the state program of Explicit Health Care Guarantees (GES, in its Spanish acronym) of the Ministry of Health. This program seeks, for all priority pathologies, including BD, to ensure access, timeliness, quality, and financial protection in the required interventions (MINSAL, 2012). It also establishes guarantees for diagnosis, treatment, and follow-up, ensuring equity and efficiency in health provision in both public and private systems.[3]

With the appropriate treatment, people with BD can manage the disorder well and regulate the mood variations that characterize it. These mood swings are also alternated with periods of euthymia. Euthymia, as its etymological sense indicates (Liddell & Scott, 1940), is a state of well-being or mood regulation. Contrary to what is commonly thought, BD can debut or occur without necessarily presenting a manic episode. Even more, when there have been such episodes, their occurrence decreases in older adulthood (Kraus et al., 2019), with the period of emerging adulthood and middle adulthood being the periods of the life course in which this disorder can express itself with greater severity (Sajatovic et al., 2004).

Despite the advancement of psychiatric treatments that contemplate the indication of mood regulators, antipsychotics, and, in refractory cases, electroconvulsive therapy (ECT), psychological therapies and interventions, individual and family, and the development of psychosocial programs—such as psychoeducation—continue to be as or more important (e.g., Yatham et al., 2018) in the proper management of the disease. This is because, in addition to protecting from stigma, they improve self-esteem, the sense of self-efficacy, hope, motivation, and adherence to treatments. In addition, it has been seen that these interventions lift the barriers to

[3] The health system in Chile is mixed, composed of a public sector and a private sector. The public sector is managed by a state insurance called the National Health Fund (FONASA) and covers most of the population, especially people with lower incomes, offering care in the network of public hospitals and health centers. The private sector is funded by the Health Pension Institutions (ISAPRES), which finance the health benefits of those who can pay higher premiums, offering access to private health centers and clinics. Both sectors operate in parallel, with differences in access, quality, and financing of services (Superintendency of Health, n.d.).

access to many therapies since stigma and self-stigma, shame, efforts to hide symptoms, and experiences of discrimination often prevent people with the diagnosis from attending health centers, being, among others, one of the factors that influences the delay of a diagnosis and the timely start of treatment (Geddes & Miklowitz, 2013; Perlick et al., 2001).

The background presented so far for the research incubator that I want to illustrate here allows us to outline a research problem and ask initial, broad, and exploratory questions, such as: What can be the best conditions for developing psychosocial support opportunities for people diagnosed with BD? What can be the representations and experiences related to BD in patients, their relatives, treaters, primary health care doctors, psychology students, health career students, etc.? What are the stigmas associated with BD and the internalized stigmas in people carrying this diagnosis? What are the everyday strategies and practices for coping with the disease? What effectiveness and value do patients assign to psychoeducation and the formation of support networks and groups?

For its part, at the Center for Research in Clinical Psychology and Psychotherapy of the Faculty of Psychology at Diego Portales University, of which I am a researcher, we had proposed, gathering previous studies, a programmatic line of research on the subjective construction of mental health problems and disorders and their treatments (e.g., Duarte et al., 2019; Tomicic et al., 2020). This focuses on experiences related to mental health difficulties and their psychological and psychotherapeutic treatments; we seek to understand the particular experiences of illness and mental health difficulties of patients, relatives, treaters, and their social environment, which provides knowledge that allows for improving their treatment, destigmatizing, and reinforcing coping experiences that promote well-being in patients and their surroundings.

With all that said, the foundations were robust enough to develop and compete for research funds to delve into some of the exploratory questions I listed in the previous paragraph, which suggest studies with qualitative methodologies. However, I needed the time conditions to start a new project. I was still implementing research funded by the National Agency for Research and Development of Chile (ANID) on culturally competent psychotherapy with people of sexual and gender diversities (Tomicic et al., 2019/2023). I had assumed a management position at the university, was working with my colleague from CEPPS, Javiera Duarte, on a project of hers (Duarte, 2021/2023), among other tasks linked to regular academic activity. Yet, I felt the impulse to research BD. So, what could I do? I also told myself I would involve my undergraduate students in this challenge.

Bipolar Disorder Research Incubator: Experience Teaching Qualitative Research in the Psychology Career

The training plan of the School of Psychology at Diego Portales University considers five years of extension in which students acquire theoretical and practical knowledge that contributes to what is regarded as three pillars or dimensions of the psychological discipline: the psychosocial dimension, the dimension of clinical psychology, and research and knowledge production in psychology. In the third year of the career, students receive training in research with qualitative methodologies, dedicating the first semester in the Research III course to the elaboration of projects and the second semester in the Research IV course to the execution of their approved projects. Likewise, the Research III and IV courses have six sections, each in charge of a professor, who proposes a thematic framework from which students develop their research. Obviously, the subjects are theoretical-practical, and at the end of the second semester, the teams of students who carry out the research present their findings at the "UDP Psychology Students Research Congress"[4] (see Fig. 17.1) and

Fig. 17.1 Photographs of the VII UDP Psychology Students Research Congress—2022, in which they present in poster format and presentations their research works (Photographs are available on the website of the Faculty of Psychology of Universidad Diego Portales: https://psicologia.udp.cl/congreso-de-investigacion-estudiantes-psicologia-udp/)

[4] Diego Portales University, Faculty of Psychology (n.d.). Congress of Research Psychology Students, UDP. Retrieved on October 11, 2024, from https://psicologia.udp.cl/congreso-de-investigacion-estudiantes-psicologia-udp.

communicate them in the form of a scientific article, with the best of each section being published in the "Book of Undergraduate Psychology Student Research UDP"[5].

As can be assumed, the Research III and IV courses, part of the training line in Research in Psychology, are preceded by the Research I and II courses, in which students design and implement studies with quantitative methodologies. This sequence of courses constitutes incubators per se since they employ a Project-Based Learning strategy (PBL; Bell, 2010) that, consequently, immediately integrates theory and practice and, therefore, the transmission of knowledge acquires the character of mentorship.

In the case of Research III, it is expected that students will understand and apply research approaches and qualitative analysis to elaborate and communicate a research project at the end of the course. Thus, they develop skills for collaboration and teamwork, oriented to the production and communication of knowledge of social and disciplinary relevance in different areas of psychology, and promote the ethical responsibility of basing decision-making in professional practice on scientific evidence. For its part, in Research IV, it is expected that at the end of the semester, students will understand and apply techniques for selection, collection, and qualitative analysis for the execution of a research project, and along with continuing to develop skills for collaborative teamwork, they are oriented to the production and communication of results of social and disciplinary relevance in different areas of psychology. These objectives assume that qualitative methodologies can only be fully learned within the framework of research and in convenience with an object of study that needs to be explored and progressively defined as students insert themselves in the field and manage to establish, in a limited way, processes of participant selection, collection, and qualitative analysis (Ravitch & Carl, 2021).

Qualitative Research Incubator: Knowledge Production on Bipolar Disorder

During the years 2021 and 2022, the students who enrolled in my section of Research III and IV (see Fig. 17.2) carried out research with qualitative methodology within the thematic framework of the subjective experience of BD. As I have already mentioned, this was deliberate, so the incubator was started in 2021, to which other projects were added, which I will detail later.

After two years had passed, the course assistants and I asked us in which directions the knowledge about BD produced by the students with their research had advanced and how the learnings about qualitative methodology had nourished their training as future professional psychologists. Our goal was then to get a general view of the results obtained in the studies on the subjective experiences of BD

[5] Diego Portales University, Faculty of Psychology. (n.d.). Publications of Students School of Psychology, UDP. Retrieved on October 11, 2024, from https://psicologia.udp.cl/publicaciones-de-estudiantes-escuela-de-psicologia-udp.

Fig. 17.2 2022 assistant team, seated from left to right: Maite Aedo, Katherine Guerrero, Martín Hernández, Felipe Alarcón and Fabián Ahumada (Photography by the author)

carried out by the students, as well as the main learnings acquired for their future professional practice in clinical psychology and psychotherapy.

To answer this objective, we first reviewed ten qualitative studies developed by ten teams of students between 2021 and 2022. The set of research involved 26 participants, 12 of whom had a diagnosis of bipolar disorder. Each student was responsible for interviewing a participant in person or remotely, according to the restrictions imposed at that time by the pandemic. The students analyzed the interview transcripts following the procedures of open coding and axial coding of Grounded Theory (Charmaz, 2014; Levitt, 2021). The ten research protocols were reviewed and approved by the Research Ethics Committee of the Faculty of Psychology of Diego Portales University, and all participants signed informed consent before being interviewed.

Table 17.1 shows that the results of the ten studies were grouped into three thematic areas.

Regarding BD and stigma, the results of the three research studies classified under this topic concluded that stigma, in the case of BD, tends to manifest in the workplace, in the constitution of the self, and in self-image. Self-demands and the concealment of the diagnosis are ways of expressing and dealing with internalized stigma, which is experienced in the workplace as "breaking the hand of fate" and results in the reinforcement of self-stigma (see Avilés et al., 2021). Furthermore, stigma is observed in the dilemma of "being bipolar or having the diagnosis of bipolarity," offering this latter way of defining the relationship with the disorder and the possibility of integrating BD as a part of the self (Cruz et al., 2022).

Table 17.1 Research grouped by thematic areas

Research	Authors
Bipolar disorder and stigma	
Being Bipolar or Having Bipolar Disorder: Construction of Self in Chilean Women Diagnosed with Bipolar Disorder I or II	Cruz et al. (2022)
Experience of Stigma in Older Adults Diagnosed with Bipolar Affective Disorder	Ahumada et al. (2023)
Employment Integration and Stigma After Diagnosis of Bipolar Affective Disorder: A Qualitative Study	Avilés et al. (2021)
Bipolar disorder and meaningful relationships	
A Step to the Side Without Leaving You Behind: Life in a Relationship with a Bipolar Affective Disorder Diagnosis	Aravena et al. (2022)
"To be a Friend of Someone with Bipolar Affective Disorder is…": A Qualitative Study from the Perspective of Friendship	López et al. (2022)
Bipolar Affective Disorder is Not My Middle Name: The Role of Family Perception in the Construction of Personal Self-Concept	Contreras et al. (2022)
The challenge of being diagnosed with Bipolar Affective Disorder: The Uniqueness of the Experience	Aedo et al. (2021)
Narratives of Children of Mothers Diagnosed with Bipolar Affective Disorder	Cifuentes et al. (2021)
Bipolar disorder and gestation	
Beyond Bipolar Affective Disorder: Experiences of Midwives in the Care of Pregnant Women with Mood Disorders	Araneda et al. (2022)
¿Relief or Stigma? Voices of Women About Their Pregnancy with Bipolar Affective Disorder	Díaz et al. (2022)

Regarding the five qualitative studies on the topic of BD and significant relationships, the students researched with families, children, partners, and friends of people diagnosed with bipolarity (Aravena et al., 2022; Cifuentes et al., 2021; Contreras et al., 2022; López et al., 2022). In addition, they asked people with the diagnosis about their significant relationships (Aedo et al., 2021). Perhaps one of the most important results is the positive aspect of the diagnosis when it is no longer hidden or is identified, and when this occurs outside the realm of stigmatization. Clarifying the diagnosis can provide relief and facilitate asking for emotional containment support.

Lastly, regarding the topic of bipolarity and perinatal, the results of the two studies conducted indicate that the support of others is significant and crucial for pregnant women with the diagnosis of BD to better face the challenges of the disorder at this life milestone, such as the relapses of depressive or hypomanic episodes. After the diagnosis, women actively seek to educate themselves about the disease, worrying about the use of medications and the possibility of transmitting BD to their children (Díaz et al., 2022). However, there is a lack of knowledge about BD among midwives, attributed to insufficient training in mental health. Self-taught training has been key for midwives to acquire skills, but the need for formal education in this area is emphasized. In addition, some perceptions that midwives have about pregnant women with BD influence the care they receive, with some seeing the patients as cooperative and attentive. In contrast, others perceive high levels of anxiety and desperation (Araneda et al., 2022).

So far, and in global terms, two years of incubating qualitative research on BD have taught us that the presence of stigma in the environment and the perception of lack of support lead to the concealment of the diagnosis, reinforcing stigmatizing beliefs and images that align with internalized stigma. On the contrary, the identification of the diagnosis as something that one has and not as something that one is promotes psychoeducation. Hence, the resources available to people diagnosed with BD play a significant role in determining their relationship with the disease. Regarding the environment, emotional support emerges as the form of support most desired in various contexts.

Qualitative Research Incubator: Acquisition of Relevant Skills for Future Professionals in Clinical Psychology and Psychotherapy

As previously mentioned, training in qualitative research at the undergraduate level offers learnings about the object of study—BD in this case—and the students, as young researchers and future psychology professionals in the clinical and psychotherapeutic area.

In the context of the qualitative research course, one of the teaching assistants[6] conducted five brief interviews with students who had already approved the course in 2021 and 2022 to inquire about what they had learned. The five interviews were transcribed, anonymized, and interpreted through a thematic analysis (Braun & Clarke, 2021).

The five students interviewed at the end of the Research III and IV courses, who belonged to some of the ten groups, stated, firstly, that taking both courses allowed them to have the experience of transferring research to practice. They learned this by translating the research findings to their future professional practice, integrating knowledge and techniques, understanding people in their context, valuing flexibility in interaction, and employing teamwork to enrich interventions. Along with this, they learned the importance of constantly searching for information, using the coding strategy to interpret and organize it systematically, and, in turn, contributing to the stigmatization of mental disorders.

Together, from the perspective of the interviewed students, the learnings mentioned earlier allow qualitative research to have a real and applicable clinical value. Finally, but not less importantly, the students mentioned having also learned firsthand about the ethical commitment in qualitative research by assuming the

[6] I gratefully acknowledge Katherine Guerrero for her valuable contribution as an assistant in the Research III and IV courses during the years 2021 and 2022, as well as for conducting the interviews with the students and the thematic organization of these.

responsibility of conducting rigorous studies that respect and benefit people, taking care to ensure that the results faithfully reflect their reality, interpreting honestly and accurately the narratives of the people, respecting their history and personal experience. As the following excerpt deepens, one of the interviewed students:

> To have a more compassionate understanding of the person's situation. To understand a little more about what is happening instead of just focusing on the fact of what is happening. And I found that this is super significant because, in the end, people are not just their actions, not just their deeds; they are much more than that, they are much more complex. Understanding bipolar disorder specifically, understanding the family's fears, also helps not to judge people's decisions so much (Student, 2022).

Bipolar Disorder Research Incubator: Undergraduate Elective Practice and Narrative Systematic Review of Scope

Once the Research III and IV courses were completed, some undergraduate students approached the Center for Research in Clinical Psychology and Psychotherapy (CEPPS) to express their interest and willingness to continue researching BD. We agreed to develop an undergraduate course called Elective Practice under the center's auspices, in which they conducted a systematic review on peer support in people diagnosed with bipolar disorder (Vásquez et al., 2022).

Diego Portales University has designed Elective Practice courses to provide a formative space where undergraduate students can connect with research centers. As their name suggests, and unlike Research III and IV courses, for example, Elective Practices are courses students choose to take and are not part of the mandatory academic offer. They can be understood as incubators because they seek students to apply what they have learned in other courses of their careers, develop new practical learnings about the professional and academic field of the discipline, and relate to professionals or researchers that allow them to expand their professional networks. For this, within the framework of Elective Practices, students work for a semester on some academic or professional project led by a teacher, hoping that during this experience, undergraduate students will participate in the substantive aspects of a research project.

In the framework described above, we agreed with the students that the objective of the Elective Practice would consist of creating a systematic review protocol and subsequently implementing it, to present their results at an SPR International Congress[7] and the Psychotherapy Congress in Chile[8] (see Fig. 17.3).

At this point, with my colleague from CEPPS, Javiera Duarte, we introduced the interested students to the method of Scoping Reviews, as a form of scientific literature research that allows mapping the existing evidence in broad research areas, especially when we are keen to explore a wide topic of interest (Munn et al., 2018).

---

[7] Society for Psychotherapy Research https://www.psychotherapyresearch.org.

[8] Chilean Congress of Psychotherapy, Reñaca http://www.congresopsicoterapia.cl.

Fig. 17.3 Carla Vázquez received the Honor Distinction for the Poster: Effectiveness of a peer support intervention for people with bipolar disorder and their families: Qualitative analysis of the perspective of facilitators (Maité Aedo, Victoria Díaz, Francisca Avilés, Carla Vásquez, Alemka Tomicic, Javiera Duarte, and Claudio Martinez) at the 16th Chilean Congress of Psychotherapy and 14th Latin American Congress of Research in Psychotherapy, 2023, Reñaca, Chile (Photography by the author)

The main function of the Systematic Review, which we proposed to the students as a project for their Elective Practice, is to identify gaps in knowledge, clarify concepts, and explore, as I said before, the available literature with a general question. Although it is not strictly a qualitative research method, its narrative character allows for describing and synthesizing relevant studies and integrating descriptive and contextual findings. In addition, scoping reviews can constitute, per se, incubators of questions leading to qualitative research—as I will show next, this was the case.

Thus, in the context of an Elective Practice, together with the undergraduate students, we developed a scoping review to compile and understand the available evidence on the characteristics of peer support interventions, their effects, and their effectiveness. Like in the research course, in the process, the students learned about conducting scoping systematic reviews, using databases, determining inclusion criteria and selecting publications, extracting relevant information for the purposes of the review, and realizing a narrative synthesis.

The data production process and the results of the scoping review carried out with the students allowed us to take a further step in configuring a qualitative research incubator in BD. Specifically, 25 reviewed and analyzed publications concluded that the evidence indicates that BD is a serious mental illness of early onset and that people who carry this psychiatric diagnosis face high levels of stigma and disability. It was also found that peer support can occur naturally among people with BD, be mediated by a trained peer, be in peer-led support groups, or be in group psychoeducation programs guided by peer support with clinicians. It was also confirmed that patients with BD highly value peer support as part of their treatment due to its positive effects such as, for example, the development of greater self-control, an increase in the feeling of self-efficacy, adherence to treatment, self-esteem, hope, and sense of belonging (Vásquez et al., 2022).

The students titled the scoping review on peer support in BD, "It feels like you're not alone: Peer support for patients with bipolar disorder," and from this advance in the incubator, we began to take an interest in the topic of peer support for people diagnosed with BD and to think, already as a team, about how to investigate it in its particular form of implementation in Chile.

Bipolar Disorder Research Incubator: Qualitative Study on Peer Support with Institutional Funding

As I have said before, BD is a chronic mental illness that can be managed with pharmacological treatment, psychotherapy, and/or psychosocial interventions (Arrieta & Santos, 2019). Evidence shows that peer support positively impacts their treatment (Kelly, 2018; Martínez et al., 2019; Marzani & Price Neff, 2021; Vieta et al., 2018), which was confirmed by our previous research. In Chile, peer support groups have been implemented since 2020—at the beginning of the pandemic—comprising approximately 1500 people, known as Peer Support Circles (CAPs) (Proudfoot et al., 2012), which are under the auspices of *Fundación Circulo Polar* [Polar Circle foundation]. The CAPs provide support, guidance, or information to participants with BD diagnoses in common, especially those recently diagnosed. The peer facilitators use their experience to teach practical strategies and promote lifestyle changes so that group members can manage their illness more autonomously (Kelly, 2018; Martínez et al., 2019; Vieta et al., 2018).

We were particularly interested in analyzing the effectiveness of the CAPs based on the evaluations made by their participants. This new step in the incubator required more than undergraduate research courses; it needed students integrated into our research center (CEPPS) and the teaching and mentoring work of my colleague and me directed at these students. By this, I mean that we required funds to cover the operating expenses of the study—transcription of interviews, dissemination of results, and economic compensation to the students, now moving to the role of research assistants. We applied for a Priority Research Fund from the Millennium Institute of Research in Depression and Personality (MIDAP)[9] of Chile.

[9]The Millennium Institute for Research in Depression and Personality (MIDAP), is a scientific center funded by the Millennium Scientific Initiative of the National Scientific Research and Development Agency (ANID) of Chile. MIDAP is made up of psychologists, psychiatrists, and professionals from various areas of the social sciences and health who seek to generate knowledge based on a multidimensional understanding of depression in interaction with personality, to maximize the effectiveness of interventions by identifying the agents and mechanisms of change involved in prevention, psychotherapy, and rehabilitation.

Following the logic of research-oriented by and for practice (Castonguay et al., 2013; Castonguay & Hill, 2023; Fernández-Alvarez et al., 2024), we established an alliance with the Polar Circle Foundation not only to contact and conduct interviews with the support group participants (CAPs), but also to develop a relationship of collaboration and active participation in the development of the research, promoting triangulation and contextualization in the construction of interview scripts, of the analyses, and of the feedback and dissemination of the results[10] (see Figs. 17.4 and 17.5).

Fig. 17.4 Teams from Polar Circle Foundation and CEPPS-MIDAP at the 5th Anniversary of Polar Circle (October 19, 2024). From left to right: Psychiatrist Jorge Cabrera (Co-founder Polar Circle), Francisco Encina (Co-founder Polar Circle), Elizabeth Veas (Manager of Support Circles—CAPS), Matías Paredes (Measurement Analyst Polar Circle), Marcela Verni (Director of Quality of Life Polar Circle), Alemka Tomicic (Researcher CEPPS-MIDAP), Javiera Duarte (Researcher CEPPS-MIDAP), Flavia Gal (Founder President Polar Circle), Rodrigo Valenzuela (Executive Director Polar Circle) (Photography available on social networks of Polar Circle Foundation: https://www.linkedin.com/posts/circulopolarong_fundaciaejncaedrculopolar-caedrculosdeapoyo-activity-7254831525278400512-GG_H?utm_source=share&utm_medium=member_desktop&rcm=ACoAADbw5DMBOBVe-1wd0tBeie4qNxB_kJHBjI4)

[10] For example, for the dissemination of the results, an animated capsule was developed with the CEPPS research team and the Polar Circle Foundation team, with the main results of the study, which was launched at the Foundation's anniversary celebration on October 19, 2024, after which it was distributed through the social networks of Polar Circle, CEPPS, and MIDAP.

Fig. 17.5 Frames from the animated capsule for the dissemination of the results of the MIDAP FIP research, titled "Support Circles, Research, and Hope". This capsule is the result of the joint work of the team from Polar Circle Foundation and the team of researchers from CEPPS and MIDAP for the elaboration launched to be distributed at the celebration of the 5th Anniversary of Polar Circle (October 19, 2024) (Script: Flavia Gal; Designs: Marcela Verni; Animation: Bernardo; Participation: Rodrigo Valenzuela, Javiera Duarte, and Alemka Tomicic)

We conducted 16 qualitative interviews with CAP participants, with men and women, both in roles of peers and expert peers, from the different geographical macro-zones of the country. The interviews were transcribed in full and analyzed using the open coding of the Grounded Theory analysis model (Charmaz, 2014; Levitt, 2021).

The findings of this study were organized into three major categories: benefits of participating in the CAPs, the conditions for good functioning of the CAPs, and challenges and limitations faced by the CAPs. Through the first category, we realized that the participants identified many benefits, with accepting the diagnosis and gaining self-esteem central to facing stigma and self-stigma. On the other hand, a central aspect that emerged from this research was that for the good functioning of the CAPs, it is crucial to have the possibility that the members of the CAPs get to know each other in person. Here, the online origin of the CAPs due to the pandemic has been installed as a barrier to this condition, which the participants desired. And, finally, related to the above, and perhaps one of the central difficulties observed, were the problems with communicating and trusting peers in an online context, in which it is easier to reproduce concealment practices due to self-stigma (Tomicic et al., 2024).

In conclusion, and as for the benefits, the agency seems to be the factor that best gathers and reflects the participants' experiences. Presence is a modality frequently desired and often is perceived as the one that best contributes to active participation, even when barriers to achieving it are described. The results of this study made us think that a possible solution is to opt for a mixed modality, which allows balancing the need to establish spaces of trust and mutual knowledge with the creation of relationships of continuity, compatible with the time limitations faced by participants (Tomicic et al., 2024).

On the other hand, the expert peers pointed out that, throughout their work in the foundation, they learn and teach about psychoeducation and have protocols and the support of both the board and other facilitators for handling complex cases. There is no fixed standard for the implementation of interventions or a strict organization of activities; peers have the freedom to modify and adapt interventions according to the needs and characteristics of their group, which can hinder the creation of a unified model that is valuable in terms of effectiveness (Tomicic et al., 2024).

From these results, we also learned that it is important to consider aspects such as cultural competence and sensitivity, stigma management, and the value given to the peer bond, which allows the transfer of knowledge related to the therapeutic alliance in psychotherapy to this form of psychosocial intervention.

As I mentioned before, the results of this study were shared with the team from Polar Circle Foundation, who found that these resonated deeply with their experiences of direct work with peer groups. This motivated both teams to develop an informative capsule about CAPS, which, in addition to fulfilling one of the products committed to for the funding of the study, served a fundamental purpose in terms of dissemination (see https://youtu.be/ui0V76n7sKU?si=8iqvZGEO-bae47Ij).

Incubator for Developing Practice-Oriented Qualitative Research and Culturally Competent Clinical Practice: Final Reflections

In this case, the idea of a qualitative research incubator oriented towards producing clinical and mental health knowledge has multiple advantages when considering producing evidence for clinical practice and, eventually, a sensitive and culturally competent psychotherapy.

First, and as I argued at the beginning of this chapter, the incubator allows for developing continuous and articulated research programs, integrating multiple projects of different scopes and magnitudes. This enables, in turn, strengthening the methodological consistency and ensures the disciplinary and social relevance of each of the studies and the research program as a whole, eventually facilitating the transfer of the knowledge generated towards training and practice.

Secondly, the incubator offers an environment where students, both undergraduate and postgraduate, can explore in-depth and a gradual approach to mental health problems, such as, in this case, bipolar disorder, offering a comprehensive understanding of complex subjective experiences, such as those linked to stigmatization and self-stigmatization. The above can encourage, in those who are part of the incubator, the creation of culturally sensitive, contextualized, and adjusted clinical and psychosocial interventions to the needs of the people who require them. In addition, a research incubator, like the one presented in this chapter, provides a practical learning space for students, who, while developing skills in qualitative research, acquire skills and understanding of the studied experience, contributing to their clinical psychology training. Through the teaching and mentoring spaces offered by the researchers and teachers, future professionals acquire an ethical and sensitive understanding of the otherness of those who carry diagnoses of mental disorders.

Furthermore, the idea of an "incubator" can go beyond the training of students, extending to the incubation of projects that, eventually, consolidate as programs. Hence, the incubator is a learning space for undergraduates, postgraduates, young researchers, assistants, or even senior researchers and a knowledge incubation space. This approach emphasizes its role in developing innovative ideas and projects, regardless of the role of those who participate in this space. In the Latin American context, this incubator acquires special relevance, as we often face limited access to resources and our research scope. For example, MIDAP (Research Institute on Depression and Personality, from the Millennium Scientific Initiative of the State of Chile) could be understood as an incubator that has grown and has become a solid platform for generating knowledge and developing significant research initiatives.

Thirdly, and equally relevant as the previous points, is the fact that the generation of qualitative knowledge, in this case about bipolar disorder, not only has an academic scope but also gradually but directly impacts the promotion of effective interventions. Thus, for example, the scoping systematic review developed within the framework of the research incubator allowed us to expand the knowledge base on peer support interventions for people diagnosed with bipolar disorder. On the other hand, the analysis of the experience of peer support groups in the Chilean context—the CAPs of the Polar Circle—favored and promoted reflection with the counterpart people of the Foundation on the possibility of developing forms and models of intervention adjusted to the realities that were expressed in the different interviews.

Together, the development of a qualitative research incubator on bipolar disorder with undergraduates in the context of the regular training plan, within the framework of a research center of the Faculty of Psychology UDP and under the wing of a broader research institute, shows that qualitative research can develop culturally sensitive knowledge on specific and relevant topics for psychology (Charmaz & Belgrave, 2012; Denzin & Lincoln, 2018). The learnings derived from qualitative research are helpful in linking research, training, and practice on topics such as mental health and related disorders (Altimir et al., 2022; Beidas & Kendall, 2010). The main competencies, both for qualitative research and for initial professional practice, are those involved in conducting interviews and descriptive and relational analysis, both as ways of approaching the understanding of the other from their subjectivity (Energici et al., 2024).

References

Aedo, M., Arancibia, J., Magendzo, T., Sandoval, C., & Urquiza, V. (2021). El desafío de ser diagnosticado con TAB: La singularidad de la experiencia [The challenge of being diagnosed with BD: The uniqueness of the experience]. In *VI Congreso Online de Investigación de Estudiantes de Psicología*. Escuela y Facultad de Psicología, Universidad Diego Portales, Santiago, Chile. Disponible en el libro de abstracts en https://psicologia.udp.cl/cms/wp-content/uploads/2023/07/Libro-VI-Congreso-de-Investigacion-2021.pdf

Ahumada, F., Morales, B., Sánchez, E., Scheiding, M., & Valdebenito, D. (2023). Ocultamiento del diagnóstico: Experiencia de personas mayores diagnosticadas con Trastorno Afectivo Bipolar. En Escuela de Psicología UDP (Ed.), Libro del VI Congreso de Investigación de Estudiantes de Psicología 2021. Universidad Diego Portales. Recuperado de. https://psicologia.udp.cl/cms/wp-content/uploads/2023/07/Libro-VI-Congreso-de-Investigacion-2021.pdf

Altimir, C., Mantilla, C., & Serralta, F. (2022). Practice-based evidence: bridging the gap between research and routine clinical practice in diverse settings (Evidencia basada en la práctica: construyendo puentes entre la investigación y la clínica rutinaria en entornos diversos). *Studies in Psychology, 43*(3), 415–454. https://doi.org/10.1080/02109395.2022.2139998

Araneda, S., Carvallo, F., Ferreira, J., Ortiz, C., & Rojas, T. (2022). Más allá del TAB: Experiencias de matronas en la atención de mujeres gestantes con trastornos del ánimo [Beyond BD: Midwives' experiences in caring for pregnant women with mood disorders]. In *VII Congreso de Investigación de Estudiantes de Psicología*, Escuela y Facultad de Psicología, Universidad Diego Portales, Santiago, Chile. Disponible en el libro de abstracts en https://psicologia.udp.cl/cms/wp-content/uploads/2023/03/Libro-de-Abstract-2022.pdf

Aravena, J. L., Gejman, B., Hevia, C., Oyarzun, F., & Pinedo, C. (2022). Un paso al costado sin dejarte de lado: Organización de la vida cotidiana en pareja cuando uno de ellos/as porta diagnóstico de Trastorno Afectivo Bipolar [A step aside without leaving you behind: Organization of daily life as a couple when one partner has a Bipolar Affective Disorder diagnosis]. In *VII Congreso de Investigación de Estudiantes de Psicología*. Escuela y Disponible en el libro de abstracts en https://psicologia.udp.cl/cms/wp-content/uploads/2023/03/Libro-de-Abstract-2022.pdf

Arrieta, M., & Santos, P. M. (2019). Trastorno bipolar [Bipolar Disorder]. *Medicine - Programa de Formación Médica Continuada Acreditado, 12*(86), 5052–5066. https://doi.org/10.1016/j.med.2019.09.013

Avilés, F., Carreño, N., Madrid, P., Pino, R., & Vidal, V. (2021). "Romper la mano del destino": Estigma y ocultamiento del TAB en el trabajo ["Breaking the Hand of Fate": Stigma and Concealment of BD in the Workplace]. In *Investigaciones de estudiantes de pregrado de psicología UDP - 2021: Investigando en un mundo en transformación* (pp. 118–153). Universidad Diego Portales. Recuperado de https://psicologia.udp.cl/cms/wp-content/uploads/2023/07/Investigando-en-un-mundo-en-transformacion.pdf

Beidas, R. S., & Kendall, P. C. (2010). Training therapists in evidence-based practice: A critical review of studies from a systems-contextual perspective. *Clinical Psychology: Science and Practice, 17*(1), 1–30. https://doi.org/10.1111/j.1468-2850.2009.01187.x

Bell, S. (2010). Project-based learning for the 21st century: Skills for the future. *The Clearing House: A Journal of Educational Strategies, Issues and Ideas, 83*(2), 39–43. https://doi.org/10.1080/00098650903505415

Braun, V., & Clarke, V. (2021). *Thematic analysis: A practical guide*. Sage.

Castonguay, L. G., Barkham, M., Lutz, W., & McAleavey, A. A. (2013). *Practice-oriented research: Approaches and applications*. In M. J. Lambert (Ed.), *Bergin and Garfield's handbook of psychotherapy and behavior change* (6th ed., pp. 85–133). Wiley.

Castonguay, L. G., & Hill, C. E. (Eds.). (2023). *Becoming better psychotherapists: Advancing training and supervision*. American Psychological Association. https://doi.org/10.1037/0000364-000

Charmaz, K. (2014). *Constructing grounded theory* (2nd ed.). Sage.

Charmaz, K., & Belgrave, L. L. (2012). Qualitative interviewing and grounded theory analysis. En J. F. Gubrium, J. A. Holstein, A. B. Marvasti, & K. D. McKinney (Eds.), *The SAGE handbook of interview research: The complexity of the craft* 2 pp. 347-365). SAGE Publications. https://doi.org/10.4135/9781452218403.n25

Cifuentes, F., Díaz, V., Farías, V., García, R., & Jeldres, C. (2021). "Lo he vivido desde que tengo memoria": Experiencias de crecer con una madre con TAB ["I've Lived It for as Long as I Can Remember": Experiences of Growing Up with a Mother with BD]. In *VI Congreso Online de Investigación de Estudiantes de Psicología*. Escuela y Facultad de Psicología, Universidad Diego Portales, Santiago, Chile. Disponible en el libro de abstracts en https://psicologia.udp.cl/cms/wp-content/uploads/2023/07/Libro-VI-Congreso-de-Investigacion-2021.pdf

Contreras, C., Ferrufino, I., Moya, M., Schilling, M. J., Sandoval, M. E., & Zamora, A. (2022). TAB no es mi segundo nombre: Rol de la visión familiar en la construcción del autoconcepto personal ["BD Is Not My Middle Name": The Role of Family Perception in the Construction of Personal Self-Concept]. In *VII Congreso de Investigación de Estudiantes de Psicología*, Escuela y Facultad de Psicología, Universidad Diego Portales, Santiago, Chile. Disponible en el libro de abstracts en https://psicologia.udp.cl/cms/wp-content/uploads/2023/03/Libro-de-Abstract-2022.pdf

Cruz, C., Gavilán, N., Fontecilla, A., Márquez, F., Schlesinger, I., & Peñaloza, F. (2022). Ser TAB o tener TAB: Construcción del self en mujeres chilenas diagnosticadas con Trastorno Afectivo Bipolar I o II. *Revista de Salud Mental y Psiquiatría, 1– 2*, 18–27.

Denzin, N. K., & Lincoln, Y. S. (Eds.). (2018). *The SAGE handbook of qualitative research* (5th ed.). Sage.

Díaz, A., Pérez, C., Salas, B., Spalinger, F., & Yau, S. (2022). ¿Alivio o estigma? Voces de mujeres acerca de su embarazo con TAB ["Relief or Stigma? Women's Voices on Their Pregnancy with BD]. In *VII Congreso de Investigación de Estudiantes de Psicología*, Escuela y Facultad de Psicología, Universidad Diego Portales, Santiago, Chile. Disponible en el libro de abstracts en https://psicologia.udp.cl/cms/wp-content/uploads/2023/03/Libro-de-Abstract-2022.pdf

Duarte, J. (2021/2023). *Episodios de encuentro y cambio en el conocimiento relacional implícito en psicoterapia [Episodes of Meetings and Change in Implicit Relational Knowing in Psychotherapy]*. Proyecto FONDECYT Postdoctoral N° 3200169. Agencia Nacional de Investigación y Desarrollo (ANID), Estado de Chile.

Duarte, J., Fischersworring, M., & Martínez, & Tomicic, A. (2019). "I couldn't change the past, the answer wasn't there": A case study on the subjective construction of psychotherapeutic change of a patient with borderline personality disorder diagnosis and her therapist. *Psychotherapy Research, 29*(4), 445–462. https://doi.org/10.1080/10503307.2017.1359426

Energici, A., Tomicic, A., & Schöngut-Grollmus, N. (2024). Qualitative research quality in Latin American vulnerable and precarious contexts. In U. Flick (Ed.), *The SAGE handbook of qualitative research design*. Sage Ed.

Fernández-Alvarez, J., Molinari, G., Kilcullen, R., et al. (2024). The importance of conducting practice-oriented research with underserved populations. *Administration and Policy in Mental Health, 51*, 358–375. https://doi.org/10.1007/s10488-023-01337-z

Flick, U. (2004). *An introduction to qualitative research* (3rd ed.). SAGE Publications.

Geddes, J., & Miklowitz, D. (2013). Treatment of bipolar disorder. *Lancet, 11*(9878), 1672–1682. https://doi.org/10.1016/S0140-6736(13)60857-0

Grande, I., Berk, M., Birmaher, B., & Vieta, E. (2016). Bipolar disorder. *The Lancet, 387*(10027), 1561–1572. https://doi.org/10.1016/S0140-6736(15)00241-X

Guba, E. G., & Lincoln, Y. S. (1994). Competing paradigms in qualitative research. In N. K. Denzin & Y. S. Lincoln (Eds.), *Handbook of qualitative research* (pp. 105–117). Sage.

Kelly, T. (2018). Prospective: Is bipolar disorder being overdiagnosed? *International journal of methods in psychiatric research, 27*(3), e1725. https://doi.org/10.1002/mpr.1725

Kraus, C., Kadriu, B., Lanzenberger, R., Zarate, C. A., & Kasper, S. (2019). Prognosis and improved outcomes in older adults with bipolar disorder: A review. *International Journal of Geriatric Psychiatry, 34*(9), 1287–1300. https://doi.org/10.1002/gps.5180

Levitt, H. M. (2021). *Essentials of critical-constructivist grounded theory reaserch*. American Psychological Association.

Liddell, H. G., & Scott, R. (1940). *A Greek-English Lexicon* (9th ed.). Clarendon Press.

López, M., Pidal, C., Reitze, V., Salazar, M., & Vicencio, S. (2022). "Ser amiga de una persona con TAB es...": Un estudio cualitativo desde la perspectiva de la amistad ["Being a friend of a person with BPD is...": A qualitative study from the perspective of friendship]. In *VII Congreso de Investigación de Estudiantes de Psicología*, Escuela y Facultad de Psicología, Universidad Diego Portales, Santiago, Chile. Disponible en el libro de abstracts en https://psicologia.udp.cl/cms/wp-content/uploads/2023/03/Libro-de-Abstract-2022.pdf

Lopez-Jaramillo, C., Lopera-Vasquez, J., García-Cebrián, A., & Palacio, C. (2015). Bipolar disorder in Latin America: Challenges and opportunities. *Bipolar Disorders, 17*(6), 645–654. https://doi.org/10.1111/bdi.12321

Martínez, O., Montalván, O., & Betancur, Y. (2019). Trastorno Bipolar. Consideraciones clínicas y epidemiológicas [Bipolar Disorder. Clinical and Epidemiological Considerations]. *Revista Médica Electrónica, 41*(2), 467–842. https://www.medigraphic.com/pdfs/revmedele/me-2019/me192n.pdf

Marzani, G., & Price Neff, A. (2021). Bipolar disorders: Evaluation and treatment. *American Family Physician, 103*(4), 227–239.

Ministerio de Salud de Chile (MINSAL). (2012). *Ley N° 19.966: Régimen de Garantías en Salud (GES/AUGE) [Law No. 19.966: Health Guarantees Regime (GES/AUGE)]*. Biblioteca del Congreso Nacional de Chile. Recuperado de https://www.bcn.cl/leychile/navegar?idNorma=229834

Ministerio de Salud de Chile (MINSAL). (2017). *Encuesta Nacional de Salud 2016-2017: Primeros Resultados [National Health Survey 2016-2017: First Results]*. Chile.

Munn, Z., Peters, M. D. J., Stern, C., Tufanaru, C., McArthur, A., & Aromataris, E. (2018). Systematic review or scoping review? Guidance for authors when choosing between a systematic or scoping review approach. *BMC Medical Research Methodology, 18*(1), 143. https://doi.org/10.1186/s12874-018-0611-x

Perlick, D. A., Rosenheck, R. A., Clarkin, J. F., Sirey, J., Salahi, J., Struening, E., & Link, B. (2001). Adverse effects of perceived stigma on social adaptation of persons diagnosed with bipolar affective disorder. *Psychiatric Services, 52*(12), 1627–1632. https://doi.org/10.1176/appi.ps.52.12.1627

Proudfoot, J. G., Jayawant, A., Whitton, A. E., Parker, G., Manicavasagar, V., Smith, M., & Nicholas, J. (2012). Mechanisms underpinning effective peer support: A qualitative analysis of interactions between expert peers and patients newly diagnosed with bipolar disorder. *BMC Psychiatry, 12*, 196. https://doi.org/10.1186/1471-244X-12-196

Ravitch, S. M., & Carl, N. M. (2021). *Qualitative research: Bridging the conceptual, theoretical, and methodological* (2nd ed.). Sage.

Sajatovic, M., Blow, F. C., & Ignacio, R. V. (2004). Age-related differences in the course and treatment of bipolar disorder in a VA medical center population. *American Journal of Geriatric Psychiatry, 12*(3), 314–322. https://doi.org/10.1176/appi.ajgp.12.3.314

Superintendencia de Salud. (n.d.). *Cómo funciona el sistema de salud en Chile [How does work the Health Sistem in Chile?]. Superintendencia de Salud*. Recuperado de https://www.superdesalud.gob.cl/orientacion-en-salud/como-funciona-el-sistema-de-salud-en-chile/

Tomicic, A., Duarte, J., Aedo, M., Díaz, V., Vasquez, C., Avilés, F., & Martínez, C. (2024). Effects of a peer support intervention for individuals with bipolar disorder and their families: A qualitative analysis of a chilean experience. In *SPR 55th International Annual Meeting*. Ottawa, Canada.

Tomicic, A., Martínez, C., Rodríguez, J., & Barrientos, J. (2019/2023). Desarrollo de un Modelo Comprensivo de Psicoterapia con Pacientes LGBT: Estudio Cualitativo de las Experiencias de Pacientes y de Psicoterapeutas [Development of a Comprehensive Psychotherapy Model for LGBT Patients: A Qualitative Study of the Experiences of Patients and Psychotherapists].

Proyecto Fondecyt Regular N°1190270. Agencia Nacional de Investigación y Desarrollo (ANID), Chile.
Tomicic, A., Martínez, C., Rosenbaum, C., Aguayo, F., Leyton, F., Rodríguez, J., Galvez, C., & Lagazzi, I. (2020). Adolescence and suicide: Subjective construction of the suicidal process in young gay and lesbian Chileans. *Journal of Homosexuality, 68*(13), 2122–2143. https://doi.org/10.1080/00918369.2020.1804253
Vásquez, C., Díaz, V., Avilés, F., Duarte, J., & Tomicic, A. (2022). "It feels like you're not alone": Peer support for bipolar patients, a review. In *53rd International Annual Meeting of the Society for Psychotherapy Research (SPR)*. Denver, USA. Virtual mode.
Vieta, E., Salagre, E., Grande, I., Carvalho, A. F., Fernandes, B. S., Berk, M., Birmaher, B., Tohen, M., & Suppes, T. (2018). Early intervention in Bipolar Disorder. *The American journal of psychiatry, 175*(5), 411–426. https://doi.org/10.1176/appi.ajp.2017.17090972
World Health Organization (WHO). (2017). *Depression and other common mental disorders: Global health estimates*.
Yatham, L. N., Kennedy, S. H., Parikh, S. V., Schaffer, A., Beaulieu, S., Alda, M., et al. (2018). Canadian network for mood and anxiety treatments (CANMAT) and international society for bipolar disorders (ISBD) 2018 guidelines for the management of patients with bipolar disorder. *Bipolar Disorders, 20*(2), 97–170. https://doi.org/10.1111/bdi.12609

Index

A. Tomicic, J. D. Soto (eds.), *Qualitative Research in Clinical Psychology and Psychotherapy in Latin America*, https://doi.org/10.1007/978-3-031-90782-1

The manufacturer's authorised representative in the EU is Springer Nature Customer Service Centre GmbH, Europaplatz 3, 69115 Heidelberg, Germany. If you have any concerns regarding our products, please contact ProductSafety@springernature.com

Printed and bound by CPI Group (UK) Ltd, Croydon, CR0 4YY
30/09/2026
02225584-0013